INVENTING AMERICA'S FIRST IMMIGRATION CRISIS

CATHOLIC PRACTICE IN NORTH AMERICA

Series editor:

—

John C. Seitz, Associate Professor, Theology Department,
Fordham University; Associate Director for Lincoln Center,
Curran Center for American Catholic Studies

This series aims to contribute to the growing field of Catholic studies
through the publication of books devoted to the historical and cultural study
of Catholic practice in North America, from the colonial period to the present.
As the term "practice" suggests, the series springs from a pressing need in the
study of American Catholicism for empirical investigations and creative
explorations and analyses of the contours of Catholic experience. In seeking to
provide more comprehensive maps of Catholic practice, this series is committed
to publishing works from diverse American locales, including urban, suburban,
and rural settings; ethnic, postethnic, and transnational contexts; private and
public sites; and seats of power as well as the margins.

Series advisory board:

Emma Anderson, Ottawa University

Paul Contino, Pepperdine University

Kathleen Sprows Cummings, University of Notre Dame

James T. Fisher, Fordham University (Emeritus)

Paul Mariani, Boston College

Thomas A. Tweed, University of Notre Dame

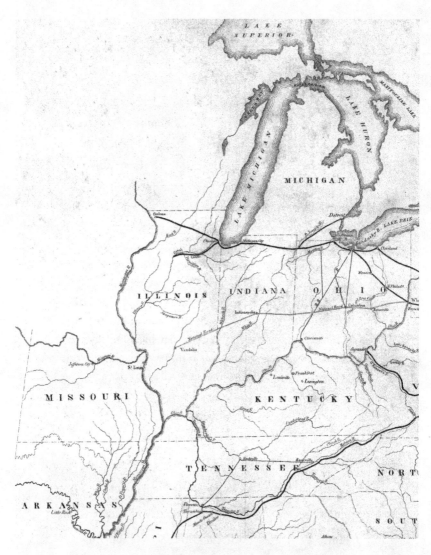

Map of the Upper Mississippi and Ohio River valleys, ca. 1840.

Inventing America's
First Immigration Crisis

Political Nativism in the Antebellum West

Luke Ritter

FORDHAM UNIVERSITY PRESS

NEW YORK 2021

FRONTISPIECE: Edward Weber & Co. *Map shewing the connection of the Baltimore and Ohio-Rail-Road with other rail roads executed or in progress throughout the United States.* [Baltimore Lith. of Ed. Weber & Co. 184–?, 1840] Map. https://www.loc.gov/item/gm70002855/.

Fordham University Press also publishes its books in a variety of electronic formats. Some content that appears in print may not be available in electronic books. Visit us online at www.fordhampress.com.

Library of Congress Cataloging-in-Publication Data available online at https://catalog.loc.gov.

Printed in the United States of America

23 22 21 5 4 3 2 1
First edition

S | H
M | P
The Sustainable History Monograph Pilot
Opening up the Past, Publishing for the Future

We are eager to learn more about how you discovered this title and how you are using it. We hope you will spend a few minutes answering a couple of questions at this url: **https://www.longleafservices.org/shmp-survey/**

More information about the Sustainable History Monograph Pilot can be found at https://www.longleafservices.org.

To my beautiful wife, Debbie:

This is for you. It's all for you.

To my bouncing boys, Louis and Peter:

You are the future. I will always love you.

CONTENTS

Introduction

WHY HAVE AMERICANS EXPRESSED concern about immigration at some times but not at others? In pursuit of an answer, this book examines America's first nativist movement. Open immigration and citizenship persist in the United States because Americans have historically believed their principles are universal. The founding generation made it radically easy for immigrants to become full American citizens. Boards of education provided free public schooling for foreign-born children. A host of benevolent organizations raised enormous amounts of money to assist newcomers to the states. U.S. cities announced to the world that they were open for business. Citizens made these efforts to spread the American gospel of "Capitalism, Protestantism, and Republicanism." Political nativism—the exception—replaced tolerance—the rule—when Americans panicked that assimilation, conversion, and economic progress were not happening quickly enough. The first self-proclaimed nativists in the United States seized the reins of political power at the national level for only a few years between 1854 and 1856, but the tactic they employed, namely identifying "outsiders" as the source of their various anxieties, has persisted as a useful political tool.

Nativism is the idea that a certain group of people can be identified as original to, or the rightful heirs to, a geopolitical territory; consequently, "natives" claim the privilege of deciding who belongs and who counts as an "outsider" based on supposed foreign connections.[1] The case could be made that nativism in this sense is universal. Nativist movements stress the interests of the locally born as a priority over nonnative, or foreign-born, people (for example, "Americans First"). Political nativism describes the coming together of nativism—the belief in inheritance—and a nativist movement—the reemphasis on "natives first"—to induce measurable political changes. At its core is the innate human desire to feel at home. What people need to feel "at home" varies across time and space but often entails economic stability and some combination of uniform behaviors, values, religious beliefs, language, or race. It must be noted that nativism does not always entail racism, although the intensification of race-based ideas and acts often corresponds to a rise in political nativism.[2] Nativists fashion themselves as protectors of local attributes against perceived foreign threats in their midst and are often willing to take extreme actions.[3]

America's first nativist movement responded to the rapid influx of roughly 4.2 million European immigrants between 1840 and 1860. Immigrants composed up to 15 percent of the total population of the United States. These figures do not take into account second-generation immigrants—that is, children born to immigrant parents on American soil.[4] Most of these newcomers were German or Irish. Not only did they speak different languages, but they also harbored diverse cultural customs and ideas, approached politics in alternative ways, and worshipped within different religious traditions. While the vast majority of white Americans born on American soil worshipped in Protestant Christian churches, approximately 95 percent of all Irish immigrants after 1840 were Catholic, while more than 30 percent of Germans were as well.[5]

Political nativism gradually emerged within the ranks of the American Republican, or "Native American," Party in the mid-1840s, the Know-Nothing Order in the 1850s, and the National American, or "Know-Nothing," Party between 1854 and 1858. In the election of 1856, the presidential candidate running on behalf of the American Party received roughly 22 percent of the popular vote. The American Party thus became the second-largest third party in American history. Its official platform demanded raising the residency requirement for citizenship from five to twenty-one years, supported only native-born Americans for office, and resisted all who would pledge a higher allegiance to a foreign church or state than to the U.S. Constitution.[6] Certain anti-immigrant thought patterns in the antebellum era have since been repeated, especially amid demographic changes due to immigration, yet much of the historical context for American nativism, and thus its meaning, has varied across time and place.[7]

Before the 1960s, much of the relevant scholarship disregarded antebellum nativist propaganda as mere cultural panic or xenophobia. In the classic book on the subject, *The Protestant Crusade, 1800-1860* (1938), historian Ray Allen Billington argued that American nativism originated in and was driven by English prejudices and religious fanaticism.[8] Historian Richard Hofstadter famously equated political nativism to paranoia.[9] With *Strangers in the Land* (1955), historian John Higham inaugurated a more nuanced line of inquiry about what American nativism has revealed about society across time and place. He argued that Americans are more likely to endorse political nativism when they perceive threats to their social status within the nation.[10] Higham changed the way scholars treated American nativism, historian Jason McDonald observed, as "not just the preserve of 'crackpots' but a major characteristic of American public opinion." Rather than religious fanaticism, a common desire to identify and solidify proper roles within the nation motivated these movements.[11] Much of the scholarship since Higham has focused on nativism as a national identity-making process.[12]

Historian Tyler Anbinder's seminal book, *Nativism and Slavery* (1992), attributed the rapid rise and demise of the American Party between 1854 and 1856 to the sectional crisis over slavery. Political expediency was the primary factor, according to Anbinder. After the collapse of the Whig Party in 1854, many ex-Whigs in the North courted the Know-Nothings because they initially promised antislavery and antialcohol reforms. Although most members were indeed anti-Catholic and xenophobic, once party leaders downplayed the issue of slavery, ex-Whigs in the North left the American Party for the solidly antislavery Republican Party.[13] Anbinder's account of political nativism still holds much of its original value. As it focuses primarily on the Northeast, however, it does not entirely explain why so many proslavery and neutral-on-slavery Americans in the western border states supported Know-Nothingism. As most studies have focused on the coasts, historians have not yet produced a complete explanation for why residents of the North American interior espoused political nativism when they did and why the nation's bloodiest election-day riots erupted in western cities, namely the St. Louis Election Riot of 1852, the St. Louis "Know-Nothing" Riot of 1854, the Cincinnati Election Day Riot of 1855, the Chicago "Lager" Riot of 1855, and the Louisville "Bloody Monday" Riot of 1855.[14]

During the antebellum era, Americans often thought of the West in three parts, the *Far* West, like California, which became the destination of some migrants after the Mexican-American War in 1848, the Trans-Mississippi West, or the territory west of the Mississippi River, and the *First* West, the region in the interior touched by the Mississippi River and its tributaries. Unless otherwise noted, all references to the "West" in this study generally refer to the Upper Mississippi and Ohio River valleys.[15] Several regional factors rendered the "First West" a rather distinct place. Residents experienced ceaseless migration, rapid growth, a large and active German immigrant population, and a politics of compromise between the slaveholding states of Kentucky and Missouri and the free states of Illinois and Ohio. American-immigrant tensions increased in the western border states regardless of their slaveholding status, precisely in the areas where immigration from Europe surged.[16] In focusing on the antebellum West, this study illuminates the cultural, economic, and political issues that originally motivated American nativism and explains how it ultimately shaped the political relationship between church and state.

The antebellum nativist movement aspired to replace local tribalism, regional sectionalism, and religious factionalism with a national identity based on a set of shared American values, but immigrants challenged the status quo.[17] Chapter one explains how unprecedented levels of immigration, the evangelical revivalism of the "Second Great Awakening," and rapid westward expansion reignited fears of Catholicism as a corrosive force. For native-born Americans living in the mid-nineteenth century, the successful assimilation of German and Irish immigrants, many of whom were Catholic, was not a foregone conclusion. The United States thus became a testing ground for what happens when a pluralist nation committed to universal democratic principles encounters an unexpected host of immigrants with unpopular beliefs. Native-born Americans often expressed more concern about European immigration to the West than to any other region of the country because Catholics and immigrants would influence new towns there as they took shape. European immigrants did not spread out evenly across North America; rather, they followed regular pathways of settlement and concentrated in northern and western cities. Much has been written about their influence in big port cities like Boston, New York, and Philadelphia; immigration to bourgeoning western cities like Chicago, Cincinnati, Louisville, and St. Louis occurred at a rapid rate as well. Fifty percent of all immigrants who came to the United States during this period arrived at the port of New Orleans before they began their journey up the Mississippi River.[18] By the time of the Civil War, 60 percent of St. Louis's population of more than 160,000 was foreign born.[19] These daily arrivals fueled the astonishing growth of previously nonexistent Lutheran and Roman Catholic churches, seminaries for priests, Catholic schools, and German and Irish groceries and pubs. In entire quarters of the city, one could hardly hear anything spoken other than German or English in an Irish brogue. Foreign-born residents increasingly influenced state and national election cycles. Many Americans believed that the outcome of religious competition in the West would decide the fate of the republic.

Catholics remained primary targets, but chapter two explores an ensuing culture war that circumscribed various immigrant customs deemed culturally corrosive by native-born Americans. Schools performed the vital function of teaching children the values that supposedly united Americans into one nation. Because many Americans insisted on using the King James Bible as a textbook in public schools, an essentially theological disagreement between immigrants and the native born became a national dilemma. Likewise, local leaders utilized Sunday closing laws to prevent Catholic feasting and German-style recreation on the Lord's Day. The Sunday laws not only enabled native-born Americans to define the requirements for national belonging but also compelled immigrants of all backgrounds and creeds, ironically enough, to unite politically against Sunday regulations and thus mainstream "Americanness." This process was most clearly observed among the German population in the antebellum West. The school and Sunday controversies directly motivated the rise of political nativism in the mid-1840s.[20]

Chapter three explains the power of nativist rhetoric to mobilize disaffected voters across the country. Rhetoric emphasizing the incongruities between the beliefs and behaviors of native-born Americans and immigrants signaled simultaneously a national-identity crisis and a solution. In the American nativist mindset, Protestant forms of Christianity, as opposed to Roman Catholic practices, formed the basis of American values and behaviors. To this end, nativists developed a mythical, nationalist story that rendered Catholicism incompatible with true Americanism and Christianity.[21]

Chapter four examines the intermittent phase of secret nativist fraternalism during the early 1850s. To this day, especially little is known about the Order of Know-Nothings in the West. Shedding new light on the inner sanctums of such orders has proven particularly difficult because Know-Nothings attempted to confound outsiders with misinformation. The extant evidence, including minute books and private correspondence, reveals, on one hand, continuity with the political nativism of the mid-1840s and, on the other, the forging of a new political response to an increasingly polarized and volatile nation. The fraternal secrecy of these organizations exhibited a hallmark of American nativism: the tendency of its most ardent supporters to take drastic measures to protect their communities against unwanted outside influences. Another hallmark of American nativism, which the Know-Nothing movement in the West well attested, has been the tendency of nativists on the fringe to mimic the very behaviors and tactics they have projected upon their enemies. Their version of secret democracy featured as a perverse imitation of popular anti-Catholic motifs.[22]

Scholars have attributed political nativism during the antebellum era to cultural paranoia, social anxiety, and political expediency. Much less examined are the ways in which economic motives contributed to it. During the late 1840s and early 1850s, Americans in urban areas resented higher expenditures on poorhouses, prisons, mental asylums, police, and other institutions that expanded to serve immigrants. Chapter five argues that the outbreak of political nativism in western cities provides a representative example of the relationship between immigrant conditions, the election riots of the mid-1850s, and the dramatic rise of the American Party. Cultural issues and the potential increase in immigrant voting power intensified economic-related resentment among the native-born population and resulted in the widespread outbreak of political nativism.

Chapter six explains why Know-Nothingism, while rhetorically powerful, struggled to overcome certain longstanding regional disputes, legislative limitations, and political circumstances. The debate over slavery raised seemingly insurmountable sectional disagreements. The increasing violence at the polls ironically forged the very thing nativists had feared: a coalition of Americans and immigrants, German and Irish, Catholic and Protestant, rallied together against the nativist onslaught. Moreover, the American Party tried to garner broad political support at the national level for immigration reform and additional social controls, but even contemporaries who sympathized with some of their fears rejected their policy goals as "un-American."[23]

Public discourse eventually forged the transformation of base anti-Catholicism within the nativist movement into a greater commitment to the ideal of church-state separation. Despite its hallmark bigotry, the nativist movement yielded a relatively more inclusive American civil religion in which it did not matter if one was Protestant or Catholic, only that each citizen pledge his highest allegiance to the U.S. Constitution, the guarantor of religious freedom. Nothing in this rearticulated formulation required an explicitly "Protestant Christian" language. Nativists in the West cast their net so wide by the end of 1854 that even German and Irish citizens, Catholics and Jews, could potentially embrace their principles, which they increasingly did during the Civil War era. Religious prejudices remained, but the country's first bout of nativism culminated in a renewal of Americans' commitment to the separation of church and state.[24] These otherwise subtle developments are clearly observed in the antebellum West.

Native-born Americans compelled Catholics and immigrants who might have otherwise shared an affinity for monarchism to accept American-style democracy; Catholics and immigrants compelled many Americans to accept a more inclusive definition of religious freedom. During the era of anti-Catholic revolutions in 1840s Europe, the Roman Catholic Church hierarchy remained uneasy about the compatibility of democracy with its teachings and ecclesiastical structure. Political nativism in the United States might have seemed like another dark mark against secular democracy, yet Catholic American leaders around the country constructed a series of powerful arguments contra political nativism. "Catholic Americanness" developed in this milieu as a direct response to more exclusive versions of nationalism. American democracy, U.S. Catholics joined together in arguing, was the best mode of government for Catholics because, unlike some of the European regimes, it at least ensured their religious freedom.

That claim remained a debatable point, but the very act of asserting it seemed to warm Catholic immigrants to the idea of making America a new home. The constitutional principle of free exercise of religion was something with which both sides could firmly agree.[25]

Religious freedom thus became a panacea for many significant contests over individual rights long before U.S. courts bore anything resembling the power they gained at the turn of the twentieth century. The principle doubled as a catalyst for ethnic inclusion. Religious acts are often indistinguishable from cultural or ethnic customs, and thus the right to express one's religious beliefs became indistinguishable from the freedom to express one's cultural heritage or ethnicity in public spaces. By appealing to Americans' special valuing of religious liberty, immigrants secured the potential to choose a path of gradual integration into U.S. society at a time when constitutional law did not necessarily guarantee equal treatment of newcomers, minority groups, or people of color.[26]

Nativists underestimated the resiliency of America's democratic institutions. The ensuing debates between Americans and immigrants transformed U.S. political culture to yield an expanded, more inclusive, and more resilient system of democracy. The right to free worship has historically served as one of the most reliable sources of individual freedom in the United States. It is no wonder, then, why Americans have often framed their respective causes in the language of religious liberty. Overall, this study offers valuable insight into the historic role of nativism in American politics. The epilogue sheds light on present-day concerns regarding immigration, including the role of anti-Islamic appeals in the elections of 2016.

INVENTING AMERICA'S FIRST IMMIGRATION CRISIS draws on a vast assortment of literature in archives spread across the Midwest, including rare books, campaign paraphernalia, court records, minute books, newspapers, political pamphlets, private correspondence, religious tracts, sermons, speeches, and state congressional records. The region generated its fair share of nativist propaganda as well as immigrant responses in German, Irish, and Catholic communications, both public and private. Primary-source materials from the Chicago Historical Society, the Newberry Library in Chicago, the Cincinnati Historical Society, and the Cincinnati and Hamilton County Library Records feature prominently, as do records housed at the Missouri State Archives, Missouri History Museum, Pius Library at Saint Louis University, Olin Library at Washington University, and Western Historical Manuscript Collection at the University of Missouri.

A fellowship from the Filson Historical Society afforded me the opportunity to research their rich archives in Louisville, Kentucky. The William E. Foley Fellowship provided me a second chance to mine the St. Louis criminal-court records housed in the Missouri State Archives. I am grateful to the Department of History at Saint Louis University for generously funding several research trips and to the Department of History and Philosophy at Troy University for sponsoring paper presentations at numerous conferences. Special thanks to the *Journal of American Ethnic History*, *American Nineteenth Century History*, and the *Missouri Historical Review* for permitting me to include research published in past issues of their journals.[27]

Many wonderful people assisted me during this project. I am much indebted to my dissertation advisor, Lorri Glover, a wise teacher, ruthless editor, and devoted friend. I have appreciated the consistently good advice of my colleagues at Saint Louis University, especially Scott McDermott, who commented on every chapter of my dissertation while he worked on his own. I am thankful for Maura Farrelly and Katie Oxx, both of whom offered crucial feedback on early drafts of my book manuscript. Special thanks to my colleagues at Troy University for their support. The editors and readers at Fordham University Press recommended substantial revisions that vastly improved the quality of this book, for which I am deeply grateful.

CHAPTER I

The Valley of Decision

If we gain the West, all is safe; if we lose it, all is lost.

—Presbyterian minister Lyman Beecher, 1830

THE AMERICAN REVOLUTION TRANSFORMED a social system founded on appearance, aristocracy, and church affiliation into one based on a shared set of values. Rather than luck of birth, certain values determined one's belonging to the American nation: the belief in natural rights to life, liberty, and property; the belief in the sovereignty of the people; the belief in promotion by merit; and the belief in an individual's freedom to think whatever one wants to think without the threat of persecution from the state, to say whatever one wants to say, to print opinions in public forums, to assemble with likeminded individuals, and to petition the government to change undesirable policies. These were the building blocks of modern democracy enshrined in the U.S. Constitution. To believe in them was to belong.[1]

One of the most radical elements of the U.S. Constitution was its neutrality on religion. The governments of France and Spain officially privileged the Roman Catholic Church; the king of England doubled as the head of the Church of England. But the United States became one of the first modern countries to deliberately *not* select an official state religion. The unamended Constitution, ratified in 1788, mentioned religion only once (in Article 6, clause 3): "No religious Test shall ever be required as a Qualification to any Office or public Trust under the United States." The delegates at the Constitutional Convention knew exactly what this meant: men of all religious persuasions could serve as government officials.[2] The founders ushered in a new degree of toleration for a plurality of religious denominations. Although men who claimed membership in the Episcopalian Church composed the majority, the convention itself represented a diversity of religious affiliations, including Congregationalists, Quakers, Lutherans, and Methodists. Two Catholics signed the Constitution, Daniel

Carroll of Maryland and Thomas Fitzsimons of Pennsylvania. At least thirteen of the thirty-nine signers were affiliated with the Order of Freemasons.[3] Furthermore, the First Amendment to the Constitution, ratified in 1791, ensured that the federal government would not prefer or persecute one religious group over another: "Congress shall make no law respecting an establishment of religion, or prohibiting the free exercise thereof." It was determined then, at least at the national level, that religion would remain a private matter.[4]

Although the delegates to the Constitutional Convention established a secular federal government that could not endorse one religion in particular (or any religion for that matter), this did not mean that Americans wanted to completely remove religion from all governmental functions. From state constitutions down to the level of city ordinances, local American law often has invoked God and privileged Christianity, namely Protestant forms of Christianity. Massachusetts maintained an official state religion, Congregationalism, until its highest state court deemed this unconstitutional in 1833. Connecticut also chose Congregationalism as the state's official religion until adopting a new constitution in 1818. New Hampshire at the same time permitted only five official state religions, none of which were Roman Catholic.[5]

U.S. courts eventually forced the disestablishment of preferred religious denominations in American states. In this way the United States matched the countries around the Atlantic Ocean in its level of religious tolerance under law. The United Kingdom, for example, passed the Catholic Emancipation Act of 1829, which after centuries of persecution finally permitted Catholic citizens to vote, hold office, and generally practice their religion without harassment. Catholic France likewise removed punishments for Huguenots (French Calvinists) in the country. Just as Catholicism retained privileges in France, as did Anglicanism in England, mainstream Protestant denominations in the United States continued to enjoy and expect preferential treatment, especially at local levels.[6]

Hypothetically, anyone could become an American citizen. The U.S. government provided immigrants a simple pathway to citizenship after five years of residency. State governments enforced their own, often more lenient rules for naturalization. As a result of the Northwest Ordinance of 1787, an open-state policy in the West permitted residents, once they constituted a population of 60,000 in a given territory, to apply for admission as a new state in the American union. Territorial and state governments could determine residency requirements for enfranchisement. Most western states allowed immigrants to vote after merely two years of residency and a declaration of their intent to naturalize. In an attempt to attract laborers, some, such as Indiana, naturalized immigrants upon arrival. Open immigration, westward expansion, and state-directed naturalization policies ensured the emergence of a radically diverse American citizenry.

By the 1830s, the unexpectedly rapid pace of immigration and western settlement posed a serious challenge to American national identity. What exact values would unite such a diverse array of peoples spread across the North American continent? Who did and did not belong? Rapid demographic change and territorial expansion triggered America's first nativist movement.

Despite religious pluralism in America, anti-Catholic sentiment figured prominently in nineteenth-century conversations about immigration policy and western settlement. Many European immigrants to the United States affiliated with the Roman Catholic Church, while most native-born Americans embraced some form of Protestant Christianity. Americans' anti-Catholic prejudices were part of the legacy of bygone centuries of theological divergence dating back to the Protestant Reformation. Theologically, Catholic doctrines traditionally emphasized the collective over the individual in matters pertaining to salvation. Historically and politically, Roman Catholicism had grown in prestige and power around the world alongside monarchical systems of government. The American Revolution raised additional concerns about the compatibility of Roman Catholicism with a democratic form of government.

Mass immigration, rapid westward expansion, and fervent religious revivalism reawakened the anti-Catholicism that had been so stark in the colonial era. The Upper Mississippi and Ohio River valleys, what most Americans thought of as the "West," became a significant site of intense competition between Protestant and Catholic migrants, with the entire fate of the American experiment seeming to hang in the balance. Americanism became tied to visions of conquering the West with American customs and values.

The Mississippi Valley as National Crucible

The generation of Americans huddled along the East Coast around the time of the American Revolution imagined the lands west of the Appalachian Mountains as a vast "wilderness," majestic and treacherous, trafficked by Indians but nonetheless a desolate and uncharted place. And it was all theirs for the taking, at least according to the terms of the Treaty of Paris of 1783, which granted the newly formed American republic a massive endowment of formerly British-occupied territory below Canada, above Spanish Florida, and stretching all the way west to the Mississippi River. Then in 1803 imperial pressures compelled the ruler of France, Napoleon Bonaparte, to sell the Louisiana Territory west of the Mississippi River, approximately 827,000 square miles, to President Thomas Jefferson's administration for fifteen million dollars. In just twenty years' time, the United States doubled in size and then doubled again. Before the Revolutionary era, very few Anglo-Americans ventured beyond the Kentucky and Ohio Territories. The acquisitions of 1783 and 1803 motivated rapid westward expansion thereafter.

The presence of indigenous Americans; native-born French and Spanish colonists; centuries-old Dominican, Franciscan, and Jesuit missions; and other sundry groups—this populated West—did not square well with American designs. Many of the French and Spanish-speaking creole inhabitants of major hubs like New Orleans and St. Louis remained even after their mother countries had withdrawn. When Anglo-American migrant John Fletcher Darby approached St. Louis from the east bank of the Mississippi River with his family in 1818, he marveled at the "striking and imposing appearance" of this formidable town of 4,000 French Catholic residents. French fur traders Pierre Laclede and Auguste Chouteau had founded the city in 1764, twelve years before Americans declared their independence, and named it in honor of their monarch's patron saint, King Louis IX. Darby remembered that the residents' "strange habiliments, manner, and jabbering in the French language ... had a new and striking effect upon myself and the other children, coming as we did from the plantation in the Southern country." Even "the negroes of the town all spoke French," he gawked, and attended mass too.[7]

Darby became the mayor of St. Louis seventeen years later. By that time, in 1835, the entire region was undergoing a profound transformation in character from being predominantly indigenous American, French, and Catholic to Anglo-American and Protestant Christian. When the United States acquired the vast territory west of the Mississippi River, the Missouri region had no Baptist, Methodist, or Presbyterian churches. By 1836, each denomination represented more than 200 congregations, and over two-thirds of Missouri's population affiliated with one of these Christian sects. Americans took this as confirmation that all of the land drained by the Mississippi River and its tributaries belonged to them as their "new Canaan," a popular allusion to the land promised to the ancient Jews in the Old Testament.[8]

The founding generation welcomed immigrants to join the American experiment, participate in democratic government, and settle the West.[9] Indeed, the availability of land in the North American interior attracted a steady stream of immigrants from Europe. After the states ratified the Constitution, approximately 15,000 immigrants, the majority of whom were white Protestants from the British Isles and enslaved Africans, arrived in the United States annually.[10] In 1790, when the total population of the original thirteen states and the brand new states of Kentucky and Tennessee reached 3,929,652 (including 757,208 black slaves), Americans with Irish ancestry constituted about 8 percent of the total population and German Americans 7 percent, while figures for residents with familial ties to Holland, France, Sweden, and elsewhere were substantially smaller. Most residents who were not British or African were born in America.[11]

Watered by the world's fourth-largest river system, the Upper Mississippi and Ohio River valleys offered fertile soil and teeming wildlife.[12] Before the advent of railroads, American migrants concentrated in the booming cities of Cincinnati, Louisville, and St. Louis because they lay at the epicenter of river traffic in the interior. Chicago boomed later in the 1850s once the construction of canals and railroads increased opportunities for trade. During most of the antebellum era, Cincinnati ranked as the sixth-largest city in the United States, followed closely by St. Louis.[13] The population of the Old Northwest increased from 1.5 million in 1830 to 7 million in 1860, constituting over 25 percent of America's total white population.[14]

Charles B. Boynton, an agent of the American Reform Tract and Book Society and minister of the Congregationalist Church, provided a mental image to describe development in the region at the time. "If we start at St. Louis and draw a semi-circular line northward and round to Pittsburgh, it will enclose a system of Railways north of the Ohio [River]," Boynton explained, which "bear commerce to Cincinnati and concentrate upon her as their focal point." If one completed the southern half of the semicircle, "there is a Southern system of Railways pointing inward upon Cincinnati." The main metropolises dotting the map of the West included Cincinnati; the Ohio River town of Louisville, 100 miles southwest; the Mississippi River town of St. Louis, 300 miles west of Cincinnati; and finally the Great Lakes port of Chicago, 300 miles north. The rivers and railroads connected the dots. By the 1850s, Chicago, Cincinnati, Louisville, and St. Louis had become significant commercial and cultural centers. It was with a profound sense of the region's interconnected expansion that Reverend Boynton noted that the West's "pulsations for good or evil will be felt throughout the land."[15]

Policymakers did not expect immigrants to travel to developing western states so rapidly and in such great numbers during the 1840s. Between 1840 and 1860, approximately 4.2 million immigrants arrived in the United States, 1.7 million of whom came from Ireland and 1.3 million from the German Confederation. The British constituted the next-largest immigrant group.[16] The population of

TABLE I.I. Nativity of Immigrants as Reported by the U.S. Census Bureau in 1850 and 1860

	1850 Census	Percentage of Immigrants	1860 Census	Percentage of Immigrants
Ireland	961,719	43.51%	1,611,304	38.94%
Germany	573,225	25.94%	1,301,136	31.45%
England	278,675	12.61%	431,692	10.44%
British America	147,700	6.68%	249,970	6.05%
France	54,069	2.44%	109,870	2.66%
Scotland	70,550	3.19%	108,518	2.63%
Switzerland	13,358	0.60%	53,327	1.29%
Wales	29,868	1.34%	45,763	1.11%
Norway	12,678	0.57%	43,995	1.07%
China	758	0.03%	35,565	0.86%
Holland	9,848	0.45%	28,281	0.68%
Mexico	13,317	0.60%	27,466	0.66%
Sweden	3,559	0.16%	18,625	0.26%
Italy	3,645	0.17%	10,518	0.26%
Other countries	37,870	1.71%	60,145	1.45%
Total	2,210,839		4,136,175	

SOURCE: Joseph C. G. Kennedy, ed., *Population of the United States in 1860; Compiled from the Original Returns of the Eighth Census,* (Washington, DC: Government Printing Office, 1864). NOTE: The 1870 census added some more to this number. The numbers for 1860 were 4,138,697, and for 1850 they were 2,244,602.

the West became relatively diverse as many newly arriving Europeans bypassed the East Coast, sailed straight to New Orleans, moved up the Mississippi River, and settled in interior states like Illinois, Kentucky, Missouri, and Ohio.

Cultivating his own farm in what is now Montgomery County, Missouri, in 1824, German immigrant Gottfried Düden promoted the region as a safe haven for those seeking to escape oppressive and overpopulated areas in the German Confederation. According to Düden, lush and undeveloped Missouri was an ideal location for a new *Vaterland* in America.[17] Many new immigrants responded and formed long-lasting, German-speaking communities in remote agrarian towns such as Augusta, Hermann, and Marthasville.[18] During the 1830s, explicit corporatist settlement schemes included, for example, one German-speaking group from Rhenish Bavaria in the German Confederation that intended to purchase a large tract of land west of the Mississippi to establish a "New Germany" in America. This "New Germany," they imagined, could attract German immigrants and eventually apply as the twenty-fifth state of the Union. Another settler society announced its intention, in a pamphlet published in 1842, to reserve a large tract of land in the West exclusively for Catholic refugees from Ireland, which they hoped might eventually become a new Irish state.[19] Both attempts failed.

Most immigrants settled in highly populated urban areas. Those who traveled out west tended to concentrate in greater numbers in Illinois and Ohio, especially near Chicago and Cincinnati. Two-thirds of all immigrants to the South settled in Kentucky, Louisiana, and Missouri, and most of those concentrated in the bourgeoning cities of Louisville, New Orleans, and St. Louis. Agrarian settlement in the country required money the newcomers seldom had, while the booming cities offered semiskilled workers employment.[20]

German immigrants were slightly more likely on average to settle in the West than were their Irish counterparts. One traveler from the East Coast observed, "The German population of these western cities are as much the ruling element as the Irish are with us."[21] Between 1848 and 1850, when the arrival of immigrant "Forty-Eighters" peaked, 34,418 Germans settled in St. Louis alone; many of them stayed and contributed to the distinct German character of the city.[22]

Even though immigrants concentrated in urban areas near native-born Americans, assimilation continued to be a gradual, often multigenerational process. Distinctly ethnic districts emerged in Chicago, Cincinnati, Louisville, and St. Louis, and entire portions of cities revolved around newly built immigrant stores and churches, including the "Over-the-Rhine" district in Cincinnati, "German Broadway" in North Chicago, "Butchertown" in Louisville, "New Bremen" in North St. Louis, the "Kerry Patch" in Central St. Louis, and "Carondelet" in South St. Louis. Americans expressed concern that the rapid influx of German and Irish immigrants to western cities would not provide the proper incentives for assimilation. While serving as the director of the Western Literary Institution, Calvin Stowe argued in 1835, "Nothing could be more fatal to our prospects of future national prosperity than to have our population become a congeries of clans, congregating without coalescing."[23] As the immigrant populations of

TABLE 1.2. U.S. Population, 1850

	Total (White)	"Colored"	Foreign-born	Percentage of foreign-born to total white pop.
United States	19,553,068	3,638,808	2,244,602	11.48%
Midwest				
Illinois	864,034 (11th)	5,436	111,892	13.23%
Missouri	592,004 (13th)	90,040	76,592	12.94%
Ohio	1,955,050 (3rd)	25,279	218,193	11.16%
Kentucky	761,413 (8th)	220,992	31,420	4.13%
Northeast				
New York	3,048,325 (1st)	49,069	655,929	21.52%
Massachusetts	985,450 (6th)	9,064	164,024	16.64%
Pennsylvania	2,258,160 (2nd)	53,626	303,417	13.44%
South				
Louisiana	255,491 (18th)	262,271	68,233	26.71%

SOURCE: Kennedy, *Population of the United States in 1860*. NOTE: The total population does not include persons, enslaved or free, classified as "colored." The chart features the percentages of the foreign-born population to the total white population. The ranking of each state according to population includes "colored" and enslaved persons.

western cities began to outnumber the native born, one self-proclaimed "Native American" complained that "the valley of the Mississippi will not long be American in the character of its population, if it now is."[24]

Mass immigration from Europe boosted the Catholic population in the United States from 150,000 in 1815 to 1 million in 1850. That same year, while the Catholic Church claimed 1 million members in the States, there were approximately 1 million Presbyterians, 2.7 million Methodists, and 1.6 million Baptists. After 1840 nearly 95 percent of all Irish immigrants worshiped in a Catholic Church, as did over 30 percent of German immigrants. By 1860, the Catholic Church in the United States claimed about 3 million members, which meant that Catholics constituted approximately 11 percent of the total free population.[25]

TABLE 1.3. U.S. Population, 1860

	Total (White)	"Colored"	Foreign-born	Percentage of foreign-born to total white pop.
United States	26,922,537	4,520,784	4,138,697	15.37%
Midwest				
Illinois	1,704,323 (4th)	7,628	324,643	19.05%
Missouri	1,063,509 (8th)	118,503	160,541	15.1%
Ohio	2,302,838 (3rd)	36,673	328,249	14.25%
Kentucky	919,517 (9th)	236,167	59,799	6.5%
Northeast				
New York	3,831,730 (1st)	49,005	1,001,280	26.13%
Massachusetts	1,221,464 (7th)	9,602	260,106	21.29%
Pennsylvania	2,849,266 (2nd)	56,949	430,505	15.11%
South				
Louisiana	357,629 (17th)	350,373	80,975	22.64%

NOTE: The total population does not include persons, enslaved or free, classified as "colored." The chart features the percentages of the foreign-born population to the total white population. The ranking of each state according to population includes "colored" and enslaved persons. SOURCE: Kennedy, *Population of the United States in 1860.*

Unlike in the East, Roman Catholic missionaries had been ministering in the Mississippi Valley for a long time, since the seventeenth century. Catholic leaders in the region persisted in expanding their unique imprint on western culture. The "Catholic revival" of the mid-nineteenth century motivated new evangelism in North America. Catholic revivalists campaigned to increase the number of the church's parishes, schools, and societies precisely to safeguard Catholic Americans from prodding Protestant missionaries and the day-to-day temptations of American secularism.[26]

Fearing the influence of migrating Anglo-American Protestants in the previously Catholic French-and-Spanish-controlled Mississippi River valley, Bishop Louis Dubourg of New Orleans, for example, recruited Roman Catholic missionaries from Europe. Italian priest Joseph Rosati came to America in 1816 in

TABLE 1.4. Foreign-born Population in Cities, 1860–70

	1860			1870		
	Total (White)	Foreign-born	Percentage of foreign-born	Total	Foreign-born	Percentage of foreign-born
United States	26,922,537	4,138,697	15.37%	38,558,371	5,567,229	14.44%
Midwest						
Chicago	109,260	54,624	49.99%	298,977	144,557	48.35%
St. Louis	160,773	96,086	59.77%	310,864	112,249	36.11%
Cincinnati	161,044	73,614	45.71%	216,239	79,612	36.82%
Louisville	68,033	22,948	33.73%	100,753	25,668	25.48%
Northeast						
New York	1,072,312	488,306	45.54%	1,338,391	563,812	42.13%
Boston	177,812	63,791	35.88%	250,526	87,986	35.12%
Philadelphia	585,529	169,430	28.93%	674,022	183,624	27.24%
South						
New Orleans	168,675	64,621	38.31%	191,418	48,475	25.32%

SOURCE: Kennedy, *Population of the United States in 1860*. NOTE: The total population for these cities in 1860 and 1870 include persons labeled as "colored." The statistics do not count second-generation immigrants—that is, citizens born in the United States with at least one parent of foreign birth. Of the total U.S. population, 28.25 percent had at least one parent of foreign birth. This chart includes Brooklyn as part of the greater New York City Metropolitan Area.

TABLE 1.5. German Immigrant Population in the Urban West, 1850

1850	Total Population	German Immigrants	Percentage
St. Louis	77,860	22,340	29%
Cincinnati	115,435	34,000	29%
Louisville	43,194	18,000	42%
Chicago	29,963	6,000	20%

NOTE: These figures are approximate estimates and include second-generation German Americans, or those born to immigrant parents on American soil. For additional statistics on German immigrants to the region, see Leonard Dinnerstein, *Natives and Strangers: Ethnic Groups and the Building of America* (New York: Oxford University Press), 88; Seventh Census of St. Louis, 1850, in Olson, *St. Louis Germans,* 14–15; Carl Wittke, "The Germans of Cincinnati," *Bulletin of the Historical and Philosophical Society of Ohio* 20, no. 1 (Jan. 1962): 3; and *Louisville Journal,* Oct. 8, 1853, in Sister Agnes Geraldine McGann, "The Know-Nothing Movement in Kentucky," *Records of the American Catholic Historical Society* 49, no. 4 (Dec. 1938): 300. See also Hartmut Keil and John B. Jentz, eds., *German Workers in Chicago: A Documentary History of Working-Class Culture from 1850 to World War I* (Urbana: University of Illinois Press, 1988); and Rudolf A. Hofmeister, *The Germans of Chicago* (Champaign, IL: Stipes, 1976).

response to Dubourg's call. When Rosati first observed St. Louis in 1817, a year before Darby's arrival, about four thousand French residents occupied the town. The sole Catholic church, built forty years earlier, was poorly furnished. It lacked doors, windows, and a solid floor. The priests there slept on the ground and wrapped themselves in buffalo skins during the winter. Rosati's efforts during the early years of St. Louis contributed directly to the perpetuation and growth of the city's unique Catholic heritage. Rosati took charge of the Episcopal See of St. Louis in 1818 and was consecrated bishop in 1824. As migrations to the West increased, Catholic leaders placed the city at the center of a new archdiocese in 1827, which included all of Missouri, most of Illinois, and all of the settled territory north of the state of Louisiana.[27]

The completion of the "Old Cathedral," as it is colloquially known in St. Louis, evidenced Bishop Rosati's remarkable success in promoting Catholicism in the West. The building design completely remodeled the drafty French Catholic Church on Third Street. Rosati took personal responsibility for financing the project, campaigned relentlessly for aid from local benefactors, and eventually solicited architects George Morton and Joseph Lavielle to design the new Greek Revival–style stone cathedral. Morton and Lavielle also designed the city's first

courthouse. The architectural style of the new cathedral was deliberately modeled after contemporary U.S. civic buildings to stress the "Americanness" and
legitimacy of Catholics in America. Elaborate pageantry accompanied the dedication of the church on October 26, 1834. A large parade, including three militia
companies and the Jefferson Barracks military band, celebrated the dedication.
Four bishops, twenty seminarians, twenty altar boys, and thirty priests led the
services. Eight days of high masses followed, with sermons in both English and
French. St. Louis parish membership rose rapidly after the building opened.[28]

Catholic leaders carried out similar plans in early Kentucky and Ohio. The
Diocese of Bardstown, just outside of Louisville, became the first inland diocese
of the Catholic Church in 1808. The Episcopal See moved later to Louisville in
1841. The first bishop of Bardstown, Joseph Flaget, laid the cornerstone of the
Basilica of St. Joseph in 1816, and by 1823, the new cathedral, also in the Greek
Revival style, stood as a testament to Catholicism's growing influence in the region. The cathedral's main school, Saint Joseph's College, quickly grew into one
of the West's major Catholic institutions for higher learning. In 1838 Bishop Guy
Ignatius Chabrat of Bardstown informed Bishop Rosati that "notwithstanding
all the efforts our enemies have made and the slanders they have endeavored to
propagate against us, our institutions are in a more prosperous and flourishing
state than they ever have been."[29] One year later Bishop Chabrat exulted, "all
our institutions are filled with pupils and in the most prosperous way the violent
efforts of our enemies against them have completely failed."[30]

The relative strength of Catholicism in the interior of North America appealed to European immigrants. In the 1830s both the bishops of the archdioceses of Bardstown (Kentucky) and Cincinnati wrote letters home encouraging
immigrants to settle in the Ohio River valley. These newcomers tended to follow
similar settlement pathways. The success of Catholicism in the West apparently
inspired immigrants in eastern cities to migrate westward. Furthermore, the
bishop of Boston at the time, Benedict Joseph Fenwick, believed anti-Catholic
sentiment in his city compelled Catholics to resettle in western cities, which
were thought to be more religiously tolerant. They fancied Bardstown (later
Louisville), Cincinnati, and St. Louis as safe havens for their faithful. Bishop
Fenwick intimated to Bishop Rosati in 1837, "The persecuting spirit that prevails
here is driving all our best Catholics to your Missouri."[31]

When Bishop Rosati died in 1843, upward of 40 percent of St. Louis residents worshiped in a Catholic church. His successor, Irish bishop Peter Kenrick,
whose brother, Francis Kenrick, served as the bishop of Philadelphia, observed,
"As no city in the United States enjoys greater opportunity for the practice of

TABLE 1.6. Growth of the Roman Catholic Church in Cincinnati

	Dioceses	*Bishops*	*Churches*	*Priests*	*Seminaries*	*Colleges*
1835	13	14	272	327	12	9
1844	21	26	675	709	22	15

the Catholic religion, so there is none that expresses Catholic life and Catholic character better than St. Louis." Indeed, for its reputation as a Catholic hub, St. Louis received the moniker "Rome of the West."[32]

The construction of Catholic institutions increased at a rapid rate as did the immigration of Catholic Europeans to the West. In 1844 one Cincinnati newspaper noted the dramatic rise of Catholicism nationwide in just ten years' time. The tendency of these immigrants to settle in urban areas made their presence especially striking. Cincinnati claimed seventy Catholic churches, Louisville forty, Chicago thirty-eight, and St. Louis thirty-seven, this in addition to numerous ecclesiastical and lay institutions for men and women in each city. The *Catholic Telegraph* of Cincinnati reported 65,000 parishioners in the Archdiocese of Cincinnati, 40,000 in Louisville's vicinity, and 50,000 in Chicago.[33] The Catholic Church in America also estimated about 57,400 conversions to the faith between 1830 and 1860. Most of these converts were also immigrants.[34]

Why Did Americans Fear Catholicism?

Although on paper the United States tolerated the Catholic religion, Americans at the time of the Revolution were not really sure where their toleration ended, nor did they have to consider it since the Catholic population along the East Coast was negligible. Most of them considered Roman Catholicism an Old World religion on its last leg before extinction. American Catholicism was so marginal at the time of the Revolution that most people outside of Maryland, southern Pennsylvania, and cities such as Boston, Philadelphia, and New York City had little to no actual contact with Catholics.[35]

As the descendants of the British Empire, Anglo-Americans had theological, historical, and political reasons to worry about Roman Catholicism. Theologically, for all their similarities, Catholics and Protestants have fundamentally disagreed over whether salvation is essentially personal or collective. Catholic doctrine builds on the basic belief that the Roman Catholic Church, that organization managed by the pope in Rome and the officially anointed bishops, mediates salvation between God and lay people, while most Protestant churches uphold the tenet that salvation is a process that occurs between God and the individual without intercession. Historically, after the Reformation of the six-teenth century, Catholics and Protestants took up arms against one another in a series of ongoing religious wars. During the colonial era, British citizens on both sides of the Atlantic were taught from a young age that the Catholic nations of Europe posed the greatest threat to their country, especially France and Spain.

Politically, the Roman Catholic Church upheld the bloodline monarchies of Europe for centuries, and in many countries its clerics doubled as spiritual and political leaders. In America, Catholic clerics aided in the Spanish and French colonization and subjugation of Native Americans. In both Europe and Amer-ica, the church owned vast amounts of property, which remained under control of officially sanctioned leaders. Americans could site many examples of church officials endorsing absolute monarchy. Furthermore, contemporary public state-ments issued by various popes and bishops appeared to condemn the democratic revolutions of the late eighteenth and early nineteenth centuries.[36]

As descendants of the Revolution, Americans typically worried that Ca-tholicism—that is, the dogma of the church, not necessarily of every single self-proclaimed Catholic—contradicted the shared set of values that grounded their democracy. During and after the Revolutionary War, they shared a belief in self-government and certain intrinsic rights, namely the individual's right to personal liberty and private property. The ecclesiastical system of the Catholic Church seemed like a top-down hierarchy rather than an institution controlled by the people, although the church was much more decentralized than Ameri-cans thought. The church's commitment to private property ownership seemed weak as it insisted on controlling vast amounts of property in both Europe and America, rather than turning over control to a board of private trustees, as was the norm for American religious organizations. The Roman Catholic Church taught a natural-law theory, which posited that all humans were made in the image of God and thus could know the difference between right and wrong even in the absence of Catholicism, but any "individual" rights came from God specifically through the church. Americans shared a commitment to certain in-dividual freedoms, including the freedom to worship, speak, and print freely and the right to assemble and petition authorities. They believed that Catholicism, as dogma, discouraged individual adherents from thinking, speaking, printing, or assembling independently.[37] Catholic dogma did require a degree of subservi-ence to clerical authorities. Native-born Americans thus worried that Catholics among them served as potential "links in the great chain that is fastened to the foot of the papal throne," as argued in the *Republic: A Magazine for the Defence of Civil and Religious Liberty;* since laymen "are bound to obey their church; they believe it can do no wrong."[38] As a reverend working for the American Home Missionary Society put it: "The cardinal principle of the Latin Church is the destruction of man's individuality and manhood in all the higher functions of his moral nature. He cannot think, judge, believe, choose, address God, or govern himself in the department of his religious interests." Put this way, Catholicism seemed to threaten the very social foundations of the United States.[39]

Dogmatic statements officially mandated by Roman Catholic councils included two especially offensive claims: 1) there was only one true Church, that which the pope and bishops presided over; and 2) the leader of that one true Church, the pope in Rome, held special spiritual and temporal powers. Orestes Brownson, an Anglo-American convert to Catholicism, openly admitted in his newspaper, the *Quarterly Review,* which bore the endorsement of Pope Pius IX as well as nearly every American bishop and was generally thought to be the official organ of the Catholic Church in America, "The Pope is the proper authority to decide for me whether the constitution of this country is or is not repugnant to the laws of God."[40] Brownson explained that one should submit one's mind to that which is true. If it was true that Jesus Christ established the Roman Catholic Church and gave its leadership certain powers—and he believed it was—then it stood to reason that Catholicity "*cannot be carried to excess.*" Roman Catholicism "is not one system among many. It is simply the truth, and nothing but the truth. *It excludes all not itself: it recognizes no rival:* IT WILL BE ALL OR NOTHING."[41] The logic was consistent, but those who did not share Brownson's faith recoiled at his militancy. Individual Catholic and Protestant Christians might be able to coexist, but how could a consistent advocate of Catholicism in principle tolerate a plurality of religions? As a Catholic American who supported religious freedom, Brownson, of course, had much more to say about that.[42]

The pope interpreted divine law as the spiritual head of the church and likewise claimed the temporal power to dispense his followers from their allegiance to any government he deemed hostile to that law, an authority several popes in the past had actually invoked. What if the current pope declared the U.S. government heretical and released his subjects from their oaths as citizens? Americans wondered, as the Catholic population grew to several million in the mid-1850s, would Catholic Americans rally to the Roman pontiff's call to arms? Questions such as these often represented a misunderstanding about the actual

ideas Catholic populations held about dogma and papal power, for even Catholics hotly debated among themselves the limits of the temporal powers of the
pope and later the nature of the doctrine of papal infallibility. For Catholics in
the mid-nineteenth century, the line between church and state authority was
rather ambiguous. As Americans struggled with their own ideas about national
versus state powers, fears of Catholic nationalism grew especially potent.[43]

For these reasons, Americans frequently called into question Catholic loyalty
to the Constitution and the "building blocks" of democracy enshrined therein.
In the event of a conflict between Roman Catholic doctrines and U.S. principles, Americans worried that church leaders would "go against our country and
for the Pope," as one pastor bemoaned. If following Catholicism meant holding
a higher allegiance to the pope in Rome than to the U.S. Constitution, then "a
man can no more be a Papist and a true and loyal American citizen than he can
serve two masters," Reverend Nicholas Murray taught. "He must be either a bad
patriot or [a] Papist."[44] Protestant Christians did not have to choose between
their faith and their country, Americans reasoned, but Catholics did.

The Evangelical "Valley Campaign"

Evangelical Christian Americans, inspired by the recent revivals of the "Second Great Awakening," envisioned the incorporation of the American West as
a crucial part of a larger foreign-missions movement to proselytize to all nations
and peoples. From afar, Christians imagined the vast region as a blank slate and
open field, where American settlers could leave petty denominational conflicts
behind and band together for the expansion of Protestant Christendom. But
migrants actually encountered highly contested ground. Evangelical missionaries expressed deep concerns about secularism, pluralism, and Catholicism.[45]
One agent of the American Home Missionary Society, for example, described
Cincinnati as "truly a most mighty Sodom, not in size but in *wickedness*." Reverend Charles Peabody, an agent of the American Reform Tract and Book Society,
believed the city was "even almost as bad as New York." Likewise the reverend
described St. Louis as a "great bustling and wicked city" in which "the Romanists have long had almost the entire control."[46] "Infidels, Deists, Unitarians, Papists and a hundred other heretical Sects and demi-Sects and semi-Sects and
anti-Sects are rank as weeds over the whole country," one Scottish American
Presbyterian merchant in Louisville bemoaned in 1840.[47] Scores of religious
tracts detailed the apocalyptic scenes awaiting Americans if they allowed such
"irreligion" to thrive in the West.[48]

Early reports warned Christians that the region had become a barbarous, uncivilized place where vice held sway over an ignorant, irreligious, and superstitious population.[49] The first official survey of religious institutions in the West, the Schermerhorn-Mills report of 1814, conducted on behalf of the American Bible Society, yielded grim findings: "There are districts containing from twenty to fifty thousand people entirely destitute of Scriptures and of religious privileges," Mills and Schermerhorn observed during their tour. "The whole country from Lake Erie to the Gulf of Mexico is as the valley of the shadow of death."[50] As early as 1820 one arrival to Louisville feared that "vice and immorality appear to be gaining ground here.... [W]ickedness abounds and religion is a stranger."[51] Reverend Peabody also sent home alarming reports of the influence of morally destitute migrants. Almost all of Ohio, he remarked, "is a complete moral wilderness. Few churches & schools are here & the population is generally poor & ignorant."[52] Likewise, the American Home Missionary Society alerted "our eastern people" to the "omnipresent sense of poverty" in "the West."[53]

The "Valley Campaign" channeled energy and resources from New England's major benevolent societies and religious organizations toward the establishment of Christian institutions in "the immense Valley of the Mississippi, which is to be the future theatre of our greatness," as Reverend Abel Stevens, a campaign leader in Boston in 1834, preached.[54] "There is perhaps no place which presents so great an opportunity to doing good," Presbyterian evangelical Joshua Belden wrote home from St. Louis in July 1830. "The scepter of Dominion is soon to pass from the East to the West. The inhabitants of this valley are soon to sway the destinies of the Nation."[55] While in Boston, Lyman Beecher became one of the Valley Campaign's chief advocates, dedicating an entire series of treatises on the subject, of which *A Plea for the West,* published in 1835, proved the most popular.[56] In a letter dated July 8, 1830, Beecher told his daughter that he longed to move to Cincinnati, "the London of the West," because "the moral destiny of our nation, and all our institutions and hopes, and the world's hopes turns on the character of the West.... If we gain the West, all is safe; if we lose it, all is lost." Beecher practiced what he preached. In 1832 he took the dual appointment as president of Lane Theological Seminary in Cincinnati and pastor of the city's Second Presbyterian Church.[57] A vast network of missionaries and societies responded to Beecher's call because they believed that the fate of the United States hinged on their success.

Missionaries focused their efforts on wresting the valley from the grasp of the Roman Catholic Church. In 1832 an Illinoisan warned about "the prospect of the Roman Catholic religion getting the ascendency in our beloved country" by "gaining ground in the valley of the Missippie."[58] In 1830 the *Fifth Annual Report* of the American Tract Society pleaded for sponsorship, without which "the progress of error and vice at the West . . ., the progress of Romanism, together with open and disguised infidelity," would leave "the world fallen—America ruined."[59] Despite "all the Protestant effort," another migrant wrote home despairingly in 1843, Catholics in Louisville and Cincinnati "embody a population whose only conformity to the divine will" was to "multiply."[60] The American Home Missionary Society therefore urged the planting of "the Gospel in those rich regions, which God has so remarkably wrested from the despotisms of Romish intolerance, and thrown into our hands."[61] Anti-Catholicism, then, gathered momentum in mid-nineteenth-century missions literature.[62]

Certain evangelical groups espoused a postmillennial eschatology that invested the incorporation of the American West with cosmic meaning. Postmillennialists believed a thousand-year period, the millennium, would precede the Second Coming of Jesus Christ, or the Last Judgment, although denominations differed on the exact timing of the events described in various apocalyptic passages in the Bible. They included Baptists, Congregationalists, some Methodists, and "New School" Presbyterians such as Beecher, as well as a host of emergent "nondenominational" sects, including more fringe groups like the Millerites, Jehovah's Witnesses, and Seventh-Day Adventists. Adherents looked for "signs" of the end times foretold in the Bible.[63] A doomsday passage in Revelation 17 prophesied the downfall of the great "whore of Babylon," or the "Beast," before the Second Coming. Postmillennialists interpreted the beast as the same "Antichrist" mentioned in other parts of the Bible. They believed the pope was the Antichrist. The original Westminster Confession, drafted by the Church of England in 1646 as a universal statement of reformed belief, made this anti-Catholic doctrine perfectly clear. Chapter 25.6 states explicitly that the Roman Catholic mass is idolatrous and the pope is the Antichrist. The First Presbyterian Church in America adopted the Westminster Confession in 1729 as a doctrinal standard with which all ministers had to approve. (The Presbyterian Church in the United States ultimately removed this specific anti-Catholic language in 1903).[64]

A peculiar interpretation of the book of Daniel fueled much of the anti-Catholic eschatology. Reverend Samuel Schmucker believed that in Daniel's strange vision in the seventh chapter, the four beasts represented empires, with the fourth bearing "ten horns" referring to the Roman Empire, which was split into ten kingdoms by 536 A.D.[65] Daniel prophesied that the Messiah, or Christ, would arise in the fourth empire. Schmucker believed the first coming of Jesus Christ in the Roman Empire fulfilled this prophecy. Daniel also prophesied that a "little horn," or a little kingdom, would arise among the other ten, absorb three of them, and usher in the reign of the Antichrist. Schmucker believed the Roman papacy was the little horn, since the pope "acquired territory and became a temporal ruler or king, a *politico-religious prince.*" He interpreted the triple papal tiara as an unintentional "emblem of the three kingdoms . . . as tokens of the crowns of Odoacer, of Theodoric and [of] Alboin!" The pope also fit Daniel's description of the Antichrist as "diverse" from all other rulers because, according to Schmucker, "he is both priest and king, combining in himself both secular and ecclesiastical power!"[66] According to Cincinnati's Reverend Boynton, another confirmation of the theory that the pope was the Antichrist was that the "beast" mentioned in Revelation 17:9 "sitteth on the seven hills," and Vatican Hill was situated across the Tiber River from the legendary Seven Hills of Rome. Thus, the papacy, Boynton proclaimed in one 1847 sermon, was the same archenemy true Christians had always faced. The Roman Catholic church under the direction of its "chief engineer," the pope, would continue to lead Christians astray until the end of the world.[67]

Since the late nineteenth century, biblical scholars have been aware that the book of Daniel was probably not written by the Daniel of legend during the Babylonian exile in the sixth century B.C. Instead, most scholars date the book to around the second century B.C. during the Jewish Maccabean Revolt. Early nineteenth-century Protestant theologians failed to see, however, that the author's messianic references were not to a future first-century messiah (Jesus Christ) but to the deposed High Priest Onias III, who the author of Daniel hoped would restore the desecrated Second Temple of Jerusalem. The "little horn," or the Antichrist, described in the apocalyptic portions of the book actually referred to the contemporaneous Greek king of the Seleucid Empire, Antiochus IV Epiphanes. In 167 B.C. Antiochus desecrated the Second Temple by erecting an altar to Zeus.[68]

Catholic theologians, who typically did not embrace postmillennialism, more easily connected Daniel's prophecies to the Maccabean Revolt because they drew on critical information from 1 and 2 Maccabees, deuterocanonical books appearing in the Catholic Bible but not in the Protestant one. First Maccabees offers reliable historical information on Antiochus's desecration of the Second Temple in 167 B.C. as well as the Maccabean movement for an anti-Hellenistic high priest to restore the temple.[69]

Apocalyptic biblical allusions nevertheless permeated evangelical western promotional literature. Beecher's Foreign Mission Society of the Valley of the Mississippi prepared the West for "the approach of the days of the Son of Man," a layered biblical allusion to the messianic figure in Daniel 7:13–14.[70] In 1832 a likeminded minister wrote Reverend Beecher, "Nowhere in all the world can you do half as much to impart and disseminate such views as in the great Western Valley—the Valley of Decision in respect to this, and probably all other nations."[71] "Western Valley" here referred to the Mississippi Valley; "Valley of Decision" frequently appeared as a biblical allusion to the "Valley of Jehoshaphat" described in Joel 3:14, also known as the "Valley of Destruction" or "Decision." In drawing a comparison between the Mississippi Valley and the "Valley of Decision," this minister situated the American West as the millennial location of the final conflagration. Postmillennialists literally interpreted Joel's account as the fate that awaited not only the Jews but also all of God's chosen people at the very end of the world. In this Valley of Decision, according to the postmillennialists' exegesis, God's chosen people would finally be separated from the "wickedness" of the "multitudes" of "heathens" around them. In the last days "the sun and the moon shall be darkened," Joel divined, "and the stars shall withdraw their shining." Then God's wrath will pour forth: "The Lord also shall roar out of Zion, and utter his voice from Jerusalem, and the heavens and the earth shall shake." God's people who survive the conflagration afterward gain paradise: "the mountains shall drop down new wine, and the hills shall flow with milk, and all the rivers of Judah shall flow with waters, and a fountain shall come forth out of the house of the Lord, and shall water the valley of Shittim."[72] The evangelical Valley Campaign stood to bring "the Millennium to the very doors." The final showdown would not be between ancient Hebrews and Pagan Moabs, but rather between "true" and "false" Christians in North America.[73]

By the mid-1830s, anti-Catholicism had reached a fever pitch in popular media. A sensational book written by Samuel Finley Breese Morse in 1835 captured the anti-Catholic vitriol. Today most people remember him as the inventor of the telegraph (Morse Code is named in his honor), but he was well known at the time as the nation's most prominent advocate for immigration reform. Morse's *Foreign Conspiracy Against the Liberties of the United States* quickly became a bestseller. The young inventor claimed to have discovered a secret papal plot to destroy the American republic from within. Emperor Ferdinand I of Austria and Pope Gregory XVI of Rome conspired to carry out the deed through a three-step process, Morse announced: first, they would raise special funds to build Catholic institutions in the American West, where Protestant institutions were scarce; second, they would employ Jesuits to warp the minds of America's youth in Catholic schools (by day) and infiltrate government entities (by night); and third, clerics in America would, upon receiving the command from Rome, incite Catholic immigrants to mass insurrection. Several at the time called into question the validity of Morse's evidence, but the book rose above its critics' concerns and became a vital component of Americans' popular imagination. Many became convinced—seriously—that the allegations were true.[74] "The Jesuits and their Ursuline sisters are in their seminaries," a writer using the pseudonym "Native American" wrote in 1835, "silently weaving the winding sheet for our liberties."[75]

Another self-proclaimed nativist and ex-Catholic priest, Samuel B. Smith, published a sensational book only a year after Morse's *Foreign Conspiracy,* playing on fears of Catholic expansion in the West. In *The Flight of Popery from Rome to the West,* Smith elaborated on a Rome-led immigrant conspiracy to snatch control of the Mississippi Valley. The scheme, he alleged, aimed at founding a new Catholic kingdom in the American West just as the democratic revolutionaries in Austria and Italy were poised to drive Emperor Ferdinand I of Austria from his throne and the pope from Rome. The "popish intrigues" Smith listed included alleged secret meetings behind the closed doors of Jesuit schools, in which Catholic leaders plotted the overthrow of America, and secret inquisition chambers and tunnels beneath Catholic cathedrals, with weapons stashed there for the impending uprising.[76]

Reverend William Wiener claimed that the insurrectionists had already chosen St. Louis as the site for the first action because the "French papists" had named it after King Louis IX, a crusader and one of the most renowned military figures in Catholic hagiography.[77] Smith took the conspiracy theory one step further: he claimed that the pope intended to move the Vatican across the Atlantic to St. Louis or perhaps Cincinnati; he could not be sure. "Every Romish temple that rises in the West," Smith warned, "will swell the Jubilee of Popish triumph, till the day rolls on, when the distant Valley of the West will toll the death of our Republic."[78]

Conclusion

The rapid development of the antebellum West wrought conflicting views: some considered the settling of the Mississippi and Ohio River valleys a sign of God's blessing to the United States; others saw it as a potential source of subversion from within. The Valley Campaign's "revival plea" intermingled hope for the perfection of Christian unity and the Second Coming of Christ with fear for a nation that remained unresponsive to the supposed lack of morality in the West. Many believed the American West was the final battleground upon which the fate of their nation would be decided. Religious competition in the region continued to forge American national identity, especially once American-immigrant disagreements over value-laden school policies and Sunday laws triggered a veritable culture war.

CHAPTER 2

Culture War

We find in many States, cities, and towns, an open war
on the part of our Catholic fellow-citizens against the use of the Bible.

—Lewis D. Campbell, American Party rally speech, 1855

The attempt to substitute for our Protestant Sabbath a Catholic holiday,
to make it a day of parade and show and amusement, to accustom our children
to its desecration, is only a part of the general attack upon our institutions.

—Charles B. Boynton, *Address before the Citizens of Cincinnati*, July 4, 1855

MANY AMERICANS REACTED VISCERALLY to instances in which immigrant groups challenged the status quo.[1] Catholics remained primary targets, but an ensuing culture war circumscribed various immigrant customs that native-born Americans deemed culturally corrosive. Public schools served the interests of promoting nationalism and inducing assimilation during the era of westward expansion. Implicitly Protestant Christian school curricula, however, repelled Catholics, Germans, and Irish. Immigrant resistance to the use of the King James Bible in American public schools entailed a controversy reaching beyond the domains of pedagogy or theology. From the perspective of native-born Americans, the successful assimilation of Catholics and German and Irish immigrants was not a foregone conclusion. The mid-nineteenth-century school controversy directly motivated America's first political nativist movement, which associated Protestant Christianity with American greatness and promoted the mandatory use of the King James Bible in schools as the primary way to convert Catholics, Germans, and Irish to American national values.

Likewise, Sunday regulations in the United States defined the requirements for national belonging. Local leaders utilized Sunday closing laws to prevent Catholic feasting and German-style recreation on the Lord's Day. Immigrants of all backgrounds and creeds, ironically enough, united politically against Sunday regulation. This process was most clearly observed in the urban West. Upon arrival, immigrants from distant provinces of the German Confederation discovered cultural bonds and political solidarity as German Americans.

Immigrants of various religious persuasions frequently rejected standard American curricula and Sunday regulations. Catholics, Germans, and Irish formed their own educational and cultural institutions to meet demand, and immigrant political solidarity expanded. Implicitly Protestant Christian biases repelled many Catholics and immigrants from the very institutions designed to induce their assimilation.

The Limits of "Nonsectarian" Education

The founders of the United States mandated public schools in order to prepare young pupils for exercising their American citizenship. They believed that universal literacy and basic knowledge formed the basis of a healthy, self-governing republic.[2] In his "Bill for the More General Diffusion of Knowledge," Thomas Jefferson explained that the best way to foster representative government was through the meritorious selection of officeholders "without regard to wealth, birth or other accidental condition." Education, rather than bloodlines or titles, he believed, could elevate the status of all men regardless of birth.[3]

Jefferson proposed a three-tiered system of state-sponsored education in Virginia, including three years of state-funded primary schooling, free tuition for select boys at twenty regional academies, and even free tuition for undergraduates at the University of Virginia.[4] The education of women was not in his purview. Legislatures repeatedly rejected Jefferson's plans for education as well as similar plans drafted by the first six presidents of the United States—including George Washington, who bequeathed his own money for founding a national university in the District of Columbia—because many property owners objected to paying taxes for anything other than primary schools. Besides, those who could afford it preferred enrolling their children in status-affirming private academies.[5]

Public schools lacked funding and institutional standards. Many states and territories did not address this problem in full earnest until the 1840s. The Northwest and Southwest Ordinances of 1787 and 1790 mandated public schools in western districts, but westward expansion occurred at such a rapid rate during the early nineteenth century that school construction could not keep up with migrating populations. Immigration from Europe, moreover, added the complication of educating non-American and non-English-speaking inhabitants in the territorial West, which fell under the U.S. government's jurisdiction.

While state governments lagged behind, American religious organizations quickly took up the mantle of education in the West. Church-affiliated societies in the East raised enormous amounts of money for the development of Sunday schools in needy areas, raising over $200,000 by 1827. By 1830, Joshua Belden, a missionary in St. Louis, celebrated the Presbyterian Church's mission "to establish Sunday Schools in every settlement in this valley, within the short space of two years." For him, the education of westerners was "fraught with greater consequences to the Nation than any ever before adopted."[6] Not until 1840 did state-funded common schools begin to supplant Sunday schools, and even then only gradually and unevenly over the next couple of decades.

Due to the plurality of Protestant sects in America, educators typically adopted a policy of "religious civility," by which Christians might put aside denominational differences and unite for the sake of making the illuminating light of knowledge available to all Americans. Public-school administrator and instructor Calvin Stowe (husband of Harriet Beecher Stowe, Lyman Beecher's daughter) believed "that notwithstanding the diversity of sects, there is common ground, on which the sincerely pious of all sects substantially agree."[7] The Western Literary Institute, founded in Cincinnati in 1831, vowed to educate students "of all climes and languages and religions under heaven."[8] American educational institutions frequently demonstrated a commitment to nonsectarianism, insofar as participants fell under the umbrella of Protestant Christianity.[9] Numerous evangelical coalitions allied for the educational development of the West, including the American Sunday School Union, the American Bible Society, the American Education Society, the American Tract Society, the American Home Missionary Society, and the American Protestant Society. Some organizations were blunter about their designs, such as the Evangelical Alliance to Overthrow the Papacy.[10]

In 1827 Mary Sibley and her husband, George, founded a Presbyterian academy for young women in St. Charles, a Missouri River town about thirty miles north of St. Louis.[11] Together, the couple composed a living metaphor for American citizenship: Mary, a dedicated believer, represented the religious character of the republic; George, an avowed agnostic, represented the civil. Mary accommodated her students of different backgrounds by keeping her religious zeal at bay, and George promoted the Christian principles that supposedly supported American democracy. The original Lindenwood charter proposed a course of instruction "Intellectual, Moral and Domestic, based on the Settled principles of the Christian Religion, and carefully adapted to those on which are founded the free institutions of our Country."[12] Lindenwood School affiliated with the Presbyterian Church, but its official circular promised parents that teachers would not attempt to indoctrinate students in the theology of infant baptism and predestination; rather, the Sibleys guaranteed that all lessons would be nonsectarian, or at least broad enough to encompass the views of nearly all trinitarian Christian denominations in the region, Baptists, Congregationalists, Methodists, and Presbyterians alike.

It was no secret to anyone that knew her: Mary Sibley was among the most avid of believers. Her Sunday activities included attending a morning Bible study and two separate sermons, one at her Presbyterian church at 11:00 A.M., and another at the local Methodist church at 2:30 P.M.; organizing prayer meetings in the late afternoon; and teaching a "Sabbath School for Slaves" in the evening. Sibley also ran a 9:00 A.M. Sunday school session for the Presbyterian church in the town, which maintained strong ties to St. Louis minister William Potts. During the week, she worked for the Female Benevolent Society disseminating Bibles and religious tracts. She ardently supported temperance and raised awareness of alcohol abuse once she finished her weekly duties for the local Bible club, the Foreign Mission Society, and the American Colonization Society. In her spare time Sibley wrote religious articles for Elijah Parish Lovejoy's *St. Louis Observer*.[13]

The same could not be said of her husband and Lindenwood School cofounder, George Sibley. Unlike his apparently pious wife, George remained "incredulous as to the truth of the Christian religion," to use his own words from a letter he wrote to an acquaintance. He was for most of his life an avowed agnostic, a crucial factor, it would seem, in the decision of at least a few secularly minded southern gentlemen to send their daughters to Lindenwood School.[14] One concerned parent, William Russell, expressly requested that his daughter not waste any of her study time on religion nor her playtime on "revivals or night meetings," which he believed were far "too exciting to the students." The recent memory of his two nephews neglecting school in nearby Belleville, Illinois, to attend such revivals haunted him still. "I don't know that there have been such meetings in St. Charles," Russell told the Sibleys, "but I object to any youth under my charge going to them either day or night." He called such revivals a "contagious disease," the "wickedness of bigot makers," and ultimately "a prostitution and straight forward service of the devil."[15]

George Sibley and his benefactors never renounced the teaching of Christian values, so long as they were not presented from a particular sectarian, or denominational, point of view. This is why concerned parent Russell could rail against "night meetings," rant about teachers who dare "to catechize or to lecture about matters of religion," yet insist that his daughter attend "Church on Sunday, or, at an appropriate time, to read the Bible."[16]

Providing education in western Sunday schools initially functioned as a generic Christian charity for the "destitute." In many places churches were the only organizations offering primary education to "many thousands of poor and vagrant children," George Sibley observed. He believed that Sunday schools were also "*anti-sectarian* in [their] construction, object and tendency" because they aimed to teach children "the first rudiment of education" and inculcate them only in the "*undisputed* doctrines" of Christianity. According to his wife, Sunday schools generally received "the sanction of all the principal Protestant sects." Local Germans of all creeds took advantage of free Sunday School lessons to learn rudimentary English. In the summer of 1832, Mary Sibley celebrated how the "cabin" in which she taught on Sundays housed "mostly Dutch children" ("Dutch" was a common moniker for "German"), although she complained in private about German Catholic children missing school when bishops from New Orleans visited St. Charles.[17]

Although Mary Sibley promoted nonsectarian education as faithfully as her husband, she nevertheless possessed quite different reasons for it. She was sickened to see Presbyterians, Methodists, and other evangelical Christian groups in the area bickering over "doctrinal points which every sect admit not essential to Salvation."[18] Part of her disgust with Protestant infighting was that it distracted fellow educators from combating their common foe: the Roman Catholic Church. Catholic immigrants started arriving in the West in greater numbers during the 1820s. The Jesuit-run Saint Louis University, founded in 1818, had thrived in the city. And other Catholic schools quickly emerged there as well. German Catholics began to settle upriver in St. Charles. Sibley argued in an article for the *St. Louis Observer* that "the Jesuits and Romans are for the most part anything but Christians." Furthermore, "Jesuits, Papists, and Infidels," Mary warned, would be "united in the latter days against the Children of God to stop the progress of the Redeemer's cause."[19] She recorded her growing disgust with Catholicism in her personal diary. When a Jesuit priest dropped by her residence requesting financial support for the construction of a new convent, Mary refused to greet him and stewed instead up in her room. George went outside, graciously received the priest, and even donated a couple of dollars to the cause. What could be more inimical to her vocation, she wondered in private, than the arrival of Catholic immigrants "under the influence of the Roman priest?"[20]

Sibley documented her several attempts to convert the German Catholics in St. Charles. When one family refused to receive propaganda from the Female Benevolent Society, she slipped a tract into a book on their shelf anyways. Another time she sat for hours witnessing to a dying Catholic woman who was so ill she could hardly speak. Sibley regularly passed out German-language religious tracts to her students, prepared with the help of German translators within the St. Charles auxiliary of the American Tract Society. When Catholic passersby walked in and out of sight, she prayed silently "that God would enlighten the minds of all deluded persons." She also admitted in her diary that she was most anxious to teach young ladies from New Orleans so "they may carry home some of those principles of the Christian religion which are so little known to the inhabitants of the Catholic districts of Louisiana."[21]

Mary Sibley believed that in order to convert European immigrants to the American worldview, educators must first rescue the Catholics in their midst "from the dark superstitions of the Romish Church." One of the stories she wrote down in her diary is particularly revealing. In 1832 she promised one Mrs. Hunt, the Catholic mother of two new recruits to Lindenwood School named Theodosia and Julia, that she would not induce the girls "to abandon [their] religion." But at one point she wrote a pointed letter to the mother expressing her concern that Theodosia's Catholicism "will prevent her from progressing very rapidly in her studies." The implication in the letter was that Protestantism was a system of thought completely compatible with critical intellectual development, while Catholicism was fundamentally opposed to free and open inquiry. Sibley claimed that the student's Catholicism would do nothing more than to "secure her from the contamination of what you consider heretical opinion." She wrote Mrs. Hunt also that her younger daughter, Julia, was an exception among Catholic students because she "has a mind that will lead her to demand the why's and wherefore's"; Julia, Sibley prodded, "will likewise be more apt to become a Protestant, if she ever turns her attention to the subject of religion."[22] How this minute encounter immediately affected Mrs. Hunt and her girls remains unknown, but it certainly did not stand alone. Mary Sibley's exchange embodied the attitudes of many American educators in the region.

Presbyterian minister Elijah Parish Lovejoy first came to St. Louis in 1827 to found a day school and evangelize against Catholicism, which was "spreading in our country to an alarming degree, and this too entirely by foreign influence."[23] Reverend Lovejoy today is better known as the editor of the antislavery *Alton Observer* in Illinois and as the first "martyr of abolition," but he devoted more time to mission efforts than politics.[24] He served as the secretary of the Missouri and Illinois Tract Society, which promoted Bible reading, tract distribution, temperance, and Sunday schools. As an editor of the *St. Louis Observer,* Lovejoy urged his fellow countrymen to guard against "the hordes of ignorant, unedu-cated, vicious foreigners who are now flocking to our shores, and who, under the guidance of Jesuit Priests, are calculated, fitted and intended to *subvert our liberties.*"[25] He also condemned Protestant parents who sent their children to Catholic parochial schools since Catholic management of "schools, nunneries and colleges for the especial benefit of Protestants," the reverend warned, was part of "a covert, crafty design."[26]

Like the Sibleys at Lindenwood, David Todd Stuart, Presbyterian minister and head of the Shelbyville Female College located thirty miles east of Louis-ville, Kentucky, described his academy as nonsectarian and admitted Catholic girls, although he believed "an institution should have some decided religious character." One day he invited a reverend to address the "girls on the subject of Romish Female Schools." Reverend Ropeter "requested our girls to form a society and make our school a life-member of the Evangelical Society," Stuart wrote in his journal. He appointed several students to raise money for the Evan-gelical Society to combat Roman Catholicism in the West. This might have been awkward for the Catholic students in attendance, but "Lavinia Winchester—a Catholic," Stuart mentioned in his journal, "took his remarks in good part."[27]

Catharine Beecher, the daughter of Lyman Beecher, raised funds for the Western Female Institute in Cincinnati for the explicit purpose of preventing Catholic convents from gaining control "of an ungoverned, ignorant, and un-principled populace."[28] A fellow educator based in Philadelphia, Sarah Josepha Hale, raised alarm over the growing number of Catholic convents in the West. "Female education must be provided for," she warned, "otherwise convents will increase, and Catholicism become permanently rooted in our country." Good republican households required good Christian mothers, Hale argued, and Catholic convents corroded the ability of women to teach their children Amer-ican republican values.[29] Evangelical Christians who contributed to the surge of benevolence, voluntarism, and revival in the early nineteenth century generously sponsored educational initiatives in the West to ensure that people of all classes and creeds could read the Bible for themselves.[30]

The King James Bible as a Textbook

Public schools performed the potentially vital function of teaching children American values. In order to promote unity over division in a religiously plural nation, American educators committed themselves to "non-sectarian" education. Educators insisted that the Bible, without note or comment, was universal, like American values; the Bible transcended "sectarian" principles so that the only teachers guilty of undue sectarianism were those who used scripture to preach on specific doctrines. Because Americans insisted on using the King James Version of the Bible in public schools, however, pedagogical and theological disagreement between native-born Americans and immigrants became a national dilemma.

Pedagogically, American educators generally agreed that the King James Bible should be included in American curricula, but as professor of American Studies Laurence Moore pointed out, they were confused about how exactly instructors should use scripture, whether as a textbook or devotional book. Moore identified "two distinguishable rationales for Bible reading": the first stressed the various applications of biblical truths to other, secular areas of school instruction, while the second emphasized biblical studies as an extracurricular, devotional practice. Generally speaking, the educators in the Common School Revival of the 1840s and 1850s did not support the Bible as a textbook on its own but as a supplemental source for lessons in arithmetic, geography, grammar, history, and other subjects. Frequent pedagogical and theological disagreements between immigrants and Americans, Catholics and Protestants, and among Protestant Americans forged the transformation of the use of Bible from an applied source offering periodic instruction in general Christianity to a devotional source serving primarily civic purposes. The Bible increasingly served as a token of reverence for the supposed principles of the American nation, much like the pledge of allegiance ritual at the beginning of the school day.[31]

Theologically, Germans preferred to read Martin Luther's German-language translation. Moreover, most Catholics refused to let their children read the King James Version because the Catholic Church had maintained a running ban on it since its publication in 1611. The Vatican also upheld bans on other "Protestant translations" prohibited by Pope Pius IV in the Index of the Council of Trent of 1559. Although Pius eventually gave his permission for vernacular translations of the Bible, he decreed that Catholics should read only translations approved by the holy office. Many Catholic leaders considered reading "Protestant" translations a grave sin that could potentially result in excommunication. They constantly turned away Bible tenders, tract evangelizers, Protestant ministers, and educators for this very reason. Catholic parents across the United States pleaded with state boards of education to allow their children to bring their own pope-approved Bibles to school. If not that, then they asked them to exempt

Catholic pupils from reading the King James Version in class. If no other option could be found, then they wanted to remove Bible study from common school curricula altogether.[32]

Americans took special umbrage with immigrants' resistance to the King James Bible because to them it represented the Reformation, religious ingenuity, and freedom in the English-speaking world. First of all, Americans argued that the King James Version offered a more accurate English translation based on better Greek sources than the Roman Catholic Church–approved Douay-Rheims Version, which was based on St. Jerome's fourth-century Latin translation, also known as the Vulgate. King James I's English translation of the Bible, finally completed in 1611, replaced many of the old traditional interpretations and statements of Catholic dogma with new commentary. Furthermore, in keeping with German reformer Martin Luther, the scholars commissioned by King James rejected the canonicity of several Old Testament books. The Catholic Bible still includes six books that King James's scholars expunged, including Tobit, Judith, First and Second Maccabees, the Wisdom of Solomon, and Baruch. Protestant theologians refer to these as the Apocrypha, or works of "dubious authenticity."[33]

The very ability to update translations of the Bible and adjust the canon became a significant part of Protestant American Christianity itself. "Nowhere did the marriage between Protestantism and the Enlightenment produce more lively offspring," historical theologian Mark Noll has pointed out, "than in the American appropriation of the Bible." Americans endorsed the "open Bible" concept. They assumed that the scriptures were perspicuous and that ordinary people could glean essential "truths" from passages without any theological commentary, reference tools, or clerical guidance. The particular hermeneutic of Bible reading in the United States implicitly entailed a narrative about American identity: that American citizens had the right to read the Bible for themselves, and that they should, lest they fail to practice what inspired their unique sense of independence in the first place.[34] Most Americans associated reading the Protestant Bible with what one nativist writer later christened the country's "*holy principle*"—that is, private judgment.[35] Even as an agnostic, George Sibley defended Bible reading in schools because the "civil and religious rights to read and study and investigate its truth" undergirded the "national character" of the people of the United States.[36] According to Presbyterian minister Nicholas Murray, a few basic components united America's Christian denominations: "an open Bible, repentance towards God, [and] faith in our Lord Jesus Christ, without any intervening power between the individual soul and God." According to Murray, "religion in this land is a personal matter—just what the Bible makes it." The

ability of individual citizens to access the Protestant Bible and interpret it themselves paralleled the independence of mind required in American civic life, while
the mediation of priests, Murray claimed, seemed incompatible in principle with
American democracy.[37]

   While a public policy of implicitly Protestant Christian instruction might
have placated most native-born Americans, immigrants presented a challenge.
In addition to opposing the King James, many immigrants also expressed concern about exposing their children to the anti-European, anti-Catholic narratives in American textbooks. History texts in primary schools emphasized the
"historical" tendency of Catholic Europe to produce ignorance and superstition,
infidelity and bloodshed. One of the more widely used geography textbooks
taught students, *"In most Roman Catholic countries,* the people are forbidden to
read the Bible, and many other books; and while there is often a large number
of learned men, the people are generally very ignorant."[38] Samuel Putnam's 1828
Sequel to the Analytical Reader identified Protestant John Huss as "a zealous
reformer from Popery. . . . He was bold and preserving; but at length, trusting
himself to the deceitful Catholics, he was by them brought to trial, condemned
as a heretic, and burnt at the stake."[39] An explicitly anti-Catholic textbook for
youngsters became popular in Massachusetts, going through a total of seven
editions between 1844 and 1850: *The Trial of the Pope of Rome, the antichrist or
Man of Sin described in the Bible, for high treason against the Son of God, before
the Right Hon. Divine Revelation, the Hon. Justice Reason, and the Hon. Justice History.*[40] Catholic parents complained about biased history and geography
texts in the common schools. One group in New York, for example, petitioned
the Public School Society: "Many of the selections in their elementary reading
lessons contain matter prejudicial to the Catholic name and character. . . . The
term 'POPERY' is repeatedly found in them. This term is known and employed
as one of insult and contempt towards the Catholic religion."[41]

   Indeed, during the antebellum era, American public schools hardly ever embraced pure secularism. Americans typically agreed with educator Horace Bushnell that their public schools ought "to be Christian schools." The American educational system, once reformed, could uphold "one school and one Christianity,"
Bushnell explained, and thus "cement the generations to come in a closer unity."[42]
In most state-funded schools, passages from scripture formed the content basis
of lessons in courses such as English grammar, French, geology, Greek, history,
Latin, natural philosophy, reading, and spelling.[43] Boards of education encouraged instructors to focus on passages from the Bible that reinforced American
principles. Massachusetts educator Horace Mann campaigned relentlessly for

nationwide state-funded public education, with uniform curricula and facilities for immigrant and native-born Americans alike. Mann believed, in a manner not too far removed from Jefferson, that common schools for common people vindicated "all rational hopes respecting the future."[44] This vision built on what one historian called a "characteristic American faith" that common education would "ensure that public deliberation would begin at a sufficiently high level to be instructive in practice as well as theory."[45] Mann continued to mandate Bible-based curricula, during his campaign to enforce uniform standards and curricula nationwide. Thus, the Common School Revival established a public school system that scholars have since described as "openly Christian, avowedly nonsectarian, and implicitly Protestant."[46]

Boards of education in nearly every county mandated the use of the King James Bible, without note or comment, as required curriculum. Most American boards, after all, included Christian ministers. In St. Louis, for example, William Renshaw served as both the president of the Missouri Sunday School Union and of the Board of St. Louis Public Schools.[47] At the same time in Cincinnati, William S. Ridgley, pastor of the city's First Presbyterian Church and chairperson of the Young Men's Bible Society of Cincinnati, also served on the board of public schools.[48] James Young Scammon, founder of the New Jerusalem Church in Chicago, the first Swedenborgian church established in the area, presided as the president of the Board of Chicago Public Schools from 1843 to 1845. William Jones, Scammon's co-member at the Chicago Lyceum and a brother at New Jerusalem, also served as president of Chicago's school board twice, between 1840 and 1843 and again in 1851. Numerous other examples could be provided for almost every town in America.[49]

Americans interpreted immigrant resistance to the King James Version as the undue influence of foreign clerics. They recalled the apparent effect of the availability of the Bible in sixteenth-century Europe. The Roman Catholic Church considered unapproved translations heretical, and Protestant reformers avidly read the Bible in the vernacular and used passages to condemn Catholic doctrines. Similarly, Americans in the nineteenth century believed an open Bible would compel Catholic citizens to challenge their church's doctrines. Reverend Murray predicted in one of his widely read anti-Catholic books that "the circulation of the Bible will be the death of popery." "Everything in the Bible is simple," he claimed, and "not a word is said about popes, patriarchs, cardinals, metropolitans, prelates, or of the duty of implicit obedience to their authority."[50] John A. Gurley promoted an open Bible in his Cincinnati newspaper, *Star in the West,* to annihilate the "superstition of Catholicism."[51]

Numerous Bible societies in the West received a steady stream of donations from benefactors in the East simply to make the scriptures available, without comment or note. Early organizations, such as the Rehoboth Society in Cincinnati, raised substantial funds to circulate Bibles for "the suppression of vice and immorality."[52] The Louisville and Vicinity Bible Society, founded as an auxiliary to the American Bible Society in 1836, distributed nearly 6,000 Bibles annually.[53] The Young Men's Bible Society of Cincinnati, also an auxiliary of the American Bible Society, distributed 30,610 copies in just two years (1842–44); at the time, Cincinnati's entire population was approximately 50,000.[54]

Distributing agents made special efforts to press King James Bibles on Catholics. When one agent came upon such a household in Louisville in 1839, the man told him he wanted "no Protestant Bible." Seeing that the householder's daughter was eager for a copy, the agent "handed her a New Testament." Her father then remarked, "When we lived in New Albany, Iowa, this girl went to the Presbyterian Sunday School, and now she cannot be content without a Testament . . . poor thing, let her have one anyhow, it will not hurt her." The Louisville and Vicinity Bible Society counted this a major victory against the degenerating influence of Catholicism in the city.[55]

It had to be the King James, Reverend Edward P. Humphrey told his congregation in 1852, because Catholic versions included extensive commentary, or "Jesuitical" sophistry, as he put it. Humphrey acted as the chairman of the Board of Domestic Missions of the Presbyterian Church. Catholics had been trained, he insisted, to relinquish individual common sense and reason to the discretion of their priestly authorities. Before even attempting to read their Bible, Humphrey claimed, parishioners were instructed to "study the acts of Councils in thirty-one folio volumes, consulting carefully the Papal Bulls in eight volumes, and the Decretals in ten volumes, . . . 'the unanimous consent of the fathers' through their thirty-five volumes; then study diligently the acts and doings of the saints, in fifty-one volumes; then, after you have read, learned and inwardly digested the solid contents of these one hundred and thirty-five mortal folios—all in canonical Latin and Greek—go up and down the earth, chasing the phantoms of apostolical and ecclesiastical traditions, and thus you ascertain what is the truth of God." A rule of interpretation such as this, argued Reverend Humphrey, confounded the meaning of the scriptures and "set up the clergy as the authoritative expounders of God's word."[56]

Not only did Catholic immigrants resist the use of the King James Version, but many also refused to matriculate in American schools altogether. In *A Plea for the West,* Beecher argued that the Catholic clergy induced the "aversion to instruction from book, tract, or Bible" as part of their design "to prevent assimilation and perpetuate the principles of a powerful cast." He believed Catholic parents withheld their children from American public schools to avoid "the ordeal of an enlightened public sentiment" and "the searching inspection of the public eye." If only these immigrants "mingled in our schools," Beecher bemoaned, "the republican atmosphere would impregnate their minds." If they could read the Bible, then "their darkened intellect would brighten." If they could "think for themselves" and cut ties with the Pope, then "we might trust to time and circumstances to mitigate their ascendancy and produce assimilation."[57] Beecher believed only *American* education would properly assimilate foreigners in the West. Primary schools and colleges, he told the faculty and students of Miami University in Cincinnati, functioned as "the guardians of liberty and equality." To remove the King James Bible from American schools, Beecher warned, "is as anti-republican as it is unchristian."[58]

Father Edward Purcell, brother of Bishop John Baptist Purcell of Cincinnati, offered full responses in the *Catholic Telegraph,* the official organ of the Archdioceses of Cincinnati and Louisville. First of all, the priest pointed out that the distribution of the King James Bible in particular was "offensive to the Catholics" because the church considered it "an erroneous translation, particularly in several doctrinal points." He could scarcely conceive of an act "of more imprudent insolence than that of an individual in the capacity of a Bible distributor intruding on the privacy of the domestic Catholic circle for the purpose of soliciting their perusal of a work which they deem spurious."[59] Furthermore, Purcell criticized "the right of privately interpreting" scriptures as untenable because there was no conceivable end to individual interpretations, and private judgment alone seemed powerless to condemn "false" interpretations of the Bible. Here, he cited the "radical" sects of the Millerites and Mormons.[60] According to Purcell, the church's teaching authority helped unite Catholics against many "errors," while Protestant denominations succumbed to factionalism and infighting.[61] He argued it was fitting for ordained priests to interpret scripture because they typically received more exegetical training than the average layman. Ultimately, he believed priests received a special charism from God to interpret his Word. In a letter to the editor, Phebe Daugherty, a Catholic educator who at the time raised funds for a new convent for the Sisters of Visitation in Lancaster, Ohio, cited Malachi 2:7 to justify clerical oversight: "the lips of the priests shall keep knowledge, and they shall seek the law at his mouth."[62]

According to Purcell, Catholics could freely choose whether or not to read the Bible or to abide by Catholic doctrines. Actually, most Douay-Rheims Bibles included a 1778 letter by Pope Pius VI, which stated, in part: "[Scriptures] are the most abundant sources which ought to be left open to everyone, to draw from them purity of morals and of doctrines—to eradicate the errors which are so widely disseminated in these corrupt times."[63] Purcell took special offense at the purported mission of Cincinnati's Western Protestant Association to deliver Catholic immigrants from clerical oversight. In one of their meetings in 1843, "much was said about the opposition of Catholicity to human freedom," he reported. "We were all charged with a desire to destroy the liberties of the country; it was said that we were enemies of the Bible, lovers of ignorance, hostile to the institutions of the United States and inimical to the principle of toleration." Purcell retorted that Catholics did not want to attend Protestant worship services, not because they were afraid of priests, but because they thought such ceremonies were ridiculous: "Attend Protestant worship! Listen to some man make a speech and a prayer and call that worship! Resign all pretension to Truth and follow the innumerable doctrines of Protestantism, all contradicting each other as if God was a Liar!" Numerous Catholic immigrants in Cincinnati wrote the *Catholic Telegraph* to express their approval of Purcell's sentiments, and a group of laymen even organized monthly protests against the Western Protestant Association.[64]

Cincinnati's Catholic Society for the Diffusion of Useful Knowledge ridiculed apparent Protestant divisiveness along the lines Purcell laid out in his newspaper. In 1840 one tract circulating in the city taught a didactic lesson in which a man expecting to enter heaven approached Jesus on the Day of Judgment. Christ asks him, "Hast *thou* given ear to the teaching of *that church* which I established?" The man responds, "Lord, *that* church fell into gross errors, and corruptions, and damnable idolatry: and I would not believe its doctrines, but *protested* against them." Jesus and the "protesting Christian" exchange several more lines, and Christ accuses him of being "*faithless*" for failing to trust his promise to preserve the church (Matthew 16:18). The tract cites the Douay-Rheims translation of 1 Timothy 3:15: "the church of the living God, the pillar and ground of the truth."[65]

Catholic Education

For the most part, Catholic educators in the region focused on retaining coreligionists more than converting western inhabitants. Church leaders did not have the grip on their charges that Anglo-American Protestants often assumed. Initially, Catholic leaders struggled to reign in a confused, decentralized, and occasionally rebellious network of clergymen. Bishop Chabrat of Bardstown,

Kentucky, constantly complained of insubordinate priests and unfit teachers. Addressing Bishop Rosati of St. Louis, he lamented, "you well know that there are in Kentucky some clergymen who have very curious ideas concerning Episcopal authority." In another letter he declared, "it is high time to make some of our clergymen here understand what is meant by *promitto obedientam* [pledge of obedience]."[66] In 1826 Bishop DuBourg became so fed up with intransigent French Catholic clergy and dissidents that he resigned his post. Vatican administrators divided DuBourg's archdiocese into two dioceses, one based in New Orleans and the other in St. Louis, appointing Rosati as first bishop of the latter. They offered him the bishopric of New Orleans, but he refused.[67]

Catholic institutions in the Mississippi Valley also faced a chronic shortage of resources. As evangelical societies in the East poured funds into education projects in the West, the bishops of Cincinnati and St. Louis requested funds from international benefactors, particularly from Austria's Leopold Foundation and the Propagation of the Gospel in America, founded in 1829. Aid arrived, but in the smallest of sums. Samuel Morse nevertheless exploited the connection as his chief example of an Austrian-led, Roman Catholic conspiracy to subvert U.S. sovereignty in the West.[68] Catholic institutions relied primarily on local wealthy benefactors, such as philanthropist John Mullanphy, whose generous contributions enabled the construction of the first Catholic hospital west of the Mississippi in St. Louis. Over time they drew a steady stream of donations from middle-and working-class German and Irish Catholic immigrants as well.[69]

In 1830 Bishop Edward Fenwick of Cincinnati started a campaign to raise funds for Catholic schools to serve the "superabundant population of ancient Europe" streaming into the United States. He urged his colleagues to "make haste; the moments are precious." The bishop contemplated that "America may one day become the centre of civilization" and asked, "shall truth or error establish there its empire?" He further worried, "If the Protestant sects are beforehand with us, it will be difficult to destroy their influence."[70] In only four years' time, the competition seemed to intensify. Fenwick's successor as bishop, John Baptist Purcell, noted with alarm how many Catholic children had taken to attending Protestant-managed schools. "So many little children are perverted," he fretted, "in consequence of their parents sending them to Presbyterian Schools" while the "Bigots [are] growing fierce in their opposition to Popery." Upon Bishop Purcell's recommendation, clergymen urged parents to send their children to Catholic schools, if they could.[71]

Bishop Rosati of St. Louis revitalized the floundering Saint Louis College, founded by Bishop DuBourg in 1818, by inviting Jesuit seminarians to run the school. The Jesuit Order experienced a small revival in the Americas beginning in 1814 after decades of suppression.[72] Officially chartered in 1832, Saint Louis University became the second-largest Jesuit university in the United States.[73] With Rosati's help, the school's first Jesuit president, Father Peter J. Verhaegen, oversaw the education of hundreds of pupils each semester. In 1832 Father Pierre Jean DeSmet secured the shipment of numerous texts from Belgium, which formed the foundation of the university's world-class library. Four years later Jesuits founded a school of medicine, which soon conferred the first medical degree west of the Mississippi. At Bishop Rosati's request in 1827, the Sacred Heart nuns, under Mother Rose Philippine Duchesne, transferred from Florissant, Missouri, to open a girls' school in St. Louis. Many of the city's wealthiest Catholics sent their daughters to Sacred Heart for their education.[74]

While Saint Louis University thrived, seven Catholic churches offered tutoring for pay and several seminaries that educated young students. The city at the time claimed nine public schools "free-of-charge," yet St. Louis Catholics also managed to offer free private education on a temporary basis. By 1845, there were four "Catholic free schools." One was attached to St. Francis Xavier Church on Saint Louis University's campus; another was apparently privately run by a charity. The Sisters of Charity also taught a free school for girls, and the Convent of the Sacred Heart hosted another.[75]

Despite ministers' warnings, it was not uncommon for well-to-do Protestants to send their boys and girls to Catholic academies. In the West private Catholic colleges especially enjoyed the reputation of being among the premier higher-learning institutions. In the spring of 1844, former governor of Missouri William Carr Lane, for example, sent his son Victor to Saint Louis University. The young man consoled his mother, who had grown anxious after reading accounts of Jesuit conspiracies in the news, that the priests were devout and pleasant. "You can see me," Victor Lane jested, "without thinking that the old priests are watching you through a keyhole or crack." He related one slightly disturbing detail, however: a Catholic boy had borrowed a Bible and taken it to mass on Sunday, and "afterwards they gave him a penance for that; now what you think of that!" At that same mass during the homily, Father Farrell condemned Catholic parents "who allowed their children to go where there was a chance of their hearing the Syren voice of heresy." Saint Louis University maintained a relatively high reputation, and Catholic schools in the region continued to serve as a viable alternative to public schools.[76] Catholic education in the West intensified the mid-nineteenth-century school controversy and fomented a national debate about the compatibility of Catholicism with American democracy.[77]

Sunday Observance & Ethnicity

As with the reading of the King James Bible, Americans equated Sunday observance to civic duty. Although federal and local courts completed the legal disestablishment of any one organized religion by 1833, local Sunday laws enabled native-born Americans to enforce a specific set of doctrinal beliefs and practices regarding the Sabbath.[78] Immigrants of all backgrounds and creeds, however, resisted Sunday regulations. Americans repeatedly cast immigrants who challenged these traditional ways of observing the Sabbath as the "other" – regardless of whether they were Catholic, Protestant, atheist, Irish, or German. "Ethnicity" is a social construction by which the dominant culture assigns certain people groups nondominant, or minority, status.[79] Ethnicity serves as an invisible and shifting line between the dominant culture and the "others" whose "foreign" customs reveal where the boundaries of the dominant culture end.[80] In this way native-born Americans and immigrants both contributed to the "dual construction of ethnicity." Immigrant communities discovered new ways to negotiate the "ethnicity" to which Americans relegated them.[81] The social conflict over Sunday regulation in St. Louis, with its large population of immigrants from the German Confederation, provides a striking illustration of this phenomenon.

When the Fourth of July happened to fall on a Sunday in 1852, St. Louis authorities postponed all public celebrations of the national holiday until Monday, July 5, to avoid violating the Sabbath. On July 4, however, several thousand German immigrants paraded three miles outside the city and celebrated Independence Day the German way. Their ringleader, Heinrich Börnstein, was a self-proclaimed "freethinker" who had immigrated to St. Louis in 1848. In his local German-language newspaper, the *Anzeiger des Westens* (Advertiser of the West), he promoted the "great popular festival with song, music and dancing, games, enjoyments and fireworks."[82] Fearing retaliation, German militia companies in the parade kept "their weapons loaded and cocked," and members of German societies carried revolvers and Bowie knives. Those men who "could not lay hands on a weapon" armed themselves with "at least two pounds of hard gravel packed in a stocking." Beginning at six o'clock in the morning, the German crowd, wearing the colors of the American flag, marched silently to avoid disturbing Sunday church services. They arrived outside the city two hours later. "When we finally left the city limits," remembered Börnstein, "the bands struck up stirring triumphal marches [and] every person felt that Germans had won a great victory and overawed our opponents." The celebration lasted until the

break of dawn on Monday morning, "precisely when the Americans were com-
mencing their celebration of the Fourth of July—on the fifth."[83]

Although the day passed without violence, many Anglo-Americans condemned this German American Independence Day parade as a desecration of
the Sabbath and the nation. One local observer accused them of parading "not
so much to celebrate the anniversary of our National Independence, as to have
a frolic on a leisure day."[84] Local residents demanded the criminal prosecution
of the participants under the Sunday laws. These laws were binding, a writer in
the *St. Louis Republican* reminded readers, even when the Fourth of July fell on
Sunday. He cited Missouri state law, which assigned the crime of a misdemeanor
to "every person who shall willfully, maliciously, or *contemptuously* disquiet or
disturb any congregation or assembly of people, met for religious worship." He
also cited a broader city ordinance, which declared it unlawful "for any *Military
Company,* or any procession, or any body of persons to march or pass through
the streets of the city on Sunday, accompanied by the sound of music."[85] A third
commentator demanded that the Germans "desist hereafter from all such attempts to do violence to public opinion."[86]

Not all German immigrants agreed with Börnstein's radical positions on
politics and religion, but the parade's symbolism resonated with a broader
cross-section of the city's German Americans. It demonstrated their general dis-
taste for Sunday regulation and marked the transformation of such resentment
into popular protest.[87] When German immigrants flooded the United States in
the 1840s and 1850s, the deep cultural differences between them and native-born
Anglo-Americans became obvious on Sundays. Simply put by one journalist, "In
Germany, Sunday is kept in one way and in the United States in another." He explained, "Natives of Continental Europe—whether Protestants of Catholics, it
matters not, invariably regard Sunday as a day of pleasure, recreation, and enjoy-
ment." On the other hand, "an immense majority of the [Anglo-American] people" honored the Sabbath "as a day of rest, of religious exercise, and of abstinence
from labor and public diversions of every kind."[88] As historian Steven Rowan has
argued, "Most Germans probably felt more concern about pressure against their
German life-style than about political restrictions, and it was easy to get a crowd
together to protest temperance laws or restrictions on Sunday entertainment."[89]
Historian Stanley Nadel has argued that the most important political issue for
German Americans was "the defense of their right to recreation." The "staples of
German-American life," he explained, were "beer and Sunday social activities."[90]
In his book *Memoirs of a Nobody,* Börnstein observed that politicians risked
losing the "entire German vote" if they advocated the prohibition of alcohol on

the Sabbath.[91] For these immigrants, celebrating the Lord's Day in their own way came to mean assimilating on their own terms. Sunday observance thus became a symbol of both resistance to dominant American culture and solidarity among the German American minority.[92]

To explain why the dispute over Sunday regulation contributed to the forging of German American identity in the mid-nineteenth century, one must first understand the differences between penitential English Sabbatarian forms of Sunday observance and Continental feasting traditions. Catholics and Protestants in Europe upheld Sunday as a crucial part of the religious and social rhythm of life, and almost everyone celebrated Sunday as a feast day. This meant that the first day of the week was a church-sanctioned, leisurely celebration with generous servings of food, beer, and wine. By the 1580s, however, English Calvinists, called "Puritans," had come to view Sunday as more than just a holy day mandated by the Church of England but rather a divine and perpetual institution wholly consistent with the Jewish Sabbath. Anglicans called those Puritans who supported Sunday absolutism "Sabbatarians" to distinguish them as a rebellious reform group within the Church of England. Sabbatarians strictly observed Sunday through penitential and somber inactivity to more closely reflect Jewish observance of the holy day in remembrance of the seventh day of creation, when God rested. Sabbatarianism became an especially formative doctrine among the Puritans and other English Protestant sects who settled in the American colonies.[93] In short, the majority of Anglo-American Protestants frequently observed Sunday through personal, quiet, and sober reflection, while almost everyone else in the Christian world celebrated the day communally.

State Sunday laws, or "blue laws" as they were called, codified American Sabbatarianism in the legal system.[94] Every state in the American republic held strict laws, some dating back to the colonial period, that were specifically designed to ensure the honoring of the Lord's Day. Upon its admittance to statehood in 1820, Missouri's government followed suit by prohibiting on Sunday the disturbance of religious assemblies, labor, horseracing, cockfighting, playing cards or games, and the sale of alcohol. These statutes carefully referred to Sunday as the "Sabbath." The state's Sunday laws comported with the American Sabbatarian view that both labor and play violated the Christian day of rest.[95]

Despite flares of opposition and even federal intervention, the Sunday laws endured because the majority of native-born Americans identified with a common Sabbatarian strand. In 1810 the first American Sabbatarian campaign of the nineteenth century erupted in response to a federal law that forced the postal service to remain open on Sunday, despite state legislation that prohibited labor on that day. The evangelical Christian group behind the effort identified themselves as Sabbatarian reformers. In their view the federal government risked "divine displeasure" by disrupting strict Sabbath observance. Invoking the biblical commandment to "remember the Sabbath day" and "keep it holy," these reformers reaffirmed the "transcendent reality of sacred time."[96] Through the 1830s and 1840s, as the Second Great Awakening swept Americans into churches, the postal issue continued to unite many Christian denominations in a moral crusade for Sunday reform. Although they did not succeed in forcing the federal government to close the post on Sundays, moral reformers were successful at regulating other Sunday activities at the local level.[97]

For most German immigrants, the mere existence of Sunday laws in the United States did not surprise them as much as their strictness and the local attitudes that encouraged their enforcement. In most provinces of the German Confederation, the state prohibited selling alcohol during church-service times, but "Sabbath-breaking" was a charge reserved for those who missed church to drink and publicans who kept their taverns open illegally during those hours. Unlike their American counterparts, the German laws did not prohibit Sunday drinking. Entire congregations visited drinking establishments regularly on Sunday afternoons and special feast days during the week. Many families devoted their free hours on the weekends to the church and the tavern, the culture of which was primarily one of leisure.[98]

Although German temperance advocates condemned drunkenness in *Trinkliteratur* (drinking literature), they rarely rejected drinking or tavern going entirely, unlike mid-nineteenth-century teetotalers in England and the United States.[99] Actually, taverns were important meeting places in which German families celebrated special religious occasions, men demonstrated their manliness, publicans extended hospitality, and citizens discussed politics and socialized. Tavern culture was generally the main arbiter of social engagement, both in rural and urban communities. The social status of drinking places ranged from exclusive gentlemen's clubs to courser working-class locales. Many public taverns served a variety of social groups; masters could be found drinking with their apprentices, householders with their servants, and patricians with artisans. Since the authorities considered alcohol a crucial part of public life, they rarely charged taverngoers with the crime of drunkenness. "The problem was not that drunkenness laws were not enforceable," explained one historian, "but that they were not enforced." The middling artisans who fled the potato rot and the political turmoil in Germany for America in the 1840s had experienced Sunday reform efforts that focused on moderation, not abstention. They took for granted that a leisurely visit to the local tavern after Sunday church services was a customary part of the weekly cycle of life and that official policies on drunkenness were unlikely to be enforced.[100]

American pietists, including evangelicals, Sabbatarians, and temperance advocates, found it difficult to understand why German immigrant ritualists, Lutheran as well as Catholic, cared so deeply about the freedom to drink and socialize on Sundays. Even German evangelical Christians supported Sunday drinking. The moral campaigns of Sabbatarian and temperance reformers actually worked to unify various immigrant factions against Sunday regulations.[101] For Germans in America, Continental religious traditions formed a more powerful unifying force than denominational affiliation with Anglo-American groups. They "were not about to abandon their traditions of imbibing," explained historian John Bodnar, because Sunday rituals "involved ways of life."[102] Ultimately at stake was the very rhythm of life, the weekly cycle upon which people ordered their days into sacred and secular periods of work, worship, penance, and play.[103]

German-managed breweries and taverns became integral parts of immigrant life in American cities. Germans owned fifteen of St. Louis's sixteen breweries in 1850. The Seventh Census of St. Louis showed that the First Ward, which included Soulard in South St. Louis, included 8,832 German immigrants out of a total 13,677 residents. German heritage thus accounted for 64.6 percent of the ward's population.[104] "There was no lack of taverns" in Soulard, remarked Ernst D. Kargau. During the work week, taverners would *ring a bell* or strike a *Chinese gong* to announce that lunch was being served." When a new keg arrived, "work was dropped in order to get a fresh glass of the new tapping."[105] The northern St. Louis district of New Bremen was also well known for its German character. In 1850 the Fifth and Sixth Wards, which included New Bremen, had an ethnic German population of 31.5 percent and 31.9 percent respectively. The taverns in both were just as busy on Sundays as any other day.[106]

To avoid conflicts with local authorities, many urban-dwelling Germans frequently traveled outside city limits to observe Sunday their traditional way. Chicago, Cincinnati, Louisville, and St. Louis saw a mass exodus of Germans on Sundays to recreational beer gardens and festival grounds. Although the German Confederation had a custom of retreat to the countryside on the Lord's Day, nothing on the American scale had ever been seen there. This exodus represented not only a retreat from the urban environment but also an escape from the city's Sunday laws. German immigrants experienced Sunday drinking and socializing outside the city, therefore, as a figurative and literal escape from

American culture. "In the good old times," Kargau reminisced, the beer gardens on the outskirts of St. Louis "were the rendezvous for German families." One of these suburban retreats was directly west of downtown in the Prairie des Noyers, another north in New Bremen, and a third south of the Soulard District of Carondelet. They were initially unclaimed public grounds where Germans could dance, drink beer, eat sausages, sing, and enjoy theatrical performances. Some of these gardens eventually became public parks, but German farmers and businessmen eventually owned most of them. In 1852 Börnstein's Fourth of July coterie held its Sunday festival in a clearing called Lindell's Grove, now the site of Saint Louis University. These suburban gardens, explained Kargau, allowed Germans "to enjoy life in their own way." Anglo-Americans rarely participated, for the "German concept of entertainment and amusement" seemed "extremely strange" to them. "Many years passed before one saw an American in our summer gardens," observed Kargau, "no matter whether on Sunday or week days."[107] St. Louis Germans also spent Sundays at nearby vineyards.[108]

This trend of escaping to suburban spaces on Sundays occurred in most major cities with concentrated immigrant populations and eventually became an institution of German American life. Kargau believed these Sunday observances contributed to the "Germanization of our Anglo-American fellow citizens."[109] A writer from Cincinnati reported that it had become customary for German Catholic glee clubs, "accompanied by a crowd of others," to travel "out of the city by steamboats and carriages, to a place called Bald Hill." There, a large crowd regularly drank alcohol, played music, and sang along.[110] In 1844 one New York journalist remarked on the stark contrast between Boston's "Puritan character" of Sunday observance and New York's Germanic influences. "At least twenty thousand people," he estimated, "pass the Sabbath in the fields," and "drinking places in all directions in the suburbs have overflowing custom on that day."[111]

These suburban retreats offered a compromise between German Americans who desired to transfer their traditional Sunday customs and Anglo-Americans who wished to preserve the American Sabbath in the cities. As *Harper's Weekly* observed, "Nothing prevents [Germans] going to the country on Sunday and drinking lager beer, and giving and going to concerts or shows among their own people."[112] The beer gardens became more sophisticated by the end of the 1850s, as benefactors transformed them into botanical gardens. In 1859 one writer celebrated the fact that these gardens now rivaled "anything of the kind in Germany" and could be found "in the suburbs of almost any American city." Those that commonly surrounded "all the cities" were typically maintained by German farmers, while richer families from the cities paid "for the privilege of enjoying its walks and breathing the fragrance of its flowers." The benefactors of the gardens regularly sponsored balls, dances, theater, sports, and served beer on Sunday.[113]

Exponential urban growth and the concentration of immigrants in almost entirely German-speaking neighborhoods heightened the culture war. German newcomers increasingly gravitated toward St. Louis for work instead of braving settlements in its hinterlands. Even those who sought refuge in the countryside found the growing city difficult to avoid. St. Louis grew from a total population of 16,469 in 1840 to 77,860 in 1850. Between 1848 and 1850 alone, 34,418 German immigrants arrived in the city.[114] One who settled in Belleville, Illinois, explained: "Here in the West, St. Louis must be considered the central gathering place of the Germans. This is the immigrant's first destination; from here he makes scouting trips out into the country to search for a place to settle; he returns to this city time and again."[115]

German artisans seeking temporary jobs in St. Louis in the hope of settling elsewhere found it difficult to migrate, and the expanding metropolis incorporated its immediate surroundings systematically through the mid-nineteenth century. The city absorbed German immigrants who had deliberately elected to settle outside its limits during a series of annexations. In one of the first of these additions, in 1841, the city annexed the French and German community of Soulard, about two miles south of downtown. As a direct result, German Americans became new eligible voters with a stake in city politics.[116] The extraordinary experience of Emil Mallinckrodt, an immigrant from the province of Dortmund who purchased a thirty-nine-acre farm just north of St. Louis in 1840, illustrates how newly settled German communities rapidly succumbed to urban sprawl. In the spring of that year, Mallinckrodt worked tirelessly to cultivate everything needed for subsistence: cabbages, carrots, wheat, melons, onions, potatoes, a variety of fruits, and grapes for wine. He also planted a row of tree seedlings that he had lugged across the Atlantic. Later that year Mallinckrodt wrote his brother in Dortmund that "the Metropolis St. Louis, is building itself around us, and in a few years we shall be living in a reliable city." The following spring he informed his brother that the city limits were merely "within a distance of five minutes from our place." His land had suddenly become valuable, and he quickly sold one lot for $300 in the fall of 1841. In the winter of 1844, Mallinckrodt reported to his brother that he had sold more land to a porcelain-and-starch factory and rented lots to ten families. That same year the city annexed the rest of his neighborhood. In the summer of 1846, Main Street ran through Mallinckrodt's property, and he sold fifteen more building lots. So, within a decade Mallinckrodt and his family had become integrated into St. Louis and its bustling economy. In 1855 the city incorporated the rest of the German district to the north, which locals called New Bremen due to its many settlers from the free German Confederation city of Bremen.[117]

Increasing American opposition to German Sunday recreation in St. Louis compelled Börnstein to build a coalition against the blue laws. After having failed to purchase a farm in central Missouri, he returned to St. Louis to become the chief editor of the popular *Anzeiger des Westens*. Börnstein, who considered himself a member of the "free-thinking" bourgeois, formerly had tried to avoid "public places and taverns" because, he opined, "the mean, raw tone prevailing there repelled me."[118] As an atheist he criticized German Christians and virulently opposed Roman Catholicism, which could be readily observed in his anti-Catholic novel, *The Mysteries of St. Louis* (1852), modeled after Parisian Eugene Sue's "big city horror novel," *The Mysteries of Paris* (1843). Börnstein supported "*German* Sunday" as a "day of joy," unlike "the American Sunday of the Puritans." If German Sunday was "wholly and totally at home in America," he wrote in *Mysteries of St. Louis,* then "bigotry, false devoted-ness and sacred hypocrisy would soon quit and much in this country would be better." German radical Friedrich Münch, Missouri state senator and translator of the only English edition of Börnstein's *Mysteries*, pointed out that "the village tavern is the most common rendezvous for the people," not for "intemperance, riot and murder," but "to discuss their private matters, their village affairs, the politics of the country, nay, even to criticize the last sermon of their village preacher." In Germany one "walks through the far-spread fields and meadow grounds" where the people "are merry indeed, in spite of their hard every day's work," but in America, Münch lamented, "Sunday is silent death."[119]

Like Börnstein, Münch spent his political career emphasizing the positive aspects of "German nationality" that supposedly connected all Germans in the West to the fatherland. Münch declared in 1859, "The German nationality has already planted itself so deeply in the western states of the Union that the traces of German blood, German industry, and German spirit can never be obliterated." Even so, he believed that the old culture would diminish over time, "especially if there is no continuing pressure of immigration to maintain an inner spiritual link with the Mother Country that refreshes our Germanity." Two years before the outbreak of the Civil War, Münch forecast the future separation of the Union into four distinct parts—the Northeast, the South, the "states along the Mississippi valley," and the Far West. "St. Louis will someday be the capital of an empire of fifty million free people," he mused. "It lies in the Germans' power to make this coming Mississippi Union essentially German, so that it could reach a helping hand across the ocean to a coming German Republic."[120]

Radicals like Börnstein and Münch invoked the ire of the majority of fellow immigrants for their anticlerical views, but they found great success in promoting German culture and building a political coalition against Sunday regulation. On July 4, 1852, as Börnstein led his parade through St. Louis, German societies in several other cities, such as Cincinnati, Milwaukee, and New York, also organized Sunday parades to feign the solidarity of the German American population.[121] In addition to running the *Anzeiger* newspaper, Börnstein eventually came to own "three large beerhalls leased to tavernkeepers," a beer garden, and a brewery. He also kept a saloon on the first floor of the *Anzeiger* press, which remained open on Sunday. Kargau remembered this tavern as being "one of the favorite gathering places for the German citizens." On Sunday evenings "a great many people came" for the concerts and good beer from Eimer's brewery in Belleville, Illinois. By 1859, Börnstein's Philodramatische Gesellschaft (Philodramatic Society) performed theatrical plays in saloons as well as vacant churches.[122]

While numerous German American groups met on Sundays, not a single Anglo-American society advertised Sabbath meetings. In St. Louis the German Benefit Society, German Roman Catholic Benevolent Society, and St. Vincent's German Orphan Association, for example, congregated on Sunday afternoons. The German Turner Societies met "on Sundays to harden their bodies by playing ball, exercising and swimming," these *Turnervereine* officially resolving to oppose "all prohibition laws" and all politicians who "identified with any nativistic organization or party."[123] The founding convention of the Allgemeine Arbeiterbund (General Workers' League) in Philadelphia in October 1850, which included delegates from St. Louis, demanded the repeal of all Sabbatarian laws.[124]

Native-born Americans reasoned that, in demanding the repeal of Sunday laws, Germans pushed toleration to its limit. Congregationalist minister Boynton in Cincinnati called German Sunday "a general attack upon our institutions." He hailed the "Protestant Sabbath" as "one of the mightiest instruments in Christian civilization." He opposed any immigrant who attempted "to substitute it for a Catholic holiday, to make it a day of parade and show and amusement, to accustom our children to its desecration." According to Boynton, German Protestants who feasted on Sundays unwittingly transferred Catholic culture to America.[125] Even non-Catholic immigrants from Europe, nativist Alfred B. Ely argued, could transmit *Catholicized* "habits of mind."[126]

European immigrants presented Americans with the special dilemma of effectively enforcing Sunday legislation, especially the prohibition on Sunday liquor sales. Native-born observers often objected to the lax enforcement of the Sunday laws in western cities. While touring the West, one proponent of the Puritan Sunday tradition noted the German affinity for "bringing the customs of their Faderland with them." On Sundays in St. Louis, the "Lager bier gardens [were] in full blast," which to him were "rather strange doings, that to a Puritan."[127] Another observer from the East discovered on his first Sunday morning in St. Louis that "this was not a Puritan town." He noted that "the saloons were all open on Sunday, and some theatres," and that German "customs as to Sunday observance had much influence on the whole city."[128]

St. Louis city authorities began to crack down in the 1850s. Between 1850 and 1853, the criminal court saw an unprecedented 484 cases of selling liquor on Sundays, by far the most commonly enforced blue law, in which approximately 50 percent of defendants had surnames of Germanic origin. Still, the professional police force at the time was hopelessly incapable of adequately enforcing the Sunday closing laws. In 1850 the population of St. Louis had reached roughly 80,000 people, but the police force consisted of only thirty full-time officers and thirty or so ad hoc volunteers. On October 14 Mayor Luther M. Kennett declared, "something is necessary for the suburbs, beyond our jurisdiction—where the dishonest and disorderly prowl about without fear of interruption, and even maltreat, with impunity, in broad day, and especially on the Sabbath, such quiet and well disposed citizens, as they may chance to encounter." He wanted to "give the city police power to keep order and make arrests throughout the county."[129] The number of cases of illegal liquor sales on Sunday continued to rise in the following years as city administrators expanded the police force.[130]

Börnstein's open opposition to Sunday regulation brought the *Anzeiger* under the scrutiny of a St. Louis grand jury in 1853. Börnstein recounted the semiannual session as being "so cleverly packed against the Germans that temperance men and Sabbath-bats had the majority." On September 9 the criminal court accused him of advertising illegal Sunday events in his newspaper. Most German immigrants accused of selling liquor on Sundays pled guilty and paid the fine of five to ten dollars, plus legal fees. But Börnstein refused to take the oath, and the jury charged him with contempt of court. "In the Matter of Henry Boernstein," the court clerk remarked on September 9 in the Criminal Record books, "Contumacious Witness before the Grand Jury." The next day the court discharged him from prison because no other German-language readers were willing to testify against him.[131]

Similar crackdowns occurred in Chicago, Cincinnati, and Louisville. The Sunday issue came to a head in 1855, once the American Party gained political offices. As historian Tyler Anbinder has shown, Sabbatarians and temperance advocates aligned with the American Party in the mid-1850s because they all opposed immigrants drinking on Sundays.[132] In 1855 the newly elected Know-Nothing mayor of St. Louis, Washington King, dramatically increased the city's police force to both combat street violence and more effectively enforce the Sunday laws. According to Richard Edwards's history of the city, King "was the first mayor who put in effectual force the Prohibitory Sunday Liquor Law." Although previous mayors had periodically enforced this prohibition, King developed a reputation for tenaciously restraining the "indecorum which had so long desecrated the Sabbath."[133] Börnstein recalled the King administration thus: "Crass nativism and intolerant temperance oppressed the entire population with an iron hand" as "trial followed trial against German tavern-keepers and against any use of publican establishments on Sunday." These measures forced several establishments to shutter their windows on Sunday, but private parties continued to serve alcoholic beverages in secret. Some taverns defiantly kept their back doors open.[134] These renewed drives for enforcement occasioned "much bitterness," according to Kargau, "even brutal attacks and bloody fights."[135]

Although political and religious disagreements fragmented German American communities, immigrants shared a Continental orientation toward certain recreational customs, which became especially significant in building ethnic and political solidarity for Germans within American culture.[136] Despite apparent ideological differences, the ensuing Sunday dispute continued to unite German communities against the American Sabbath. Through social meetings in taverns, cultural celebrations in beer gardens, and political resistance to Sunday laws, immigrants from various provinces in the German Confederation forged a lasting ethnic identity in the United States.

Language

Language difference presented an additional barrier between native-born Americans and immigrants. The prevalence of the German language in the Mississippi Valley seemed to reinforce cultural differences. During the mid-nineteenth century, immigrants settling in the West created a vast network of German-language institutions. These people attended German-language church services and followed developments in German-language newspapers. Many parents enrolled their children in German-language schools, which used Luther's translation of the Bible. German-language societies, like the *Turnervereine,* were tremendously popular throughout the region.[137]

In Cincinnati German-language speakers concentrated in a district of the city known as "Over-the-Rhine." In Chicago, German immigrants settled in a northern district known as "German Broadway." In Louisville German and Irish immigrants lived in "Butchertown." According to Kargau, in many portions of South St. Louis one "could imagine himself transplanted to Germany, for one heard only German spoken here." One could travel from Chouteau Avenue in midtown about eleven miles south to where Jefferson Barracks is presently located "without hearing anything else than German." In the New Bremen district, "one often imagines one is in Germany," Mallinckrodt observed, "when one hears low German and the patter of wooden shoes clattering on the streets."[138]

Americans considered English-language acquisition the mark of assimilation. Nativists argued further that fluency in English should be a requirement for voting. It was the opinion of Willis L. Williams, a land attorney in Missouri, that residents unable to speak English could not rightly understand American politics and should not vote. "Feller citizens!" Williams addressed residents of Hillsboro, Missouri, in an impromptu speech:

> Will any man in this krowd tell me that a Dutchman [German] ought to vote? No: there a'nt a man here who will say so. As I cum down here from Saint Lew the other day, I cum up to a house and called out to the man that I wanted some buttermilk, and dog on't, if he could understand what I sed. *Nix furs tey* ["they Know-Nothing"]. Couldn't say buttermilk. A Dutchman who don't know what buttermilk is! I say no foriner should have a *right* to vote; if should *I wish I may be cut.* (Great applause and shouts of hurrah for "buster").[139]

German Americans criticized the nativist claim that immigrants needed to acquire fluency in English to properly understand American politics. They also took offense at the nativist policy of a twenty-one-year residency requirement for citizenship. Such Americans "believe they are the ones who have received the mind of God," wrote an anonymous author of a German-language pamphlet circulating in Ohio in 1849. "The nativists maintain that the German immigrant, although still diligent in school in Germany, nonetheless knows nothing more than the newborn American child, and that he even will need as much time to understand as an American child to grow into a man."[140]

American nativists grew especially alarmed when German-language speakers united for political purposes. Not only did German immigrants protest cherished Anglo-American institutions, such as public schools, the King James Bible,

and Sunday closing laws, but they did it in German. The German language facilitated the political solidarity of immigrants in America.

Conclusion

Political nativists included teaching the Bible in common schools and preserving the American Sabbath in their party platforms. One official Know-Nothing
platform from 1854, for example, among other things called for:

> A pure American Common School system. . . .
> War to the hilt on political Romanism. . . .
> Hostility to all Papal influences, when brought to bear against the
>   Republic. . . .
> The amplest protection to Protestant Interests.[141]

In depicting Catholic and immigrant resistance to the reading of the King James
Version of the Bible in public schools as an assault on American freedom, the nativist movement crystallized the accepted wisdom of Protestant Americans into
a political ideology. They weaponized significant elements of American culture
to serve their own nationalist agenda.

Antebellum political nativism ironically set the stage for the creation of the
very hybrid ethnic-American political identities they had feared. These activists
announced the "ethnic" boundaries against which German and Irish immigrants felt compelled to resist. Initially, immigrants from various parts of the
German Confederation did not necessarily have strong national attachments
to one another. German Protestants disliked German Catholics as much as in
any other ethnicity or nationality. The heightened intensity of disagreement
between native-born Americans and immigrants, however, welded together German immigrants of all sorts so that, by the mid-1850s, one could witness even
German Catholic priests joining with German freethinkers as fellow German
Americans in common cause against American nativism. Those pressing for
Protestant Christian curricula and Sabbatarianism actually repelled immigrants
from the very institutions they purported to be necessary for Americanization.

Immigrants didn't want to conform to what nativists wanted them to do

CHAPTER 3

The Power of Nativist Rhetoric

The Natives are up, d'ye see . . .
They have seen a foreign band,
By a servile priesthood led,
Polluting this Eden-land,
And the graves of the patriot dead.
The boy and the bearded man,
Have left the sweets of home,
To resist a ruthless clan—
The knaves of the Church of Rome.
The Natives! The Natives!! The Natives!!!

—Know-Nothing campaign song, ca. 1855

AMERICANS DEFINED THE UNITED STATES as a group of people who shared certain values and value-based traits.[1] The antebellum nativist movement used immigrants as a measuring apparatus for nationality since Americans chronically disagreed among themselves along partisan and denominational lines. As such, nativists pointed to foreigners to declare "we're not like *that;* in contrast, this is what we believe and how we behave." Rhetoric emphasizing the incongruities between the beliefs and behaviors of native-born Americans and immigrants signaled both a national identity crisis and the solution simultaneously.

Opposition to immigration entered politics during the mid-1830s and became a potent rallying tool over succeeding elections. In the American mindset, Protestantism, as opposed to Roman Catholicism, formed the basis of American values and behaviors. As French political thinker Alexis de Tocqueville put it during his tour of the United States in 1835: "Americans so completely confuse Christianity and freedom in their minds that it is almost impossible to have them conceive of the one without the other."[2] To this end, American nativists developed a mythical, nationalist story that rendered Catholicism incompatible with true Americanism and Christianity.[3]

Origins of Political Nativism

At the most basic level, a "nativist" is one or all of the following: 1) a person who believes they are the rightful heir to a geopolitical territory; 2) a person who emphatically favors "natives first" over and against "outsider" influences, perceived or real; and/or 3) a person who demands political policies that effectively prioritize the native-born to the detriment of the foreign-born and their offspring. Hypothetically, even a native-born American might not possess the values and traits that qualifies one as a "rightful heir"; on the other hand, a foreign-born citizen might display the faculties of mind worthy of U.S. citizenship. In some sense, then, the label "nativist" is a misnomer because so-called nativists did not necessarily believe one's birth in the United States automatically qualified one as a worthy representative of Americanism. In targeting unwanted immigrants and residents, Americans have articulated positive assertions of principle grounded in a broadly felt national and religious identity. Political nativism has often presumed criteria beyond one's chance of birth for national belonging.[4] Throughout American history, most Americans have at least occasionally met the basic definition of a "nativist." Many have avoided the label "nativist," however, since it is commonly used in the pejorative sense to identify a person who irrationally opposes immigration and foreign-born residents.

More specifically in the antebellum context, "nativist" often described a person who either joined an independent anti-immigrant political party or society or deliberately voted for native-born candidates because they vowed to reform the naturalization requirements for citizenship. The term became popular after the 1835 publication of Samuel Morse's *Foreign Conspiracy Against the Liberties of the United States*. Morse marshalled a new political group in New York. His cohort called themselves—or rather were called by others—the "nativists," and their grassroots campaign for immigration reform became known as the nativist movement. These people vowed to withhold their vote for any public official who was not born on American soil, regardless of party affiliation. In 1836 Morse made an unsuccessful bid for mayor of New York City under one of the country's first nativist tickets. His widely read treatises stressed the relationship between "foreign" and "Catholic." He demanded stricter immigration laws on the conviction that "the *Conspirators* are in the *foreign importations.*" "Innocent and guilty are brought over together," Morse calculated; "we must of necessity suspect them all."[5]

Until the formation of the independent American (or Know-Nothing) Party in 1854, the political action of choice among nativists was to vote en masse for a native-born American candidate, whether Whig, Democrat, or independent, who promised to resist Catholic and foreign influence in local affairs. Nativists made their intentions known by publicly endorsing certain candidates before elections. It is difficult to discover who attended the early nativist party rallies and even harder to account for the members of the top-secret Know-Nothing Order, which formed in the 1850s.[6]

Even if one could identify all the members of the hundreds of nativist organizations that existed between 1830 and 1860, it would not entirely account for the influence and power of nativism across the United States as a system of beliefs and a nationalist narrative. A cross-section of society, ranging from eminent politicians to ministers and ordinary laborers, supported immigration reform for nativist reasons, though many of them may have never voted for a "Native American" or "Know-Nothing" ticket. Many Americans patronized nativist newspapers and entertained a host of anti-Catholic conspiracy stories. Political nativism entailed much more than voting for a party; it entailed a system of thought that pervaded American religion and politics.[7]

The first episodes of nativist political action took place in the nation's earliest immigration hubs, New York City and Philadelphia. In 1840 a Catholic faction in New York asked the city to allocate part of the public funds toward Catholic parochial schools. Governor William H. Seward, recognizing the abysmally low attendance of Catholic children in American primary schools, seemed willing to oblige. Irish Catholic voters in New York City under the direction of Archbishop John Hughes formed an independent ticket, nicknamed the Carol Hall Party, that favored public monies for Catholic schooling. Hughes insisted it was a "principle of American government" that the U.S. Constitution's religious-freedom clause was broad enough to guarantee Protestants the right to read the King James Bible and Catholics to read the Douay-Rheims Version. It was a compromise intended to preserve the religious integrity of each side. He pleaded, "I have never asked or wished that any denomination should be deprived of the Bible, or such version of the Bible, as that denomination conscientiously approved—in our Common or Public Schools."[8] Hughes insisted, however, that forcing Catholic children to read a spiritually outlawed version of the Bible constituted a violation of their "legal rights of conscience." Since the reading of the Protestant Bible violated the religious conscience of Catholics, proponents of sending some school funds to Catholic institutions based their arguments on the right to freedom of worship.[9]

But Americans argued that any removal of the Bible from common schools or the splitting of public school funds with parochial education actually violated their right to free worship. To nativists, political action like that of the Carol Hall Party seemed to affirm their worst fears of Catholic intervention in American political affairs. In 1841 one nativist writer criticized Catholics for selfishly demanding "a portion of their own money for the education of their own children, in their own Religious Faith!!!"[10] At the time, this critic asserted, no Protestant sects campaigned for special parochial-school funding. No Americans expected Methodists or Presbyterians, for example, to request special public funding for their Sunday schools or seminaries. The school controversy isolated Catholics not only as the largest Christian religious group principally opposed to reading the King James Bible in common schools but also as the only Christian denomination in America asking for special public funding. Nativists insisted Archbishop Hughes's independent ticket amounted to an all-out assault on the Bible and American freedom.

This is when a group of Americans officially formed the American Republican, or Native American, Party. The Executive Committee of the American Republican Party in New York vowed to make the "Holy Bible, without sectarian note or comment," available to children "in or out of school."[11] The public school controversy quickly spread to other states, and Native American parties formed in almost all major cities between 1843 and 1850.

As the debate raged, nativists recommended amending the U.S. Constitution to exclude foreigners from the polls for an extended period of time. Nearly all Americans admitted the need for some period of acculturation preceding citizenship. The American Republican Party preferred a twenty-one-year probationary period before immigrants could vote. After all, native-born Americans had to wait twenty-one years from birth before they could vote. The policy was meant neither to sully the image of the United States as a safe haven for the destitute nor to interfere with the ability of newcomers to work. Nativists recognized the importance of immigrant labor to the development of America's economic infrastructure.[12] Additionally, nativist leaders proposed literacy tests, enhanced naturalization oaths, and other ways of weeding out foreign "feelings" and "prejudices." Henry Winter Davis of Maryland argued that the naturalization laws should be reformed to "require a knowledge of and attachment to the Constitution as the condition on which citizenship is conferred."[13] Kentucky nativist James Wallace recommended a naturalization tax *"so heavy that few can pay."*[14]

The controversy intensified in nearby Philadelphia as well and eventually erupted into one of the most brutal anti-Catholic riots in American history, resulting in more than twenty deaths between May and July 1844. Nativist fears heightened in 1842, when Bishop Francis P. Kenrick of Philadelphia requested an exemption from reading the King James Version for Catholic students either by excusing themselves from the classroom or bringing in their own translation. The state government seemed to comply in the controversial Maclay Bill of 1842, which prohibited funds to any schools that taught "religion," though as historian Ray Allen Billington has shown, the Central Committee of Education, composed almost entirely of Protestant ministers, continued to mandate the reading of the King James Bible.[15] In the summer of 1844, nativist mobs attacked German and Irish Catholic homes and the seminary of the Sisters of Charity, and they burned down two Catholic churches, St. Michael's and St. Augustine's.[16] Even the burning of the Ursuline convent in Charlestown, Massachusetts, ten years earlier paled in comparison. "We have never known Catholic intolerance to go so far," one Cincinnatian lamented.[17] According to a lengthy article on the history of anti-Catholicism in America in the *U.S. Catholic Magazine,* Catholics in Philadelphia believed the violence was the result of false rumors raised by nativists, who assumed "the Catholics wished to exclude the Bible from the common schools." Catholic voters everywhere, the author noted, "never asked that the Bible be excluded from the schools, but merely that their own children, if forced to read the Bible at all, might be allowed to use the Catholic version." Thus, the author remarked ironically, "a new politico-religious party was organized, called the Native American, for the special defence of the Bible!"[18]

Political nativism spread westward. During the 1840s, nativist tickets appeared in elections in all of the West's major metropolises, including Chicago, Cincinnati, Louisville, and St. Louis. Like their cohorts in the East, the American Republican Party in the West formed because "the integrity and perpetuity of our free Institutions are in imminent peril."[19] The "American Republican Manifesto" thus asserted a constitutional right to restrict immigration to preserve American institutions.[20] As in Philadelphia and New York during the 1844 elections, many Whigs in the West "dropped their own ticket, and voted *en masse* for the Am. Republican candidate," as reported by one newspaper in Columbus, Ohio. Although Democrat James K. Polk carried Cincinnati in November, every American Republican candidate for Congress won in Columbus.[21] In Louisville one German newspaper reported that the Catholic and immigrant populations defected entirely from the Whig Party because of the "incendiary *natives* of which the *whole* Whig Party of Louisville consists."[22] A Whig-nativist coalition in St. Louis elected nativist Peter G. Camden mayor in 1846. One year later the Native American Party in Kentucky independently nominated Stephen Fitz-James Trabue to "bring about a remedy for the evils growing out of foreign immigration."[23] Trabue failed to secure a seat in Congress in 1847 and 1849, but Kentuckians elected Whig candidates Charles Morehead and Humphrey Marshall, both of whom were renowned nativists who later joined the Know-Nothing Order.[24] Nativists continued to operate inside both of the major political parties.

Many nativist leaders in the West sponsored Bible societies and evangelical clubs. Hamilton Rowan Gamble, for example, served as the president of the Missouri Bible Society.[25] He eagerly contributed to the Sibleys' Lindenwood Female College and volunteered as a trustee for the Second Presbyterian Church. Gamble saw no conflict of interest between his religious activities in St. Louis and his political support of the emergent Native American Party. He later served as a national delegate of the American Party of Missouri in 1855 and became the provisional governor of the state during the Civil War.[26] Peter G. Camden won the race for mayor of St. Louis in 1846 on an American Republican ticket dedicated to keeping the Bible in common schools.[27] In 1841 a Baptist minister named Hinton baptized him in Chouteau's Pond in St. Louis.[28] Thereafter, Camden joined the Missouri Bible Society alongside Mary Sibley's favorite Presbyterian minister, William Potts, as well as Presbyterian reverend Artemus Bullard, who served alongside Lyman Beecher in the Foreign Mission Society of the Valley of the Mississippi during the 1840s.[29]

The opponents of political nativism had clear political incentives to depict the nativists as a strange, marginalized group, but in reality nativist political leaders were well-connected. One disturbed political commentator in St. Louis considered Camden's coterie there a confused and fleeting party: "He was elected by a mad faction, and may our Heavenly Father forgive them, for they knew not what they did."[30] But Camden's faction swayed politics in the city for over a decade. At least one of the men on his ticket, Luther M. Shreve, who at that time served on the board of the St. Louis Lyceum, a large library and hall for intellectual debates, later became a delegate to the Grand Know-Nothing Council of Missouri during the height of nativist success in 1855. These Bible-believing nativists remained important political figures with broad community support.[31]

For over a decade in Cincinnati as well, renowned nativist James D. Taylor campaigned for a "Free Common School System" and an American Party in that city. Taylor also organized Bible drives as a trustee for the First Presbyterian Society in 1843.[32] That same year he established Cincinnati's premier nativist newspaper, the *Dollar Weekly Times,* for the stated purpose of protecting American institutions against "the insidious wiles of Catholicism."[33] Under the mantra "Free Thought, Free Schools and Free Speech!" Taylor led an independent "Free Ticket" in the spring 1853 municipal election to oppose the splitting of school funds to pay for Catholic schools. He did not win because there were two other "free school" tickets more popular than his.[34] Later, in 1855, the city's Know-Nothings, who had swept the previous year's elections, nominated Taylor for mayor. Western nativist leaders forged decades-long political careers, interrupted only by the Civil War. They raised public awareness of the negative cultural, economic, and religious effects of immigration in the American West.

Christian American Myth

American nativism became rhetorically potent because its leading proponents told a compelling origin story of the United States, replete with powerful religious symbolism. Popular nativist books, newspaper articles, pamphlets, and political propaganda promoted a Christian American myth. That myth served as a framework for how Americans should interpret the past, and it provided "lessons" for contemporary society. Nativists saw independence, individualism, and Protestantism as historically and inseparably linked. They attributed the success of American democracy to the harmonious meeting of Protestant, specifically "Bible-based" and "Puritan," ecclesiastical principles with the civic principles enshrined in the U.S. Constitution. While the Christian American myth sustained a sense of belonging to a uniquely free and Protestant nation, it likewise constituted a guiding framework—a measuring stick—by which Americans decided who did and who did not belong. It helped nativists justify an immigration policy aimed at restricting European Catholic access to U.S. citizenship.

"God gave this country to our fathers and us a *Protestant* land, and we will keep it thus!" Cheers lifted from the Cincinnati crowd gathered in College Hall after Charles B. Boynton, a Congregationalist minister, delivered the line. On this Monday, July 5, 1847, schools were closed and work suspended to celebrate Independence Day. Americans held their national holiday on the fifth that year so as not to disturb Christian assemblies on Sunday, July 4. The widespread local policy at the time, of respecting the Christian Sabbath, added weight to Boynton's claim that the United States was a "*Protestant* land." His address attracted "Native Americans" advocating for a stricter immigration policy. The eastern agent of the American Tract Society, Reverend Charles Peabody, met Boynton during his travels and noted, "he always carries along with him the popular feeling," though "he has on quite too much steam for his own good."[35]

In the spring elections of 1847, a substantial number of these native-born white Americans defected from their traditional parties and voted instead for an independent "Native American" ticket. Those supporting political nativism in Cincinnati included English-speaking citizens, white, native born, rich and poor, and many recent migrants to the West of various affiliations. Boynton stressed the lengthy "historical" record of Catholic Europe's antagonism to American ideals. "The Protestant Republic cannot dwell in peace with Rome," he claimed. Granted, there were many immigrants "noble and valuable," but Boynton worried about "the criminals, the paupers, the sabbath-breakers, the main supporters of infidelity" in their midst, those who together might produce a *"general influence"* of moral degeneracy. Only an extended residency requirement could ensure the naturalization of fully Americanized—by which he meant *Protestantized*—immigrants. So complete was the harmonic relationship between the American state and Protestant Christianity, Reverend Boynton proclaimed in his speech, that "Puritanism, Protestantism, and True Americanism are only different terms to designate the same set of principles."[36]

The nativists of the antebellum era set out to prove that Protestant Christianity was the root cause of the most desirable American national "attributes." Three published works in this historical-political genre explicitly connected the nativist movement's version of American heritage to Puritan ancestry. Boynton, a Cincinnati minister and spokesman for the Native American Party, published a collection of his public remarks in 1847. That year the country witnessed more than just its first "nativist tickets"; 1847 also saw some of the first nativist fraternal orders emerge. Bostonian Alfred Brewster Ely, a leader of one of the original secret nativist societies, the Order of United Americans (OUA), likewise published his reflections on the history of America in 1850. Marylander Anna Ella Carroll's anti-Catholic works sold many copies between 1854 and 1856, the height of Know-Nothing power. Boynton, Ely, and Carroll spoke before different crowds, in different regions of the United States, and at different times, each of them representing a stage of development in the antebellum nativist movement. Yet a mythical story seemed to connect them across time and place and audience. Each author traced the birth of American principles to early Puritan New England, promoted Protestant America as providentially blessed by God, and condemned Catholic Europe as being against the stream of historical progress.[37]

Puritanism, in particular, held a special ascendancy in Boynton's mind. He believed the Puritans of New England were the first group to strike the correct social balance between church and state because they used the Bible as their sole guide. Boynton depicted Catholicism as Puritanism's antithesis. "From the moment the Papacy was born," the reverend declared in his address before the Native American Party of Cincinnati in 1847, "it declared war against Puritanism, for Puritanism is older than Rome." By "Puritanism," Boynton meant a timeless principle of social organization that kept both ecclesiastical and civil spheres of government democratic in their operations and separate in their functions. Early Christian churches were "private associations," in his view. "Popery" changed that. Only three hundred years after Jesus founded the Christian church, it "proved false to its trust" when Roman emperor Constantine made Christianity legal.[38] In 325 Constantine summoned the Council of Nicaea, which established a uniform doctrine, known as the Nicene Creed; set the date for Easter; and ordered the promulgation of canon law. According to Boynton, this was when the "terrific power" of the papacy arose. Then, "for a thousand years and more, truth and liberty were crushed together" as the "Roman hierarchy" attempted to suppress the modes of faith and government "born of the Bible."[39]

This narrative formulation set up the Protestant Reformation magnificently as the single moment in which the true Christians in hiding finally brought forth the light of knowledge. It was these reformers, after all, who insisted on printing the Bible in vernacular translations. Englishman John Wycliffe first translated the Bible for readers who could not read Latin, the official language of the Catholic Bible and the church. The English Protestant Reformation soon followed under King Henry VIII in the 1530s. Still, the Reformation was not complete, Boynton observed; the powers of good (religious liberty) and of evil (religious despotism) remained at war. England shamefully slipped back into old "popish" ways under the tyrannical rule of the Anglican Church. And so it was not until a century later when Puritan Oliver Cromwell—"England never saw a greater or a nobler man," Boynton claimed—led the English Puritan Revolution, inaugurating the English Civil Wars, during which that country supposedly reached a height of moral character it never again attained.[40]

This portion of the narrative prefigured English America as the next and final site of reformational progress. On February 22, 1850, the OUA invited an itinerant minister to ring in the 118th anniversary of George Washington's birthday.[41] Reverend Ely's lengthy speech charmed the rowdy nativist crowd. The first half was a 12,000-word history stressing the special influence of puritanical forms of civil and ecclesiastical government on the development of American liberty, followed by another 12,000 words describing the imminent dangers of foreign immigration. "We are as an Order," Ely announced, "opposed to the encroachments of foreign influence, and are desirous of sustaining a policy purely American—a Bible-based, Law-loving, Liberty-built policy."[42]

During the Dark Ages, a time periodization Ely applied to the 1,204 years between Emperor Constantine's recognition of the Christian religion in 313 and the beginning of Martin Luther's Reformation in 1517, true Christianity existed only in hiding because "the Bible was shut up from the people." "Religious Despotism" enslaved all of Christendom "with the cross in one hand, and bloody sword in the other," Ely recounted. Without direct access to the Bible, ignorance prevailed. True Christianity lay a fledgling in wait. Only a few believers, by the special grace of God, remained unadulterated by the "whore of Babylon," the Antichrist mentioned in Revelation 17 and 18, which many Protestants interpreted as a reference to the pope. These few "awaited the time when the hand of Providence should rake them out and the breath of Heaven blow them into flame to consume alike the despotism and the despot, the tyranny of church and of state."[43]

Puritanism in America, distant from the influences of the pope and the English monarch, finally established an egalitarian society with a truncated religious system. True Christian modes of society and government "burst forth in the Puritan forests" of New England, Ely proclaimed. The "Puritan meeting-house" inculcated "the principles of a Republican Christianity" as the colonists adopted "the very forms of stern simplicity, rejecting all notions of sacramental efficacy and priestly intercession." Their reverence for the biblical doctrine of "justification by faith alone" engendered unparalleled individualism. In the "Puritan school-house," teachers used "the Bible as the first textbook" and imparted knowledge "under rules of wholesome discipline—where the mind was early trained to think, to investigate, to decide upon, and to act independently and fearlessly." The Puritan way of organizing education, politics, religion, and society, he claimed, induced a natural progression of equality, individual accountability, and self-government, all of which led, inevitably, to the American Revolution. Ely admitted that the English Puritans had at least one flaw: they loved liberty too much and at times became overzealous in their pursuit of justice.[44]

Anna Ella Carroll's *The Great American Battle; or, The Contest between Christianity and Political Romanism* (1856) became one of the most popular among the new wave of nativist books flooding the U.S. market during the height of Know-Nothing power. It adorned the personal libraries of prominent nativist leaders alongside copies of Lyman Beecher's *Plea for the West* (1835) and Maria Monk's *Awful Disclosures* (1836).[45] Carroll's editor, Horace Galpen, believed *The Great American Battle* was calculated to "restore the poor, blinded Papists, in bondage to priestcraft, to their native original right of freedom of conscience" and to show Catholics the "freedom of Bible Republican independence."[46] Former U.S. president and 1856 American Party presidential nominee Millard Fillmore endorsed Carroll's *"good cause."* J. W. Barker, president of the Know-Nothing State Council of New York, proclaimed the book "a complete success." Another renowned New York nativist leader, Erastus Brooks, labeled Carroll a "true American Woman," while Louisville journalist George D. Prentice believed her book exhibited "a striking illustration of the truth that an intellectual woman, though she may not have the privilege of voting at the polls, can teach men how they should vote." Carroll sold her 365-page magnum opus for the bargain price of one dollar; Americans bought tens of thousands of copies.[47]

The enthusiasm over *The Great American Battle* had at least as much to do with the author as with the content. Anna Carroll descended from one of the nation's oldest and most influential Catholic families. Nativists were thrilled to count in their throng the granddaughter of Maryland statesman Charles Carroll, the only Catholic to sign the Declaration of Independence—whose cousin, John Carroll, became the first U.S. Catholic archbishop in 1789. Her father, Thomas King Carroll, an Episcopalian, served as governor of Maryland in 1830. Although some in the family converted to the Episcopal Church after the Revolution, including Anna's father, many members of the Carroll family continued to practice their ancestral religious heritage from English Catholics in the seventeenth century.[48] Carroll's middling position between two religious traditions, her advertisers alleged, made her more sensitive to the potential pitfalls of excessive anti-Catholicism. Horace Galpen, author of the book's introduction, claimed, "The subject of this book is no fiction." He believed it transcended contemporary anti-Catholic works, riddled with conspiracy and vitriol, by warning instead against the entire *"system* of Popery."[49] Carroll wrote in the preface: "Connected as I am with those holding the Roman Catholic as well as the Protestant faith, it would not be consonant with reason or taste to arraign them!— and though myself a Protestant.... I honor that paternal ancestry of which I in common descended with the amiable, distinguished, and worthy Archbishop who bore my name, the first in the United States, and one of the heroic signers of our Independence."[50] In *The Great American Battle* and a lesser-known work published that same year, *The Romish Church Opposed to the Liberties of the American People,* she labored to persuade Catholic Americans that Roman Catholic doctrines were inherently incompatible with Americanism.[51]

Like Boynton and Ely before her, Carroll attempted to unite all Americans, regardless of regional origin, under a Puritan ancestral story. "Americans, let us see how the first stones were gathered," she challenged her readers. Like Boynton and Ely before her, she began her story of America with the Puritans in seventeenth-century England. They "were assailed day and night by the ministers of the ecclesiastical tyranny" under the reign of Queen Elizabeth and her successor, King James I. They escaped to Amsterdam, where they laid plans to transplant to America to worship freely and "advance the Gospel in the New World."[52] One hundred of these pious "pilgrims" embarked for America on the *Mayflower* and landed on the Rock of Plymouth in December 1620.[53] After "prayer and thanksgiving to almighty God," they consented to the Plymouth Compact. In Carroll's estimation, the implications of this minute affair were profound: "This, Americans, was the first *republic* erected in America," she proclaimed, "and is the most remarkable instance of the true spirit of liberty upon the record of history."[54] Carroll opined, "For five thousand years this vast continent lay upon the bosom of the deep, occupied by untutored man." Europeans had no conception of the size of the North American continent at the time, yet their singular desire "for freedom to worship God" resulted in "the unparalleled development of liberty." She deemed the Protestant American conquest of the continent "our 'manifest destiny.'"[55]

In locating the seeds of the American principles of civil and religious liberty in Plymouth, Carroll deliberately overlooked her native Maryland, founded in 1634, where Catholics and Protestants initially enjoyed de facto religious freedom. The Plymouth Colony was not even the first English settlement in North America. Englishmen seeking gold and a strategic port to combat Spanish hegemony in the Atlantic founded the fledgling colony of Jamestown in 1607.[56] Among the many colonial French and Spanish settlers on the continent, Carroll singled out in her retelling only the French Huguenots, Calvinist refugees from France who founded a short-lived community in Florida in 1564 near present-day Jacksonville. "The same God which had taken the English Pilgrim and set him on Plymouth Rock," she claimed, "led the French Huguenot to the South. It was the genius, the heroism, the instinct, of liberty."[57] But for the most part, Carroll and her cohorts preferred not to give mention to the well-known existence in America of other European groups who were Catholic and had been there much longer than the British colonists, not to mention the indigenous peoples who had been there even longer.[58]

Another nativist author attempted to account for the holes in Carroll's story. The same year Carroll wrote *The Great American Battle,* a nativist from Ohio published an extensive history of Catholicism and Protestantism in America titled *The Outlook of Freedom: or, The Roman Catholic Element in American History.* In this 400-page history, Justin D. Fulton interpreted the development of the entire continent as a "battle" between the religions. "This is the first attempt," he claimed in the introduction, "to trace the elements of Romanism and Protestantism as they have met face to face to try swords on a new field." From Columbus to the arrival of the Puritans to the Louisiana Purchase (1803) to the U.S. war with Mexico (1846–48), Fulton described America as the scene of a cosmic contest pitting free Protestantism against despotic Roman Catholicism, the historic "foe to freedom, of truth and of humanity" and "secret ally of a foreign despotism." Fulton concluded, after reviewing the "facts," that Protestants were destined to win in North America.[59]

As the advocates of the Christian American myth sought to establish their version of events, no other founder was more frequently appropriated and contested than George Washington. Almost immediately after Washington's death in 1799, American authors began composing stories about his life and death that suited the memory of an exceptionally religious founding. Preachers everywhere depicted Washington as a singularly pious Christian, whose enduring personal faith in Jesus Christ had saved the American republic from otherwise sure destruction. It yet remains unclear what exactly Washington actually believed about God. Regardless, Americans throughout the United States adorned their homes with depictions of the "Father of the Country" and revered his image "like a saint's icon," as historian Edward Lengel has pointed out. Popular primary-school readers borrowed fabricated accounts of the first president's piety from "Parson" Mason Locke Weems's 1800 biography, *Life and Memorable Actions of George Washington,* a bestseller. The Sunday School Union also disseminated curriculum detailing moral tales of Washington's faith during the American Revolutionary War, all based on no real evidence.[60] Nativist pamphlets frequently (mis)quoted Washington's instructions to one sentinel while the Continental Army encamped at Valley Forge: "Put none but Americans on Guard To-night." He never said it.[61]

America's largest nativist organization at the beginning of the 1850s, the OUA, vowed to educate the public about Washington's true religious legacy. At its exclusive meeting on February 22, 1850, celebrating Washington's birthday, Reverend Ely of Boston invited all Americans to "meditate upon the life and character of this 'perfect just man,' till they learn to emulate his virtues and become thoroughly imbued with his spirit." The name of Washington, Ely proclaimed, rose "above every name, . . . a name ever dear, and interwoven, with the most hallowed associations! [A] character that seems to acquire, if possible, new luster with each succeeding year!"[62] Initiated members took home elaborate certificates, each measuring more than three feet long and two feet wide, adorned with images of the beloved Father of the Country. The OUA granted one award to a New Yorker, who later moved to Cincinnati, in 1850 that included richly detailed portrayals of quintessential Revolutionary events—the British retreat from Concord, the Battle of Bunker Hill, the signing of the Declaration of Independence—and the inauguration of President Washington. Amid these grand depictions appeared Washington kneeling in prayer at Valley Forge encampment.[63] Also included was a sketch of a humble wooden schoolhouse overlooking a harbor. The students had just been let out for the day, while ships of commerce hoisting U.S. flags sailed in the distance. The caption for this image read: "Patriotism and Education, our country's hope."[64]

The nativist movement reinforced the legend of Washington as a man of faith and all but christened him as America's first saint. One popular nativist organ celebrated Washington as the great "Bible General," the founding fathers as the first "Bible Congress," and the founding generation as devoted Christians who "prayed to no licentious Pope—to no mere man" and "took the Protestant Bible as their guide."[65] Reverend Boynton of Cincinnati attributed the allegedly Christian values of the U.S. Constitution to "our great puritan statesman, George Washington."[66] In the first chapter of *The Romish Church Opposed to the Liberties of the American People* (1856), Anna Carroll likewise claimed that the founders recognized "the Protestant religion as the support of this government." She included Washington's alleged supplication to "that Almighty Being" in an address at the conclusion of the Revolutionary War in 1783 as well as Benjamin Franklin's benediction during the Constitutional Convention.[67]

The nativist movement also depicted Washington as a nativist. The Washington they envisioned patriotically opposed foreign influence in America. The official constitution of the OUA vowed to honor "the precepts and warning legacy of our immortal Washington, to 'beware of foreign influence.'" The society also believed that his true legacy promoted the prevention of "ignorant and vicious foreigners from exerting an undue influence" over the country.[68]

Nativists often misapplied quotations to serve their agenda. The line "beware of foreign influence" referred to Washington's 1796 Farewell Address, in which he famously announced his retirement from the presidency after serving two four-year terms. It became one of the most frequently cited quotations of a founding father in nativist literature, yet it was hardly verbatim. Washington actually said: "Against the insidious wiles of foreign influence (I conjure you to believe me, fellow-citizens) the jealousy of a free people ought to be constantly awake, since history and experience prove that foreign influence is one of the most baneful foes of republican government." In the context of the Farewell Address, the president referred specifically to the danger of forming a diplomatic alliance with any foreign nation in Europe during the French Revolutionary Wars. The "foreign influence" of which he warned referred to English and French diplomats who even then still tried to prod the United States into the European war. If Washington was thinking about "foreign influence" within the republic, it was that of French or pro-French revolutionaries trying to stir up Americans to support their cause. Washington's successor, John Adams, had the same concerns in mind when he oversaw the passage of the infamous Alien and Sedition Acts of 1798, which among other things temporarily raised the residency requirement for naturalization to fourteen years (instead of five).

Another popularly cited passage derived from Thomas Jefferson's *Notes on the State of Virginia* (1788), in which he momentarily expressed concern about the potential for immigrants to render the American Republic "a heterogeneous, incoherent, and distracted mass."[69] Jefferson also wrote these words in the context of American foreign policy regarding the French Revolution. The key political debate of his day revolved around whether the United States should lend support to the French revolutionaries, to England, or to remain neutral, the very same issue that concerned Washington and Adams. Nativists also claimed precedents for their proposed twenty-one-year residency requirement in the Alien Act of 1798. "No nothing measures originated of old John Adams," Kentucky nativist James Wallace explained to his brother, "and were advocated strongly by our Father [Washington]." The founding fathers, he claimed, "always held this right to be preserved by the constitution."[70]

Nativists invoked the founding fathers to persuade Americans that Catholicism also threatened the republic. One Virginian, writing under the pseudonym "Madison," accused his generation of lacking vigilance. He regretted that his fellow Americans had become an unsuspecting people who "look upon popery" in the same light as "other Protestant denominations." He warned, "This is the MISTAKE WHICH MUST BE CORRECTED, or all is lost." If only native-born Americans would remember the example of their founding fathers, "Madison" argued, they too would support anti-Catholic legislation. "The revolutionary fathers," he recounted, knew well "the character of the papacy and the treachery of papal princes."[71] Boynton told a nativist crowd in Cincinnati that the Puritan faith had been "baptized with the American name," for the founders had designed the U.S. Constitution to "preserve a Christian, Protestant, Democratic State." The biggest threat to the perpetuation of American principles, in the reverend's view, was Catholicism. He for one believed that the United States was the first Christian nation to successfully liberate itself from papal dominion. The founding of the United States brought the entire world "to the final struggle—the death-grapple—in which Romanism or Protestantism and Liberty must die." If the country failed to survive, Boynton warned, popery would again deliver the world to darkness.[72] The nativist movement grew in popularity during the antebellum era because it not only drew on old fears but also asserted positive beliefs about American identity.

Religious Freedoms

For Americans, the language of freedom was especially evocative. The founders had demanded religious liberty in the Constitution to protect the people from subjection to the rule of a particular state-preferred church. In the early republic, separation of church and state meant first and foremost the sustained resistance to any denomination becoming the official religion of the government, as in Anglican England and Catholic France. "Protestantism" was no single organized religion but a diversity of Christian sects operating independently of one another so that it went hand in hand with religious pluralism. Americans promoted common Christian rituals in government functions but resisted the ascendancy of any one sect in political affairs. Generally, those who had grown accustomed to denominational competition supported church-state separation as not only necessary but also ideal. The church, separated from the state, could elevate its members above the ambition, greed, and power supposedly inherent in temporal affairs. The state, in turn, would be kept in check by an upstanding Christian citizenry.[73]

Many Americans assumed there was (and would always be) a permanent Protestant majority in the United States. It was the responsibility of citizens, they claimed, to gradually and peacefully direct the ship of state on a course consistent with divine law. Any sectarian disputes should be resolved democratically. As a democratic state was founded on the will of the people, Christianity, Reverend Abel Stevens asserted before his congregation in Boston in 1835, could operate "upon the most simple and elementary principles of society." Christian ethics ought to "enter essentially into its most complex institutions . . . moulding and shaping its institutions."[74] Without "the Christian Religion [as] the foundation of all good Government," as Daniel Raymond, editor of the *Western Statesman,* reasoned in the 1842 mission statement of the nativist-leaning Cincinnati newspaper, "our political shipwreck is not far off." He further asserted, "It is therefore the duty of every good Christian to exercise his whole influence upon the Government."[75]

Why, then, did the nativist movement wish to deny certain freedoms to Catholic Christians? Nativists argued that Catholics could not be trusted because their allegiance to the pope in Rome might trump their devotion to the U.S. Constitution. They feared that self-identified Roman Catholics wanted instead to unite their church's hierarchy with the federal government and extirpate Protestant heretics. Nativists worried that another inquisition could begin in America on a simple command from the Vatican. Boynton pointed out in his 1847 Independence Day speech that the separation of church and state was "of great delicacy of structure." Of course, Presbyterians might dominate one electoral district, Congregationalists another, but many Americans thought the arrival of numerous Catholic immigrants raised superseding concerns. Boynton pinpointed the conundrum, wondering "whether to guard ourselves against Rome is intolerance or righteous self-defence."[76] Could the young republic embrace the newcomers and *Americanize* immigrants influenced by "popery" in a timely manner, if, indeed, it was possible at all?

Americans recognized limits to religious liberty. At the time, Mormonism was popularly thought to be beyond those limits insofar as it promoted polygamy, and nativists argued Catholicism might as well exist beyond the threshold of reasonable toleration as well. While a good Mormon had to recognize polygamy, a good Catholic was compelled to acknowledge "the *temporal power of the Pope.*" Without limits, even the polygamous faith of the Mormons, one nativist from Virginia reasoned, could claim immunity "under the broad shield of the freedom of religion!"[77] "The papal is not like the Christian religion," a Native American argued, "IT IS A POLITICAL ORGANIZATION."[78] As such, it could be legislated against.

At this point in history, many drew a distinction between "Catholicism" and "popery." According to U.S. law, Catholic Americans had the constitutional right to worship as they wished, but they had no right to inject their church's influence into political affairs. This was the difference between "Catholics" and "papists" according to Reverend Nicholas Murray, an Irish ex-Catholic priest and vocal nativist: the former attended mass but voted according to the dictates of their own conscience, while the latter strove to abide by the dictates of the pontiff in Rome in public and in private.[79] The distinction did not allay popular

worried they were faking it

fears that Catholic citizens could easily feign allegiance to the Constitution. "Popery and Christianity are just as opposite as is the truth and its caricature," Murray claimed in a sermon delivered in the same New York hall where Reverend Ely had spoken before the OUA on Washington's Birthday in 1850. Murray explained that for Protestant Americans the oath to the U.S. Constitution was inviolate because it consummated the perfect harmony of civil and religious liberty as espoused in the Bible. Catholic Americans who pledged their allegiance to that same Constitution, however, were rendered duplicitous by their tenets of faith, which demanded their undivided allegiance to the temporal and spiritual authority of the pope.[80]

In response, Catholic authors flipped the Christian American myth on its head. Their historical narratives often stressed the Catholic role in the development of America and the U.S. Constitution. These outspoken proponents of Americanism often claimed post facto that the Roman Catholic Church had always been committed to American values, that the adherents of Catholic dogma were the truest Americans. In his 1842 work, *Protestantism and Catholicity Compared,* Reverend Jaime Balmes of Spain offered an influential counternarrative to American claims that their version of Christianity alone signaled human progress. He asserted that "the progress which has been made since Protestantism has been made not by it, but in spite of it." Balmes nodded to the many Catholic clerics who had been ministering to the inhabitants of the American West for centuries. He cited the brutality of the French Revolution as evidence of the logical end of the secularism some Americans seemed to be espousing.[81] Bishop of Louisville Martin Spalding followed suit, arguing that Protestantism "has really done little for the cause of human freedom" because basic U.S. principles, including freedom of thought, trial by jury, habeas corpus, and fair taxation, all derived from Catholicism. The faith's age-old observance of the freedom to do right guarded against "libertine" pluralism, or liberty without a moral compass.[82]

Counter Arguments

Catholic counternarratives connected American freedom to developments, not in New England, where English Puritan leaders "hung Quakers, burned witches, proscribed and drove from their territory all who were not of the number of the elect," as one Cincinnati Catholic wrote, but instead in the English Catholic colony of Maryland.[83] From its founding in 1634 under the Catholic Lord Baltimore's two sons, George and Leonard Calvert, until the Glorious Revolution of 1689, Maryland remained the only colony in English North America that extended religious toleration to Protestants and Catholics alike. Although the Puritan overthrow of the Catholic-dominated government there in 1689 drove Catholic worship underground, Maryland Catholics retained leadership positions and persisted in their faith privately in their homes.[84] In a brief history titled *The Day-Star of American Freedom; or, The Birth and Early Growth of Toleration in the Province of Maryland* (1855), George Lynn-Lachlan Davis claimed that the Maryland charter's provision for religious toleration, written at a time when other colonies forbid Catholic priests from even entering their domain upon pain of death, placed it "in advance of every State upon the continent." It was Maryland, not Plymouth, that made America. Marylanders "planted that seed which has since become a tree of life to the nation, extending its branches and casting its shadows across a whole continent."[85]

Catholic newcomers quickly laid claim to the American Revolution and asserted their right to enjoy free worship. Their ideas about American freedom constituted a substantial component of the political dialogue. Irish Catholic Thomas D'Arcy McGee emphasized Catholicism's historic contributions to the American Revolution in *The Catholic History of North America*. He featured a letter written by Bishop Charles Carroll to Washington praising the president for his service to "our country" and his "respect for religion." Washington responded, "I presume that your fellow-citizens will not forget the patriotic part which you took in the accomplishment of their revolution and the establishment of their government." Washington longed for Roman Catholics to "enjoy every temporal and spiritual felicity" in the United States throughout the years to come.[86]

In a blistering critique of Boynton, titled *Reverend Cha's B. Boynton on Nativism: Reviewed by an American Citizen,* one Cincinnati Catholic accused the nativists of distorting the past to serve their ends. The author argued that Catholics in colonial Maryland demanded a clause about religious freedom in the U.S. Constitution despite Puritan attempts to proscribe them. Furthermore, the church's clerics, the Cincinnati Catholic asserted, would never speak on political matters during mass or try to sway parishioners to vote for one candidate or another, unlike Boynton, both an outspoken nativist and a Congregationalist minister. Catholics understood that bringing politics into mass undermined their faith. The writer took special offense at Boynton trumpeting the "Native American" cause from a pulpit and challenged the minister to produce "the chapter and verse in the Bible in which the Savior has commissioned you to preach politics, setting man against man."[87]

The Cincinnati Catholic further criticized Reverend Boynton's religiously narrow association of Washington with Puritanism and "the monster Cromwell." According to the writer, Cromwell had "waged a cruel, bloody, unrelenting warfare against the church in which our country's father [Washington] was raised and instructed [the Anglican Church]." Boynton had defined Puritanism negatively by "its *uncompromising hostility to Rome*," but the Cincinnati Catholic rejoined, "Would it not be better to set Rome straight, and convince her of her errors, than to be thus uncompromisingly hostile to her, hostile even to death?" Alluding to John 8:3–11, the writer recounted how Jesus demurred condemning an adulteress, then suggested "perhaps the Puritan is not his disciple." If Puritanism was so opposed to monarchies, then perhaps it failed to grasp Jesus' commission to "'teach *all* nations'" (a reference to Matthew 28:19). After all, "Christianity has been propagated and has flourished under every form of government, and so it will continue." The Cincinnati Catholic argued that Reverend Boynton's notion that American principles sprang from Puritans in New England failed to acknowledge the historical reality that Christian "principles were known and acted upon in Europe, long before Columbus set foot upon the New World." "Really, Mr. Boynton," the reviewer concluded his lengthy critique, "you are too shallow." It was the height of impudence to tell the Roman Catholic Church it was "incompatible with liberty" at "this late hour," since "for eighteen hundred years it has been the religion, frequently the only religion of republics and monarchies, both absolute and limited."[88]

Catholic Americans displayed their patriotism in public to prove their loyalty. On Washington's Birthday the *Catholic Telegraph* published a eulogy to the president, "the purist patriot that ever guided the destinies of a nation." It called upon all, regardless of nationality or religion, to "preserve in purity the memory of him who was 'first in war, first in peace and first in the hearts of his countrymen.'"[89] Every Fourth of July, Catholic Americans lined the streets to join in the celebration of the Revolution "to testify their respect for their independence and their gratitude for the blessings of the only free government on earth." Many of them, Purcell claimed, happily embraced "the political principles of our revolution."[90] A certain strand of Catholic Americans even entertained the myth that the Virgin Mary had graced the general in a miraculous vision at Valley Forge and that Washington converted to Catholicism on his deathbed.[91]

The public discourse compelled a reevaluation of the meaning and limits of church-state separation. The principle of religious freedom clearly served the interest of Catholic Americans, who wished to observe their faith without persecution. Father Purcell, editor of the *Catholic Telegraph,* assured Catholics in the West that "the pretexts [nativists] assume—that the country is in danger, that Catholics are foes to liberty, are undermining the Constitution, etc.—cannot hide, even from those who believe them, the fact that Catholics are persecuted for conscience sake." The nativists "banded together to proscribe us," he charged, not for violating any laws of the country, but merely "for *being Catholics*."[92]

Catholic priests persistently disavowed collusion with any political party and refused to intervene in matters outside the generally accepted scope of pastoral instruction. Archbishop Hughes of New York, one of the most cited exemplars of "political Romanism," assured the public, "I have never, in my life, done any action, or uttered a sentiment, tending to abridge any human being, of all or any of the rights of conscience, which I claim to enjoy myself, under the American Constitution." He rejoined that he did "nothing more than is done by clergymen of other denominations." Besides, the archbishop declared, Catholics did not seek to interfere with any religious tenets of other Christian denominations.[93]

Eventually, Catholic apologists compelled some native-born Americans to reappraise the Christian American myth. In an 1852 speech, a Whig state senator of Illinois, James Morrison, a native-born American, unraveled the very core of the Christian American myth. Morrison questioned the premise: "It is asserted that ours is a Protestant country, but are our institutions Protestant in their origin?" He continued: "I venture the assertion that not one of them is," rather, "the modern Representative form of Government is traceable to the Roman Catholic Councils." To prove this shocking claim, he recounted the American Revolution, which "was accomplished by Catholic aid," as an example of the church hierarchy's disposition toward democratic states: "her rule is silent, individual opinion begins, revolution may ensue." Morrison disregarded papal incursions into state affairs in the past as a matter of historical circumstance: "The Catholic Church teaches obedience to legitimate government, so long as that government rules within the limits of reason and justice. This is her principle, founded as she says, upon the divine law." Alluding to the escalating sectional crisis, Senator Morrison retorted that Catholic Americans were even more loyal to the American republic than many Protestants because their faith bound them to legitimate rulers, regardless of "irritating" congressional acts.[94] He thus rejected almost every key ingredient of political nativist rhetoric and offered a more inclusive understanding of American republicanism. Catholics found many other Anglo-American friends like Morrison who despised political nativism.

Conclusion

Ironically, the nativists of the 1840s actually fulfilled their own prophecies of "Catholic-foreign influence" in U.S. politics by excluding Catholics and immigrants alike from the major narratives and institutions that generated national identity. Their assault on the Roman Catholic Church stimulated a social spiraling effect: nativists sought to protect the American principle of religious freedom from the inroads of "political Romanism," but pervasive anti-Catholic sentiment compelled Catholic Americans to foreground their version of American religious freedom. "Religious freedom" became the rallying call of Catholics and nativists alike, and the misunderstandings between both sides seemed only to increase every time a respective representative staked out a claim.

One newspaper editor informed readers in St. Louis, "If the Catholics ever gain (as they surely will do, though at a distant day) an immense numerical superiority, *religious freedom* in this country is at an end." The line appeared in one of the city's premier pro-Catholic newspapers, the *Shepherd of the Valley*. The archbishop of St. Louis, Peter Richard Kenrick, endorsed the newspaper without reservation. When they read the line, most American nativists saw only one possibility: this was evidence of a literal Catholic conspiracy to destroy American democracy in the West. They quoted this controversial line from the *Shepherd of the Valley* over and over again, and readers around the country grew ever more convinced of a "papist plot." The writer, a pious St. Louis Catholic, actually wrote the phrase sarcastically. Catholics read the line as it was intended, as a play on the kind of proscriptive "religious freedom" the nativists wanted. Ironically, nativist writers misread the line as an affirmation of their deepest fears.[95]

CHAPTER 4

The Order of Know-Nothings and Secret Democracy

When you fight the devil, you have a right to fight him with fire.

—Know-Nothing congressman William Russell Smith, Jan. 15, 1855

P OLITICAL NATIVISM DURING THE 1840s fomented a public back-
lash.[1] Americans and immigrants alike accused its adherents of bigotry.
The nativist movement afforded Catholic spokesmen the opportunity
to promote the compatibility of their faith with Americanism. Nativists in
response retreated from the political limelight and reformulated their strategy.
During the late 1840s and early 1850s, many of them around the country secretly
orchestrated the spectacular rise of the fraternal "Know-Nothing" Order. This
turn to secrecy exhibited a hallmark of American nativism: its most ardent
supporters tend to take drastic measures to protect their communities against
unwanted outside influences. Nativism itself is not necessarily incompatible
with American democracy. Such movements on the fringe, however, often do
not meet democratic standards.[2] Nativists opted to covertly achieve their political aims rather than pursuing the openness and transparency normally encouraged in modern democracies.

Another hallmark of American nativism, to which the Know-Nothing
movement in the West well attested, is the tendency of those on the fringe to
mimic the very behaviors and tactics they have projected upon their enemies.
The Know-Nothing version of secret democracy perversely imitated popular
anti-Catholic motifs.[3] Members of the order turned to ritualistic fraternal secrecy to combat the clandestine plotting they thought must have been going
on behind closed doors in Jesuit universities and Roman Catholic councils, attempting to fight secrecy with secrecy. Many at the time noticed the irony. "If
you hate the Catholics because they have nunneries and monasteries, and Jesuitical secret orders," railed one Democratic senator from Virginia, "don't out-Jesuit
the Jesuits by going into dark-lantern secret chambers to apply test oaths. If you

hate the Catholics because you say they encourage the Machiavellian expediency of tellin' lies sometimes, don't swear yourselves not to tell the truth."[4]

The actual content of these secret nativist meetings sheds important light on Know-Nothingism itself as a grassroots movement. But uncovering this has proven difficult because members attempted to confound outsiders with misinformation. To this day, especially little is known about the Order of Know-Nothings in the West. The extant evidence, including Know-Nothing minute books and private correspondence, reveals, on one hand, continuity with the political nativism of the mid-1840s and, on the other, the forging of a new political response to an increasingly polarized and volatile nation.[5]

Where Did All the Nativists Go?

Nativists began to vanish from the public eye around 1848, a year in which immigration levels reached unprecedented highs. Around the same time, locals started reporting odd insignia painted on the sides of buildings as well as folded paper notes randomly discarded about town. One passerby sent a reporter a list of secret "passwords" he discovered beneath a bench somewhere in Ohio in 1854: "MAS L EUGK XQU MX LQVF MAT P PCCK TOU MT LOVL."[6] There were rumors of mysterious assemblies. Wives reported that their husbands were disappearing in the middle of the night. Some fretted that they had joined the Masons or some other "sacrilegious" fraternal order.

A secret fraternal society was indeed gaining ranks, and when reporters cornered alleged members for an interview, they all responded the same way: "I know nothing." New York reporter Horace Greeley referred to the new order as the "Know-Nothings" for the first time in print in the *New York Tribune* issue of November 10, 1853. The nickname stuck.[7] Americans' fascination intensified in the spring of 1854 when these "Know-Nothings" influenced the outcome of city and state elections across the nation and even formed independent tickets during the summer of 1854. The secrecy and political meddling of the Know-Nothing Order provoked a firestorm of opinionated articles in the press. Only with the power of hindsight and access to private correspondence and Know-Nothing records can one be sure what they were up to.

There were many other nativist societies in the 1850s, but the Order of Know-Nothings was unique because it required its members to disavow membership. Eventually, the order became the single most influential of these organizations because it aimed to secretly influence elections.[8] The organization apparently originated in the Order of the Star Spangled Banner (OSSB), also known as the

Sons of the Sires of '76, which Charles Allen founded in New York in 1849. Another nativist group, the Order of United American Mechanics (OUAM), operated separately in the Mississippi Valley under the leadership of dime novelist Ned Buntline but eventually merged with the OSSB sometime in the early 1850s.[9] The OSSB acquired the nickname "Know-Nothing" as early as May 1853.[10] To be admitted into this order, at least at the beginning, an initiate had to be male, white, native born, at least twenty-one years old, and a Protestant Christian.[11]

Misinformation and false reports exaggerated the strangeness of the Know-Nothing Order. A St. Louis newspaper, for example, reported that early societies held séance-like midnight ceremonies in wooded areas outside city limits to avoid detection. One investigator supposedly discovered a Know-Nothing oath "misplaced" at one of these ritual sites:

> I, _____, hereby swear (hold up your right hand) this my oath to endure forever and a day after (raise your right leg) that if I catch a Roman Catholic (shut your right eye) alone in the woods (bat your left) or some out-of-the-way place, that I will pound him into a jelly, or chop him into sausages. I will eat him without pepper or salt and in this way endeavor to annihilate the whole tribe of worthless rapscallions—so help me teapot.[12]

Since the members of the order were apparently sworn to secrecy, they could not do much to dispel vicious rumors. So nativists got in on the joke. Under the pseudonym "Know Something," one such writer confounded contemporaneous reports on Know-Nothing activities by spreading grotesque misinformation. Claiming to be a former member of the order, he pretended to reveal that his cohort actually went by the codename "Babelorium"; that the order's three degrees of membership were titled "Mumsome," "Mummore," and "Mummost"; and that, during meetings, the head of the order presided atop a buffalo, "clothed in the wardrobe of an Indian chief in his wigwam." The penalty for violating fidelity to the order, "Know Something" continued, was an unimaginable racking: the offender's "hide suspended on a liberty pole till dried to a whisp, then taken down and pounded to powder, and the powder to be put into a fifty pounder to be fired off on the ensuing Fourth of July."[13] Americans on the outside could not tell if they were supposed to laugh or take alarm.

Many felt more disturbed than baffled. In 1854 Lemuel C. Porter of Louisville left a record in his diary that bespoke his utter bewilderment at the Know-Nothings' increasing popularity in Louisville: "It is a Singular circumstance that now in the middle of the nineteenth century the most republican & protestant nation on earth should feel such dread of Catholics as to justify a wide spread secret organization the main object of which is to guard American institutions against their baneful influences."[14] David Todd Stuart, a Presbyterian minister and head of Shelbyville Female College, worried about the popularity of the movement in his Kentucky hometown. He "formed a bad opinion" of a fellow minister in Louisville for becoming "an enthusiastic 'Know-Nothing.'" When Stuart returned to Shelbyville on August 8, 1854, an acquaintance cornered him to deliver a cryptic message: "there was a Society of Know-Nothings in the town—that he was a member—and that a gentleman would call on me Thursday evening." The minister wrote later in his diary that he "felt perplexed and despondent" that men he respected had invited him "to join the Know-Nothing Society."[15]

Yet others enthusiastically signed up. One cavalier student of Miami University near Cincinnati, Albert Seaton Berry, wrote his cousin in September 1854 that there were many Know-Nothings in the area and that he had joined them. He had been "secreted smugly away in their domicile, cogitating on the principles of republican government and foreign immigration and the naturalization laws—under the new *modus operandi*." He made light of his plunge "down the deep black hollow" and proclaimed without reserve that "the star of Know-Nothingism is at its zenith here [in Cincinnati]." He boasted three hundred members in his local lodge, including esteemed fellow students and professors. He believed that prospects for the order were bright in his home state of Kentucky too. He also belonged to the Lincoln Lodge in Lincoln County, Kentucky, southeast of Louisville, where, he told his cousin, "I first beheld the star of K.N. rising above the horizon which since had shone so brightly in my eyes."[16]

Membership only cost fifty cents, and native-born westerners of all classes joined in remarkable numbers. In August 1854 the Know-Nothing Grand Council of Ohio, which directed the surrounding states before each formed their own executive state bodies, reported 138 subordinate councils in the state of Ohio, 15 in Kentucky, 10 in Missouri, and 5 in Indiana.[17] The nativist editor of the *Hannibal True American,* Thomas A. Harris, served Tea Party Council no. 1, Missouri's first official Know-Nothing lodge, as a delegate to Ohio's grand-council session in July 1854. When he returned home, he was elected vice president of the Grand Council of Missouri and oversaw the formation of eighteen local chapters by November 1854. The following year Harris presided over more than 274 councils.[18] Membership kept rising. The secretary of the Ohio Grand Council estimated 830 councils in his state by January 1855. In June of that year, Grand President Thomas Spooner reported 1,195 Ohio councils, with an aggregate membership of 130,000.[19]

Jesuit Conspiracy

Popular tales of Catholic conspiracies against the American republic played a major role in motivating nativists' turn to secrecy. In this way those who joined the Know-Nothing orders in their hometowns became obsessed with the secretive power they had attributed to Catholic hierarchy, ritual, and Jesuit intrigue. Know-Nothings justified their modus operandi on, first, the disproportionate influence of Catholics and foreigners in elections, and, second, the supposed covert Catholic agenda to destroy the republic. Know-Nothings masked their political cause in a veil of secrecy to fight unseen Catholic powers. As renowned Kentucky nativist Garrett Davis put it in an 1855 speech in Louisville: "Let Know-Nothingism keep abreast with Jesuitism. Let us fight the Devil with fire."[20]

Americans were avid readers of Catholic conspiracies, including the nun tales of Maria Monk and Rebecca Reed and the Jesuit plots imagined by Morse in *Foreign Conspiracy Against the Liberties of the United States* (1835) and Samuel B. Smith in *The Flight of Popery from Rome to the West* (1836). In these false stories, nuns were accused of sexual misconduct with priests, aborting their children and discarding the corpses into a pit in the basement of their convent.[21] Jesuits were charged with laying plans for a bloody inquisition in America—arming German and Irish Catholics, fortifying cathedrals with cannons, and constructing secret inquisition chambers beneath.[22] The "conniving Jesuit" functioned as a powerful motif in the anti-Catholic genre. Ever since the infamous Gunpowder Plot of 1605, when Guy Fawkes and a small group of militant Catholics tried to blow up King James I in Parliament and restore a Catholic monarchy in England, Jesuit operations bore the stigma of secrecy and treachery. Although the only Jesuit executed by English authorities was Father Henry Garnet, whose alleged involvement in the plot has since been cast into doubt, the term "Jesuit" became highly charged with connotations of betrayal, lies, secrecy, and treason.[23] As Reverend Abel Stevens remarked, it was "a name that rings with horror on the ear of the patriot."[24] Jesuit intrigues were so wily, Reverend Samuel Schmucker warned his congregation, that one of its sworn members "may even pretend to be a convert to a Protestant church in order the better to promote the interests of popery."[25] The order's creed caused particular alarm because, unlike secular priests, its adherents took a special vow of obedience to the pope.

In one popular tale, British soldiers found a paper tucked away in the pocket of a dead Irish priest. The British had won the Battle of Arklow that day in June 1798, outside Dublin. The priest named Murphy, a known leader of the Irish rebels, carried to his death a list of articles of faith for Roman Catholic clerics—the complete, unabridged version for priests' eyes only.[26] The creed stated some of the already widely known dogmas of the Roman Catholic Church, yet it also included peculiar articles never before seen in print. It opened with supplications identifying the pope as the "the Lord God" who had the divine power to "make vice virtue, and virtue vice." Then it went on to denounce "heretics" and to stipulate the following:

9th We are bound not to keep our oaths with heretics, though bound by the most sacred ties.

10th We are bound not to believe their oaths, for their principles are damnation.

11th We are bound to drive heretics with fire, sword, fagot and confusion.

12th We are bound to absolve, without money or price, those who imbue their hands in the blood of a heretic.

As soon as they finished reading, another soldier discovered a second article on the Irish priest's person. It turned out Father Murphy was a member of the Jesuit Order. This document instructed Jesuits to establish colleges in "opulent cities," to accumulate great wealth, and to conceal "the real value of our revenues." Even more alarming, it encouraged them to use their money to "artfully worm themselves" into the coterie of government officials, so "that we may have their ear" and "easily secure their hearts."[27]

The story was fictional, completely made up. Whether or not he knew it, publisher G. A. Seigneur, a French ex-Catholic priest turned American colporteur (a peddler of religious books), was at the tail end of a trans-Atlantic game of telephone. The tale's origins traced to the militantly anti-Catholic Orange Lodge in Ireland. A patron of that society wrote up the story and submitted it to the local Irish Protestant newspaper. A British subscriber passed it on to an anti-Catholic newspaper in London. During a weekly scan for noteworthy news from London, an American reporter copied the story for an article in New York's premier anti-Catholic newspaper, the *Protestant Vindicator,* sometime between 1836 and 1839. At no point did any of the journalists attempt to corroborate the story. Enter Seigneur, who rediscovered the news story in the *Vindicator* while in New Orleans nearly two decades later. He then traveled the Mississippi Valley in 1854, selling the tale in his twenty-five-cent compilation, *A Startling Disclosure of the Secret Workings of the Jesuits.*[28] Nearly all of the stories of Catholic misdeeds were recounted in a similar manner.

Americans bought many Catholic conspiratorial works such as Seigneur's. Journalists in mid-nineteenth-century America took stories of such intrigue

seriously and constantly pressured Jesuit superiors to turn over their "real" clerical oaths, assuming the official materials released to the public were a cover.
An investigator supposedly got his hands on an "authentic" copy in 1855 and
published it immediately. According to this document, Jesuits vowed to uphold
the pope's "power to depose heretical kings" and renounce "any allegiance as due
to any heretical king, prince, or state, named Protestant." The Jesuit candidate
was required to do his "utmost to extirpate the heretical Protestants' doctrine,
and to destroy all their pretended powers, regal or otherwise." All this was followed by a solemn pledge "to keep secret and private all her [the church's] agents'
counsels." Jesuit authorities' insistence that the document was a fabrication fell
on deaf ears.[29]

According to Reverend Charles Boynton of Cincinnati, the Catholic conspiracy in America was the inevitable outcome of the "*one central principle* of
the Papacy": imperial domination of the Earth. It was the Catholic Church's
"solemn duty to overthrow all Protestant or other opposing governments, and
exterminate utterly every faith but her own." Boynton asserted that the dogmas
of the church even permitted the Catholic hierarchy "to employ any means for
the glory of God, because treachery and fraud, even the violation of oaths, private murder, or destruction by war, are all justified by the holy end which she
has in view." It was not the Catholic "religion" he sought to proscribe, Boynton
claimed, but "a politico-ecclesiastical Corporation of priests and Jesuits . . . under
the direction of a foreign power." [30]

As the real presence of Catholics and Catholic institutions in the West expanded rapidly between 1845 and 1855, especially in developing cities, the Know-
Nothing Order presented itself to westerners as the only antidote.[31] A resident
of Ohio named Sidney Maxwell mentioned in his diary in September 1854 that
he believed the Catholics in his state "have been working themselves into our
offices of government." He vowed to prevent Cincinnati's government from
falling "into the hands of Romanists."[32] Four months later, after penning this
timely entry in his diary, Maxwell celebrated the remarkable rise of the Know-
Nothings. On January 1, 1855, though apparently not a member himself, he
mentioned that the group's activities "were entirely secret" yet believed he could
properly discern the main object of the new party: "to fill our offices with none
than native born Americans—to extend the time of naturalization, and to watch
with the utmost vigilance the operations of the Roman Church in this government." Maxwell noted with admiration that "this new organization had found
soil in Ohio, it appears, that was suited to its growth."[33] In Cincinnati one lawyer
remarked that the order "termed out of doubt—*Know-Nothing*" was poised to

"break down all foreign control and influences, particularly that of the Roman Catholic," which he evidently thought was "a commendable undertaking and worthy to be carried out to its utmost extent."[34] In Louisville a doctor penned in private that the order's opposition to Catholics and foreigners was "truly American" because "the foreign influence has been banefully felt for a number of years . . . in our large cities & Demagogues have given them this consequence by pandering for their support thusly giving them in many cases the balance of power in elections."[35] A wide cross-section of westerners lent their support to the Know-Nothings.

Nativist leaders in the West believed Catholicism in the United States had grown too powerful for ordinary democratic measures. "Already have [papists] overwhelmed the old native American party in the United States," renowned Kentucky representative Garrett Davis charged, which therefore "proved by their strength the necessity of a more potent body—*even the secret and mysterious order of the Star Spangled Banner.*" The Know-Nothings of Kentucky nominated Davis for governor in 1855, then for president of the United States in 1856. Davis believed his order combated two formidable forces: one, the "swarms of demagogues," and two, the "world-wide hierarchy that boasts of its antiquity, its unchangableness, and its infallibility," the Catholic Church. The order's "mode of action," he claimed, "is to isolate and nationalize the American people from the corrupting effects" of these two forces.[36] Davis explained that through "concentrated native American voting," Know-Nothingism counteracted "the spirit of the papacy, [which] undoubtedly, interferes with native Americanism." It was impossible, he reckoned, "to conceive how it is wrong for the native Americans to interfere back again, by moral and spiritual means with the papists." Davis proclaimed, "Let the subordinate and grand councils of the Patriotic Fraternity oppose the Beastly Monster," and "as long as we live, let us ever prefer Christianity to Popery, 'Liberty to power.'"[37]

"Rigged" Elections

Loose naturalization laws, which varied by state, made it remarkably easy for European immigrants to gain enfranchisement, especially in the West. The state governments of Illinois, Kentucky, Missouri, and Ohio proved especially eager to attract settlers to their states and accordingly adopted a policy of allowing immigrants to vote after only one or two years of residency simply by declaring their intent to naturalize in five years' time. Acquiring voting rights in these states required the mere expression of one's intent to become an American citizen.

Eager to attract immigrant workers, one of the least populated western states, Indiana, actually waived all residency requirements and expediently naturalized immigrants upon arrival.[38]

Know-Nothings chastised native-born "demagogues" who allegedly pandered to immigrants. The word "demagogue" derives from the Greek (*demos* means "people," and *ago* means "carry/manipulate"—so "people's manipulator") and refers to a rabble-rousing populist who appeals to the base passions of the lower classes. It was a bad word in nineteenth-century America. Nativists claimed "unassimilated" foreigners fueled demagoguery. They rallied to exterminate corrupt political machines and preserve America's most important institution: the vote.[39] As Reverend Alfred Ely put it, the ballot constituted nothing less than "our very *sanctum sanctorum*," and as such, suffrage "should not only be preserved inviolate but it should be guarded with the severest caution."[40]

In *The Origins, Principles, and Purposes of the American Party,* Know-Nothing Henry Winter Davis of Maryland condemned the Democratic Party in particular for consistently pandering to immigrants. Indeed, that party consistently drew more than 75 percent of the immigrant vote.[41] James Chapman, a former Democrat and the minister of the Southern Methodist Episcopal Church of Tennessee, demonstrated the problem in his exhaustive book *Americanism versus Romanism; or, The Cis-Atlantic Battle between Sam and the Pope* (1856). Even though the proportion of immigrants to the entire population was small, Chapman showed how immigrants' solidarity within one party, in this case the Democratic Party, gave them disproportionate political power. The native-born American vote typically split in half between the Whig and Democratic Parties. The numbers suggested that the foreign-born population, however, was not so evenly divided between the two parties.[42] Democrats generally secured above two-thirds of the foreign-born vote, often just enough to swing elections in their favor. By 1850, more than 90 percent of Irish Americans nationwide voted for proslavery Democrats, with roughly 80 percent of German Americans voting for them as well. In cases when two Democratic candidates competed, Germans preferred the one with a more moderate position on the extension of slavery in the West.[43] The growing power of this so-called "foreign bloc" of voters became apparent in elections held in urban areas in the North and West, where major metropolises hosted disproportionately large immigrant populations. Most Germans and almost all Irish voted Democrat, so as a group they played a decisive role in mid-nineteenth-century elections, especially at local levels.

Statistically speaking, Roman Catholic citizens tended to vote en bloc for the same candidate, typically a Democrat. More than 95 percent of Catholic immigrants nationwide voted Democrat after 1845. They composed significant percentages of foreign populations in urban areas. Since Democrats relied on the immigrant vote, they therefore depended on Catholics for victory. This could be witnessed in many American elections, Davis asserted, as "demagogues" found loyal immigrant voters, or "mercenaries" as he called them, in the solid "faction of the political papists."[44] Reverend Chapman asked "whether it is their nationality, their personal feeling, or their Catholicism that causes them to coalesce at the polls?" The fact of Catholic bloc voting proved with "almost unquestionable certainty," Chapman claimed, that the pope in Rome held sway over American elections. "The German and the Irish socially hate each other," he offered as an example, "but if they are *Catholics,* they always *vote* alike."[45]

If the elections were already rigged in this fashion, then nativists figured they had no choice but to do some rigging of their own. In their minds, Catholic bloc voting necessitated dark-lantern politicking. For all their celebration of democracy, the nativists were among the first to admit that the American system of government had a disturbing flaw for them: if left to their own devices, Catholic American voters would also mold American institutions. On one hand, nativists placed the blame on the "demagogues" who tried to win the German and Irish vote. It was "not that we fear their numerical strength," nativist Reverend Sam Chapman remarked, "but their influence over time-serving and self-interested politicians." On the other hand, nativists believed Catholic leaders were then plotting to destroy their opposition, infiltrate the U.S. government, and eventually bring about the nation's demise.[46]

The modus operandi of the nativist movement revealed a strange fascination with the stigmatized "Catholicism" nativist authors had been imagining. Contemporary observers often dismissed Know-Nothingism, however, as a smokescreen for political agendas its members wished to keep hidden. Whigs believed Democrats in the order were trying to destroy the Whig Party, while Democrats believed the Whigs in it looked to do them in. Some charged that the order was secretly a tool of northern abolitionists; others accused the Know-Nothings of being in league with the southern "slavocracy." But what exactly did the Know-Nothings attempt to accomplish?

A Peek Inside Know-Nothing Councils

Members of the Know-Nothing Order vowed to vote in unison for a political candidate who was native-born and Protestant Christian, their purpose being to limit Catholic and foreign influence in politics. The Know-Nothings initially did not conspire with one political party in particular. According to the State Council of Missouri's previously top-secret *Ritual of the Order,* its president delivered an address to initiates after the conferral of the first degree, wherein he explained their reason for gathering: "foreign influence has been making steady and alarming progress in our country." On the one hand, the Know-Nothing Order continued the work of earlier patriotic societies such as the Order of United Americans (OUA): "good and true men have devised this Order as a means of disseminating patriotic principles, of keeping alive the fire of national virtue, of fostering the national intelligence, and of advancing America and the American interest." On the other, it broke with tradition by organizing independently and politically to check "the stride of the foreigner and alien" and to thwart "the deadly plans of the enemies of our Republican Institutions."[47]

The 1854 constitution of the Grand Council of Ohio obliged members to make this pledge:

> I, _____, hereby solemnly swear eternal fidelity to the vows I have taken in this Order. I also swear that I will advance the interests of every native born American citizen, especially the members of this Order, to the entire and absolute exclusion of all aliens and foreigners, and more especially those who belong to or approve of the Roman Catholic faith. So help me God![48]

Here in the official 1854 version, the "Roman Catholic faith" was explicitly denounced. Thus, from its inception, the Know-Nothing Order functioned as a safe haven for anti-Catholics. Members could express such beliefs openly among comrades without having to fear public scorn. Through 1854 and the first half of 1855, only white, native-born Protestant Christian men over the age of twenty-one were admitted to a council. The order barred men who were married to a Roman Catholic woman. The Grand Council of Ohio, the West's first state Know-Nothing council, on August 1, 1854, resolved to establish the following criteria for membership: "any person born within the jurisdiction of the United States, of Protestant parents, and raised and educated under Protestant influence, and who has not a Catholic wife, shall be eligible to membership in this order."[49]

Initiates began their symbolic journey into the inner sanctums of the organization by facing the marshal, who guarded the entrance to the lodge. He asked, "Do you believe in a Supreme Being, the Creator and Preserver of the universe?" Answer: "I do." Then the initiate made a solemn pledge of secrecy upon the "Holy Bible and Cross." The marshal first asked for his age and where he was born. If the candidate was twenty-one years or older and a native of the United States, the marshal then queried as to whether he wanted to liberate public schools "from all sectarian influence" (the proper response being "I do"), whether he submitted his private judgment and civic duties to "the authority of any man or set of men on earth, either lay or ecclesiastical" (response, "I do not"), and whether he was willing to resist foreign influence in American political affairs (response, "I do"). If the initiate answered the questions correctly, the marshal permitted him into the council room, where the vice president gave him the first-degree passwords, signs, and handshakes.[50]

The first-degree oath required members to vote only for native-born Protestant Americans, to resist foreign political influence in general, and to keep the order and its membership a secret. The second degree called upon members to imitate the "brilliant deeds of patriotism of our fathers, through which [we] received the inestimable blessings of civil and religious liberty," and, above all, to keep alive "the deathless example of our illustrious WASHINGTON." The third degree bound members to preserve the union of the United States at all costs. At each conferral, new passwords and signs were conveyed. At the end of the conferral of the third degree, the president explained the meaning of the member's symbolic passage: the dangers to American liberty came from within; immigrants in their midst brought "imminent peril."[51]

Not until March 1854 did any Know-Nothing groups attempt direct action. In 1852 Pope Pius IX had donated a marble stone to be incorporated in the Washington Monument in Washington, D.C. John F. Wieshampel raised outcries against the use of the stone in the national monument. His widely circulated pamphlet *The Pope's Stratagem, "Rome to America!"* underlined the pope's recent efforts to "interfere" in the American civic order.[52] On March 6, 1854, a small Know-Nothing mob stormed the storage shed in the capital where the "Pope's Stone" rested. They poisoned the guard dog, bound and gagged the guard, dragged the marble block to the Potomac River, and cast it into the water. Several newspapers reported that before capsizing the marble into the river, the Know-Nothings pounded off several chunks and stole them away.[53]

Two months later, on May 17, the biggest grand council meeting of Know-Nothings in the West to date congregated in Cincinnati. Delegates from all over the region converged in the Queen City. Robert Morris from Lodge no. 9 in Portsmouth, Ohio, brought two rare gifts that thrilled the councilmen. One member immediately moved "the thanks of this Grand Body be returned to Bro. Morris" for the generous contribution of the items. Upon another motion, the grand council resolved to keep the gifts in their "permanent possession."[54]

One of the mementoes was a small chunk of marble, which Morris claimed was an authentic piece of the original "stone which Pope Pius IX contributed to the Washington Monument." This was a diabolical symbol sure to enflame the ire of Catholic Americans. The Grand Council of Ohio was not the only group to seemingly endorse the theft and destruction of the Pope's Stone. Know-Nothing councils in Chicago, Cincinnati, Louisville, and St. Louis each hailed the group of twenty men who sunk it as true patriots; several of them also claimed to possess authentic pieces of the stone. For the anniversary of its capsizing in the Potomac, the Grand Council of Missouri even organized the Committee on the Washington Monument to join hearts with the rioters in Washington, D.C., and preserve the symbolic purity of the national icon.[55]

The other memento was a Roman Catholic relic upon which the original members of the Grand Council of Ohio apparently swore their first oaths to the Know-Nothing Order. Catholics venerated relics, and if this one actually was authentic, they would have certainly condemned the order as the most heinous and sacrosanct group in the whole of the country. That added to the Know-Nothings' revelry. Morris claimed that this relic "had been taken from one of the Catholic churches of Philadelphia during the riot which took place there a number of years since." Here, he referred to the Philadelphia Riot of 1844, during which nativists tore down and carried away various holy items stationed in St. Augustine's and St. Michael's Cathedrals before they burned both to the ground. What happened to the consecrated paraphernalia had remained a mystery until now. Morris told the group, "Catholics claimed that the wood of which it is composed is a part of the true cross upon which our Savior was crucified."[56]

We may never know whether these artifacts were authentic, but we can glimpse the intended message behind their ritualistic appearance. The relic and the rubble were insignia, "mementoes" as they called them, that the Ohio Know-Nothings reappropriated as their own crypto-Catholic icons and relics. For the Know-Nothing council, the chunk of marble stolen from the Washington Monument and the relic stolen from a cathedral in Philadelphia represented in microcosm the destruction of Roman Catholic designs. The insignia also symbolized the necessity of taking direct action against Roman Catholic intervention in state and public affairs. These Know-Nothing councils did not necessarily condone rioting and property damage as much as they lent their support to an ethos, that they were serious, a force to be reckoned with, like Rome; that they cared not one iota for Catholic religiosity, miracles, and holy items; and that demagogues, Catholic voters, and political office seekers should take heed of the order.

Even in secret, the Know-Nothings tried to practice what they preached—a pure democracy. Although shrouded in mystery, their councils were in some ways more democratic than the existing two-party system. As historian John Mulkern has pointed out, Know-Nothings envisioned their radically democratic lodge networks as "the ultimate expression of republicanism."[57] When it came to voting for political candidates, members felt their individual vote carried more representative weight in these lodges than in the traditional nomination processes within Whig and Democratic caucuses. "Each party [has] its secret agents in Washington—meeting in dark conclave," one Know-Nothing representative explained; "mysterious inuendos of conspiracy are uttered with low tones and smothered breath, and all justified, commended, practiced, and applauded."[58] Indeed, the two political parties each harbored a core group of influential and powerful leaders, wielding backing and money, who often swayed the course of the nominations. Things were different in Know-Nothing councils. In August 1854 the Grand Council of Ohio formed a separate Committee on Elections, which resolved immediately to model the order's inner election procedures purely on the U.S. Constitution so that even "the choice of nominees for all offices" would be "elective by the people." Know-Nothings in the West resolved that each subordinate council would send one delegate for every three hundred members to the state council to serve as legislator. Unlike in the Whig and Democratic processes, where the convention selected candidates, Know-Nothing officials from the county to national levels were nominated by popular vote.[59]

Moreover, Know-Nothing votes were recorded on secret ballots at a time when elections still practiced voting viva voce ("by word of mouth"; that is, voice vote). Many still defended the old system because, as one Missourian put it, voting out loud prevented "bad and ignorant voters" from gaining "impunity from public shame or private resentment in consequence of voting as their own malignant passions may dictate." This commentator believed that "the secret ballot is anti-republican—it encourages men to give votes they would not dare avow, and of which they would be ashamed, if known." Interestingly, those in favor of the voice vote criticized the secret ballot for enabling political nativism.[60]

During Know-Nothing elections, the candidate with the simple majority of votes won the nomination, and all members then vowed to vote for the nominee in the upcoming election. A tie was settled by lot.[61] In the case of a vacancy, the president of the order sent out his nominee in secret to all the subordinate councils, and each had the opportunity to approve or reject his selection. Annual elections were held for executive councilmen, including the president, vice president, secretary, treasurer, and so on. The Committee of Elections structured the process this way because they believed it was "the best course to secure, spread and strengthen American principles, as recognized by this Order." The Know-Nothings envisioned a highly individualistic democratic process.[62]

The leaders of the order expected individual members to comport themselves in a manner becoming good republican citizens. The Ohio Grand Council included a clause in its constitution that required members "to possess good moral characters." The constitutions of Ohio and Missouri included passages to prevent possible "demagoguery" within Know-Nothing councils so that politicians could not pander to the order during campaigns. The Missouri Grand Council, for example, passed a special restriction in 1855 barring membership for anyone currently running for office to discountenance "demagogism" and prevent the order from "being used as an instrument for promoting interested and selfish ends."[63]

If one could peek inside the Grand Councils of Ohio and Missouri, one would witness procedures that paralleled the most solemn of congressional sessions. According to the Ohio council's "Rules of the Order," meetings began with the seating of the president and the pounding of a gavel: "at the sound of the gavel there shall be a general silence, under the penalty of a public reprimand." Then came a roll call of officers, an orderly presentation of the delegates' certificates, the reading aloud of the previous meeting's minutes, the reports of the committees, and then the conferral of degrees upon new members and any "new business." The "presiding officer," the rules stated, "shall preserve order and decorum" at all times. No member was to interrupt another while speaking. Before making a motion or speech, each member had to rise and ask the permission of the presiding officer, who could accept or deny the request. Slander was forbidden, as was personal attacks on fellow members.[64]

The first meeting of the Grand Council of Missouri, on September 29, 1854, established similar procedures. Missouri's Know-Nothing delegates first ratified the order's constitution, voted on the next meeting date, and amended the bylaws and rules. On October 19 and 20 they met again in St. Louis in the hall of Yorktown Council no. 11, where they spent two tedious days revising drafts of bylaws and proceeding through the several nominations for various seats in the executive council and the national convention (to be held in June 1855). Only after the day's sessions did the delegates leave parliamentary procedure behind to share one another's company at "a sumptuous [dinner]." They made patriotic toasts into the early morning hours, and the company was "entertained by the happyness interchanged of anecdote and friendly tolkens."[65]

Like U.S. congressional sessions, Know-Nothing councils opened with prayer. Clergymen, of course, joined the order. It seemed natural for the Grand Council of Missouri to invite the minister of St. Louis' First Methodist Church, Charles B. Parsons, "to open sessions of this council each morning with prayer."[66] The Know-Nothings of St. Louis probably requested Reverend Parsons because of his personal connection to Solomon Smith, president and state delegate of Valley Forge Council no. 14 in the city.[67] Parsons saw no reason why his religious duties should interfere with an opportunity to oblige Smith, "an old friend."[68] Another Christian minister from that state privately urged Missouri Whig politician George R. Smith to join the Know-Nothing Order: "I am a life member, so far as I understand their aims and objects. I am not one *of them,* but am one *with them,* and if alive and well, expect on the day of the 'fight' to record my vote in favor of the sentiment, 'None but Americans shall rule America.'" Little did the reverend know that George Smith was already a member of the order, representing the district of St. Louis for the Grand Council of Missouri.[69]

Masonry, Odd Fellowship, and Know-Nothingism

The whole structure of the Know-Nothing Order, including its dark-lantern rituals, borrowed from Masonry. The Order of Free and Accepted Masons began as a respected club for elite men in early America. Freemasons included at least nine of the signers of the U.S. Constitution and such esteemed patriots as George Washington, Benjamin Franklin, and Paul Revere. Before the mid-1830s, a rare few considered the secrecy and exclusivity of Freemasonry undemocratic. The nation's first president, after all, was a master mason, the highest rank of the order, in Fredericksburg, Virginia.[70]

During the Second Great Awakening, a new generation of evangelicals like Charles Grandison Finney, formerly a Mason himself, denounced Masonic secrecy and ritual. After his conversion to Christianity in 1824, Finney condemned Freemasonry as at best a diversion from the faith and at worst a "counterfeit religion." He organized an anti-Mason crusade that lasted well into the mid-nineteenth century. In *The Character, Claims and Practical Workings of Freemasonry,* Reverend Finney accused the order of drawing young men away from religious conversion and toward a fraternal initiation that only mimicked in some ways the ethos experienced in church gatherings: the fear of hell, the obstacle of personal ineptitude, the hope in personal transformation, and the perseverance of brotherly love.[71] Masonic rituals created a kind of "liminal experience," an in-between space, exotic but reflective of mainstream hopes and fears. It hardly escaped the anti-Masons' notice that the ratio of church attendance in the 1840s figured two females for every male. Apparently, many young men chose fraternities over churches.[72]

Catholic leaders had warned their charges for centuries not to join secret societies under pain of excommunication. The church hierarchy consistently opposed secret orders such as Masonry and Odd Fellowship. They pronounced it a mortal sin to join any society requiring an oath of initiation that bound members to hold higher allegiance to the order than to their ecclesiastical authorities and to withhold details of their membership from the clergy in the confessional booth. This hostility to secret societies traced back to the earliest Roman Catholic councils anathematizing Gnosticism. According to Father Edward Purcell: "It is distinctly known to all Catholics, that their church does formally and unreservedly condemn all Secret Societies, whose members bind themselves by solemn oaths . . . to fellowship or secrecy."[73] To be reconciled to God, an individual had to clear his conscience to his confessor.

The Catholic Church took the matter so seriously, Purcell explained in 1849, that "if a Catholic should die whilst attached to the order of Odd Fellows, we would not attempt to interfere with his funeral." In other words, the Catholic hierarchy refused to admit those who died as members of secret societies into its consecrated burial grounds, implying that committed Masons and Odd Fellows could not enter heaven. Catholics acknowledged the right of such societies to exist and recognized their charitable contributions, but they also claimed the right to exclude such orders from their own places of worship. Although Freemasonry made use of scriptures and Christian doctrines, Purcell argued it was not a true religion because its object was the promotion of its members, not the defense of "the word of God and the peace of his Church."[74] The rituals of Masonic societies, moreover, obviously "ridiculed the Scriptures and mocked at religion," incorporating mock antiphons and creeds and referring to their superiors as "High Priest" and the like.[75]

The Masons and Odd Fellows began a campaign of their own in an attempt to build bridges with concerned Christians. They embraced a new semitransparency, publishing many of their proceedings.[76] Curious readers could see firsthand that Masons respected God in the opening invocations, "thou hast promised that where two or three are gathered together in thy name, thou wilt be in the midst of them," and that their constitutions outlined democratic procedures for members, with each individual casting ballots to elect members to office.[77] They claimed the attendance of "many thousands of devoted and consistent Christians and church members," including clergymen.[78] One member celebrated a new hall in St. Louis as a "temple of practical Christianity," referring to the Order of Odd

Fellows as a "great and spreading church," harboring both "the priest of science" and the "priest of religion." The author believed the motto of the order—"Friendship, Love and Truth"—epitomized the "true spirit of Christianity."[79]

Society officials appealed openly to the wives of members. One leader of the Independent Order of Odd Fellows, the second-most-popular secret fraternal society in the Mississippi Valley, reminded outspoken female dissenters in 1846, "your nature is different." While men were naturally aggressive and prone to selfishness, the author claimed, "your Creator has already endowed you with the feelings and sentiments peculiar to Odd Fellowship." Men needed Odd Fellowship, in other words, to "elevate them to the standard of your own."[80] The exclusivity and secrecy offered sincere pursuers of the truth the assurance that the men to whom they committed their fraternal love were indeed upright fellows.[81]

By 1853, the city of St. Louis listed ten major Masonic lodges, as well as three German ones, and ten lodges of the Independent Order of Odd Fellows. There were many more subordinate lodges. There were also eight councils of the United Ancient Order of Druids and at least five councils of the nativist Order of United American Mechanics in St. Louis alone.[82] In 1855 Chicago counted one council of the OUA, sixty Odd Fellows' subordinate lodges, one hundred of the Independent Order of Good Templars, and over 150 Masonic lodges.[83]

Many of these organizations' members joined the Know-Nothing Order the following year. Philip Swigert of Frankfort, Kentucky, to give a specific example, presided as the grand sachem of the Grand Lodge of Kentucky in 1845 before he served as an executive officeholder in the Know-Nothing Grand Council of Kentucky in 1855.[84] A prominent St. Louis delegate to the Know-Nothing National Council in 1855, Archibald Gamble, had been a Mason since Missouri became a state in 1820.[85]

Know-Nothings copied the structure of Masonic degrees, governance, and lodges. Instead of incorporating the numerous degrees of these lodges, though, Know-Nothings reduced those conferred to just three. Instead of "Grand Lodge" and "Grand Master," Masonic terms, Know-Nothings used "Grand Council" and "Grand President." Instead of the executive positions of "Warden" and "Deacon," Know-Nothings used "Marshal" and "Instructor." Instead of "Guardian," they used "Sentinel." Many subordinate lodges of Freemason, Odd Fellows, and Know-Nothings were named after U.S. founders and Revolutionary events, including Washington, Franklin, Bunker Hill, Valley Forge, and Plymouth Rock, which were the most popular.[86] The Know-Nothing Order of Cincinnati even solicited the Odd Fellows to publish their initial proceedings (abridged) in 1854.[87]

Employing a tactic familiar to Masonry, members of the Know-Nothing Order argued that secret fraternal societies like theirs actually promoted free-thinking and that this was precisely why the Roman Catholic Church forbid its congregants to join them. According to these spokesmen, Catholic leaders' outcries only proved that Know-Nothing countermeasures accomplished the intended effect of undermining the very secrecy the church had traditionally relied upon.[88] They further argued that the Catholic religion demanded "a more submissive obedience to its guides, a greater dependence upon authority for its direction and conduct, and a closer inter-relation of personal sympathy and identity of end and object, than any other fraternity in our land."[89] One Know-Nothing outside Chicago pointed out with disgust that a member of the Catholic Church faced excommunication and ostracism simply for being "sworn not to tell what he knows about the Masons, or any of their sort of secret duins." If Masons were good republicans, and Catholics could not be Masons, he therefore reasoned that Catholics could not be good republicans. "If they made em no nothins," an Illinoisan argued in 1854, "they couldn't be Catholics." If a Catholic were ever elected to office, then "all the Pope hes got to du to pull down the hull fabric of our Government and build himself up onto it is to tell such fellars to du it." He concluded, "'Pears to me it's the Catholics that go agin the Constitution and the no nothings is agin *them,* just because they are agin the Constitution."[90]

In 1854 nativist author S. D. T. Willard, using the pseudonym "A Foe to Despotism," sold 20,000 copies of his propaganda piece *Red Cross of Catholicism in America,* which elaborated on a Catholic conspiracy to infiltrate Know-Nothing councils. Willard argued that church leaders claimed duplicitously to oppose secret orders in public while plotting "in secret conclaves" themselves. "Hear that, ye Odd Fellows," Willard warned: "Admit no Roman Catholics into your noble order, for as sure as they should learn your secrets and proceedings, an account of them would be transmitted by the first opportunity, to his unholiness, the Pope."[91]

Like their Masonic counterparts, Know-Nothing propagandists in 1854 and early 1855 tried to persuade the public that the secret rituals of the order hid nothing sinister. One such propaganda piece, a 350-page novel titled *The Know-Nothing?,* hit the presses in Cleveland, in 1855. The anonymous author painted a rosy picture of Know-Nothingism. The protagonist of the story, Mr. Lamont, appears in an anonymous western town seeking members for a mysterious club. "The *name* of this order I cannot tell you now; *but hear me,*" he tells one recruit, "I have information to impart that *will startle you.*" The recruit, Edward Buford, selects friends to come with him to a secret midnight meeting. They attend on his word that the order is "consistent with true principle, sound morality, and genuine patriotic feeling."[92] During the first meeting, Mr. Lamont affirms "the duty of every good citizen to look abroad ... to see where evils exist" and correct them. He gives them simple signs and passwords to indicate their membership in the group and promises to reveal more the following meeting. At the second meeting, he encourages the men to shun selfishness and pledge "obligations that will make us continually stand by and love each other." Lamont urges them to avoid slander against their brothers, to help one another in business, and to watch over the families of deceased brethren. In a delightful twist, Mr. Lamont is revealed to be Edward Buford's biological brother, not immediately recognizable because he had spent several years abroad. This plot device stresses the familiarity of Know-Nothingism in western locales, suggesting that members were friendly neighbors rather than mischievous outsiders.[93]

The novelist wrote the story in part to insulate Know-Nothings from the accusations of anti-Mason female protesters. One Illinois reporter, for example, recorded local women's concern with the order: "The wimmen, all tu once, got to complainin that the men fokes stayed out nights till ten or leven oclock, and fur a week or so back every boddy hes bin a talkin about the no nothings bein in the neighborhood."[94] So, late in the novel, when one new recruit returns late at night, his wife accuses him of forsaking her for a scandalous club. "It's nothing more nor less than this outlandish Know-Nothing society that is leading all the men away from their duties," she yells. If he refuses to convince his married friends to quit the order, she threatens, the women of the town would form a society "that will make you cook your own dinners, make your own shirts, and take care of yourselves in general!" But the following week, she is "put to shame" when it comes to light that Know-Nothings have cared for the widow and son of a deceased member of the order, ministered to the poor, fed orphans, and spread kindness and goodwill throughout the town. The novel ends with the rosy conclusion that the Know-Nothings had elevated the western town to "'a city set on a hill,' casting abroad a bright and glorious light" for the rest of America to emulate.[95]

Looking inside the Know-Nothing councils in the West reveals how anti-Catholicism remained a key aspect of the movement. Nativists justified their secrecy on the grounds of a Catholic conspiracy to subvert their liberties. This secrecy allowed them to avoid accusations of bigotry from their enemies and prepare a new political strategy. The Order of Know-Nothings invoked the "greater good" of American unity and purity. Cloaking their actions in secrecy nevertheless appeared suspect to many. Over the ensuing years of the order's existence, Know-Nothings confronted challenging, potentially devastating criticisms.

Know-Nothingism as "Un-American"

Many Americans excoriated nativist secrecy as un-American. Purcell, a Catholic priest based in Cincinnati, thought it especially revealing that native-born Americans chose secrecy as their ploy to "end popery" in a free republic, where Protestants in fact dominated "the Press, the Publishing houses, the Public School Fund, the Universities, and popular prejudices." Perhaps it suggested that nativists were insincere about their love of democracy.[96] A Protestant reverend in Ohio agreed with Purcell that the "secret Democracy" of the Know-Nothings served as a cover for "plotting schemes and in the dark working vigorously to the injury of our country's common good."[97] The minister prodded, "Pretend, do they, to oppose Catholicism?" He thought it more likely they were in league *with* Jesuits than against them. A Missourian likewise denounced Know-Nothingism as cowardly and could only imagine that the nativists had sunk so low because they wished to conceal "monstrous bigotry and intolerance." The order had merely added "religious bigotry and jacobinical secrecy" onto the "ostensible principles" of the "old Native Americanism."[98]

Orestes Brownson of Boston asserted that the order was essentially anti-Catholic, rather than authentically and positively "nativist." Brownson, an Anglo-American convert to Catholicism and editor of the premier Catholic journal in the United States, argued the distinction in his *Boston Quarterly Review.*[99] His essays were dispersed so widely that they appeared as common stays in private western libraries.[100] In an article titled "Native Americanism," Brownson defined nativism as a natural and necessary preference for one's own country over others. He admitted that immigrants from Germany and Ireland did not automatically share a sense of allegiance to the United States like native-born Americans and agreed that some foreigners needed time to assimilate, although he hesitated to offer an opinion on immigration policy. He instructed Catholic Americans to beware, then, "of confounding the proper native American feeling with the anti-Catholic feeling." He asserted that true "Native Americanism is as strong in the bosom of American Catholics as it is in the bosom of American Protestants." Vitriolic exchange between "No-Popery leaders" and Catholic immigrants had made out nativism and anti-Catholicism to seem like the same thing.[101]

In targeting Know-Nothing secrecy, Catholic Americans emphasized their own transparency. This was precisely what nativists wanted to counteract, but their decision to hide from the public limelight discredited them. One Missourian pointed out this exact dilemma: "Secrecy is no doubt an element of strength; it is also a source of weakness. When the order and its principles are attacked, there is nobody to defend—nobody belongs to it."[102] Under the pseudonym "foreigner," one writer asked in 1854, "What are they afraid of?" How could reasonable people honestly worry that "two to three millions of Catholics" were both able and willing to "murder all the nineteen millions of protestants in the twinkling of a broomstick?" The author concluded that Know-Nothings ultimately gathered in secret because "they feel and know that their object is to oppose the laws of the country, and their machinations will not bear the light of day, or the scrutiny of their fellow citizens."[103]

Hardline Democrats and Whigs likewise denounced the entire movement as bigoted. In an address widely circulated by Democrats in 1855, Governor Henry A. Wise of Virginia took more offense at the "religiously intolerant" Know-Nothing Order than the purportedly decrepit and outdated Roman Catholic Church.[104] "Yes, sir," a representative from New York concurred, "a class of men are springing up in the politics of this country more bigoted, intolerant and proscriptive than the inquisition in Spain."[105] The national Democratic platform officially condemned the Know-Nothing Party as contradictory to "the liberal principles embodied by Jefferson in the Declaration of Independence, and sanctioned in the Constitution" because it applied "an adverse political and religious test" for political office holding. Democrats considered this "political crusade in the nineteenth century, and in the United States of America, against Catholics and foreign-born" as inimical to "the spirit of toleration and enlightened freedom which peculiarly distinguishes the American system of popular government." The Democratic convention thus aligned with Catholic Americans in opposing "all secret political societies, by whatever name they may be called."[106]

Conclusion

The *Columbian* newspaper in Ohio announced the first ever "Holy Church Democratic State Ticket" in its October 11, 1854, issue. Archbishop Purcell of Cincinnati appeared as the nominee for Ohio's director of public works, Pope Pius IX for the office of supreme judge. The newspaper's editor called it the "Pope's Ticket." It was exactly what the nativists had prophesied would occur, yet it was another Know-Nothing sham.[107] The Roman Catholic Church in America did not condone such uniting of church and political interests, but the idea that it could, that it might, continued to animate the Know-Nothing

Order. Their perception, that a "Pope's Ticket" was imminent, led to an actual Protestant ticket under the Know-Nothing Party. The nativists beat the Catholics to it.

Such Know-Nothing antics suggested a place for the nativist movement on the fringe of American politics and society, but political nativism returned to the fore dramatically in 1854 after its adherents formulated a new strategy. The unique political circumstances of the mid-1850s emboldened and transformed the Know-Nothing Order into a political organization capable of garnering massive, nationwide support.

CHAPTER 5

Crime, Poverty, and the Economic Origins
of Political Nativism

Already our Northern, Eastern and Southern cities are filled
to overflowing, with poor, diseased and degraded immigrants. . . .
Let us begin to do something now. Delay is dangerous.

—Native American Party of Kentucky, 1847

D URING THE ANTEBELLUM ERA, nativists believed that immigrants caused negative economic as well as cultural effects.[1] They emphasized the correlation between crime and immigration from Europe. Rampant drunkenness, prostitution, and vagrancy among immigrant populations rendered urban societies less financially and morally viable, they claimed. Dangerous and dirty immigrant neighborhoods made cities less safe and clean, they claimed. At the time, Massachusetts and New York appear to have been the only states to actually deport immigrants who became public charges. Massachusetts alone deported 50,000 Irish during the 1850s. The rest of the states were forced to provide assistance for destitute refugees.[2] Indeed, city administrations increasingly took responsibility for the mentally disabled, orphans, young prostitutes, and a host of other public charges, all on the taxpayer's dime.

Scholars have attributed political nativism to cultural paranoia, social anxiety, and political expediency.[3] Much less examined are the ways in which economic motives have contributed to its periodic rise. More recent anti-immigrant movements, after all, appear to respond to upswings in immigration especially when there are discernable changes to economic as well as cultural conditions. In comparing nativist movements in twentieth-century France, Germany, and the United States, political scientist Joel Fetzer has argued that "the critical economic variable seems to be real disposable income instead of unemployment. Not armies of the unemployed but rather something associated with a thinner collective

pocketbook seems more likely to boost overall levels of opposition to immigration." The availability of public resources based on tax monies, such as funding
for public schools and other metropolitan projects, factors into "real disposable
income." Periods of economic "hardships" need not take the form of unemployment or a decrease in wages: diminishing public resources and increased city taxes
for the benefit of others can render one's after-tax income less valuable. This vital
distinction can serve scholars who wish to study the economic consequences of
immigration for antebellum American cities, when unemployment was relatively
low. Data collected from the U.S. Census Bureau, mayoral and police reports, and
criminal-court records indicate that these newcomers, or rather the ways in which
authorities handled them, caused a subtle decrease in Americans' real disposable
income. During the late 1840s and early 1850s, Americans resented higher expenditures on poorhouses, prisons, mental asylums, police departments, and other
institutions that expanded to serve immigrants.[4]

As most studies on nativism have focused on the coasts, historians have not
yet produced a complete explanation for why westerners joined the ranks of the
National American, or "Know-Nothing," Party in such great numbers in 1854
or why the nation's bloodiest election-day riots erupted in western cities, namely
the St. Louis Election Riot of 1852, the St. Louis "Know-Nothing" Riot of 1854,
the Cincinnati Election Day Riot of 1855, the Chicago "Lager" Riot of 1855, and
the Louisville "Bloody Monday" Riot of 1855.[5] The outbreak of political nativism in St. Louis provides a representative example of the relationship between
immigrants' conditions, the election riots of the mid-1850s, and the dramatic
rise of the National American Party. Cultural issues and the potential increase
in immigrant voting power intensified economic-related resentment among the
native-born population and resulted in the large-scale outbreak of political nativism in 1854.[6]

Immigration, Crime, and Poverty Statistics, 1850–1870

Data collected from the U.S. Census Bureau and local institutional records indicate that immigrants exhausted urban resources at disproportionately high rates.
The local dimension of the following quantitative analysis focuses on St. Louis, a
city that provides an especially illustrative example. Despite informational gaps,
the following data yield significant insights about the relationship between immigration, crime, poverty, and political nativism in the antebellum West.

The overall population demographics provide the context for social change.
According to official reports from the U.S. Census Bureau in 1850, 2,244,602

foreign-born residents constituted 11.48 percent of the total white population of 19,553,068. These figures do not include second-generation immigrants, that is, children born to immigrants on American soil. By the time of the 1860 census, 4,138,697 foreign-born residents constituted 15.37 percent of the total white population of 26,922,537.

Although New York topped the charts, the most populous states of the First West rivaled levels of immigration in Pennsylvania, the second-most-populous state. Immigrants in Missouri, the thirteenth-most-populous state in 1850, composed 13 percent of the total white population, but they increased their share to 15 percent in 1860, when Missouri was the eighth-most-populous state.

The population of immigrants in major cities reliably exceeded the national average of 11.48 percent in 1850 and 15.37 percent in 1860. By 1860, Chicago, Cincinnati, and St. Louis actually surpassed the ratio of immigrants in New York City. Immigrants in New York City composed 46 percent of its total white population of 1,072,312. Those in Cincinnati composed 46 percent of that city's total white population of 161,044. Immigrants in St. Louis composed 60 percent of the city's total white population of 160,773. Finally, immigrants in Chicago composed 50 percent of the city's total white population of 109,260.

According to the U.S. Census Bureau, which provided general statistics on the number and demographic composition of prisoners, immigrants were disproportionately represented in American prisons. The census of 1850 counted 6,737 total inmates nationwide. Although immigrants constituted nearly 9.7 percent of the total population, they accounted for about 35.8 percent of all prisoners. In 1860 the census reported 19,086 total inmates. Although immigrants constituted almost 13.2 percent of the total population, they accounted for nearly 46.9 percent of all prisoners. The number of foreign-born prisoners remained disproportionately high throughout the 1860s and 1870s.

The census records reveal that immigrants composed a disproportionately large percentage of prisoners in states with foreign-born residents. In 1850 New York topped the list with 1,288 reported inmates, 49.61 percent of whom were foreign born, followed closely by Massachusetts with 1,236 prisoners, 47.17 percent of whom were foreign born. In New York immigrants constituted 25.80 percent of the total population in 1860 and 58.43 percent of prisoners. In Massachusetts immigrants constituted 21.13 percent of the total population in 1860 and 44.20 percent of prisoners. The states of the First West experienced similar conditions. In Missouri immigrants constituted 11.23 percent of the total population in 1850 and 69.44 percent of prisoners; by 1860 they accounted for 13.58 percent of the total population and 41.96 percent of prisoners.

TABLE 5.1: Percentage of Foreign-Born Population, 1850–1870

	1850	1860	1870	
	Percentage of foreign born to total *white* pop.	Percentage of foreign born to total *white* pop.	Percentage of foreign born to total pop.	Percentage with at least 1 foreign-born parent
United States	11.48%	15.37%	14.44%	28.25%
Midwest				
Illinois	13%	19%	20%	39%
Ohio	11%	14%	14%	32%
Missouri	13%	15%	13%	27%
Kentucky	4%	7%	5%	11%
Northeast				
New York	22%	26%	26%	51%
Massachusetts	17%	21%	24%	43%
Pennsylvania	13%	15%	15%	33%
South				
Louisiana	27%	23%	9%	18%

SOURCES: Joseph C. G. Kennedy, ed., *Population of the United States in 1860; Compiled from the Original Returns of the Eighth Census* (Washington, DC: Government Printing Office, 1864); Francis A. Walker, ed., *A Compendium of the Ninth Census, June 1, 1870; Compiled Pursuant to a Concurrent Resolution of Congress, and under the Direction of the Secretary of the Interior* (Washington, DC: Government Printing Office, 1872). NOTE: The percentages to the total population for 1850 and 1860 do not factor in persons, enslaved or free, classified as "colored." The chart features the percentages of the foreign-born population to the total white population. The percentages to the total population for 1870 factor in all persons labeled as "colored." Decimals have been rounded to the nearest whole number.

Local reports in St. Louis provided a more detailed account of the problem. Between 1850 and 1859, 48 percent of felons incarcerated in the Missouri Penitentiary at Jefferson City were foreign born, although immigrants represented approximately 13 percent of Missouri's total population.[7] The St. Louis City Workhouse, which incarcerated low-level offenders, reported 404 inmates over a six-month period in 1853 at an annual expense of $18,655.11. Of these, 87.87 percent were foreign born. Forty-nine white native-born Americans stayed in

TABLE 5.2: Foreign-Born Population in Cities, 1860–1870

	1860			1870		
	Total (White)	Foreign born	Percentage of foreign born	Total	Foreign born	Percentage of foreign born
United States	26,922,537	4,138,697	15.37%	38,558,371	5,567,229	14.44%
Midwest						
Chicago	109,260	54,624	49.99%	298,977	144,557	48.35%
St. Louis	160,773	96,086	59.77%	310,864	112,249	36.11%
Cincinnati	161,044	73,614	45.71%	216,239	79,612	36.82%
Louisville	68,033	22,948	33.73%	100,753	25,668	25.48%
Northeast						
New York	1,072,312	488,306	45.54%	1,338,391	563,812	42.13%
Boston	177,812	63,791	35.88%	250,526	87,986	35.12%
Philadelphia	585,529	169,430	28.93%	674,022	183,624	27.24%
South						
New Orleans	168,675	64,621	38.31%	191,418	48,475	25.32%

SOURCES: Kennedy, *Population of the United States in 1860*; Walker, *Compendium of the Ninth Census.* NOTE: The total population for these cities in 1860 and 1870 include persons labeled as "colored." The statistics do not count second-generation immigrants—citizens born in the United States with at least one foreign-born parent. This chart includes Brooklyn as part of the greater New York City Metropolitan Area. In 1870 28.25 percent of the total U.S. population had at least one parent born outside the United States.

TABLE 5.3: Demographic of Prisoners, 1850

	Total inmates on June 1, 1850	Foreign-born prisoners	Foreign born in total pop.
United States	6,737	35.79%	9.68%
Midwest			
Missouri	180	69.44%	11.23%
Illinois	252	34.92%	13.14%
Ohio	133	23.31%	11.02%
Kentucky	52	21.15%	3.20%
Northeast			
New York	1,288	49.61%	21.18%
Massachusetts	1,236	47.17%	16.49%
Pennsylvania	411	27.98%	13.12%
South			
Louisiana	423	43.26%	13.18%

SOURCE: Kennedy, *Population of the United States in 1860*. NOTE: These figures are based on the number of current inmates in the census year as of June 1, which represents a sort of average of the number and demography of inmates in U.S. prisons and workhouses. Houses of refuge for juvenile offenders are not included in the survey. The total population figures include persons, enslaved or free, labeled as "colored."

the prison, with the ethnic breakdown of the remaining inmates being 227 Irish; ninety-eight German; eleven Mexican; nine English; seven French; and three Scottish. In 1855 the workhouse incarcerated 983 inmates throughout the year at an expense of $19,593.64. Of these prisoners, 69.2 percent were male and 89.5 percent were foreign born. Ninety-two white and eleven "colored" Americans spent time in the prison, with the rest of the population consisting of 706 Irish, 122 German, fifty-one English, thirteen Mexican, twelve French, and nine Scottish inmates. Reports from later years likewise indicated the overrepresentation of immigrants in the penal system.

Local police reports illuminate the root causes of the imbalance. During the 1840s and early 1850s, American police forces were remarkably decentralized and frequently incapable of widely enforcing city ordinances. They specialized, rather, in policing perceived "problem" areas. Mayor Luther M. Kennett reported

TABLE 5.4: Demographic of Prisoners, 1860

	Total inmates on June 1, 1860	Foreign-born prisoners	Foreign born in total pop.
United States	19,086	46.86%	13.16%
Midwest			
Ohio	623	57.46%	14.03%
Missouri	286	41.96%	13.58%
Kentucky	232	36.64%	5.17%
Illinois	485	35.46%	18.96%
Northeast			
New York	6,882	58.43%	25.80%
Massachusetts	2,679	44.20%	21.13%
Pennsylvania	1,161	34.88%	14.81%
South			
Louisiana	849	57.71%	11.44%

SOURCE: Kennedy, *Population of the United States in 1860.* NOTE: These figures are based on the number of current inmates in the census year as of June 1, which represents a sort of average of the number and demography of inmates in U.S. prisons and workhouses. Houses of refuge for juvenile offenders are not included in the survey. The total population figures include persons, enslaved or free, labeled as "colored."

on May 13, 1850, "The police at present consists of a Captain, three Lieutenants, and thirty-six privates of the night guard, and one Lieutenant and nine privates of the day guard, in all *fifty*." At the time, the total population of the city was approximately 80,000.[8] Most of these police officers worked part time. The turnover rate was high. The officers lacked uniforms and the sort of professionalism that came to characterize the police force after the reforms of 1855. They typically took orders from the mayor, who, regardless of party affiliation, insistently directed the police force to focus their energies on the prevention of three crimes that the public considered a menace: vagrancy, public drunkenness, and prostitution. The focus on these crimes in particular accounted for the vast imbalance of arrests between the native and foreign born.[9]

Residents of any given district, including those foreign born, elected the men they wanted to police their neighborhood and removed them if they wielded

TABLE 5.5: Demographic of Prisoners, 1870

	Total	Foreign-born prisoners	Foreign born in total pop.	"Colored" prisoners	"Colored" in total pop.
United States	32,901	26.53%	14.44%	24.49%	12.66%
Midwest					
Ohio	1,405	27.54%	13.98%	8.97%	2.37%
Missouri	1,623	25.02%	12.91%	19.96%	6.86%
Illinois	1,795	23.57%	20.28%	7.97%	1.13%
Kentucky	1,067	9.28%	4.80%	41.52%	16.82%
Northeast					
Massachusetts	2,526	48.89%	24.24%	5.50%	0.96%
New York	4,704	43.49%	25.97%	7.12%	1.19%
Pennsylvania	3,231	21.63%	15.48%	13.74%	1.85%
South					
Louisiana	845	3.20%	8.50%	42.37%	50.10%

SOURCES: Kennedy, *Population of the United States in 1860;* Walker, *Compendium of the Ninth Census*. NOTE: These figures are based on the number of current inmates in the census year as of June 1, which represents a sort of average of the number and demography of inmates in U.S. prisons and workhouses. Houses of refuge for juvenile offenders are not included in the survey.

too much authority. For that reason, officers often looked like the residents they policed. Even the position of "private"—a common patrolman—was an elected one. Extant sources agree that the St. Louis Police Department represented the ethnic makeup of the city's white population. In 1854 St. Louis resident Henry Hitchcock described the "regular city police" as "almost all foreigners."[10] The official department roster in the St. Louis city directory of 1854 appears to corroborate Hitchcock's claim. At least half of the force bore surnames of non-English origin. Out of the ninety-two police officers listed by the directory that year, twenty-three bore surnames of obvious Irish origin—such as Boggers, Cullin, Downey, Doyle, Finnegan, Gannon, Higgins, Hickey, M'Donald, and O'Riley—and thirteen of obvious Germanic origin—including Becker, Busch-kamper, Coogel, Kesler, Klunck, Kruglan, Prigge, Roeder, and Schultz. Several

TABLE 5.6: Percentage of Foreign-Born Prisoners, 1850–1870

	1850		1860		1870	
	Foreign born in total pop.	Foreign-born prisoners	Foreign born in total pop.	Foreign-born prisoners	Foreign born in total pop.	Foreign-born prisoners
United States	9.68%	35.79%	13.16%	46.86%	14.44%	26.53%
Midwest						
Missouri	11%	69%	14%	42%	13%	25%
Ohio	11%	23%	14%	57%	14%	28%
Illinois	13%	35%	19%	35%	20%	24%
Kentucky	3%	21%	5%	37%	5%	9%
Northeast						
New York	21%	50%	26%	58%	26%	43%
Massachusetts	16%	47%	21%	44%	24%	49%
Pennsylvania	13%	28%	15%	35%	15%	22%
South						
Louisiana	13%	43%	11%	58%	9%	3%

SOURCES: Kennedy, *Population of the United States in 1860*; Walker, *Compendium of the Ninth Census*. NOTE: These figures are based on the number of current inmates in the census year as of June 1, which represents a sort of average of the number and demography of inmates in U.S. prisons and workhouses. Houses of refuge for juvenile offenders are not included in the survey. Decimals have been rounded to the nearest whole number.

TABLE 5.7: Population of St. Louis Workhouse, 1852–1872

	Total committed	Annual expense	Portion male	Portion foreign born	Portion "colored"
1853	404 (6 months)	$18,655.11		87.87%	
1855	983 annual	$19,593.64	69.18%	89.52%	1.12%
1858	1,180 (6 months)	$25,600.71	95.7%		
1863	1,902 annual	$16,752.63	49.84%		
1866	1,736 (6 months)	$33,182.36	56.97%		
1869	2,982 annual		68.71%		
1870	1,225 (6 months)	$10,086.55 (6 months)	57.88%	66.78%	12.24%
1871	1,707 (6 months)	$34,521.93	63.15%	65.55%	12.65%
1872	2,322 annual		58.31%	70.93%	16.93%

NOTE: The full fiscal year stretched from April 1 to March 30 of the following year, although there were variations from year to year. The superintendents of the St. Louis Workhouse often submitted six-month reports in October, some of which included demographics of inmates. These figures represent the most detailed reports in the *Mayor's Messages* between 1847 and 1872, housed in the St. Louis Room of the St. Louis Public Library.

other surnames suggest Dutch, French, Scottish, and Swedish origins.[11] Henry Börnstein, German immigrant and editor of the *Anzeiger Des Westens,* celebrated "the introduction of German citizens" to "the municipal police that had been previously dominated by Irishmen and French Creoles."[12] An 1871 report honoring veterans of the force initially appointed between the years 1835 and 1857 categorized sixteen of the nineteen men as foreign born, or about 84 percent, most of them originally from Ireland, with two from Germany and one from Austria.[13] Actually, St. Louis patrolmen were often accused of being *too* sympathetic to foreign-born perpetrators. In 1855 Know-Nothing mayor Washington King blamed the "foreignized police" for failing to prevent riots that erupted in immigrant neighborhoods.[14]

Starting in the late 1840s, city officials grew especially worried about the arrival of large groups of "paupers," or impoverished individuals who became public charges. An official report from the Mayor's Office of St. Louis, for example, reported an unusually high number of foreign-born "paupers" buried in the city's

TABLE 5.8: Nativity of Inmates at St. Louis Workhouse, 1852–1855 & 1869–1872

	1853	1855	1870	1871	1872
United States (white)	49	92	257	372	282
United States (colored)	?	11	150	216	393
Ireland	227	706	576	821	1,365
Germany	98	122	128	192	212
England	9	51	53	82	37
France	7	12	12	8	9
Scotland	3	9	15	28	7
Mexico	11	13	2		
Canada			20	21	15
Switzerland			6	5	

NOTE: The full fiscal year stretched from April 1 to March 30 of the following year, although there were variations from year to year. The superintendents of the St. Louis Workhouse often submitted six-month reports in October, some of which included demographics of inmates. These figures represent the extant reports in the *Mayor's Messages* between 1847 and 1872, housed in the St. Louis Room of the St. Louis Public Library. The St. Louis Police reports in the *Mayor's Messages* offer additional demographic information about the types of persons arrested and incarcerated in the workhouse.

common cemetery at public expense between 1847 and 1850. Mayor Kennett reported on October 14, 1850, "About 800 of the emigrants landed, were paupers, and had to be supported."[15] The following year he lamented the absence of any laws "to make persons liable to a fine who bring us sick paupers from a distance, on steamboats and otherwise, to be taken care of by the city." Kennett's successor, Mayor John How, supported a new law to penalize boat captains who knowingly unloaded paupers or "insane people."[16] In 1853 Ordinance 2395, Section 9, of the *Revised Ordinances of St. Louis* empowered the mayor to appropriate funds to remove paupers from the city "who otherwise might become a greater burden to it." On November 2 the city passed Ordinance 3072, a measure "to prevent the introduction of insane persons or paupers into the city of St. Louis." According to the ordinance, health officers were required to report any impoverished or mentally disabled immigrants. The guilty transporter of such individuals could be forced to pay a fine of between $25 and $300 per person and take out a bond with the recorder to ensure their transport elsewhere. No instance of the city

TABLE 5.9: Nativity of St. Louis Police Department, 1869–1872

	1869	Portion foreign born	1871	Portion foreign born	1872	Portion foreign born
Total Officers	278	60.07%	346	59.25%	361	63.16%
United States	111		141		133	
Germany	85		99		93	
Ireland	61		93		104	
England	9				15	
France	11				4	
Others	1		13		12	

NOTE: These figures represent the extant police reports in the *Mayor's Messages* between 1869 and 1872, housed in the St. Louis Room of the St. Louis Public Library.

charging a steamboat captain for violating Ordinance 3072 has yet been found in the extant records of the St. Louis court system.[17]

Ordinance 2384 in the 1853 edition of the *Revised Ordinances* defined an illegal "vagrant" as either a homeless person or someone temporarily lodging in a beerhouse or bawdy house. This criminal category also included those convicted of "keeping a gaming table" or of burglary. For the crime of vagrancy, a person could be fined anywhere between $50 and $500. If unable to pay the fine, the vagrant would be committed to the St. Louis Workhouse.[18]

According to eyewitness testimonies, vagrants lined the waterfront of St. Louis, despite the law, and concentrated especially in the notoriously crime-ridden, impoverished boroughs of Battle Row north of Morgan Street, the Kerry Patch in the northwestern portion of St. Louis, the red-light district on Almond and Third Streets, and the Mill Creek Valley area. All of these areas were predominantly occupied by immigrants. In his later *Tour of St. Louis* (1878), Dr. J. A. Dacus estimated that thousands of "wandering boys and girls" had resided in the city, many of whom became either "sneak-thieves" or "fallen girls." "The boys in many instances become sneak-thieves," Dacus observed, and "find their way to houses of correction." Kerry Patch, the traditional Irish district located on Seventeenth Street between Biddle and Mullanphy Streets, he noted, "is celebrated for its bands of young Bedouins." Many of those who lived in Kerry Patch erected makeshift shanties "on land not their own." Even those who could afford to rent rooms in the slums, Dacus remarked, lived "in a wretched

TABLE 5.10: Nativity of Internments in St. Louis City Cemetery during Cholera Epidemic, 1847–1850

	1847–48	Portion foreign born	Portion male	1849–50	Portion foreign born
Total	576	63.89%	67.01%	1,075	80.19%
United States	208			213	
German States	140			230	
Ireland	63			222	
England	14			87	
France	10			14	
Holland	4			5	
Scotland	3			10	
Mexico	3				
Switzerland	2			25	
South America	1				
Sweden	1				
Norway				3	
Canada				5	
Birthplace unknown	127			255	

NOTE: According to a report in 1849 by Thomas Finan at the Sexton City Cemetery, out of the 774 total internments for the fiscal year June 1848–May 1849, 77.91 percent were born outside the United States, and 74.68 percent of these were male. Finan identified 358 of the total number as "paupers from the city, buried at the expense of the city." See *Message of the Mayor of the City of Saint Louis, and Reports of City Officers, Delivered to the City Council,* May 1849 (1849), SLPL.

state of poverty." The residents "are quite religiously inclined, and bestow great reverence on the pastor of the parish in which they live," he observed, but they also earned a reputation for causing disturbances of the peace, illegally hosting "dog-fights and cocking" on Sundays and even "occasionally battering up a 'peeler,'" a pejorative name for a police officer.[19]

During the 1850s, the district north of Morgan Street developed a reputation for alcohol-related crime. St. Louis residents called a particular alley occupied almost entirely by Irish immigrants Battle Row, as it was the site of numerous disturbances, including an infamous election riot in 1854. Dacus described the area surrounding the intersection of Fifth and Biddle as "a hard neighborhood." While observing the local police court one day, he mentioned how many of those charged with misdemeanors were foreign born. An Irish woman named Kate Smith, a frequent offender accused of public intoxication, conversed with the judge in a thick brogue: "An' fwhat if I was iver so drunk? The perlaceman, the spalpeen a standin' afore yer honor, is prajudyced agin me, an' he jist tuk me in onyhow." A German woman named Mina Schlessel, a first-time offender accused of soliciting for prostitution, responded to her accusers in broken English: "Vell, Ich dells you de trut. Vat you calls geelty? Ich var yust talking a leedle mit a shentlemans ven der politzeman komt und saft, 'Sie, geh mith mire.' Das is alle."[20]

Some predominantly German districts in the southern half of the city acquired reputations for breaking city laws on Sundays, public drinking, brawling, gambling, and prostitution. On Fourth Street in South St. Louis, German bars illegally hosted "Scat" or "31," a popular gambling card game.[21] Dacus commented: "On Fourth Street are situated some of the finest 'gambling hells' of the city. On Fifth and Sixth streets are numerous houses, where the sill and the 'duffers' go to dispose of whatever money they may possess." Some of the most popular bawdy houses were located on Third Street, at the intersection of Almond and Poplar Streets in the city's south-central area. Dacus expressed his sympathy for the "fallen women of the slums of Christy Avenue and Almond and Poplar streets." He bemoaned, "In these neighborhoods the low saloons are kept open from sunset to sunrise." Dacus believed that the most dangerous vagrants resided "in the neighborhood of Almond, Poplar, Plum, and a portion of Third Street."[22] The St. Louis Criminal Court's records include numerous cases arising out of confrontations at the intersection of Third and Almond.[23]

Drunken street dwellers, vagrants, and prostitutes constituted a substantial portion of all arrests and incarcerations. Before the city raised funds for a correctional facility exclusively for juvenile offenders as well as an insane asylum for the mentally afflicted, many orphans and mentally disabled people ended up in the St. Louis Workhouse. Low-level offenders spent several months laboring for little to no pay. Superintendent John Shade reported in 1847 that the male portion of convicts "have been employed for six weeks grading, hauling rock, rough paving, and Macadamizing the avenues leading to the Gravois road."[24] During the 1850–51 fiscal year, the city apportioned $15,755.82 to the workhouse to accommodate its growing population.[25] In May 1852 Mayor Kennett commended the police for landing a "large number of vagrants and other evil-doers in the Work House," but he acknowledged it was not really the proper venue for vagrants and mentally disabled people, especially for those who were underage.[26] Of the 404 total commitments to the St. Louis Workhouse between October 1852 and April 1853, 87 were incarcerated for the crime of vagrancy, 58 of whom were male and 29 female. While the men in the workhouse graded Lafayette Park, planted trees, and laid gravel for other streets around Mill Creek, "the females (of which there has been an unusually large number)," as Superintendent V. J. Peers reported, "have been employed in making clothing for the prisoners, in washing and scrubbing."[27]

Vagrants and mentally disabled people returned to the St. Louis Workhouse on a regular basis. Peers informed Mayor How that many of the female inmates in particular deliberately appeared intoxicated in public so that they could be sent to the workhouse for food and shelter. "I am led to believe," Mayor How reported on May 9, 1853, "that many of them go there as a matter of choice." St. Louisans believed a separate facility could better serve female vagrants and streetwalkers. Moreover, How expressed alarm at "the unfortunate insane, who are taken up in our streets" in increasing numbers. "We have at present no place but the Calaboose and the Workhouse for their reception," he lamented. "It is shameful to incarcerate the unfortunate beings who have been deprived of their reasoning faculties in the same prison with the vicious and depraved."[28] Men, women, children, the mentally disabled, petty criminals, and felons all mixed together in a single correction facility. It was an intolerable situation.

Mayor Kennett and his successors stressed the pressing need for a house of refuge "for juvenile offenders." On October 13, 1851, Kennett announced: "Our streets and wharves are swarming with idle dissolute children, ostensibly begging, but often detected in petty thefts, for whom we have no proper place of reception, and whose utter ruin is inevitable unless a house of refuge be provided for them." Finally, in 1854, the city raised enough tax monies to complete the St. Louis House of Refuge for young boys and girls.[29] After 1854 most young vagrants, pickpockets, streetwalkers, and felonious juvenile offenders ended up in house of refuge. Between March 1855 and April 1856, it committed 166 children; 51.2 percent of inmates were male and just over 56.6 percent were foreign born. Eighty-two of the inmates were incarcerated for the crime of vagrancy, fifty for larceny, and twenty-three for disobedience to guardians. The St. Louis House of Refuge grew to meet demand, its annual expense skyrocketing from $9,925.44 in 1856 to $39,829.00 in 1858.

If the official arrest reports of the St. Louis Police Department in the 1860s resembled those in the 1850s, which they likely did, then these extant records may provide a representative example of the typical demography of arrests in

TABLE 5.11: St. Louis House of Refuge, 1854–1872

	Total committed	Annual expense	Portion male	Portion foreign born	Portion "colored"
1855	40	$7,724.49	70.00%		
1856	166	$9,925.44	51.20%	56.63%	
1858		$39,829.00			
1861		$8,587.00			
1865		$26,829.56			
1866		$59,164.35			
1869	177		75.14%	62.71%	24.86%
1871	136	$31,714.00	71.32%	58.82%	27.21%
1872	134		82.84%	52.99%	25.37%

NOTE: The full fiscal year stretched from April 1 to March 30 of the following year, although there were variations from year to year. These figures represent the extant House of Refuge reports in the *Mayor's Messages* between 1847 and 1872, housed in the St. Louis Room of the St. Louis Public Library. This number includes all inmates whose parents are listed as "foreign-born." The St. Louis Police reports in the *Mayor's Messages* offer additional demographic information about the types of persons arrested and incarcerated in the House of Refuge and the St. Louis Workhouse.

mid-nineteenth-century St. Louis. The department maintained thorough records after 1865. In 1866 St. Louis police arrested 9,839 people. Of these, 64.5 percent were male and 52.9 percent were foreign born. By this time, the numbers of arrested "foreign born" appeared roughly proportional to the city's ethnic makeup, although these numbers did not include second-generation immigrants. St. Louis Irish-origin residents, however, were twice more likely to be arrested than those of German origin, suggesting an overrepresentation of Irish among the arrested. Irish residents accounted for just over 32.8 percent of all arrested persons. By comparison, nearly 14.7 percent of all arrested persons were born in the German States, even though these immigrants were more numerous in the city.[30]

Most of those arrested represented the poorest of the poor. The official guidelines of the St. Louis Police Department instructed patrolmen to "send persons, penniless and without homes, to the stationhouse."[31] In accordance with this policy, officers arrested vagrants on a regular basis. The most common

TABLE 5.12: Nativity of Inmates at St. Louis House of Refuge, 1856 & 1869–1872

	1856	1869	1871	1872
United States (white)	72	24	19	29
United States (colored)	?	44	37	34
Ireland	33	76	54	48
Germany	38	23	13	19
England	1	7	5	4
France	1	3	2	3
Switzerland	1		2	
Italy	2	1		1
Others	9	1	4	1

NOTE: The nativity of inmates at the House of Refuge follows the nativity of the parents. The full fiscal year stretched from April 1 to March 30 of the following year, although there were variations from year to year. These figures represent the extant House of Refuge reports in the *Mayor's Messages* between 1847 and 1872, housed in the St. Louis Room of the St. Louis Public Library. The St. Louis Police reports in the *Mayor's Messages* offer additional demographic information about the types of persons arrested and incarcerated in the House of Refuge and the St. Louis Workhouse.

TABLE 5.13: Nativity of Arrested Persons Reported by St. Louis Police Department, 1865–1872

	1866	1867	1868	1869	1870	1871	1872
Total Arrests	9,839	11,203	11,609	13,196	14,068	17,484	19,308
Portion "Colored"	5.19%	6.82%	6.77%	13.65%	11.01%	6.37%	9.18%
Portion Irish	32.83%	37.68%	34.28%	36.62%	35.78%	35.30%	36.14%
Portion German	14.69%	15.44%	17.89%	16.25%	16.90%	20.58%	15.40%
Portion English	2.34%	1.95%	2.17%	1.93%	2.06%	2.73%	1.68%
Portion Canadian	0.51%	1.00%	1.14%	1.28%	0.57%	1.83%	0.36%
Portion French	0.61%	0.52%	0.66%	0.66%	0.74%	1.09%	0.73%
Portion Scottish	0.61%	0.51%	0.65%	0.48%	0.46%	2.02%	0.42%
Portion Italian	0.56%	0.65%	0.47%	0.49%	0.31%		

SOURCE: "Arrested Persons," St. Louis Police Department Report, *Mayor's Message* (annually, 1865–72).

misdemeanor reported between 1865 and 1872 was public drunkenness. The most common felony reported was larceny. Among those arrested, the primary male occupation was laborer, while the primary female occupation was prostitute. The vast majority of arrested persons were male and single. In 1866 just over 39.7 percent of arrested persons were marked as illiterate, a mark of poverty in a highly literate city such as St. Louis. In 1864, out of 7,297 total arrests, 2,271 were for the crime of public drunkenness and 560 for vagrancy.[32] Out of 8,416 reported misdemeanors between April 1865 and March 1866, 1,576 were for public drunkenness, 1,000 for drunkenness and disturbing the peace, and 1,900 for vagrancy. Police reported similar numbers in the following years. Desperate economic circumstances accounted for most of these reported crimes.

Thus, the disproportionately high levels of poverty among immigrants from Europe best explained the disproportionately high level of foreign-born crime. The U.S. Census Bureau provided general statistics on the number and demographic composition of paupers as well as the estimated total cost on taxpayers for providing them assistance. The 1850 Census counted 50,353 paupers nationwide; total cost for their care amounted to $2,954,806. This expenditure did not include private charities and donations, only public funds. Although immigrants constituted about 9.7 percent of the total population (including those labeled as "colored," both enslaved and free), they accounted for nearly 26.7 percent of paupers. In 1860 the census counted 82,942 paupers nationwide at a total public cost of $5,445,143. Although immigrants constituted a little less than 13.2 percent of the total population, they accounted for over 39.1 percent of paupers. The number of foreign-born paupers was disproportionately high again in 1870.

Census records reveal that immigrants composed a disproportionately large percentage of paupers in all states with significant foreign-born populations. Again, New York topped the list, but the states of the First West experienced similar conditions. In Missouri, for example, foreign-born residents constituted more than 11 percent of the total population in 1850 and just over 50 percent of paupers. Then in 1860 they accounted for almost 14 percent of the total population and nearly 35 percent of paupers. In both counts immigrants were demonstrably overrepresented as public charges.

Many if not most immigrants to the United States were vastly poorer on average than their American counterparts. This was especially true of the Irish after 1840. During the Great Famine of the mid-1840s, many Irish refugees spent their entire savings on the voyage to the United States, arriving penniless. Historians have since confirmed the existence of "assisted emigration" from Ireland to America. It was not uncommon for the very Irish institutions in charge of

TABLE 5.14: Arrested Persons Reported by St. Louis Police Department, 1865–1872

	1866	1867	1868	1869	1870	1871	1872
	9,839	11,203	11,609	13,196	14,068	17,484	19,308
Most common felony	larceny	larceny	larceny	larceny	larceny	larceny	larceny
Most common misdemeanor	drunkenness	disturbing the peace	drunkenness	drunkenness	drunkenness	drunkenness	drunkenness
Portion male	64.45%	73.06%	75.04%	78.24%	79.27%	78.71%	78.31%
Portion foreign born	52.85%	58.10%	57.59%	53.82%	57.66%	68.34%	56.87%
Portion "colored"	5.19%	6.82%	6.77%	13.65%	11.01%	6.37%	9.18%
Primary male occupation	laborer	laborer	laborer	laborer	laborer	laborer	laborer
Primary female occupation	prostitute	prostitute	prostitute	prostitute	prostitute	prostitute	prostitute
Portion illiterate	39.71%	39.96%	35.70%	37.43%	31.70%	23.18%	17.9%
Portion single	74.98%	65.79%	59.94%	66.39%	63.91%	67.48%	68.59%

SOURCE: "Arrested Persons," St. Louis Police Department Report, *Mayor's Message* (annually, 1865–72).

TABLE 5.15: Demographic of Paupers, 1850

United States	Total	Foreign-born paupers	Foreign born in total pop.	Estimated total cost
	50,353	26.69%	9.68%	$2,954,806
Midwest				
Missouri	505	50.30%	11.23%	$53,243
Illinois	434	35.71%	13.14%	$45,213
Ohio	1,673	25.04%	11.02%	$95,250
Kentucky	777	11.20%	3.20%	$57,543
Northeast				
New York	12,833	55.15%	21.18%	$1,440,904
Pennsylvania	3,811	30.36%	13.12%	$232,138
Massachusetts	5,549	26.85%	16.49%	$392,715
South				
Louisiana	106	28.30%	13.18%	$39,806

SOURCE: Kennedy, *Population of the United States in 1860*. NOTE: The Census Bureau's statistics on pauperism in each city remain much disputed. Cities in 1850 and 1860, for example, organized their information on pauperism by different fiscal periods, making it difficult to compare rates. The bureau set a date of June 1 for all cities to report annual numbers as well as figures for individuals currently on state support at that time. The number of paupers is based on the number of persons receiving state support as of June 1 in the year of the census. These numbers, then, suggest an average number and demography of paupers. Officials took the aggregate cost of maintaining almshouses, workhouses, and other state-run facilities for the poor rather than counting heads, although some states averaged a cost per head in the census years of 1850 and 1860. The estimated total cost does not include private-run charities and private donations. The total population figures include persons, enslaved or free, labeled as "colored."

caring for unemployed Irish laborers to sponsor their passage across the Atlantic to North America in the hopes of eliminating destitution in their own districts. Even individual landlords paid for the passage of their impoverished tenants to America. Thus, often the poorest of the Irish poor arrived in America during the height of the Great Famine.[33]

Americans expressed concern about the rates of foreign pauperism and crime in the United States for cultural and economic reasons. Nativists emphasized a

TABLE 5.16: Demographic of Paupers, 1860

United States	Total	Foreign-born paupers	Foreign born in total pop.	Estimated total cost
	82,942	39.13%	13.16%	$5,445,143
Midwest				
Illinois	1,856	61.91%	18.96%	$196,184
Ohio	14,092	59.55%	14.03%	$311,109
Missouri	784	34.57%	13.58%	$70,445
Kentucky	899	16.69%	5.17%	$71,603
Northeast				
New York	19,215	60.10%	25.80%	$1,440,904
Pennsylvania	7,776	42.19%	14.81%	$665,396
Massachusetts	6,503	19.94%	21.13%	$579,397
South				
Louisiana	162	9.88%	11.44%	$11,395

SOURCE: Kennedy, *Population of the United States in 1860*. NOTE: The total population figures include persons, enslaved or free, labeled as "colored."

"neo-liberal" clash between the supposed ideals of American independence and the "leeches" who filled the prisons and accepted welfare from state almshouses and other charitable organizations. They envisioned "their nation as a republic of independent, industrious workers," as historian Hidetaka Hirota has explained. Ideologically, nativism equated freedom to "economic self-sufficiency." Proponents thus categorized paupers as the "antithesis of American citizens."[34] According to historian Joseph Kett, Americans especially of the Whig persuasion "linked character to capital formation and saw a high ratio of capital to labor as the basis of progress."[35] Rampant crime and poverty in U.S. cities seemed to undermine American values.

Rampant crime and poverty also exhausted scarce urban resources. Additional expenditures related to the increase in immigration compelled St. Louis authorities to raise taxes during the early 1850s. According to the auditor's report of the Mayor's Office, the annual cost of the St. Louis Workhouse more than doubled during this time, from $9,300 during the fiscal year 1848–49

TABLE 5.17: Demographic of Paupers, 1870

United States	Total	Foreign-born paupers	Foreign born in total pop.	"Colored" paupers	"Colored" in total pop.	Estimated total cost
	76,737	29.71%	14.44%	12.25%	12.66%	$10,930,429
Midwest						
Illinois	2,363	46.93%	20.28%	1.74%	1.13%	$556,061
Missouri	1,854	23.68%	12.91%	17.53%	6.86%	$191,171
Ohio	3,674	22.16%	13.98%	5.47%	2.37%	$566,280
Kentucky	1,784	6.56%	4.80%	39.46%	16.82%	$160,717
Northeast						
New York	14,100	57.78%	25.97%	4.71%	1.19%	$2,661,385
Pennsylvania	8,796	45.18%	15.48%	5.32%	1.85%	$1,256,024
Massachusetts	5,777	6.60%	24.24%	1.26%	0.96%	$1,121,604
South						
Louisiana	507	19.33%	8.50%	25.64%	50.10%	$53,300

SOURCE: Kennedy, *Population of the United States in 1860.*

to $19,593.64 during the fiscal year 1854–55. The operational budget of the St. Louis Police Department also more than doubled, from $26,499.78 during the fiscal year 1851–52 to $58,444.34 during the fiscal year 1854–55. New taxes funded this increase in the police budget to better enforce city ordinances outlawing vagrancy, prostitution, public drunkenness, and gambling as well as other laws targeting perceived "problem" areas in the city. The St. Louis House of Refuge began operating with an annual budget of $7,724.49 in 1854 to serve the juvenile vagrant population in the city, most of whom were foreign born or the descendants of immigrant parents. Over the next several years, the costs of these programs increased dramatically. During the fiscal year 1857–58, taxpayers funded an annual budget of $25,600.71 for the workhouse, $39,829 for the house of refuge, and $126,177.18 for an expanded police department. The city's administration also increasingly took responsibility for the mentally disabled, orphans, young prostitutes, and a host of other public charges—all at taxpayer expense.[36]

TABLE 5.18: Percentage of Foreign-born Paupers, 1850–1870

	1850		1860		1870	
	Foreign born in total pop.	Foreign-born paupers	Foreign born in total pop.	Foreign-born paupers	Foreign born in total pop.	Foreign-born paupers
United States	9.68%	26.69%	13.16%	39.13%	14.44%	29.71%
Midwest						
Illinois	13%	36%	19%	62%	20%	47%
Missouri	11%	50%	14%	35%	13%	24%
Ohio	11%	25%	14%	60%	14%	22%
Kentucky	3%	11%	5%	17%	5%	7%
Northeast						
New York	21%	55%	26%	60%	26%	58%
Massachusetts	16%	27%	21%	20%	24%	7%
Pennsylvania	13%	30%	15%	42%	15%	45%
South						
Louisiana	13%	28%	11%	10%	9%	19%

SOURCES: Kennedy, *Population of the United States in 1860*; Walker, *Compendium of the Ninth Census, June 1, 1870*. NOTE: The Census Bureau's statistics on pauperism in each city remain much disputed. Cities in 1850 and 1860, for example, organized their information on pauperism by different fiscal periods, making it difficult to compare rates. The bureau set a date of June 1 for all cities to report annual numbers as well as figures for individuals currently on state support at that time. The number of paupers is based on the number of persons receiving state support as of June 1 in the year of the census. These numbers, then, suggest an average number and demography of paupers. Officials took the aggregate cost of maintaining alms houses, work houses, and other state-run facilities for the poor, rather than counting heads, although some states averaged a cost per head in the census years of 1850 and 1860. The estimated total cost does not include private-run charities and private donations. Decimals have been rounded to the nearest whole number. The total population figures include persons, enslaved or free, labeled as "colored." Decimals have been rounded to the nearest whole number.

Social Disturbances at the Election Polls

During the mid-1850s, native-born Americans in urban areas responded to immigrant-induced social and economic changes with retributive crowd action. In a series of massive riots between 1854 and 1858, these mobs targeted the inhabitants and institutions they felt had burdened their homes with crime, disorder, financial decline, and immorality. It is no coincidence that each of these riots took place during the highest peaks in immigration to date and precisely as city administrations began collecting additional taxes to accommodate the newcomers. Most of the disturbances occurred on an election day, when all work was canceled so voters could assert their will at the polls. The first episodes of violence in this new wave of nativist panic erupted in the urban West. Various immigrant groups nevertheless attempted to establish their political and social solidarity in the face of such opposition.[37]

In the St. Louis Election Riot of 1852, violence erupted between Germans and Americans at an election polling place in the predominantly German First Ward. Then, the native crowd targeted well-known German establishments, including a popular tavern. The St. Louis Know-Nothing Riot of 1854, which erupted during an especially significant gubernatorial election on August 7, resulted in the destruction of hundreds of Irish bars and businesses in the Irish district in North St. Louis. The nativist crowd targeted Irish and Germans, nearby Catholic churches, and the building that housed Börnstein's *Anzeiger* printing press. In 1855 a critical Cincinnati election in which the German vote played a crucial role devolved into a citywide riot between Germans and nativists, known as the Cincinnati Election Day Riot. The Chicago Lager Riot of 1855 brought German and Irish bar owners together in a violent encounter with vocal supporters of the city's recently elected Know-Nothing administration. The Louisville Bloody Monday Riot of 1855, the deadliest of the five, engulfed that entire city on Election Day as nativists attacked German and Irish residents and businesses. In these cases self-proclaimed "nativists" targeted immigrant drinking establishments, the violence erupted on election days, and native-born Americans in the crowds attacked foreign-born residents, regardless of their actual political persuasion, religious orientation, or nationality.

St. Louis Election Riot, April 5–6, 1852

On April 5, 1852, at ten o'clock in the morning, a group of Democratic Germans and Whig Americans started brawling just outside the election polling place in Soulard, South St. Louis, a predominantly German district. The total population of the First Ward was around 16,000 people, of whom 60 percent were Germans (exclusive of second-generation immigrants).[38] How it began and who was to blame remains highly contested. Testimonies of Germans grabbing native Whig voters by the neck and rolling them over in the mud incited a crowd of vigilantes in the central part of St. Louis.[39] These reports could have easily been fabricated. At one point a German crowd did wreck a Whig carriage that sported banners for the mayoral Whig incumbent, Luther Kennett. The blood-ied coachman stumbled into City Hall and pleaded before the mayor that the Germans had prevented him from voting and had pelted him with stones.[40]

Kennett came at once to the First Ward, arriving at noon to disperse the crowds. But many Germans confronted him. They accused the mayor of ally-ing with nativists, with one angry man in the crowd yelling in his direction, "I heard you abuse the Dutch in the ferryboat."[41] Others in the crowd yelled, "Hang him; drown him!" Kennett turned his carriage around.[42] After the mayor returned safely to City Hall, unconfirmed reports circulated in the Fourth and Fifth Wards that the Germans had taken control of the Soulard polls and were not allowing any native-born Americans to vote. A crowd of about five hundred concerned citizens congregated in the streets outside City Hall. Nativist leader Edward Zane Carroll Judson, known by many as "Ned Buntline," and Bob Mc'OBlennis, a notorious gang leader and omnibus driver, rallied the crowd.[43]

At one o'clock an Anglo-American named David Robinson arrived from the First Ward and told Buntline that Germans had driven him away from the polls. Emboldened by this testimony, Buntline roused the crowd with a lively anti-German speech.[44] He mounted a white horse, then shouted to Robinson: "Come with me. I'll see that you get a chance to vote."[45] He charged forward and motioned those gathered to "follow him."[46] Mc'OBlennis tailed him in an omni-bus. Others jumped aboard the vehicle, and the rest of the crowd rushed south on Fourth Street to Soulard Market. When Buntline neared the polls, several Germans fired at him, with one bullet striking his horse. He retreated on foot as they showered him with stones and other debris, then mounted another horse and led a full assault on the marketplace. The Germans, now overwhelmed, took cover behind a nearby lumberyard on Seventh and Marion Streets and continued to shoot at the Anglo-Americans from there.[47] Before two o'clock, the native-born vigilantes took control of the Soulard Market polls. Mc'OBlennis tapped a keg of whiskey and gathered some tumblers for the bystanders. They soon lifted a second keg of whiskey from a nearby German tavern. Buntline delivered another speech as the crowd cheered and drank. Robinson later testified, "After the whiskey was brought the boys mostly drank it and became quiet."[48]

Rioters then spread out to other parts of the German district. They now targeted immigrants who had nothing to do with the earlier affray. At one point a German fired on a menacing group of Americans from a building near the intersection of Seventh and Park Streets. Someone pointed to Henry Niemeier's bar, a popular resort for residents in the district, and the crowd rushed to the establishment.[49] A young man in a fireman's outfit, Joseph Stevens, pounded on the front door with a club as others threw stones though the front windows. A German bunkered inside shot Stevens through the heart; he collapsed on the street. Americans then stormed the bar, burned it to the ground, and beat the owner, Henry Niemeier, to within an inch of his life. His pregnant wife escaped out the back door just in time. The Phoenix Fire Engine arrived to extinguish the fire, but the firemen first hosed nearby Germans instead. Then, when the company decided to work on the blaze, a rioter cut the waterline. Meanwhile, the Anglo-Americans hauled two brass howitzers toward Seventh Street and commandeered a third cannon from Captain Almstedt's militia company.[50] More men among the firefighters suffered severe wounds, as did several Germans.[51] The fighting continued until sunset. At six o'clock the city was still in a state of commotion as several fires raged on.[52]

Mayor Kennett summoned all the militia companies to quell the mobs and deputized two hundred citizens as special constables on Monday and Tuesday nights. Several militia companies guarded the *Anzeiger des Westens* building on Third Street, which housed Börnstein's newspaper, after a crowd threw several stones through the windows of the first-floor office late Tuesday night.[53] The militia and special police once assembled managed to keep order, and no more violence ensued. The St. Louis Election Riot resulted in one man dead and several others wounded as well as the destruction of numerous immigrant businesses, including the bar owned by Niemeier, a respected German American businessman. The immigrants involved in the affray represented a cross-section of the German American community.[54]

In the aftermath St. Louisans struggled to determine who was to blame for the riot. A print war between the nativist dime novelist Buntline and German freethinker Börnstein, each the editor of a local newspaper, had preceded the violent eruption on April 5. Naturally, citizens blamed them. A year before the riot, Buntline, the self-proclaimed founder of the Order of United American Mechanics (OUAM), traveled the Mississippi Valley initiating young American men into an informal branch of the order, called the Patriotic and Benevolent Order of the Sons of America. His reputation preceded him, for thousands of Americans in the West had followed his exploits in New York City, where Buntline had begun his nativist career targeting British immigrants.[55] During the Astor Place Riot of 1849, his OUAM attacked a theater on Astor Place because the director hired British actors rather than American players. In his early dime novel *The Mysteries and Miseries of New York* (ca. 1848), he depicted wealthy British immigrants as scheming villains who corrupted the city's politics and exploited American workers. By 1851, however, anti-Catholic rather that anti-British sentiment had consumed Buntline's writing. His next urban publication, the *Mysteries and Miseries of New Orleans* (ca. 1851), featured not a British villain but a Jesuit who conspired to subvert American democracy.[56] Buntline came to oppose the influx of Catholic immigrants to the United States, the speed with which they became politically active, and their growing political power.

Buntline turned to the West to recruit new members to the order because he believed the balance of power in antebellum politics hinged on winning the Mississippi Valley.[57] In 1850 he departed New York and the following year launched *Ned Buntline's Novelist* in St. Louis. While in the city, he came to the realization that German immigrants wielded as much or more political power than Catholics in the region. He therefore rallied his followers to battle German voters in South St. Louis during an especially heated mayoral election between the Whig candidate Kennett, an ally of the nativists, and Democrat Thomas Hart Benton, an ally to Germans.

That year Börnstein aspired to form a German voting bloc that could sway elections. In his *Memoirs of a Nobody,* Börnstein explained his singular goal in St. Louis: "to organize the Germans in the West into a large, strong unity in order to help them attain power and influence in the internal matters of their homeland."[58] In addition to writing for his German-language paper, *Anzeiger des Westens,* he hosted the Verein Freie Maenner ("Association of Free Men"). As a freethinker, or atheist, Börnstein devoted nearly his entire political career to opposing the Roman Catholic Church and its clerics.[59] His anti-Catholicism may have seemed "radical" to German Lutherans and Catholics, but it was run-of-the-mill in the United States. "Börnstein's career as a red menace," one biographer explained, "was short lived and long behind him by the time he reached America, and his reputation as a radical in Missouri rested on different criteria."[60] In a city with a substantial minority of German Catholics, he fanned the flames of religious antagonism within the immigrant community.[61] German American Gustave Koerner, a close friend of Abraham Lincoln at this time, criticized Börnstein's "sensationalist reports about cruelties inflicted in convents, kidnapping and other terrible misdeeds" for generating "disturbances and even

riots."[62] While conservatives from the German Confederation considered Börnstein a radical for his anticlerical and socially liberal views, American Protestants
and temperance advocates saw him as a radical for encouraging German political
solidarity and drinking on Sundays, when he kept his tavern on the first floor of
the *Anzeiger* office open for business.[63]

In the *Anzeiger* Börnstein accused Buntline of planning to take over the polls
in Soulard. Preparations for the riot, according to Börnstein, began at the end of
March, when Buntline's gang raided a German Democratic rally near Laclede
Market. Nativists assaulted another Democratic rally two days before the election. Börnstein reported that "many rowdies and members of Ned Buntline's
gang arrived in the First Ward, insulting the election judges and the Germans
waiting in line to vote. They fired pistols in the air and did everything to provoke
the Germans to some excess." Only after residents had "coolly disarmed" the
"rowdies," Börnstein explained, did Buntline spread the rumor that Germans
had taken possession of the ballot boxes. Börnstein also reported misconduct in
the Third Ward. An allegedly hostile election judge called a German voter, a Mr.
Roever, a "DAMNED DUTCH" and removed him from the polling place.[64]

When the election authority announced that Kennett had been reelected
mayor by a small margin the next day, Börnstein charged Buntline's nativists
with corruption, having allegedly smashed German ballots at the Soulard election polls.[65] Moreover, Kennett marched in a funeral procession for the fallen
fireman on Tuesday, which suggested collusion between him and the nativists.[66]
Börnstein pointed out that the First Ward, nicknamed the "Banner Ward" for
its strong support of the Democratic Party, could have carried the election for
the Democrat Benton if the riot had not occurred. The nativists, in his estimation, had performed the "crude work of disrupting and stealing elections, of
inciting election riots and falsifying votes."[67]

Buntline, of course, blamed Börnstein and the Germans for the riot. He issued a proclamation to all "Americans" in his newspaper, *Ned Buntline's Novelist:* "The events of yesterday must teach you that the institutions of our republic
cannot be maintained if you do not do your duty. Yesterday at the ballot boxes
it was Germans and foreigners against Americans! This despicable crime cannot be tolerated, and it will not be tolerated. This story has only just begun;
what happened yesterday was only the beginning of the end, and no one can say
what the end shall be. The American spirit has been awakened, and the blood
of our murdered brother will not go unrevenged."[68] Stevens, the fireman killed
outside Niemeier's bar on Seventh Street, was the "murdered brother" to whom
Buntline referred. Several hundred nativists and Whigs organized an honorary

funeral procession for Stevens the day after the riot. The procession, stretching over a half mile long, marched behind his coffin through the streets of St. Louis. Nativists carried two large banners alongside the casket. One read: "Americans! We bury our brother! Remember, how he was slain!" The other declared: "Our brother was murdered, While we mourn our loss, We remember his worth." One eyewitness, Pardon Dexter, reported that "all Kinds of Mottoes and banners were carried in procession to excite their sympathy and arouse to vengeance."[69]

Other newspapers blamed Börnstein's Association of Free Men, founded in 1851, for promoting secularism and a form of socialism the later generations would recognize as Marxism. "We believe," argued a writer for the *Missouri Republican,* the riot "was carried on by those Socialists, Red Republicans, and Infidels, whom . . . the Anzeiger, with their poetical editor, control."[70] The *St. Louis News* concurred: "Radicalism in its worst form has gained the victory— European radicalism."[71] St. Louis was, in fact, home to very few socialist-leaning immigrants, and those who existed there found fellow Germans as unwelcoming as Americans.[72] This author also touted Börnstein, who at the time of the election had only resided in the United States for four years, as an example of undue foreign influence in politics; he was not even a U.S. citizen: "his interference assumes an aspect that will rouse the blood, not only of the native born, but of those who have by time been entitled to the rights of citizenship."[73] Börnstein had also allegedly urged several foreigners who "had not attained the proper age" to "naturalize" before the April 5 elections and vote. The ire of the American press put his life on the line. Dexter remarked that Börnstein had been "notified to leave the State."[74]

The St. Louis Criminal Court actually indicted Buntline two months later on the charge of rioting, but by then he had skipped town.[75] No cases were brought against any German residents. The St. Louis Election Riot of 1852 polarized the city's politics, galvanized the nativist movement, and increased German immigrant solidarity.

St. Louis Know-Nothing Riot, August 7–9, 1854

Two years later, during a gubernatorial election on August 7, 1854, another massive riot pitted Anglo-Americans against immigrants, this time in the Irish district of St. Louis. That morning a group of Know-Nothings, escorted an election judge to the predominantly Irish Fifth Ward to check voters' naturalization papers. During an affray, an Irish boy stabbed a nativist in the stomach. One reporter called the boy a "blackguard," a common criminal, surmising that the juvenile delinquent led a small Irish gang of vagrants armed with knives and slingshots.[76] Some Know-Nothing vigilantes chased him into a row of Irish boardinghouses. Havoc descended upon the city as the initial confrontation escalated into an all-out ethnic battle. Anglo-American crowds raged against well-known Irish establishments in the Fifth Ward, and the Irish fought back.[77]

Reports estimated that over the next three days mobs numbering as high as 5,000 (out of a population of about 90,000) inflicted hundreds of thousands of dollars of damage on German and Irish businesses and homes and caused the deaths of at least ten people. The city's police force and militia units were incapable of suppressing what turned out to be the largest riot in St. Louis before the Civil War and the greatest of its kind west of the Mississippi River to date. Mayor How finally ended the fighting on August 9 by deputizing an unprecedented seven-hundred-man posse—many of whom happened to be members of the National American (Know-Nothing) Party, including two of the group's militia leaders, Captains Eaton and Cooke.[78]

A print war preceded the conflict, during which the *Missouri Republican* circulated a rumor that 2,000 foreigners intended to vote illegally in the election. On election days it was not uncommon for party leaders to escort foreign-born residents of five years or more to the courthouse so they could become "naturalized" and thus eligible to vote. Between 1850 and 1860, 17,352 immigrants became naturalized in St. Louis. New residents could also declare their "intent" to become citizens after two years of residency, which likewise qualified them to vote in local elections.

On the morning of the August 1854 election, hundreds of immigrants descended upon the St. Louis Circuit Court and Court of Common Pleas to declare their intent to become citizens so that they might vote that day. The extant records show ninety-three such declarations on August 7. Each declarant had to provide proof of two years of residence and sign a pledge of allegiance. Several who were illiterate, including an immigrant from Germany named Christy Smith and two immigrants from Ireland, Peter Coleman and Michael Gurhey, made their mark with an "x."

Worried about the potential for illegal voting, nativists in the city demanded that immigrants present their naturalization papers to prove their eligibility. There had been, after all, previously documented cases of immigrant voter fraud, both of unnaturalized immigrants voting and naturalized immigrants voting more than once, although nativists probably overstated the number of instances. On Election Day, April 3, 1848, for example, Irish immigrant Edward Murphy officially registered his naturalization with the St. Louis Criminal Court and

TABLE 5.19: Naturalizations in Missouri, 1846–1861

Year	Total immigrants naturalized	Irish immigrants naturalized
1846	Unknown	52
1847	450	78
1848	1,186	149
1849	292	49
1850	533	48
1851	678	61
1852	1,340	108
1853	656	100
1854	1,285	190
1855	1,116	175
1856	2,065	622
1857	1,393	314
1858	2,151	564
1859	1,924	431
1860	4,211	1,126
1861	Unknown	103

SOURCE: Naturalization Records, MSA.

proceeded to a ballot box—then he went to another. The court later prose-cuted Murphy for the crime of "voting more than once."[79] During an election for sheriff on August 1, 1852, both candidates were summoned to the circuit court for an investigation after a prosecutor provided "an extensive list of illegal voters."[80] The criminal court fined Thomas Tremble twenty dollars for "illegal voting" during an election on August 1, 1853. Election judges of the Third Ward recorded "two ballots of said defendant as the voter." Tremble testified that once he started drinking that day, he forgot he had already voted. The court found him guilty, for it did not matter "whether of the time he voted were drunk or sober."[81] Alcohol was a major part of election-day festivities in the nineteenth century. Most residents did not have to report for work, but the bars remained open for business.[82]

TABLE 5.20: Declarations of Intent to Become Citizens on August 7, 1854

"Intention to become a citizen" on election day, August 7, 1854 (93 entries)

August Potthoff	Hanover
John Henry Ferhaahr	Prussia
Franz Loher	Prussia
Casper Graulech	Hesse Darmstadt
John Thuman	Oldenburg
George Kormann	France
Ernes H. Elbrecht	Hanover
Charles Klausman	Baden
Henry Lienemeyer	Hanover
Frederick W. Kamper	Hanover
John Henry Elberths	Hanover
Henry Haeper	Prussia
Peter Frederick Fake	Prussia
Michael Richard	France
Philip Pollhaus	Prussia
Herman Munster	Hanover
William Menkes	Prussia
Herman H. Bockstruck	Prussia
Thomas Slavin	Ireland
John Sullivan	Ireland
Michael Quinn	Ireland
Nicholas McGraw	Ireland
Ralph Farr	Ireland
Edmund Grace	Ireland
John Hensy	Ireland
William Vaber	Prussia
Henry W. Kutemann	Prussia
Henry Sprenger	Prussia
Henry Ludwig	Hanover
Henry Beuke	Hanover
Conrad Ludwig	Hanover
William Powers	Ireland
John Mollowny	Ireland
John Henry Husemann	Prussia
Herman Henry Biermann	Prussia
George Henry Greaves	England
Richard Geeson	England
Franz Bieber	Bavaria
Patrick Fox	Ireland
Frederick Kobusch	Prussia
Frank Hupe	Hanover

James Stack	Ireland
Michael Sullivan	Ireland
Albert Heider	Prussia
Patrick Carroll	Ireland
Henry Birkmann	Prussia
William M. Murphy	Ireland
Patrick Casey	Ireland
James Morrissey	Ireland
Johannes Husch	Bavaria
Timothy Daily	Ireland
Cornelius Inwright	Ireland
Timothy Slattery	Ireland
Herman Henry Aring	Hanover
Christian Muehle	Prussia
Andrew Ford	Ireland
Bernard Fitzsimmons	Ireland
Patrick Gorman	Ireland
Patrick O'Connell	Ireland
John Murphy	Ireland
John Collins	Ireland
Joseph Simmons	England
Thomas Rourke	Ireland
Thomas McCarthy	Ireland
Patrick Malowny	Ireland
Frederick Trautmund	Prussia
William Green	Ireland
Clemens Schaap	Hanover
Andrew Carter	Ireland
Henry Wells	Ireland
Henry Huchttons	Prussia
Caspar Meyer Otto	Prussia
Michael Cleary	Ireland
Jeremiah Scandlin	Ireland
David Tracy	Ireland
Jerry Ford	Ireland
Edmund Roland	Ireland
John Caffry	Ireland
John Dougherty	Ireland
Owen Gillespie	Ireland
John Regan	Ireland
John Henry Sommerich	Prussia
John Quinn	Ireland
Daniel Maloney	Ireland
Louis Gruneman	Prussia

Henry Gruneman	Prussia
Peter Coleman	Ireland
John Duddy	Ireland
Michael Gurhey	Ireland
Christian Heister	Switzerland
Bartholomew Elward	Ireland
George Gavin	Ireland
Christy Smith	Germany

SOURCES: Aliens Declarations, Land Court, 1853–66; Declaration of Aliens No. 3, Criminal Court Records 1853–57; Declaration of Aliens, Circuit Court, 1849–56; Declaration of Aliens, 1850–65, Court of Common Pleas, MSA.

On August 7, 1854, after the initial affray at the election polls, a mob of hundreds packed an area from Fourth and Green Streets to Second and Morgan, the center of the Irish district. A Catholic guard known as the Hibernians formed a regimented line across Morgan Street to block the vengeful nativist Americans from entering a boardinghouse. A melee ensued. Rival crowds battled on Morgan Street with fists, clubs, knives, and bricks. Irishmen fired "hundreds of discharges" from the windows of boardinghouses lining Morgan.[83] Nativist crowds rampaged eastward, overtook the entire levee from Franklin to Locust Streets, and destroyed Irish businesses, especially pubs, along the riverfront. Liquor and blood streamed down the limestone bank of the Mississippi through broken glass, splintered tables and chairs, shattered porcelain, and mashed cigars. The Americans soon turned west up Locust Street, and at Second Street the Irish Hibernians fired on them. The nativists pushed them back several blocks northward and further damaged Irish dwellings from the levee west all the way to Ninth Street, wrecking an area over seven blocks wide.

The targets of the mob reveal the underlying economic concerns that gave rise to political nativism. In a letter describing the event, St. Louisan Henry Hitchcock told his relative that the disruption "was at no time either a regular party riot nor even a sectarian (anti-Catholic) mob." Small-scale affrays had been quite common. Between December 1851 and December 1853, ninety-nine individuals were charged with the crime of "rioting" in the St. Louis Criminal Court.[84] On August 7, 1854, however, mobs of thousands destroyed entire city blocks. It was the "start of civil war," reported *La Revue de l'Ouest,* a French-language newspaper based in St. Louis.[85] "Wherever an Irishman was seen on the street," observed the *Globe Democrat,* "he was pursued and most cruelly beaten." A few days later it reported, "The excited populace" demolished "well known resorts of the Irish."[86] Another St. Louis observer, George Engelmann, informed a friend that the riot "was a quarrel between the Irish and the Know-Nothings."[87] The mob targeted popular Irish businesses and dwellings on Morgan Street. Just north of there lay a sector of Irish bawdy houses and taverns known as Battle Row for its frequent gang activity. They too were destroyed. Some considered Battle Row the most dangerous district of the city, said to have hoarded the most notorious drunkards, prostitutes, and gangs in St. Louis.[88]

Rioters primarily targeted Irish drinking houses, interchangeably referred to as "coffeehouses," "pubs," "groggeries," "taverns," "saloons," "bars," or "dram shops." They found no shortage of targets along the levee. From Franklin to Locust Streets, each block averaged six drinking houses. The same ratio existed on Morgan between Fourth Street and the levee. Main, First, and Second Streets, all running parallel with the river, averaged at least two drinking houses per block.[89] Rioters destroyed over forty Irish pubs on Monday afternoon in less than thirty minutes. Hitchcock assured a relative in Nashville that "the low Irish drinking houses in the neighborhood . . . were *cleaned out*."[90] A local newspaper reported that Irish groggeries near the levee "were all more or less injured and the contents destroyed." There were whole blocks farther west of the river where rioters wrecked all the pubs in sight.[91]

Victims included Irish immigrant John Bourke, owner of a coffeehouse at 92 Front Street between Green and Morgan, officially naturalized on April 3, 1854. Bourke reported a total of $301.65 in damages. The mob destroyed two of his large looking glasses, an eight-day clock, a silver watch, seven armchairs, one glass door, eighteen cut-glass decanters, some brandy and port, and a violin and bow. John Cox, naturalized either in 1849 or 1851, owned the Crescent Exchange at 85 Front Street. On the day of the riot, he possessed a "large quantity of liquor of various qualities and kinds." He was "carrying on his said business as he rightfully might do," he testified, when his "house and premises were assailed by a mob of riotous and disorderly persons who without any just or reasonable cause or provocation whatever in the most violent disorderly and riotous manner broke open the doors . . . and forced an entrance." Once inside they "broke and destroyed the property of the plaintiff of the value of" $811.75. The crowd smashed his Chinese bottles, decanters, and looking glasses and stole away some sardines and $209 worth of cigars. Peter Sharkey, naturalized on November 2, 1852, owned a similar establishment, called the Exchange, at 90 Front Street. He claimed $343.15 in damages. The mob also sacked The America, a coffeehouse at 91 Front Street owned by Irish immigrant Thomas McGrath, who claimed $438.95 in damages. When the crowd forcibly entered the Louisiana Exchange, a coffeehouse on the levee owned by immigrants John Massoa and August Grillo, they wasted bottles of soda, absinth, cherry brandy and cordials, Burton's ale, wine, and port as well as forty-two gallons of French brandy, whisky, ten gallons of rum, 1,800 regalia cigars, and half a chest of imperial tea. Joseph Shannon, owner of the Central Exchange, a "coffee house or drinking house" at 84 Front Street, reported $247.75 in damages to his house and $28.50 worth of damage to his doors and windows. Irish immigrant William Morton Hughes, naturalized after the riot on January 14, 1856, reported $219.30 worth of damages to his boarding and coffee house at 215 North Main Street. Michael Walsh, who received U.S. citizenship on April 3, 1854, suffered damages at his grocery store at the corner of Sixth and Green Streets totaling $351.35. German immigrant Henry Heuer operated a large tavern four doors north of Pine Street on the west side of Third Street. During the "Know-nothing riots," German immigrant Ernst Kargau recalled, "Heuer was struck on the forehead with a stone, which left a deep scar, a memorial of those stormy days."[92] Later Monday night a group of Americans gutted the coffeehouse of Irish immigrant Terrence Brady at the intersection of Fifth and Morgan. This was the third time rioters had sacked his business since 1853.[93]

At 12:00 A.M. on Tuesday, August 8, a gang of "little, trifling vagrant boys" gathered at Fourth Street and marched west on Green Street, throwing stones and bricks through the windows of various Irish residences. Suddenly, a rival gang in an Irish shanty at the corner of Sixth Street opened fire. After several shots were fired "in rapid succession," Captain Blackburn's militia, known as the Continental Rangers, arrived. The Irish men in the shanty quickly redirected their fire at them. News of the shootout infuriated local residents. Captain Blackburn was lightly wounded, and four of his militiamen were severely wounded. Around the same time, a respected iron merchant, E. R. Violett, was shot to death at Ninth and Biddle Streets. A lieutenant of the night police was shot through the chest; he died the next day.[94]

The American mobs actualized cultural and political fears. A crowd of approximately 500 nativists nearly destroyed St. Francis Xavier Catholic Church, located on the Jesuit campus of Saint Louis University. Rumors spread that over 1,000 German and Irish Catholics had barricaded themselves inside the church at Ninth and Green Streets. Hitchcock explained that the nativist mob was motivated by "stories of a possible attack on the Cathedral, or the College Church (St. Xavier's, where ladies sing) and again, of arms and ammunition stored away in the same to prepare for it." The vigilantes marched west on Green Street toward the campus. They disbanded, however, once they could not find any Germans or Irish fortified inside. Indeed, Irish-born Archbishop Peter Richard Kenrick issued a proclamation during the riot "admonishing his people not to be carried away by excitement," which appeared to have some effect.[95] The rioters also besieged German immigrant Börnstein's *Anzeiger des Westens* press and threatened to burn the building to the ground, which they may have accomplished if the militia had not arrived in time to deter the potential arsonists.[96]

The scale of the violence was unprecedented, and St. Louis authorities scrambled to act. The police force, totaling sixty-three hapless officers, quickly retreated. Mayor How called upon all militia companies to defend properties, but they were not numerous enough to do so effectively. How even considered declaring a state of national emergency and requesting out-of-state help to restore order. Hearing that many in the crowd were inebriated, the mayor issued an emergency proclamation temporarily outlawing liquor sales, but that did not prevent rioters from breaking into Irish pubs and stealing away booze.[97] A posse of seven hundred volunteers finally restored order in the city on Wednesday, August 9, and the administration spent the rest of 1854 picking up the pieces. The city's legal system hardly entertained any of the cases brought by victims of the riot. Only a week after August 7, the St. Louis City Recorder's Court summarily "relieved the docket of a large accumulation of cases growing out of the late mob."[98]

Mayor How and his successor, Washington King, actually blamed the city's episode of turbulence on drunk Irish Catholic immigrants.[99] King, the first Know-Nothing candidate to run for office, campaigned in 1855 to increase the city's security from the "*mobocracy*" of the previous year.[100] Following his lead, the Missouri legislature passed an antiriot law giving mayors the power to close saloons and enforce curfews on election days or in cases of emergency.[101] King's administration stigmatized immigrants in St. Louis as disorderly, prone to alcohol abuse, and culturally backward.[102]

In the aftermath of this riot, coalitions of Germans and Irish levied enough political support, however, to compel the city's administration to distribute reparations to victims of the mobs. Rather than let citizens fall prey to the whims of vigilante crowds, city officials resolved to take full responsibility for all residents, native born and immigrant alike. Although Mayor How and Mayor King blamed the 1854 riot on immigrants and drunks, they were more receptive to immigrant pleas for justice behind the scenes. By October 1, 1855, the Board of Alderman distributed $8,149.26 total to German and Irish victims of the August riot.[103] The payment had no obvious legal precedent and indicated a new responsibility on the part of the city's government. After 1854, municipal leaders on both sides of the political aisle realized the necessity of strengthening the power and scope of the government to provide for the welfare and safety of all of its citizens.

Cincinnati Election Day Riot, April 5, 1855

On Election Day, April 5, 1855, a band of Know-Nothing rowdies aimed to "secure" the polls from voter fraud in wards of the city where Germans predominated, namely the Over-the-Rhine district in the Eleventh Ward.[104] Rumors of German schoolboys stuffing ballot boxes incited a nativist mob of three hundred to four hundred strong, which stormed the polling place of the German district and burned approximately 1,300 ballots in the Eleventh Ward. They reportedly burned several hundred more the following day. Despite the lost ballots, Democrat James J. Faran won the election by a small margin.[105]

The Know-Nothings in Cincinnati had nominated James Taylor for mayor, despite his controversial anti-immigrant and antiparochial-school policies. In a previous spring election cycle in 1853, Taylor, then the nativist editor of the *Cincinnati Times,* headed a "Free Ticket" to oppose the splitting of school funds to pay for Catholic schools. In his campaign he condemned Catholic and German immigrants for subverting the public school system in Cincinnati. He supported the use of the King James Bible in classroom instruction. He did not win the 1853 contest, but only because there were two other "free school" tickets more popular than his.[106]

Unlike the Know-Nothing mayoral candidates in Louisville and St. Louis, Taylor was firmly antislavery. Instead of continuing a path to fusion on an antislavery platform, the German citizens of Cincinnati backed neutral-on-slavery Democratic candidate Faran. Radical abolitionists, such as Friedrich Haussaurek, and traditionally Democratic German Catholics supported Faran because they disliked Taylor's nativism. One disgusted Know-Nothing spoke of the German political alliance: "When I see . . . the Hassaureks united with the Roman Catholics, all under a foreign banner, I see something in the election much deeper and more important than a question of men. It is a question of whether Americans shall govern Americans, or whether a miserable faction aided by domestic charlatans shall rule us."[107]

Chicago Lager Riot, April 21, 1855

The Chicago Lager Riot erupted five weeks after the Chicago elections in March 1855 in response to actions taken by newly appointed Know-Nothing mayor Levi Boone. Mayor Boone had achieved his election victory by allying with antislavery and temperance advocates. The Illinois General Assembly passed its version of the Maine Law, which prohibited the sale or use of alcohol in the entire state of Maine, but the bill required a special referendum of Chicago voters to pass into law in June 1855.[108] The measure would take a serious toll on the German and Irish barkeepers of Chicago, since all but fifty liquor establishments were owned by German or Irish residents.[109]

Like Washington King in St. Louis, Mayor Boone cracked down in Chicago. In his inaugural address of March 13, 1855, he denounced all at once Catholicism, foreignism, and drinking: "I cannot be blind to the existence in our midst of a powerful politico-religious organization . . ., its chief officers bound under an oath of allegiance to the temporal as well as the spiritual supremacy of a foreign despot, boldly avowing the purpose of universal dominion over this land." Against such Catholic and foreign attachments, Mayor Boone boldly announced, "*I wish* to be known as taking my stand."[110] He appointed recruits to the police force "of strong physical powers, sober, regular habits, and known moral integrity." Boone and the city council hired eighty new officers, whose main task was to enforce the city's Sunday closing laws. German tavern keepers claimed that the administration's new police force discriminated against German and Irish bars and allowed native-born publicans to keep their saloons open on Sunday.[111] With the June referendum nearing, the immigrants of Chicago decided to make a stand.

On April 21 a group of protesters, including German and Irish of all creeds, marched on city hall to demand their right to drink and serve alcohol. The "crowd of protestors marched down Clark Street armed with shotguns, knives, clubs and assorted kitchen implements," one eyewitness reported. "They were met by a solid line of 200 lawmen. A yell arose from the German contingent—'Kill the police!'—and the two armies went for each other."[112] The affray resulted in the death of one German and the wounding of several others.[113] After that, both Catholic and non-Catholic German and Irish immigrants focused on countering Boone's Know-Nothing administration. Due in part to their combined efforts, Chicago's electorate voted down the antialcohol law in the June referendum.

Louisville Bloody Monday Riot, August 6–7, 1855

Almost exactly a year after the St. Louis Know-Nothing Riot, a riot on Louisville's Election Day, August 6, 1855, erupted at the polls in an area of the city known as "Butchertown," the predominantly German First Ward. The event became known as "Bloody Monday," since it claimed the lives of over twenty-two immigrants, both German and Irish, and left many more maimed. Unlike the previous year, the Know-Nothings were now in power in Louisville. Residents of the city had elected nativist John Barbee in the April elections of that year over moderate Democratic candidate James S. Speed. The August elections now afforded Know-Nothings the opportunity to secure their power in both Louisville and the state of Kentucky, while immigrants saw their chance to join together against the American Party by turning out for the Democrats. The days leading up to the election grew increasingly tense and replete with vituperative hearsay.

Candidate Speed provided one of the most highly respected testimonies of events that fateful day. From his office above the polling place in Butchertown, where the fighting broke out on Monday morning, Speed "saw many Irish and Germans beaten in the court house." At the beginning, Speed testified, "it was not fighting man to man, but as many as could, would fall upon a single Irish or German and beat him with sticks or short clubs." Men and boys with short clubs remained in the courtyard outside the polling place to prevent "foreigners" from voting and shouted "hurrah for Marshall, hurrah for Sam," referring to Know-Nothing congressional candidate Humphrey Marshall and the mythical figurehead of Americanism, Uncle Sam. Marshall supporters had organized the affray and wore yellow tickets "in their hats or on their breasts" so others knew the candidate to whom they were allied.[114]

Tensions mounted after someone informed the crowd gathered by the courthouse, in which Speed remained bunkered, that "the germans 200 strong and armed with double barrel shot guns had taken possession of the polls in the first ward." They rushed off with a roar. Finally, at five o'clock that afternoon, Speed left his office for home. He saw on the streets "many Irishmen carried to jail all covered with blood." He also watched in horror as a group of Know-Nothings beat a young German boy nearly to death:

> The crowd on guard took after a little German. . . . He ran pursued by the crowd. He was stricken many times before he got to the court house yard gate; soon after he got into the yard he was knocked down and most unmercifully beaten. To escape the blows he crawled under the Know-Nothing stand, and from where I stood I thought the man with the iron fork stabbed him when under there. . . . They dragged him from under the stand more dead than alive and carried him to jail on their shoulders, the crowd yelling to make the damned rascal walk.

Nativists continued to guard the polls from foreign voters until it grew dark. One German who attempted to cast his ballot in the evening was thrown over a high platform, beaten with clubs, pelted with stones, and knocked out cold.[115]

Meanwhile, the fighting spilled into the Irish Eighth Ward, where the nativist mob killed and injured several residents of Quinn's Row, a street that featured many well-known Irish businesses and pubs. One eyewitness, a child at the time, remembered that on the morning of the election, "the Irish and Dutch were reluctant to go to the polls to cast their votes." He recalled a group of firemen who gathered Germans and Irish off the streets and forced them to announce before mock judges for which party they planned to vote. "If not for the know-nothing candidates, they were stood up against the fence opposite and the tongue of the Volunteer engine was aimed at their abdomens, and the volunteer election hangers on did the rest."[116]

As these accounts demonstrate, the rioters targeted German and Irish businesses and immigrants. Later, rumors circulated that German and Irish Catholics had fortified a Catholic church on Fifth Street with guns and ammunition. The mob marched on the church but decided not to burn it down after Mayor Barbee inspected the grounds himself and announced that no hostile materials were stored there.[117]

What followed in the aftermath of the Louisville election riots, and after the riots in all the other western cities, was a nativist smear campaign in the press attempting to convince readers elsewhere that German and Irish Catholics and/or socialists had somehow been responsible for the violence. One Louisville journalist in particular, George D. Prentice, editor of the pro-Know-Nothing *Louisville Journal,* aimed to persuade the public that various German and Irish gangs had tampered with ballots, submitted fraudulent votes, and incited the disturbances in the First and Eighth Wards. He claimed that Know-Nothings had only behaved admirably and honorably to restore order in the city.[118] One avid reader of the *Louisville Journal* bought Prentice's narrative wholesale, remarking in his journal: "The American Party was not the aggressors. The *Irish* and *dutch* first shot down several peacible and quiet citizens. *My opinion* the retribution was not complete."[119] Another advocate of Know-Nothingism from California, where J. Neely Johnson won the gubernatorial election on the Know-Nothing ticket in 1855, initially told an acquaintance in Louisville, "I cannot tell who are the most culpable parties when the papers from there give such contradictory versions not only of the commencement but of the whole concern."[120] Within a couple of weeks, he received a copy of Prentice's newspaper and wrote back with an altered opinion: "It is clear that the Irish and germans commenced the disturbance.... I think they were visited with a most fearful vengeance."[121]

But it was not clear who started the fighting. Several prominent newspapermen, particularly those aligned with the Democratic Party, labored to prove that it was in fact the Know-Nothings who instigated the Bloody Monday Riot.[122] If the latter were correct, then the city's Know-Nothings were guilty of the ironic charge of corrupting the ballot box.[123]

The nativist narrative of events remained influential in Chicago, Cincinnati, Louisville, and St. Louis because the American Party had acquired seats of power in those cities. After Bloody Monday, Mayor Barbee became directly involved in a committee that immediately blamed the riot on immigrants in the First and Eighth Wards. In the official minutes of the special investigative committee, the clerk revealed the committee's bias when he labeled the event the "Irish and Dutch Insurrection." The board, over which Mayor Barbee presided, furthermore ruled that the city was "not liable for the losses occasioned by the mob."[124] Behind the scenes, the Board of Alderman of Louisville followed St. Louis's example by arranging to divvy out over five hundred dollars in five-and ten-dollar increments to individuals burned out of their businesses and homes by the mobs. Of all those who received these lump sums, most of the surnames appeared to be German and Irish in origin.[125]

Conclusion

The political nativism of the antebellum era responded to a unique set of urban problems. It also unintentionally sparked a new phase of urban reform. The upswing in violence between native-born Americans and immigrants occurred at the tail end of a phase in the American city's development characterized by lax policing and a remarkably weak, poorly financed municipal government. When it came to urban reform, nativists lacked imagination about potential solutions to crime and poverty. The rapid social and economic changes of the period did not destroy American cities in the West because philanthropic immigrants, private benevolent organizations, and progressive urban planners implemented seminal programs to restore order and safety. These reforms included an empowered professional police force, prisons and workhouses for criminals, almshouses for paupers, houses of refuge for orphans, insane asylums for the mentally disadvantaged, and societies for destitute immigrants.[126]

Among the charities aiming to alleviate the suffering of impoverished migrants in St. Louis were the German Immigrant Society, founded in 1847 by Germans for Germans; the Mullanphy Emigration Society; the Daughters of Charity of St. Vincent de Paul, composed of foreign-born nuns who served mostly "German and Irish immigrants"; the Episcopal Orphans' Home; the St. Louis Protestant Orphan Asylum; the School Sisters of Notre Dame; the

Ursuline Nuns, who focused on educating German-speaking children; the Irish Sisters of the Good Shepherd, who served "fallen women" in the city; the Home for the Friendless, which became an alternative to the county poorhouse; the Girls' Industrial Home, an alternative to the St. Louis House of Refuge; and the Sisters of Mercy, who served the "young, unemployed, and unskilled women" of the Kerry Patch district.[127] Many more charitable organizations aided the downtrodden.

Meanwhile, the wealth generated by labor-intensive industrialism continued to fuel the steady economic growth of St. Louis and other American cities, funding expansive urban programs for decades to come. The City of St. Louis eventually funded the City Asylum for the Insane, the Social Evils Hospital for prostitutes, an orphanage, and a host of other organizations for the poor. Certain election reforms temporarily decreased violence at the polls. The municipal government imposed the closure of bars and instituted a curfew on the day of elections, for example. It also passed an ordinance in 1854 prohibiting naturalization within two weeks of any election.[128]

The anti-immigrant violence in the urban West drastically altered the tenor of national politics during the mid-1850s. America's first nativist movement culminated in the rise of the National American (Know-Nothing) Party, which garnered nearly 900,000 votes in the presidential election of 1856, or 22 percent of the popular vote. Urban-based westerners and southerners joined the ranks of the Know-Nothings because the party's rhetoric addressed major cultural and economic concerns. In 1855, residents elected Know-Nothing mayors to office in Chicago, Louisville, and St. Louis; Cincinnati's Know-Nothing mayoral candidate lost only by a small margin. Nativists politically mobilized with a host of complaints about immigrants and immigration policy precisely as urban dwellers experienced an economic decline in their real disposable income and panicked about the future economic security of urban environments that had not yet adapted to new social demands.

CHAPTER 6

From Anti-Catholicism to Church-State Separation

The U.S. Constitution repudiates all other spiritual sovereignty than that of God.

—Proceedings of the Grand Council of Kentucky, 1856

I N THE FALL ELECTIONS of 1854, Know-Nothing candidates unexpectedly won major political offices across the country.[1] The success of the American, or Know-Nothing, Party brought nativists out of hiding and propelled them into the national limelight. The rapid rise of their political party astonished onlookers. In just one year's time, Know-Nothing membership nationwide rose from 50,000 in May 1854 to 1 million in June 1855 in more than 10,000 lodges. The Know-Nothing Party swept the November 1854 elections in Massachusetts, occupying every seat in the state senate and all but 3 of the 378 positions in the lower house.[2] By April 1855 the American Party controlled the state governments of Connecticut, New Hampshire, and Rhode Island.[3] They won both state and congressional elections in counties throughout the South and were particularly strong in Louisiana and Maryland.[4]

Know-Nothings in the West likewise captured seats in county offices and state legislatures and sent dozens of representatives to Congress. A combined independent faction of Know-Nothings and Republicans claimed nearly all the state offices of Ohio in 1854 and 1855. The residents of Chicago, Louisville, and St. Louis elected Know-Nothing mayors in April 1855, while mayoral candidate James D. Taylor nearly won in Cincinnati.[5] Illinois and Ohio each elected two Know-Nothing representatives to Congress. Missouri elected five Know-Nothing representatives in 1855 and two more in 1856. Kentucky sent seven Know-Nothing representatives and one Know-Nothing senator to Congress in 1855 alone.[6] Know-Nothing voters turned out as far west as California, where San Franciscans elected the American Party's mayoral candidate to office in 1854. A Know-Nothing won the governorship of that state in 1856.[7] During the presidential election of 1856, the American Party's presidential candidate, former president Millard Fillmore, gained twenty-two percent of the national popular vote. The American Party made its mark as the second-largest "third party" in U.S. history.[8]

The dire timing of the political rise of the nativists did not go unnoticed. Know-Nothings believed that the future of the Union hinged on their success at uniting Americans in the North, South, and West. One leader from Missouri, Samuel H. Woodson, warned fellow Missouri nativist George R. Smith in 1856, five years before the outbreak of the Civil War, "If the American Party succeeds the Union is safe. . . . [B]ut if it fails the horrors of intestine war, and all the appalling consequences of disunion must ensue."[9] As historians have demonstrated, the American Party owed its stunning success to the North-South sectional controversy over the expansion of slavery into the West, which fomented the collapse of the Whig Party in 1854.

Yet political nativism revealed multiple axes of political and sectional realignment in the decade before the Civil War. The American Party thrived in western border states, including Illinois, Ohio, Kentucky, and Missouri, where nativists raised the banner of compromise. In the antebellum West, where anti-Catholicism and antislavery sentiment did not necessarily go hand in hand, political nativism forged a political transformation of base anti-Catholicism into the higher ideal of church-state separation. Once they came out of hiding, nativists discovered that the anti-Catholicism they had been spewing all along was better expressed in a more sanitized way as a commitment to the separation of church and state. New political platforms substituted a vague deism for previous declarations favoring Protestant interests so as to include a larger pool of faith traditions. The latest drafts of American Party platforms preferred using the term "Supreme Being" rather than "God."[10] Nativists in the West cast their net so wide that once they formed a national political party in 1854, even German and Irish citizens, Catholics and Jews, could potentially embrace their principles, which they increasingly did over the ensuing years. Religious prejudices remained, but the country's first bout of political nativism culminated in a renewal of Americans' commitment to the separation of church and state.[11]

This sanitizing process occurred in the West because Know-Nothings were more likely to work in coalitions with German immigrants, Republicans, and even French Catholics there than they were in the Northeast. Nativists in the West emphasized an important distinction: "It is not men of Foreign birth that we war against," explained President of the Ohio Order Thomas Spooner, "Our arms are, and should only be, directed against Foreignism and Romanism—those who would subvert our Institutions, and place our country under the yoke of Rome." Semantically, "Catholicism" became less charged than "Romanism" or "popery," which connoted the undue influence of clergymen in American politics.[12] Along these lines, orders in the West became the first to permit German and Irish citizens and even some Catholics into their ranks.

The rise of the American Party afforded nativist leaders the chance to refine their version of American nationalism in a way that suited the current political environment. They subtly shifted the goal of the nativist movement from pursuing an exclusive anti-Catholic state to ensuring an American state radically removed from any church influences. Thus, Americans compelled Catholics and immigrants who might have otherwise shared an affinity for monarchism to accept American-style democracy, while Catholics and immigrants compelled native-born Americans to accept a more inclusive definition of religious freedom. Together, they effectively expanded the number of religions openly condoned in U.S. politics.[13]

How Partisanship Gave Rise to the American Party

After 1850, the Second Party System, which pitted the Whigs against the Democrats, began to collapse under the weight of the politics of slavery. The newly formed American Party rose to national prominence in this milieu. Although its stance on the slavery issue was officially neutral, time would reveal clear sectional divisions within the emergent party. Its members preferred to avoid the issue and instead focus on other pressing matters, namely immigration reform. Ultimately, the deep political divisions over slavery proved unavoidable. Thus, the crisis over slavery manufactured the American Party's sharp rise and decline between 1854 and 1856.[14]

New York Whig William Seward's widely publicized speech in the U.S. Senate on March 11, 1850, added an especially controversial dimension to the debate regarding the "constitutionality" of slavery. What became known as the Compromise of 1850 (passed later that year) proposed admitting California as a "free state" barring slaveowning in exchange for several concessions to proslavery Southern Democrats, including a stricter Fugitive Slave law. Seward's Whig faction boldly denounced the compromise as a stain on American principles of freedom and equality and insisted that slavery ought to be prohibited from all western states and territories, not just California. Proslavery adherent John Calhoun and his Southern Democratic cohort, on the other hand, considered the Whig Party's "free state" western policy a violation of the U.S. Constitution. Opponents of Seward read one passage of his speech with particular alarm, where he claimed his antislavery stance was founded on "a higher law than the Constitution, which regulates our authority over [the West]. The territory is a part, no inconsiderable part, of the common heritage of mankind bestowed upon them by the Creator of the universe. We are his stewards, and must so discharge our trust as to secure in the highest attainable degree their happiness."[15] Once expressed, this morality-based policy became frustratingly divisive and eventually tore the Whig Party into antislavery, proslavery, and "neutral" ranks.

When Senator Stephen A. Douglas's Kansas-Nebraska Bill of 1854 mandated the political doctrine of "popular sovereignty" for the organization of new territories in the West, politics became increasingly polarized between those who supported the measure and those who did not. The bill's passage in the spring of 1854 sparked a mass exodus of disillusioned Whigs and Democrats into the ranks of the antiparty Know-Nothing Order, which at the time welcomed all defectors.

Many Know-Nothings in the free states of Ohio and Illinois supported antislavery as well as immigration and temperance reforms. Ideally, they hoped to vote for the party that could uphold all three of these positions. Disgusted by the Whigs' lack of resolve during the Kansas debacle as well as their seeming inability to deal with the immigration question, many in the Northwest chose to defect to the Know-Nothings to pursue both an antislavery and anti-Catholic agenda.[16]

Know-Nothingism also promised neutral and proslavery ex-Whigs and ex-Democrats in the western border states an alternative to the antislavery "higher-lawism" prevailing among Whigs in the North.[17] Relative neutrality with respect to slavery proved especially strong in Kentucky and Missouri, both slave states. A political leader in Missouri named James Rollins, for example, endorsed the American Party for resisting "unprincipled fanaticism, which a few dangerous demagogues are now inciting."[18] Luther M. Kennett, now a Know-Nothing congressman representing St. Louis, informed a fellow nativist leader in that city, Henry Williams, that unlike his opponents in the Democratic and Republican Parties, he was neither "a nullifier [n]or a black republican."[19] In 1857 ex-Whig and now Know-Nothing St. Louis mayoral candidate William Carr Lane asserted that Know-Nothings in Missouri, unlike their antislavery brothers in Illinois and Ohio, maintained a perfect balance: "Here, in what used to be the West, but which is now the centre of the Union, we do not entertain the extreme views."[20] Know-Nothings in the western border states with slavery thus fashioned the nativist movement as a guard against the volatility of extremism in the dubious forms of abolitionism, demagoguery, popery, and also proslavery advocacy.

The American Party included in its ranks former Whigs and former Democrats, whether antislavery, against the extension of slavery, or proslavery, who hoped to come together nevertheless on a certain set of shared national principles. The party's focus on the issue of immigration afforded concerned Americans a chance to step outside the political factions and feuds that seemed to be ripping the nation into various sectional parts and rediscover a source of unity. The famous nativist author Anna Carroll, for example, warned citizens in her 1856 book, *The Union of the States,* that "our national existence is in peril!" and insisted that the only way to avoid disaster was to draw on "the everlasting bond of our national life and faith and action."[21] Nativists blamed the "outside" forces of undue Catholic and immigrant influences for the political turmoil of the 1850s, at the same time attempting to define the values that united Americans.

Although Whig and Democratic defectors joined the American Party for varying reasons, it must be remembered that they all took Know-Nothing oaths. They approved its nativist platforms and cheered the speeches of its leaders. Even the most cynical Know-Nothing members gave their tacit approval to the anti-Catholic, anti-immigrant sentiment pervading the party, which in and of itself yielded significant political results. Millions of Americans found it convenient to blame the ills plaguing antebellum America, including economic recession, political partisanship and corruption, sectionalism, and the politics of slavery, on unwanted outsiders.

Wanted Outsiders: Early Western Attempts at Inclusivity and Transparency

It was in Cincinnati, not New York, where the Know-Nothing Party made its first large splash in national politics. The first "national" Know-Nothing Council convened in New York in June 1854 but attracted little attention because there were few delegates from outside the Northeast. Just five months later, in the wake of the party's sweeping victories in Massachusetts and Ohio, the Cincinnati Know-Nothing Convention drew new delegates from across the nation. Held in November 1854, it successfully established a national agenda for the order's emergence on the political scene as well as uniform eligibility requirements and terms of admittance for new members.[22]

Nowhere during the fall of 1854 was political realignment more dynamic and exciting than in Ohio, the first state to successfully cast out both major parties and usher in an independent fusion party. "Fusion" entailed the Know-Nothings in Ohio joining together with other political groups, such as the emergent

Republicans, into a broad, independent third party. Cincinnati was a hotbed of Know-Nothing activism, and residents of the city set the tenor for the most significant developments in political nativism in the region. Ohio ranked as the third-most-populous state, and the Know-Nothing Grand Council in Cincinnati served then as the central administrator of lodges in the surrounding states of Kentucky, Illinois, Indiana, and Missouri as well as Ohio. This meant that councils in the western border states were, in effect, governed by the Grand Council of Ohio throughout 1853 and 1854. Forces opposed to Douglas's Kansas Act in Ohio combined with new members of the Know-Nothing Order in a wildly unprecedented political uprising against the Whig and Democratic Parties in the state. Distraught Whigs, Democrats, temperance advocates, Free-Soilers, German Americans, Republicans, and Know-Nothings formed a massive coalition under the "People's State Ticket." Know-Nothings constituted the majority of the coalition, with Republicans a close second. These fusionists turned out for the October 1854 elections with enough votes to sweep the congressional and state contests throughout Ohio.[23] What seemed to unite all sides on the People's State Ticket in 1854 and 1855 was a general dislike of the Kansas-Nebraska Act as well as resentment toward representatives in the major parties for allowing the crisis to occur. But Catholicism and immigration were also potent political issues. By January 1855, only three months after the electoral victories of October 1854, membership in the Know-Nothing Order doubled. The national secretary of the order announced the presence of 830 councils in the state of Ohio alone, amounting to nearly 120,000 voters.[24]

The scale of the antislavery fusion movement's success in Ohio was unlike anything witnessed in American history. It was entirely distinct from Know-Nothingism in the Northeast, where nativists there did not necessarily need to rely on immigrants and Republicans for political success. During the Whig collapse in 1854, Know-Nothings in the Northeast quickly took the place of that party as the chief political rival of the Democrats. During the summer municipal elections of 1854 in Philadelphia, for example, mayoral candidate Robert T. Conrad ran as a member of the Whig Party, joined the Know-Nothing Order, and facilitated the transition from Whig to Know-Nothing dominance that year without losing an election to the Democratic Party. Conrad denounced the Kansas-Nebraska Act, vowed to appoint only native-born Americans to city positions, and promised to regulate Sunday drinking. Former antislavery Whigs in Philadelphia found a comfortable home, then, in the emergent Know-Nothing Party because they could boycott the two-party system and the Kansas-Nebraska Act while retaining their advocacy of political nativism, temperance, and stricter immigration laws. In Massachusetts the smooth transition from Whiggery to Know-Nothingism was even starker, as the order summarily swept the state elections in November 1854.[25]

Western politics produced a series of peculiar coalitions and compromises. Since the Democratic Party in Ohio was much more powerful than in Massachusetts, Pennsylvania, or other northeastern states where Know-Nothings independently won major victories, an alliance between antislavery German Americans and Know-Nothings was necessary.[26] Despite the presence of Know-Nothings in the opposition fold, even German Americans took refuge in the new fusion party. Animated by the polarizing atmosphere of party politics in the mid-1850s, German Protestants in Cincinnati who had consistently voted for antiextension Democrats for decades suddenly rallied around Kansas-Nebraska opponents within their community such as Charles Reemelin and Henry Roedter; the latter served as the editor of the *Ohio Staats-Zeitung* between 1850 and 1854. Both Reemelin and Roedter disavowed their long affiliation with "Bentonites," antislavery members of the Democratic Party who supported Senator Thomas Hart Benton of Missouri, and supported instead the People's Party under antislavery advocate Salmon P. Chase.[27] The antislavery editor of the *Daily Morning Leader* in Cleveland, Joseph Medill, rejoiced in May 1854, "The Germans are seriously with us and large numbers of native born Democrats, how many we can't tell, but the defection is general."[28]

This defection from the Democratic Party in the Old Northwest is well known and sometimes exaggerated; many German voters remained loyal to the Democrats through the Civil War. Less examined, however, is the anti-Catholic and antislavery affinities non-Catholic German Americans shared with Know-Nothings in the People's Party.[29] German Protestant activists in Ohio held several anti-Kansas-Nebraska meetings in the summer of 1854, during which they denounced the "intrigues of papal agents" in the Democratic Party as well as the southern "slave power" that seemed to be tightening its hold on Democratic agendas.[30] Actually, many non-Catholic Germans assiduously charged Pope Pius IX's administration with conspiring to influence the politics of German Catholics in America. German freethinkers did not share the Protestant religious worldview that bolstered nativist anti-Catholicism, but they did have in common the goal of limiting the influence of the Roman clergy.

Freethinking organs such as Heinrich Börnstein's *Anzeiger des Westens* in St. Louis spouted anti-Catholic vitriol and reinforced the nativist idea that European Catholicism was incompatible with American republicanism.[31] The "Free Germans" of Louisville asserted, moreover, that all religious-based legislation, including "the Sabbath laws, thanksgiving days, prayers in Congress and Legislatures, the oaths upon the Bible, [and] the introduction of the Bible into the free schools," violated human rights in general and the Constitution in particular.[32] The Jesuit priests in Börnstein's novel *The Mysteries of St. Louis* conspired to agitate the northern abolitionists against the southern fire-eaters. "We have thrown the slave question between them," mutters the Jesuit villain during a midnight rendezvous of Jesuit conspirators on Bloody Island, the notorious sandbar in the middle of the Mississippi River at St. Louis. After reciting their Marian devotions, the Jesuit superior announces, "After the next session of Congress there will be no more Whigs or Democrats, and the Union will be overthrown."[33]

A year after Börnstein published his sensational Jesuit conspiracy tale in 1853, Italian papal nuncio Gaetano Bedini toured the United States to encourage all parish boards of trustees to turn over the title of church property to their bishop. German freethinkers in Cincinnati raised awareness of Cardinal Bedini's involvement with counterrevolutionary forces during the recent democratic uprisings in Italy. Everyone "in the *Old World* have raised their hands to *swear vengeance* and *retribution*" for Cardinal Bedini's crime of executing Italian revolutionaries, one anti-Bedini broadside declared.[34] While on his tour in the United States, the cardinal specifically ordered two parishes to turn over church property ownership from their board of trustees to their bishop: one in Buffalo, New York, and the other in Cincinnati. When Bedini arrived in the Queen City in December 1853, non-Catholic German immigrants protested. A two-hundred-person mob of freethinkers decried the nuncio's presence in the city, burned him in effigy, and besieged Bishop John Purcell's residence.[35] The Cincinnati Riot of 1853 led nativists and non-Catholic German leaders alike to imagine an anti-Catholic political coalition forming in the following years. Despite the uprising, nearly all Catholic parishioners immediately submitted to the nuncio's request, including those in Cincinnati, German and otherwise.[36]

Since a Know-Nothing political landslide such as in Massachusetts was not a possibility in the western border states, where the collapse of the two-party system splintered voters into various factions, nativists there were among the first to belong to a political-fusion organization, which was anti-Catholic, antislavery, yet also inclusive of non-Catholic immigrants. It remained to be seen, however, if all sides could work together. Through the winter of 1854–55, Chase's Republicans tended to disregard the nativists. Chase was wary of the "K-N alliance" on the conviction that "there is nothing before the people but the vital question of freedom versus slavery."[37] For members of the Know-Nothing Party, however, slavery featured as one aspect of a multi-faceted problem. The slavery dilemma could be resolved by first ensuring the purity of elections from foreign influence.

Grand Council president Spooner and Ohio congressman Lewis D. Campbell, both of whom were ardently anti-Catholic and antislavery, presented fusion as the best way forward. Despite mistrust between Know-Nothings, Republicans, and ex-Democrat German American factions, Chase and Spooner reluctantly agreed upon a compromise securing Know-Nothing dominance in the resulting fusion party in exchange for Chase's nomination to the governorship of Ohio in 1855. But Campbell, who had antislavery credentials rivaling Chase that he never hesitated to recount in public, was not convinced. He had gained his seat in Congress as an ardently antislavery Whig in 1848 but converted to the nativist cause along with his brother Edwin Campbell as early as December 1853.[38] Congressman Campbell thought the "idea which they set forth so constantly that Chase is entitled to all the glory of resisting the Nebraska swindle" was "simply ridiculous."[39] For two decades, he claimed, "I have fought the fight for freedom straight through—'in Congress and out of it.'" He intimated to one correspondent, "you will not appreciate the intensity of my feelings on this subject because you do not know the little of what I have suffered in a consistent course on the slavery question."[40] Campbell likewise insisted on making a stand against undue Roman Catholic influence.

Meanwhile, non-Catholic Germans who advocated barring slavery in the West demanded that the People's Party endorse the existing naturalization laws. They were willing to work with Republicans on the slavery issue and Know-Nothings on the Catholic issue, but their request that nativists stop campaigning for a twenty-one-year residency requirement for naturalization never received adequate attention. Both Know-Nothings and Republicans frequently ignored such demands.[41] German freethinkers and Protestants begrudgingly remained allied with the Know-Nothings, like the Republicans did, because they saw no better way to defeat the Democrats. Recognizing this political reality, even the most opinionated Republican journalists kept their antinativist views private. Newspaper editor Medill privately berated the Know-Nothing "knaves and asses" and considered the election of Spooner to the "head of the K N Order a horrible political blunder." He acknowledged to correspondent Oran Follett, however, that the antislavery people "are disposed to avoid a controversy with any of the Republican papers of Ohio concerning No Nothingism."[42] In April 1855 he persisted in advising Follett and other Republican journalists to keep "from doing mischief until the fever of secret societies is past." Medill nicknamed his antislavery nativist allies the "Know Somethings" in items for the *Cleveland Daily Morning Leader.* Some German newspapers followed suit.[43]

Although the western Know-Nothings continued to push for an increased residency requirement for citizenship, they did learn to compromise with German immigrants in other ways. Fusion in Ohio was possible because nativists met immigrants halfway by making their own operations more transparent. Attempts to act in coalition with Republicans and Germans changed the Ohio Know-Nothing Order's character dramatically since its clandestine beginnings in early 1854 and contributed to its distinctness from other orders in the East.

Since Know-Nothings in the Northeast were able to achieve political success in independent rather than fusion parties, they were more inclined to defend their order's exclusivity and secrecy outright. Know-Nothingism in New York was unique from the other northeastern states because it was not former Whigs but ex-Democrats who dominated the party. They elected congressmen on an independent ticket and attempted to rally conservative "silver" Whigs and "soft" Democrats into political alliance with them. Such coalitions did not include immigrants but closely paralleled old party politics.[44] Having achieved success secretly rallying lodges throughout the state, the Know-Nothing Order in New York refused to make their politicking transparent until the major parties opened their primaries to the public. Furthermore, the New York nativists vowed to remain secret until immigrants demonstrated their desire to renounce "all attempts to embody themselves, as Catholics, to influence public policy; proclaim undivided allegiance to the civil power, and exemplify it by practice, in conformity with the theory of our Government and its laws." When in 1855 both hardline Whigs and Democrats in the New York legislature criticized the "Anti-Republicanism of Know-Nothings or American Jesuits," the New York order doubled down on the necessity of secrecy in its *Principles and Objects of the American Party.*[45]

Yet a desire for transparency prevailed in the Know-Nothing orders of the West by 1855.[46] As early as the fall of 1854, proponents of transparency within the Ohio order began pressing for internal reform. Eager to defend the society from a barrage of accusations from allies in the People's Party, President Spooner urged Know-Nothings at Ohio's state convention in 1855 to make the "proceedings, principles, intentions, objects, &c, &c" available to the public and to "no longer envelop our movements in hidden mystery."[47] He also called for "a clear and full expression of the views of Ohio upon all the national questions that have agitated the public mind," including immigration and slavery.[48]

As the alliance between Know-Nothings, Republicans, and German Protestants always stood on shaky ground, Ohio nativist leaders also campaigned
for reforms of the Know-Nothing State Council's constitution to censor the
movement's potentially volatile bigotry. Within Know-Nothing councils in
Ohio that year, delegates suggested adding additional resolutions of good will
toward immigrants. One brother from Fulton, for example, recommended a
measure to reprimand, suspend, and even expel members who engaged in "ma-
licious or wanton attacks upon any foreigner."[49] This resolution was tabled until
the following session. Since outbreaks of anti-immigrant violence threatened
to undermine the nativists' cause, Spooner reined in the subordinate councilmen to prevent further unnecessary hostility. He ordered Know-Nothings to
strictly follow the protocols of the order's constitution and to uphold an "enlarged view" of the American Party. In a memo from July 1855, which was likely
disseminated to every subordinate council in the state in response to the recent riots, President Spooner chided those members who "have fallen into the
popular error that 'Americanism' consists in mere antagonism to the Foreign
and Catholic tendencies of a portion of our population." He asserted that his
order was precisely "the embodiment of Liberty in its widest and most enlarged
sense, developed by a free education, directed by the teachings of Christianity,
with the world for its area, and the whole human family for its recipients." The
latter phrase "whole family" was significant, for Spooner opposed slavery. He
encouraged the members of the order to set aside their differences and their
prejudices against European immigrants and African slaves and rallied Know-
Nothings to advance the cause of true liberty by sustaining the Union: "let us
not compromise the high trust confided to us by attempting to circumscribe its
limits or set bounds for its action, but give it the illimitable scope indicated by
its divine origin, knowing or acknowledging no sectionalism, North or South,
East or West."[50] Know-Nothing leaders in the West thus sought to persuade
the public that their order was more antipapist than anti-immigrant and that
the recent violence against Germans was not representative of its principles as
a whole. Nativist pamphleteers in the region carefully depicted undue political
Romanism, not one's national origins of birth, as the primary danger to the
purity of American citizenship and democracy. The Know-Nothing newspaper
Cincinnati Times reminded voters on August 3, 1854, "It should never be lost
sight of that Romanism is the head and front and that Native Americanism is
secondary and contingent."[51]

Moreover, the inclusion of Germans in the People's Party compelled a revi-
sion of the requirements for membership. Medill, who became the editor of the

Chicago Tribune in 1855, noted in a private letter the precarious nature of the fusion fold in its infancy, where Know-Nothings initially did not necessarily recognize German Protestant immigrants: "the K. N.'s refuse to admit Protestants naturalized in the Councils and prescribe them the same as Catholics." Initially, the Ohio State Council had adopted a resolution on August 1, 1854: "That hereafter any person born within the jurisdiction of the United States, of Protestant parents, and raised and educated under Protestant influence, and who has not a Catholic wife, shall be eligible to membership in this Order."[52] Within a year's time, however, the state council dropped the requirement of nativity, while keeping the religious clause, to admit anti-Catholic German immigrants.[53] In June 1855 President Spooner advised Know-Nothing state delegates "to admit to membership and endow fully upon those of Foreign birth, of Protestant parentage—who were brought to this country in early age, or have resided here twenty-one years—all privileges and immunities that we claim of right should be vested in Americans."[54] During the state convention of the Grand Council of Ohio, which met in Cleveland precisely at the same time as the national convention in June 1855, the grand council resolved to "extend the hand of welcome to all such of the people of the Old World."[55]

The slaveholding states of Kentucky and Missouri immediately followed the Grand Council of Ohio's lead and in some ways carried Spooner's mandate for an "enlarged view" to its logical extent. Know-Nothings in those states as well as Illinois formed their own state councils at the end of 1854. Unlike Ohio's nativists, the recently formed Grand Councils of Kentucky and Missouri were content to let the Kansas-Nebraska Act stand, but they did support Ohio's openness to immigrants. Missouri's Know-Nothings passed a series of revealing resolutions in their respective state councils before the national convention meeting in Philadelphia. In its April 1855 session, the Know-Nothing Grand Council of St. Louis, now independent of the Grand Council of Cincinnati, actually opened membership to both immigrants and native-born Catholics.

The grand council compelled Missouri nativists to "welcome into the ranks of our party" every U.S. citizen who was born on American soil, pro-Union, and willing to pledge a higher allegiance to the U.S. Constitution than any and all foreign powers, whether political or ecclesiastical.[56] Technically, second-generation immigrants and even Catholic Americans could meet these qualifications. Northeastern Know-Nothings were stunned when they learned that some French Catholics in Missouri were taking the pledge.[57]

As opponents across the nation raised criticisms against the order's dark-lantern politics, exclusivity, rowdiness, and seeming religious bigotry, Know-Nothings in the West offered among the most salient responses. In the national Know-Nothing convention meeting in Philadelphia in June 1855, leaders in the West pressed for a national platform based on the principles of fusion, transparency, and a greater degree of religious tolerance.

The Impending Crisis and the Limits of Political Nativism

In June 1855 the entire country turned its attention to the National American Party Convention in Philadelphia. The Know-Nothings had turned out extraordinarily well in the fall and spring elections of 1854 and 1855, both at the local and national levels. Early indications suggested that leaders in the West had the ear of most national delegates. The agenda acknowledged westerners' desire to make the Know-Nothing Order more transparent and to reword resolutions so as not to completely alienate potential immigrant allies. Emboldened by the semitransparency in western orders, the National Council's majority hoped to make the order's creeds and activities apparent to the public, while keeping the passwords and grips secret.

The newly endowed national and public version of the Know-Nothing Party, rechristened the National American Party by 1855, had its fair number of internal critics. One detractor of the Cincinnati order's push for transparency suggested that the Know-Nothings there had success in early 1855 precisely because they had excited "prejudices and operated by surprise." This man, an original Know-Nothing, predicted that the very attempt at forming a national party like the Whigs or Democrats would bring about their order's downfall. The existence of a political platform seemed to contradict the very ethos of the grassroots nativist movement, which was initially "above all creed making and organization, . . . no nothing but that the *public safety* required a [group] of Patriots to act instead of talking, and to do at the moment and place of danger." Many Know-Nothing members chafed under the National Council's official approval of Spooner's call for transparency in June 1855.[58]

The position of the National Council in 1855 and 1856 on religion and slavery became the crux of the American Party movement. As one Kentuckian outside Louisville wrote in his diary, "The questions of the day are Catholicism and slavery."[59] The agenda eventually broached the matters of slavery, transparency, and the inclusion of immigrants to the order, but President E. B. Bartlett, a Kentucky statesman, permitted delegates to spend the entire first day debating a singular item: the admittance of the Louisiana delegation. The convention hesitated to recognize that state's delegates because one of its six members,

Charles Gayarré, was a known Catholic.[60] Gayarré, a Franco-American leader of the Know-Nothing Order in Louisiana, presented the council with a unique sectional problem.

Know-Nothings in the West and South had demonstrated their resolve to include immigrants and Catholics, but the northern-led "national" council the previous year in New York had elected to retain their denunciation of the Catholic religion. A heated debate over the "anti-Catholic" policy of the Know-Nothing Order and the platform's religiously prescriptive eighth article occupied the 1855 convention. The article under question resolved, "Resistance to the aggressive policy and corrupting tendencies of the Roman Catholic Church in our country by the advancement to all political stations . . . of those only who do not hold civil allegiance, directly or indirectly, to any foreign power, whether civil or ecclesiastical, and who are Americans by birth, education and training."[61] Bartlett, himself a member of the Know-Nothing Order in Kentucky, sympathized with Gayarré's plight and permitted him to speak.

Gayarré confessed his intention to test the "religious clause" in the platform.[62] He urged the council to remove the specific mention of the "Roman Catholic Church" so as not to exclude immigrants—French, Irish, German, and otherwise—who wished to worship in a Catholic church in America. He reprimanded the National Council for potentially violating the "constitutional right" of patriotic Catholic Americans. After establishing his credentials as a prominent historian and politician in New Orleans—he served as the secretary of state of Louisiana prior to the American Party convention—he sought to prove his loyalty to the nativist cause. He had joined the order alongside several other French Catholics in New Orleans early on. He subscribed to the nativist policy that immigrants required more thorough Americanization before naturalization but contended that there were Catholic American "nativists" who embraced religious liberty and rejected the "Ultramontanist" doctrine of the authority of the pope in Rome over "temporal" matters in other countries. In a manner consistent with the French Gallican tradition, Gayarré explained that his fellow native-born Catholic Louisianans "acknowledge no other power in the head of our church than one which is purely spiritual." He represented Catholic Americans who believed that the pope was entitled to dictate only spiritual matters of faith and morals, not temporal matters like politics.

The Louisiana delegate proposed to substitute the phrase "Roman Catholic" in the eighth section of the platform with new language: "Resistance to . . . *all who, whatever be their religious creed, cannot declare under oath that they acknowledge in these United States of America no other political power than that which is derived from the Federal Constitution.*" He closed with a threat that the Louisiana order might secede from the party unless the National Council expunged the offensive anti-Catholic phrasing. Although Gayarré rallied several sympathizers, particularly from the western states of Illinois, Kentucky, Missouri, and Ohio, the convention opted to keep the anti-Catholic clause and expel him. This appeased delegates from northeastern states. As a compromise, the council officially received Louisiana's five other Protestant delegates several days later.[63]

Yet Gayarré's comments lingered over the following weeks. The Louisianan had presented a poignant challenge to the prospect of national unity based on anti-Catholicism. Delegates had debated his admission because they sensed the importance of presenting a uniform stance in public. After all, Gayarré reminded them in his speech on the convention's opening day, the Know-Nothings might just need a portion of the several million votes of naturalized immigrants if they wanted their candidate to win the 1856 presidential election. The very idea of a "Catholic nativist" jarred many delegates, however, especially men from the Northeast, where "Irish" and "Catholic" went hand in hand. But what of Anglo, French, and German Catholics in other parts of the country? The Gayarré affair raised questions about what, exactly, the nativists opposed. For what reasons should they exclude naturalized Protestant immigrants or Catholic nativists? It was not a question of whether the Know-Nothings were anti–Roman Catholic power in America, but rather *which* type of anti-Catholicism the National American Party ought to endorse, and how that choice informed their interpretation of the Constitution.

Blaming Catholic "outsiders" also revealed the nativist movement's lack of cohesion on the slavery issue. Know-Nothings in the North believed Catholic immigrants contributed to the slavery controversy because they tended to vote for proslavery Democrats. The causes of anti-Catholicism and antislavery thus became linked. Know-Nothings in the South, however, tended to vote for proslavery candidates; that Catholics voted proslavery was not a matter of particular concern.[64] On July 4, 1855, in Cincinnati, Know-Nothing Charles B. Boynton had asserted that Protestantism and the U.S. Constitution were "designed for the overthrow of slavery," while the Catholic Church shared much in common with the system of chattel slavery. The American republic faced two imminent dangers, in Boynton's estimation: "Papacy and Slavery."[65] President Spooner of the Ohio Grand Council likewise declared in an official address at the beginning of 1856 that "Americanism and Freedom are synonymous terms. Foreignism and Slavery are equally so, and the one is antipodes of the other."[66]

On the other hand, Know-Nothings from slaveholding states worried about Catholics and immigrants voting for antislavery candidates. Samuel Chapman, a Know-Nothing from Tennessee, paired abolitionism and Catholicism. "Romanism is to Protestants what the [Republican Party] would be to slaveholders," Chapman proclaimed. The Republicans "pledge themselves to exterminate slaveholders by fire, the sword, and all other means of death—hold councils, and publish to the world that they will not respect even an oath made to men should they become slaveholders, and Romanists crown the Pope a sovereign, bind themselves in allegiance to him . . . and proclaim to all that they will not respect even an oath made to men, should they become heretics or Protestants."[67] Commentators in the South and West also expressed alarm over the "atheistic" freethinking Germans who openly denounced the institution of slavery. Many nativists in the West claimed that foreign-born voters agitated the slavery issue by carrying the major parties to both extremes. German freethinkers persistently campaigned for "socialist abolitionism," St. Louis nativist William Carr Lane claimed. Irish immigrants were a completely different problem. Irish Catholics supported the southern-led Democratic Party in order to uphold "papist slavery," according to Lane.[68] In regards to the slavery issue, anti-Catholic and anti-immigrant sentiment cut both ways.

On June 9 another controversial item on the agenda reached the floor of the Know-Nothing convention, article twelve. Because the slavery issue proved especially divisive, many delegates of the National Council proposed "nonintervention." This disturbed the antislavery Know-Nothings cooperating in fusion parties in the states of Illinois and Ohio, but it satisfied Bentonian Know-Nothings in the slaveholding states of Kentucky and Missouri. The same North-South sectional conflicts plaguing the other national parties also threatened the existence of the American Party.

Nonintervention meant that the Kansas-Nebraska Act would remain unchallenged and that voters in each western territory would decide whether their state entered as free or slaveholding. Antislavery Know-Nothings from several states staged a stormy protest. This sizeable minority demanded that the National Council resolve to uphold the Missouri Compromise of 1820 and thus remove the possibility of the institution of slavery extending to Kansas, Nebraska, or any other western territory. Delegates who favored the minority report included Thomas H. Ford, a party leader in Ohio, who warned the convention that if delegates refused to restore the Missouri Compromise, then more-radical antislavery advocates in the North, namely the upcoming Republicans, might overtake northern politics and destroy the American Party's nationalizing mission. But the delegations from the South, including the border states of Kentucky and Missouri, insisted on leaving the slavery issue alone. With the help of eleven sympathetic northern delegates (from New Jersey, New York, and Pennsylvania), the National Council passed the majority report 78 to 63. In other words, they voted to avoid the issue. The rest of the northern delegates voted against the twelfth article. Those from Illinois and Ohio voted with the northeastern representatives to oppose slavery's extension to the West.[69] So, a controversy about the definition of unwanted religion seemed to divide Know-Nothings on an East-West axis, while a controversy about the extension of slavery severed delegates along a North-South line.

Delegates from every free state except Pennsylvania, New Jersey, and New York refused to attend the next day's assembly. Instead, northern delegates reconvened nearby and passed new antislavery resolutions, styling themselves the "North American Party" and labeling those (the majority of delegates) who refused to join them "South Americans."[70] The remaining delegates to the National Council resolved "to abide by and maintain the existing laws upon the subject of Slavery, as a final and conclusive settlement of that subject in fact and in substance," the idea being that if there was indeed something unconstitutional about the Kansas-Nebraska Act, then it would be within the U.S. Supreme Court's jurisdiction to determine. Delegates from the southern states, including Kentucky and Missouri, considered this a conservative, middling measure that might skirt the slavery controversy. The "South Americans" further stated that Congress did not have the constitutional right to decide the fate of slavery in a territory or newly admitted state nor the power to abolish slavery in the District of Columbia. Conversely, the "North Americans" boycotted the regular convention and insisted that Congress ought to refuse the admission of any slave territory or state that had previously been declared free under the terms of the Missouri Compromise.[71] These delegates from twelve northern states, including Illinois and Ohio, defiantly resolved to support "the unconditional restoration of that time honored compact known as the Missouri Compromise" and, thus, the admission of Kansas and Nebraska as free states.[72]

The National Council continued to recognize the membership of the Know-Nothing orders in the protesting northern states. Know-Nothing councils in the North and Northwest still hoped for reconciliation, but the "North American" boycott of the Philadelphia convention sparked a key moment in their movement. Know-Nothings across the country demonstrated their relevance in politics at the local level, but once the various councils collected into a national party in late 1854, members struggled to balance sectional agendas.

By the election of 1856, most Know-Nothings in Illinois and Ohio joined with Republicans in opposing slavery, while most members in Kentucky and Missouri joined with former Bentonites in new fusion parties to maintain a "neutral" position. The intensity of the politics of slavery made it nearly impossible for these "soft" Democrats in the western border states who opposed slavery's extension to work with an increasingly ardent proextension, southern-led national party. As a result, some of these antislavery Democrats defected to the Know-Nothing Party to retain neutrality on slavery rather than dealing with more militantly proslavery southern Democrats. Agitation over the Kansas-Nebraska Act ultimately became too divisive. One Missouri Know-Nothing congressman, Samuel H. Woodson, observed with regret in a letter to one of his state's renowned Know-Nothing leaders, George R. Smith, "You [might] as well try to oppose an avalanche as the influence of this Kansas excitement."[73]

A Democratic congressman from St. Louis, Francis Preston Blair Jr., knew the Know-Nothings could hardly remain silent on the slavery issue.[74] At first they enjoyed success in the West, Blair remarked, because "of the deep seated dissatisfaction which exists in both parties"; also, in different locations in Chicago, Cincinnati, Louisville, and St. Louis, they were able to take "different sides as it suited the sentiment of the different sections." In St. Louis, he explained, "they were proslavery. In Massachusetts and elsewhere in the north they were anti-slavery." Blair saw in early 1855 that the Know-Nothings would not be able to make a compromise on slavery that would satisfy all sides so that any presidential nominee they might put forth would simply "fall between the stools."[75] He suggested that only the Bentonites could pacify westerners on both sides of the slavery issue and forge a Democratic coalition in the western border states. Unfortunately, Thomas Hart Benton, their namesake who had led antislavery Democrats in the West since Missouri became a state in 1820, died in 1858.[76]

The Legacy of Know-Nothingism

During the height of Know-Nothing success, members of the American Party scaled back their generalizing claims about Catholicism and Catholics and drew finer distinctions about which kind of Catholicism they opposed. "If we could believe that religious proscription, in any sense, shape, or form, is the fixed policy of the American party," Reverend Chapman of Tennessee vowed in 1856, "we too would at once cut ourself loose from it." Chapman was himself a "foreigner by birth," and he pledged to fight any Christian sect that attempted to meddle in politics. No Protestant Christian sects required members to pledge "allegiance to the see of Rome" it so happened, nor any other foreign ruler for that matter.[77] By 1855, many Know-Nothings publicly ceded that Catholicism—if it could be stripped bare of any special oaths to the pope and subservience of will to the Catholic hierarchy in America and if it could prove no collusion with the "foreign potentate" on any other matters besides faith—was just as acceptable in the republic as any other personal delusion. What mattered most was that Catholic citizens in America were first and foremost politically loyal to the United States and that they participated in the democratic process on their private, independent convictions alone. It was not religious proscription, Know-Nothings argued, to pass legislation guarding against the interference of a foreign clergy in the democratic political process.

The defenders of political nativism consistently denied charges levied against them that their platform violated the First Amendment of the U.S. Constitution or Article VI, Paragraph 3—"no religious test shall ever be required as a qualification to any office or public trust under the United States"—because some aspects of the Roman Catholic system, they argued, was not properly religious but political and should be treated as such.[78] One Virginia nativist, writing under the pseudonym "Madison," pleaded in 1855 that American nativism had been misunderstood, that it was in fact "as tolerant of the *religious* sentiments of *Catholics* as of *Protestants*." The American Party, he claimed, only declared eternal enmity against one particular branch of the Roman Catholic Church. Nativist opposition to ultramontane Roman Catholicism, argued "Madison," "has nothing to do with the *faith* or *worship* of the members of that division of the church, but relates entirely to certain *political* opinions." Ultramontanists, he alleged, believed in the supremacy of the pope over temporal matters, specifically "that the Pope has the power *to subvert republics, to nullify laws and to absolve both subjects and citizens from their allegiance to any sovereign or Republic which may incur his displeasure.*"[79] Members of the order followed this line. Dr. Lemuel C. Porter in Louisville explained in 1855, "The basis of [the Know-Nothing] organization is opposition to catholics and foreigners politically, not religiously or socially."[80] Chicago Know-Nothing newspaperman William W. Danenhower reminded voters in February 1855 of the semantic difference between "Catholicism" and "Romanism" in Know-Nothing propaganda. While "Catholicism" referred to a religion, "Romanism, we repeat, is not a religion; is entitled to no consideration as such; and is nothing more or less than the boldest—most shameless, and barefaced absolutism that ever cursed humanity."[81] At the same time, the Know-Nothing mayoral candidate in Cincinnati, James "Pap" Taylor, vowed his "OPPOSITION TO POLITICAL ROMANISM" and urged the order in the Queen City to resolve its "Opposition to the Papacy, whether it seeks to unite Church and State, or to sever the Government from the People, its legitimate masters."[82]

Many Know-Nothings considered the Gallican school, which denied the authority of the pope over matters of the state, as an acceptable kind of Catholicism, although it was not necessarily the predominant Catholic interpretation of papal supremacy. Reverend Chapman suggested amending article eight of the Philadelphia platform to exclude anyone who accepted "the plea that the temporal is subject to the spiritual." This meant that Gallican Catholics like Gayarré might join but not Ultramontanist Catholics who upheld the traditional view of papal supremacy. Gallicanism, "Madison" admitted, was only upheld by a few fringe factions in parts of France and Louisiana. Although the Roman Catholic Church tolerated them, most Catholic leaders "stigmatized [Gallicans] as the '*half-way house to Protestantism.*'" Catholic Anglo-and Franco-Americans like the Carrolls and Gayarrés landed under the benign category of "Catholic," while German and Irish immigrants were more often labeled as "papist," "Romanist," or "Ultramontanist."[83]

The difficulty of pinning down which form of Catholicism to legislate against took its toll on the American Party's national aspirations. While Know-Nothings in the Northeast were content with the explicitly anti-Catholic religious clause of the Philadelphia platform, many in the West thought it did too little to dispel the notion that political nativism entailed religious intolerance. While the prospect of Know-Nothing success in the 1856 presidential election still seemed attainable, northeastern party members in 1855 generally remained unmoved by the Louisiana order's plea to remove language directed at Roman Catholicism. One month after the national convention, it was time for the Grand Council of Louisiana to ratify the party's platform. They accepted all of it, with one minor qualification. Although there were some Know-Nothings, called the "blue-books," who wanted to preserve anti-Catholic rituals, on July 4, 1855, the Louisiana order struck through the anti-Catholic wording in article eight and replaced it with a version of Gayarré's proposed phrasing. They justified the edit on the basis "that religious faith is a question between each individual and his God" and that no U.S. citizens ought to face a religious test for any political station.[84]

Grand councils in Illinois, Kentucky, Missouri, and Ohio, like Louisiana, also addressed the criticisms of their political opponents by refining the anti-Catholic character of the National American Party. Illinois proved more divisive than the other western states over the religious issue. Two factions there debated the religious test: the "Sams" wanted to exclude Catholic immigrants from the order, while the "Jonathans" did not.[85] Ultimately, each of these states eventually altered the phrasing of the Philadelphia platform in their state policies and constitutions to rid the order of its bigoted reputation. The Know-Nothings of Illinois, Kentucky, Missouri, and Ohio remained suspicious of the Roman Catholic Church, but they also carried their recommitment to the church-state separation doctrine to its ultimate conclusion. Orders in these states gradually downplayed specifically Protestant religious interests, welcomed "Gallican" Catholic Americans who denied papal temporal authority, and developed a language about God that enveloped Catholics and immigrants of various religious persuasions.

By 1855, the American Party's version of civil religion recognized the "Supreme Being" and the U.S. Constitution as their twin sources of authority. References to the other persons of the Christian doctrine of the divine trinity, Jesus Christ and the Holy Spirit, vanished from the latest nativist literature, as did any suggestion that the American Party affiliated with a particular Christian sect. The American Party in Kentucky even asserted in 1856 that the U.S. Constitution "repudiates all other spiritual sovereignty than that of God." Kentucky Know-Nothings argued that the Constitution dictated all the terms of a citizen's proper role and that there was no higher law in the land or in any other foreign country than the U.S. Constitution—that only God himself trumped the document's authority over men. According to their official published literature, the purpose of their movement was "to liberate American citizens of *all* religions from foreign dominion over their wills or their acts."[86] Such a claim certainly ruled out the meddling of Catholic clergymen in American political affairs. Moreover, this sentiment, carried to its logical conclusion, potentially expelled Protestant Christian authority figures as well.[87]

According to the Missouri Know-Nothings, the Roman Catholic Church presented a particularly imminent threat to civil and religious freedom, but really any particular religious denomination might be targeted for inordinate influence in politics. One popular broadside circulating in St. Louis stated bluntly that Know-Nothings "*will oppose as enemies of Republicanism* any man or set of men, whether *Baptists, Methodists, Presbyterians, Episcopalians, Catholics, or any other denomination* who claim for their church or association by divine right, *authority or control over temporal affairs, and seek to unite Church and State.*"[88] The city's Know-Nothings assured the public that their order cared "not a fig what religious belief men have, or how they carry it out, *provided their religion is confined to religious affairs and does not teach interference in political matters.*"⁸⁹ Here was an official statement that abrogated the American Party from committing to a specific religion of any sort. No mention was made here of a specific church denomination or even Protestant Christianity in general. The sentiment spilled over into St. Louis's grand council. Solomon Smith's revised formulation of article eight appeared in the 1855 state platform of the American Party of Missouri: "religion and politics, in all countries, and under all circumstances, should be kept separate and distinct; that we most unequivocally condemn all and every species of interference, by any religious denomination, sect or church, in the civil relations either of governments or individuals, and that the political actions of every man should be controlled by the dictates of his own judgment."⁹⁰ William B. Napton remarked on Missouri's American Party platform in his diary: "so far as their great idea of hostility to Catholics and foreigners is concerned, they have so pared down what was supposed to have been their creed on these topics as to make it almost entirely unobjectionable."⁹¹

Other councils in surrounding states likewise self-edited in an attempt to avoid directly naming the Catholic Church. For example, the resolution in the *Constitution of the National American Association of Hamilton County* (Ohio) read: "Hostility to ecclesiastical influences upon the affairs of government, and especially to the interference of a foreign church and a foreign clergy; but unlimited freedom of religion disconnected with politics."⁹² Although the Know-Nothing Grand Council of Kentucky, which included renowned party leaders such as E. B. Bartlett, the president of the National Council, and Thomas Hart Clay, son of Henry Clay and the president of the Kentucky State Council, condemned all foreign attachments, the official party document welcomed all immigrants to "worship God according to the dictates of their own consciences" and to enjoy "their constitutional privileges as American citizens." In their official state platform, Kentucky Know-Nothings denounced "any foreign power, civil or ecclesiastical, as supreme over their consciences or their constitutional obligations." All good Christian Americans could agree, they claimed, "to separate church and state."⁹³ Likewise, in *The Origins, Principles, and Purposes of the American Party,* Henry Winter Davis of Maryland asserted "that the State has no right to prescribe laws for religious worship, and that no citizen of any sect has a right to make his religious views or sectarian relationship a ground of political action."⁹⁴

During a nativist rally in Cincinnati in 1856, Know-Nothing spokesman James Brooks further distanced political nativism from charges of religious bigotry: "I care not what may be a man's religion, provided he is faithful to the institutions of this country." He announced, "I make no war on Catholics of any kind—Lutheran Catholics, Catholics of the Church of England, Roman Catholics, Greek Catholics, or any species of Catholics whatsoever."[95] That same year Representative Campbell of Ohio entirely severed his political agenda from Protestant Christianity, proclaiming in a famous speech: "We are charged with making war upon the Catholic religion—a war which is said to spring from prejudice. That is untrue. I certainly have no prejudice (never having been a member of any church)."[96] In this instance, a Know-Nothing congressman from Ohio admitted before an audience of nativists that he did not attend church at all; they cheered him on anyway.

Throughout 1855 and early 1856, the Philadelphia platform retained its explicit reference to the Roman Catholic Church, but Know-Nothings in the South and West insisted on adjusting its controversial religious clause. In 1856 the National American Party Convention returned to the West, this time held in Louisville on the south bank of the Ohio River. Its members rewrote the religious article for the Louisville platform in the same vein as local Know-Nothing platforms in the region: "No person should be selected for political station (whether of native or foreign birth) who recognizes any allegiance or obligation of any description to any foreign prince, potentate, or power, or who refuses to recognize the Federal and State Constitutions (each within its sphere) as paramount to all other laws, as rules of political action."[97] Although the phrasing "allegiance to a foreign prince" remained a thinly veiled allusion to the pope, the Know-Nothings had effectively removed all explicit mention of the Roman Catholic Church.[98]

Know-Nothings in the West systematically replaced "anti-Catholic" rhetoric with the more neutral language of church-state separation. In expanding its criticism to include any domestic or foreign religious organization that sought undue influence in politics, the nativist movement yielded an American civil religion void of explicitly Christian sectarian language.[99] A graduate of Lyman Beecher's Lane Theological Seminary and copastor of the Lebanon Presbyterian Church during the 1850s in Kentucky, Thomas Horace Cleland, noticed the irony that the politics of nativism publicly debased Protestant as well as Catholic forms of Christianity. On the one hand, "the Catholics think they are proscribed by the K.N.," but, on the other, the Know-Nothings fear "allegiance in temporal to the pope." All that people seemed to care about in July 1855, Cleland regretted, was "the bringing of religion into politics, involving the Native American and Catholic question." It was almost as if, he feared, they had forgotten "there is a God or a hereafter."[100]

Conclusion: An American Party Collapses, an American Religion Endures

The polarizing nature of the slavery issue presented serious obstacles to the success of Know-Nothingism. The northern Know-Nothings who had resolved to make the restoration of the Missouri Compromise a part of the "national" platform in June 1855 met separately in Cincinnati that November. They called this Cincinnati meeting a "national" convention, but in reality only three of the twelve states that had participated in the walkout during the summer attended. Fifty-two delegates from Ohio, Illinois, and Indiana convened in the Queen City to reaffirm their stance against the extension of slavery into the West. The other nine northern state councils passed similar resolutions independently. The Cincinnati convention attempted to reconcile with the "South Americans" by affirming the property rights of current slaveholders and asking the president of the National Council, E. B. Bartlett, who happened to live just across the Ohio River in Covington, Kentucky, to attend. But this was a rather backhanded appeal to the National Grand Council, since the Cincinnati nativists proceeded to recommend resolutions opposing the extension of slavery for the next year's national platform. They also blamed the "South Americans" for the "abandonment of American principles and the disorganization of the American Party."[101]

Illinois and Ohio Know-Nothings were the most likely to remerge with the South Americans before the 1856 election. Ohio Know-Nothings hoped to override the twelfth article of the Philadelphia platform since the national convention voted to apportion delegates based on electoral apportionment in 1856. This meant that their state was entitled to twenty-three delegates at the next national convention, a big jump from the seven of the previous year. In preparation for the convention in February 1856, which was set to meet again in Philadelphia, Thomas Ware from Plymouth Council no. 8 in Cincinnati called a special state meeting to elect Ohio's delegates on January 3, 1856. He proposed a series of resolutions for the Ohio order to stand firm against the Kansas-Nebraska Act.[102] Ohio Know-Nothings could not override the national convention's neutral stance on slavery, however, and the hope of reconciliation quickly faded.

By June 1856, only a year after the Know-Nothings had established their official national platform in Philadelphia, two opposing conventions met at the same time: one, composed of neutral-on-slavery Know-Nothings from the southern border states, convened south of the Ohio River in Louisville, where delegates revised a platform retaining a neutral stance on slavery; the other, consisting of antislavery Know-Nothings from the northern border states, convened north of the Ohio River in the free city of Cincinnati, where delegates reaffirmed their opposition to slavery in the West. The members of these competing Know-Nothing conventions across the Ohio River, within one hundred miles of one another, held similar views on religion and immigration, but their inability to resolve the slavery issue demonstrated how divisive the controversy had become. The South American–led National Council refused to recognize Cincinnati's convention and actually expelled the Ohio order from the American Party. President Bartlett called a special meeting of the National Council on February 18, 1856, to secure the election of the neutral-on-slavery Know-Nothing nominee for president, Millard Fillmore, before antislavery members had a chance to protest.[103]

Alarmed by this dispute, many German immigrants in the West further distanced themselves from Know-Nothingism. Infighting among Know-Nothings and ensuing Anglo-German conflicts rendered fusion unsustainable for the American Party in the West. "If the elements of opposition [to the old parties] could only be united—we have now the state!" regretted one St. Louis nativist: "It will be quite hard to get the Irish and Germans to vote for a Know-Nothing." The rise of Know-Nothingism in the West worked in some places to unite Catholic and non-Catholic immigrants, including stridently anti-Catholic atheists such as the German freethinkers, under the broad umbrella of the newly formed Democratic fusion parties in Kentucky and Missouri and the Republican Party in Illinois and Ohio. Initially, Republicans had trouble acquiring German votes. Although German Catholics and freethinkers in Missouri held widely different views, many of them continued to vote Democratic; their vote only split when there were two Democratic candidates. In Ohio many German immigrants refused to join the Republican Party because they recognized nativists in their fold.[104] Nevertheless, the Republicans inherited the antislavery coalition in the West, including many former Know-Nothings, like one nativist from Chicago who explained in an editorial for the *Free West* on March 15, 1855: "I am still a member of the Order, and have held the highest offices in the subordinate lodges. . . . I would sooner see the whole Order, and its principles blown higher than the *seven stars,* than see it perverted to the support of the Slave power."[105]

The decline of the Know-Nothings in 1856 occurred almost as rapidly as its rise to power in 1854. After the National American Party split into antislavery (North American) and "neutral" (South American) factions in June 1855, many northern nativists joined the Republican Party. This support for Republican candidates in 1856 contributed directly to the rise of that party and the victory of Abraham Lincoln in 1860. Southern Know-Nothings held on longer. They continued to dominate elections in New Orleans, for example, until 1858.[106] During the decline of the American Party in 1856, nativists in the southern halves of Illinois and Ohio, and especially in the slaveholding states of Kentucky and Missouri, sought to fuse with groups like the Constitutional Unionists, who won a majority in Kentucky during the 1860 elections, and the Northern Democrats in Missouri. The latter group nominated Senator Douglas, who, after running the gauntlet in Congress as a proponent of compromise, had become disillusioned with the southern-led, proslavery faction of Democrats and joined the independent Northern Democratic Party based in Missouri. Douglas repudiated his own Kansas-Nebraska Act and renounced his former condemnation of Know-Nothingism to attract former members of the order. Missouri, in fact, gave its eight electoral votes to the senator in the fateful election of 1860. His comeback in Missouri reinforced the enduring divide between the antislavery nativists in Illinois and Ohio and the neutral Bentonian nativists in Kentucky and Missouri.

The Civil War interrupted everything. Any progress nativists had made and any hopes of making a political comeback came to a halt in 1861. The nativist movement may have become politically ineffective in the sectional, polarized national politics of the mid-1850s, but its legacy endured. Like both the Democrats and Whigs before them, the Know-Nothings were forced to try to appease German immigrant voters and address provocative constitutional issues. As a result, Know-Nothings from various regions of the United States made deliberate choices about the language in their platforms. Those in the West were particularly keen to remove anti-Catholic language that appeared offensive to a much-desired immigrant voting bloc. The American Party thus represented its criticism of the allegedly political side of Roman Catholicism through its commitment to the separation of church and state. Americans have since invoked church-state separation to protect democracy from unpopular religions, immigrants, and other "outside influences," but those targeted as outsiders during nativist movements have also utilized the American language of liberty.

Epilogue

The Specter of Anti-Catholicism, New Nativism, and the Ascendancy of Religious Freedom

There are not over a hundred people in the United States who hate the Catholic Church. There are millions, however, who hate what they wrongly believe to be the Catholic Church.

—Archbishop Fulton J. Sheen, Preface to *Radio Replies*, 1938

Most people who speak passionately against Shariah do not, in reality, understand it.

—"Understanding Shariah," an ICNA Project, 2012

C ATHOLIC AMERICANS, ONCE DEEMED "foreign" and "dangerous," nevertheless acquired full citizenship status and broad recognition as loyal countrymen in a matter of a few generations.[1] Appropriating the First Amendment afforded them the opportunity to stress their belonging to the republic and uphold their religious beliefs at the same time. At the turn of the twentieth century, other religious groups, including Jews and Mormons, followed the same pathways to cultural citizenship and recognition as members of the American religious establishment. In the wake of World War II, Americans were more likely to include Catholics and Jews in their conceptualization of nation, and politicians touted a new phrase to describe American values, "Judeo-Christian." President Dwight D. Eisenhower perfectly captured this new, expanded attitude toward religion in a 1952 campaign speech, famously declaring, "Our government makes no sense unless it is founded in a deeply felt religious faith—and I don't care what it is." His remark "I don't care what it is" was not meant to connote indifference but rather an acknowledgement that part of America's exceptionality could be found in its embrace of religious freedom and particularly the three great Judeo-Christian faith traditions: Protestantism, Catholicism, and Judaism.[2]

One year into Eisenhower's administration, and during the height of the Communist scare, Congress in 1954 pressed for an addition to the Pledge of

Allegiance to broadcast that Americans, unlike the Soviets, held the moral high ground because they believed in God as well as democracy. Since their aim was not to divide Americans, congressmen did not invoke the King James Bible, which would alienate Catholic Americans, or Jesus Christ, which would exclude Jews. Rather, they voted to include in the national pledge a simple invocation to a divine Supreme Being, "one nation under God." Jews, Muslims, and nearly all Christian denominations, Catholic, Protestant, or Orthodox, believe in an ultimate supernatural being. Only the Communists and atheists, congressmen reasoned at the time, would find the reference offensive.[3]

Soon after, Americans witnessed the presidential campaign of 1960 between Republican Richard Nixon and Democrat John F. Kennedy. This race resulted in the twentieth century's closest popular-vote margin, and the outcome hinged on Kennedy's ability to convince Americans that his Catholic faith would not conflict with his duties as president. Not since Al Smith ran for the presidency in 1928 had a Catholic been a contender for the White House. Many Protestant Christians, of course, still feared that a Catholic president would be suscepti-ble to the influence of the pope in Rome. Indeed, several columnists opposed Kennedy on religious grounds. But Kennedy's voice as a Catholic American held legitimacy with the broader public as long as he convincingly advocated church-state separation.

As the first Catholic to realistically pursue the White House, Kennedy's cam-paign determined to avoid Smith's political mistake of defending his allegiance to the Roman Catholic Church. As early as March 1959, Kennedy broached the subject in an interview for *Look* magazine, stating that "whatever one's religion may be," the office holder ought to prioritize absolutely nothing "over his oath to uphold the Constitution and all its parts." He strongly supported legislation up-holding the First Amendment's principle of the separation of church and state, including measures to prohibit federal aid to parochial schools.[4] Seven weeks before Election Day, at the invitation of three hundred Protestant clergymen attending the Greater Houston Ministerial Association, he addressed the issue of his personal faith. Kennedy assured the gathered Protestant clergymen on September 12, 1960, that "the separation of church and state is absolute." In an attempt to "separate the bigots from the honestly fearful," he publicly vowed that "no Catholic prelate would tell the President (should he be Catholic) how to act and no Protestant minister would tell his parishioners for whom to vote." He further pledged to keep any public office from serving as "an instrument of any religious group."[5] Radio and television broadcasts replayed his remarks across the nation over the remainder of the campaign. Seven weeks later, Kennedy became the first Catholic president of the United States. At the time, many Protestant Americans, especially the emergent Christian fundamentalists, feared that his faith remained a potential threat.[6] On the other hand, some Catholic Americans accused Kennedy of selling out. Regardless, he won the popular and electoral vote.

Kennedy's election to the presidency suggested that even Catholics could serve the country as legitimate political actors, but Kennedy only accomplished the feat through the strictest adherence to the tenets of civil religion.[7] His inaugural address of January 20, 1961, positioned his own era squarely within the civil religious tradition: "the same revolutionary beliefs for which our forbearers fought are still at issue around the globe—the belief that the rights of man come not from the generosity of the state but from the hand of God." Kennedy included powerful references to an "Almighty God," closing with the invocation, "here on Earth God's work must truly be our own." Such rhetoric has been a mainstay in politics, and one can still hear politicians uttering invocations to the Almighty.[8]

Since 1960, there hardly has remained a public space that does not fully integrate Catholic Americans. One hundred and twenty-eight years after the Know-Nothings destroyed the marble stone Pope Pius IX had donated for incorporation in the Washington Monument, the obelisk required renovation. A Catholic priest from Spokane, Washington, jumped at the opportunity to restore Pius IX's gesture. Reverend James E. Grant learned about how nativists had cast the pope's gift into the Potomac River in 1854 and acquired special permission from the National Park Service to commission a replica bearing the engraving on the original pope's stone, *A Roma Americae* ("From Rome to America"). In 1982 the replica Pope's Stone was installed in the Washington Monument, 340 feet up; it remains there today, untarnished.[9] In recent years, nearly 24 percent of Americans have identified as Catholic. They tend to split right down the middle during national elections and, apparently, participate in all political and public spaces.

The Specter of Anti-Catholicism

In 2003 Philip Jenkins and Mark Massa argued that a "new anti-Catholicism" nevertheless existed as this country's "last acceptable prejudice." Jenkins took particular offense at the portrayal of Catholics in the media and suggested that parishioners are more vulnerable to open prejudice than Jews or Muslims. He gave as an example a Boston high school Halloween party in 2001, less than two months after 9/11, in which the administration prohibited students from wearing outfits poking fun at Muslims yet presented the "most comical costume" award to two boys dressed as pregnant nuns accompanied by a third playing the priest who impregnated them.[10] In one collection of essays on the relationship between Catholicism and American culture published a year later, author Andrew Greeley claimed that anti-Catholicism is still so pernicious in today's society that "any Catholic who has walked down the beaches of the upper academy, the higher media, or the New York publishing companies will have been fortunate *not* to have encountered it." *Newsweek* editor Kenneth Woodward compared the experience of Catholics in America to that of Jews, African Americans, and LGBTQ people: "It is common for defenders of the Catholic Church like William Donohue to substitute Jews or blacks or gays for Catholics, and ask those who smear Catholics if they would dare ridicule these other identity groups in the same fashion. In general, I think that is a fair test, and I am astonished to learn that his adversaries find his questions repulsive. Clearly, Catholics are fair game."[11]

Such complaints suffer from a myopic perspective. These attempts by Donohue and others to substitute identity politics for apologetics are designed to insulate Catholicism from legitimate ideological disagreement. Moreover, Catholic studies misleadingly conflate clear instances of anti-Catholic bigotry with otherwise valid expressions of concern about Roman Catholic dogma.[12] Even if the superficial cases described by the expositors of "new anti-Catholicism" belie some lingering anti-Catholic bigotry in the United States, one might argue that the prevalence of Catholic imagery in media and all the poking fun proves the faith has become just as acceptable in the fabric of American religious pluralism as any of the other traditionally accepted religions. Many are hypersensitive about Muslim Americans because they are underrepresented as a group and several Muslim individuals have recently suffered persecutions. Catholic Americans, however, are well represented in society, and blatant instances of persecution lie in the more distant past. The tensions they may now feel as they encounter the American state and American media and the persecution complexes they acquire closely parallel the experiences of other religious Americans within traditionally accepted faith traditions. It is not uncommon for Christians in power to interpret ideological conflict through the lens of a persecution complex. After all, Christianity was founded by a persecuted religious minority whose archetypal leader was executed.[13]

Historically, Catholics have oscillated themselves between two seemingly conflicting desires: either to assert the compatibility of Roman Catholic dogma with American-style democracy or to express their alienation in modern secular society. Consider the case of Stephen Kobasa, a teacher at Kolbe Cathedral High School until 2005, when Bishop William Lori of Bridgeport, Connecticut, fired him for refusing to hang an American flag in the classroom. Kobasa objected thus: "My teaching can never take its legitimacy from any symbol except the Cross of Christ. To elevate any national emblem to that level would be for me to ignore the fundamental call of Jesus to compassion without boundaries." With the backing of Bishop Lori, the school's superintendent nevertheless fired Kobasa for "un-patriotism."[14] Bishop Lori became the archbishop of Baltimore in 2012 and thereafter led the American bishops' campaign for religious freedom and liberty of conscience in the United States. At an address at the University of St. Thomas, William Cavanaugh pointed out that this "state of affairs" is part of an age-old dynamic: "there's a frequent oscillation in the bishop's rhetoric between dire apocalyptic statements about the state of American society on the one hand and patriotic boosterish statements about America on the other."[15] Kobasa's case suggests an invisible line for religious persons in the United States, which Roman Catholic authority figures help enforce. Those like Kobasa who elevate their religion over nation, or vice versa, run the risk of ostracization.

Bishop Lori's campaign to protect Catholic-affiliated institutions from unwanted government policies relies heavily on the religious freedom clause in the First Amendment of the U.S. Constitution. Catholic bishops of America frequently assert that the existence of their religion actually strengthens American freedoms. The Archdiocese of Baltimore and the United States Conference of Catholic Bishops's official website have advertised dozens of patriotic prayers, displaying the Catholic Church of America's full devotion to the United States despite pending disagreements. One can access the widely distributed Litany for Liberty and Prayer for the Protection of Religious Liberty, and even the Patriotic Rosary. Within the Patriotic Rosary, each bead symbolizes a state in the Union. For each "mystery," to be read after every ten beads on the rosary, it invites the faithful to dwell on various quotes from the founders of the United States, including George Washington and John Adams. The fifth mystery features an 1863 quote from Confederate general Robert E. Lee.[16]

Still, many Catholic Americans have questioned the practicality of blending together nationalism and spirituality in such a way. Cavanaugh, for one, has suggested Catholics might be better off taking a more Augustinian approach to the question of national allegiance, one that emphasizes the "homelessness" of Catholicism and describes the temporal church as a group on a special pilgrimage to its heavenly home. In other words, Catholics might expect to never feel perfectly comfortable, or "at home," anywhere in the world. Particular nation-states, Cavanaugh pondered, could find ways to fit into the universal Catholic Church, not the other way around.[17] That remains to be seen. It appears for the time being that Catholic Americans have the same range of responses available as other Christian denominations.

New Nativism and Anti-Islamicism

Scholars have noticed parallels between anti-Catholicism in the nineteenth century and anti-Islamicism during the first two decades of the twenty-first century.[18] Muslim immigrants from Asia arrived in greater numbers after 1965, when the Hart-Celler Act overturned the quota system of the Immigration Act of 1924, which favored those of European national origins. Popular fears of the growing influence of Islam in the United States and the world increased dramatically after the terrorist attack on the World Trade Center's twin towers on September 11, 2001. Ensuing conflicts in the Middle East have created millions of Muslim refugees. After a temporary immigration lull during the opening years of war in the Middle East in 2002 and 2003, the United States under the Bush and Obama administrations admitted an unprecedented number of Muslim refugees into the country. In 2017 the Pew Research Center estimated a Muslim American population of 3.45 million. Between 2007, when Muslim Americans numbered 2.35 million, and 2017, the majority of their growth has been due to immigration.[19] The year 2006 marked the first in which the United States admitted, in total, more Muslim than Christian refugees. Tens of thousands from Muslim areas entered the United States each succeeding year. In 2016 the United States admitted the highest number of Muslim refugees to date, 38,901, or about half of all refugees admitted entrance that year. The greatest number of these hailed from countries with predominantly Muslim populations, including Syria (12,587), Iraq (9,880), Somalia (9,020), and Afghanistan (2,737).[20]

The more recent influx of Muslims to the United States, combined with steady media coverage of Islamic-related extremism and war in the Middle East, has induced a new American nativist movement. This culminated in 2016, with Republican Donald Trump's campaign call for a "Muslim Ban" during the presidential election of 2016. In October, a month before the election, a reporter asked Trump if he still intended to ban Muslim immigration in the United States, to which he responded: "Something is going on that's not a positive force. We are going to be looking very much at certain areas of the world. We have to be very careful with radical Islamic terror. We can be politically correct and say it doesn't matter but it does matter."[21] This worry about the more "radical" elements within Islam in other parts of the world motivated another campaign promise regarding refugees from Syria, 95 percent of whom are Muslim: "They're not coming to this country if I'm president. And if Obama has brought some to this country they are leaving, they're going, they're gone."[22] Indeed, once in office, Trump issued Executive Order 13769, titled "Protecting the Nation from Foreign Terrorist Entry into the United States," along with its second manifestation, Executive Order 13780, which have attempted to ban refugees from seven predominantly Muslim countries, including Syria, on the grounds that refugees from these countries are more likely to include covert hostiles.

Media coverage of Islamic-related extremism has amplified foreign and domestic threats in the public imagination beyond what was ever possible in the nineteenth century. In fact, the ratio of the Muslim American population to the whole in 2020 pales in comparison to the ratio of Catholic Americans who resided in the United States during the first nativist movement. Likewise, the number of immigrants admitted each year in comparison to the total population remains smaller in the twenty-first century than the amount of newcomers allowed annually during the nineteenth century.[23] Currently, Muslims represent about 1.1 percent of the total U.S. population. In 2017 Besheer Mohamed, a senior researcher for the Pew Research Center, projected an increase to 8.1 million Muslims by 2050, making up 2.1 percent of the projected total population.[24] By comparison, Catholic Americans in 1860 constituted approximately 10.8 percent of the total free population of the United States, and most of their growth had been due to immigration during a twenty-year period.[25] Even though the ratio of immigrants to the total population in 2020 is relatively smaller, immigrants bearing traditionally unrepresented faith traditions like Islam have arrived from exotic countries relatively quickly and have grabbed enough media attention to provoke an American nativist response.

While the target of bigotry and fear has changed, the American nativist style of discourse has not. Anti-Muslim sentiment often resembles the kind of bigotry and conspiracy nativists directed toward Catholics during the antebellum era. The Council of American-Islam Relations tracks a disturbing number of anti-Muslim hate crimes nationwide, information it makes available on its website.[26] "Islamophobia," insofar as it refers to anti-Muslim bigotry, is real. It is important to distinguish, however, between the latest bout of anti-Islamic xenophobia and certain ideological disagreements Americans may have with Islamic doctrines.

As with Catholicism, Americans' chief concerns with Islam have been political in nature, and accordingly they have advocated the strengthening of church-state separation. Many Americans reject Islamism, a theory of governance within Islam that holds that the Qur'an and Hadith should be the dominant sources of both religious and civil law, as fundamentally opposed to American principles. In this sense, the more refined versions of anti-Islamicism witnessed in modern America mirror the anti-Catholicism of the 1850s. Most U.S. critics of Islam target "political Islam," or Islam as an undue political force. Such has been the case in more recent efforts to ban the construction of mosques and to pass state legislation against Shari'a law.

Notice the ideological content of the 9/11 Families for a Safe and Strong America's official 2010 statement against the construction of an Islamic cultural center in lower Manhattan. They targeted as the source of their opposition the belief system of Islam and particularly the imam slated to manage the mosque: "Imam Rauf embraces Shariah, a sociopolitical system of jurisprudence based upon the Koran which supersedes manmade law and which rejects the Constitutional doctrine of the separation of church and state." Replace "Imam" with "priest," "Shariah" with "Roman Catholic dogma," and "Qur'an" with "pope" in this sentence, and the parallels between anti-Catholicism and anti-Islamicism become obvious. The statement also points out the supposed incompatibility between American values enshrined in the U.S. Constitution and Islamism: "Islamic countries that embrace Shariah and political Islam are known for brutal policies that discriminate against women, gays, and religious minorities. Shariah law is entirely incompatible with the Equal Protection clause of the 14th Amendment and would violate 1st Amendment protections of speech, assembly and the free exercise of religion."[27] Again, replace "Islamic countries" with "Catholic countries," "Shariah law" with "Catholic dogma," and "political Islam" with "political Romanism," and there is hardly any difference in the charges currently being levied against Islam today versus Roman Catholicism in the past.

These anti-Islamic arguments reveal stunning similarities with those of anti-Catholic Know-Nothings. One can hear or read about a Muslim conspiracy to infiltrate American government and society and enact Shari'a law, which some interpret as a harsh penal code akin to the Inquisition. It is not uncommon to hear the claim that Muslims hold allegiance to the Qur'an, certain religious leaders, or to their predominantly Muslim countries of origin over the U.S. Constitution. Another concern is that those raised in theocratic regimes are not equipped to understand American democracy and bear the responsibilities of U.S. citizenship. Many worry about the compatibility of Islam with core American values related to democracy, individual rights, women's rights, and religious freedom. At root there appears to be a growing concern that American homes will look dramatically different without immediate immigration reform.

Accordingly, legislatures in all but sixteen states have seriously considered passing a ban on Shari'a law. By 2014, seven states—Alabama, Arizona, Kansas, Louisiana, North Carolina, South Dakota, and Tennessee—had actually passed legislation that either explicitly banned Shari'a law by name or prohibited, in a thinly veiled reference to it, "foreign, international, or religious law."[28] Notice the justification issued by Tennessee representative Rick Womick, who claims to have studied the Qur'an: "He declared that Shari'a, the Islamic code that guides Muslim beliefs and actions, is not just an expression of faith but a political and legal system that seeks world domination." Womick explained in a speech that Shari'a "is not what I call 'Do unto others what you'd have them do unto you.'"[29]

It is yet unclear whether such bans are constitutional. In 2010, voters in Oklahoma approved a statewide ban on Shari'a law, which prohibited the state's courts from considering all foreign or religious laws as well, but in a challenge organized by the Council on American-Islamic Relations, a federal judge ruled Oklahoma's ban unconstitutional on the grounds that it could potentially violate the rights of Muslim Americans in the state.[30] The Tenth Circuit Court of Appeals upheld the unconstitutionality of the ban on January 10, 2012.[31]

The claims of the anti-Islamists might be misguided, but the act of raising these ideas does not necessarily disqualify one from the conversation. Actually, the discussion is essential to the democratic process. It seems disingenuous at this stage to conflate all Americans who worry about foreign-born terrorism and the potential for immigrants to disrupt democracy with actual anti-Muslim bigots or to crudely label those who raise ideological concerns "Islamophobes" in the same way it seems wrong for Catholics to accuse their ideological opponents of base prejudice. The historical record has shown, however, that such claims about a religion's incompatibility with American democracy are highly unlikely to pass muster for long. The more Americans become acquainted with Muslims over time, the more likely they will be to see Islamic-related extremism as aberrant and not representative of the religion as a whole. And each time Muslim Americans encounter anti-Islamists, they become even more invested in securing their rights under the First Amendment. Not only have most Americans reliably presented their disagreement with Islam as a political one—as the nativists first started doing during the antebellum era—but Muslim Americans themselves have formed their counterarguments precisely along the same lines as Catholic German and Irish Americans did.

The parallels between the response of Catholics and Muslims point to the profound historical and national significance of religious freedom in the United States. Muslim Americans have challenged these bans as an assault on their constitutional right to free worship. A popular Islamic organization recently explained, "these anti-Shariah bills are far from securing Americans from an impending threat and actually infringe upon the rights of the American Muslim community." Actually, Shari'a "demands that Muslims follow the law of the land," the author goes on to explain, citing Surah 5:1 and Surah 9:4 in the Qur'an. "This command is binding so long as they are not forced to commit an irreligious act or prevented from fulfilling their religious duties. Thankfully, this is not the case in the United States because the Constitution protects freedom of religion." In other words, the First Amendment makes it possible for Muslims who wish to uphold Shari'a to exist as U.S. citizens and exercise their right to freedom of worship. The document goes on to point out the potential for harmony between Islam and the Judeo-Christian faith tradition in the United States, as Muslims follow many of the same religious practices of Christians and Jews. Much of the available literature addressing the particular claims of anti-Islamists follows a similar line of response.[32]

The Ascendancy of American Religious Freedom

Precisely because the First Amendment constitutes a vital component of American democracy and has given rise to a vibrant history of civil religion in the United States, a few present-day observations seem warranted. It is not likely the United States will follow the direction of France, for example, which is home to five million Muslims, the largest such population in Europe. The founding documents of both countries establish separation of church and state and protections for religious persons. But the French principle of Laïcité in Article 1 has embedded the strong sentiment that the church-state doctrine protects the state *from* religion, whereas the American system has yielded a greater historical emphasis on the separation of church and state as a fundamental protection *of* religion. Muslims have accordingly found it much more difficult to express their religious beliefs in France than in the United States. In 2004 France passed Europe's first national ban on the burqa in all public spaces as well as a law prohibiting teachers and students in state-run schools from wearing religious paraphernalia like head-coverings and crosses. In 2011 Prime Minister Nicolas Sarkozy's administration doubled down on this policy with a ban on full-face veils.[33] American government and law, however, have reliably upheld the right of all religious persons to express their beliefs in public spaces. Americans highly value this principle, though sometimes it is a bitter pill to swallow.

A native-born Protestant American from the 1830s would find an American political commencement presided over by Catholic priests, female clerics, Jewish rabbis, and a Mormon choir absurd and grotesque. But this is precisely what Americans witnessed during the 2017 inauguration of the president. This is the new norm. The last several presidential inaugurations have included a cast of female clerical figures, Catholic priests, and rabbis, all of whom invoke Almighty God in public prayers. The Mormon Tabernacle Choir has sung blessings upon the United States. Soon, Americans will likely witness an imam invoke "God" at a presidential inauguration ceremony. We can anticipate more politicians who regularly include Islam as part of the ensemble of American religions. "Abrahamic tradition" or "Biblical-Qur'anic" might replace Judeo-Christian in the characterization of national values. American political culture will absorb Islam and Muslims into the fabric of the republic. It is already happening.

American nativism has compelled newcomers, repeatedly, to seek solace under the religious freedom clause of the U.S. Constitution. Unless American democracy fails catastrophically, history suggests we can reasonably assume that Islam, like Catholicism, will soon receive broad recognition in America's political and public spaces. Catholics, Jews, Mormons, Muslims, and other minority groups have expanded the horizons of religious tolerance, and all continue to demonstrate a vested interest in strengthening church-state separation in the United States of America.

Introduction

1. See John Higham, *Strangers in the Land: Patterns of American Nativism, 1860–1925* (New Brunswick, NJ: Rutgers University Press, 1955).

2. See Jan Willem Duyvendak, *The Politics of Home: Belonging and Nostalgia in Western Europe and the United States* (New York: Palgrave McMillan, 2011).

3. See David H. Bennett, *The Party of Fear: From Nativist Movements to the New Right in American History* (Chapel Hill: University of North Carolina Press, 1988).

4. Joseph C. G. Kennedy, ed., *Population of the United States in 1860; Compiled from the Original Returns of the Eighth Census* (Washington, DC: Government Printing Office, 1864); and Campbell Gibson and Kay Jung, "Historical Census Statistics on the Foreign-Born Population of the United States: 1850 to 2000," U.S. Census Bureau, Population Division, Working Paper 81 (Washington, DC: U.S. Census Bureau, February 2006): 1–119. For an example of a popular contemporary source that drew on official statistics from the U.S. Census Bureau to fairly accurately estimate the number of German and Irish immigrants between 1820 and 1855, see William J. Bromwell, *History of immigration to the United States, exhibiting the number, sex, age, occupation, and country of birth, of passengers arriving . . . by sea from foreign countries, from September 30, 1819 to December 31, 1855; compiled entirely from official data: with an introductory review of the progress and extent of immigration to the United States prior to 1819, and an appendix, containing the naturalization and passenger laws of the United States* (New York: Redfield, 1856), General Collection, CMC.

5. James P. Shenton and Kevin Kenny, "Ethnicity and Immigration," in *The New American History,* ed. Eric Foner (Philadelphia: Temple University Press, 1997), 353–73.

6. National American Party, Philadelphia Platform, June 5, 1855, in American Party, *Facts for the People! Read before You Vote!! Americans Should Govern America!!* (Published by the Executive Committee of the American Party of Tennessee, 1856), box 731, folder 2, OHS.

7. See Peter Schrag, *Not Fit for Our Society: Immigration and Nativism in America* (Berkeley: University of California Press, 2010); Higham, *Strangers in the Land*; and Bennett, *Party of Fear.*

8. Ray Allen Billington, *The Protestant Crusade, 1800–1860: A Study of the Origins of American Nativism* (1938; repr., Chicago: Quadrangle Books, 1964), 324. Dissertations

on antebellum nativism from Catholic University during Richard J. Purcell's professorship include Mary St. Patrick McConville, "Political Nativism in the State of Maryland, 1830–1860" (PhD diss., Catholic University, 1928); Sister M. Evangeline Thomas, "Nativism in the Old Northwest, 1850–1860" (PhD diss., Catholic University, 1936); C. J. Noonan, "Nativism in Connecticut" (PhD diss., Catholic University, 1938); and A. G. McGann, "Nativism in Kentucky in 1860" (PhD diss., Catholic University, 1944).

9. See Richard Hofstadter, *The Paranoid Style in American Politics and Other Essays* (New York: Alfred A. Knopf, 1952); Hofstadter, *Anti-Intellectualism in American Life* (New York: Alfred A. Knopf, 1962); Seymour Martin Lipset and Earl Raab, *The Politics of Unreason: Right Wing Extremism in America* (New York: Harper and Row, 1970); and Carleton Beals, *Brass-Knuckle Crusade: The Great Know-Nothing Conspiracy, 1820–1860* (New York: Hastings House, 1960).

10. Higham, *Strangers in the Land,* 4–11.

11. Jason McDonald, *American Ethnic History: Themes and Perspectives* (New Brunswick, NJ: Rutgers University Press, 2007), 72.

12. For more on the development of American nationality during the antebellum era, see Dale T. Knobel, *Paddy and the Republic: Ethnicity and Nationality in Antebellum America* (Middletown, CT: Wesleyan University Press, 1986); Knobel, *"America for the Americans": The Nativist Movement in the United States* (New York: Twayne, 1996); Matthew Frye Jacobson, *Whiteness of a Different Color: European Immigrants and the Alchemy of Race* (Cambridge, MA: Harvard University Press, 1998); Noel Ignatiev, *How the Irish Became White* (New York: Routledge, 1995); and Peter Kolchin, "Whiteness Studies: The New History of Race in America," *Journal of American History* 89, no. 1 (June 2002); Mae M. Ngai, *Impossible Subjects: Illegal Aliens and the Making of Modern America* (Princeton, NJ: Princeton University Press, 2004); and Schrag, *Not Fit for Our Society.*

13. Tyler Anbinder, *Nativism and Slavery: The Northern Know-Nothings and the Politics of the 1850s* (New York: Oxford University Press, 1992). For more scholarship on nativism and antebellum politics, see Ira Leonard and Robert Parmet, *American Nativism, 1830–1860* (New York: Van Nostrand Reinhold, 1971); Michael F. Holt, "The Politics of Impatience: The Origins of Know-Nothingism," *Journal of American History* 60, no. 2 (Sept. 1973): 309–31; Holt, *Forging a Majority: The Formation of the Republican Party in Pittsburgh, 1848–1860* (New Haven, CT: Yale University Press, 1969); David Morris Potter, *The Impending Crisis, 1848–1861* (New York: Harper & Row, 1976); Stephen E. Maizlish, *The Triumph of Sectionalism: The Transformation of Ohio Politics, 1844–1856* (Kent, OH: Kent State University Press, 1983); Stephen E. Maizlish and John J. Kushma, eds., *Essays on American Antebellum Politics* (College Station: Texas A&M University Press, 1982); William E. Gienapp, *The Origins of the Republican Party, 1852–1856* (New York: Oxford University Press, 1987); and John R. Mulkern, *The Know-Nothing Party in Massachusetts: The Rise and Fall of a People's Movement* (Boston: Northeastern University Press, 1990).

14. Know-Nothing riots also erupted in Baltimore in 1856; Washington, DC, in 1857;

and New Orleans in 1858. See Paul A. Gilje, *Rioting in America* (Indianapolis: Indiana University Press, 1996).

15. See Stephen Aron, *Frontiers, Borderlands, Wests,* American History Now, with a forward by Eric Foner and Lisa McGirr (Washinton D.C.: American Historical Association, 2012.

16. The tremendous growth of anti-Catholic political nativism in the slave-holding states of Kentucky and Missouri complicates Andrew H. Stern's depiction of Catholic-Protestant relations in the South as congenial in *Southern Crucifix, Southern Cross: Catholic-Protestant Relations in the Old South* (Tuscaloosa: University of Alabama Press, 2012). See also W. Darrell Overdyke, *The Know-Nothing Party in the South* (Baton Rouge: Louisiana State University Press, 1950).

17. See Knobel, *"America for the Americans."*

18. See Jon Gjerde, *The Minds of the West: Ethnocultural Evolution in the Rural Middle West, 1830–1917* (Chapel Hill: University of North Carolina Press, 1997).

19. Kennedy, *Population of the United States in 1860.*

20. See Steven Green, *The Bible, the School, and the Constitution: The Clash That Shaped Modern Church-State Doctrine* (New York: Oxford University Press, 2013); and Rush Welter, *Popular Education and Democratic Thought in America* (New York: Columbia University Press, 1962). For more on the relationship between Sabbatarianism, temperance, and nativism, see Joseph R. Gusfield, *Symbolic Crusade: Status Politics and the American Temperance Movement* (Urbana: University of Illinois Press, 1963); Robert H. Abzug, *Cosmos Crumbling: American Reform and the Religious Imagination* (New York: Oxford University Press, 1994); and Alexis McCrossen, *Holy Day, Holiday: The American Sunday* (Ithaca, NY: Cornell University Press, 2000).

21. For more on the Christian American "myth," see Allison O'Mahen Malcolm, "Anti-Catholicism and the Rise of Protestant Nationhood in North America, 1830–1871" (PhD diss., University of Illinois–Chicago, 2011); Elizabeth Fenton, *Religious Liberties: Anti-Catholicism and Liberal Democracy in Nineteenth-Century U.S. Literature and Culture* (New York: Oxford University Press, 2011); William M. Shea, *The Lion and the Lamb: Evangelicals and Catholics in America* (New York: Oxford University Press, 2004); John T. McGreevy, *Catholicism and American Freedom: A History* (New York: W. W. Norton, 2003); Francis D. Cogliano, *No King, No Popery: Anti-Catholicism in Revolutionary New England* (Westport, CT: Greenwood, 1995); Jenny Franchot, *Roads to Rome: The Antebellum Protestant Encounter with Catholicism* (Berkeley: University of California Press, 1994); Robert N. Bellah, *The Broken Covenant: American Civil Religion in Time of Trial* (Chicago: University of Chicago Press, 1992); and Billington, *Protestant Crusade.*

22. See Bennett, *Party of Fear;* Schrag, *Not Fit for Our Society;* and Franchot, *Roads to Rome.*

23. See Anbinder, *Nativism and Slavery;* Eric Foner, *Free Soil, Free Labor, Free Men: The Ideology of the Republican Party before the Civil War* (New York: Oxford University, 1970); Potter, *Impending Crisis;* Maizlish, *Triumph of Sectionalism;* and Maizlish and Kushma, *Essays on American Antebellum Politics.*

24. See Green, *Bible, the School, and the Constitution;* David Sehat, *The Myth of Religious Freedom* (New York: Oxford University Press, 2011); Fenton, *Religious Liberties;* Tracy Fessenden, *Culture and Redemption: Religion, the Secular, and American Literature* (Princeton, NJ: Princeton University Press, 2007); and Philip Hamburger, *Separation of Church and State: A Theologically Liberal, Anti-Catholic, and American Principle* (Chicago: University of Chicago Law School, 2002).

25. See McGreevy, *Catholicism and American Freedom;* Jose Casanova, "Roman and Catholic and American: The Transformation of Catholicism in the United States," *International Journal of Politics, Culture, and Society* 6, no. 1 (Fall 1992): 75–111; Steven Conn, "'Political Romanism': Reevaluating American Anti-Catholicism in the Age of Italian Revolution," *Journal of the Early Republic* 36, no. 3 (Fall 2016): 521–48; and Patrick Carey, "Recent American Catholic Historiography: New Directions in Religious History," in *New Directions in American Religious History,* ed. Harry S. Stout and D. G. Hart (New York: Oxford University Press, 1997), 445–61.

26. See Steven Green, *The Second Disestablishment: Church and State in Nineteenth-Century America* (New York: Oxford University Press, 2010); and James H. Kettner, *The Development of American Citizenship, 1608–1870* (Chapel Hill: University of North Carolina Press, 1978).

27. Luke Ritter, "Immigration, Crime, and the Economic Origins of Political Nativism in the Antebellum West," *Journal of American Ethnic History* 39, no. 2 (February 2020): 62–92; "The King James Bible as Nationalist School Curriculum amid Immigration to the American West," *American Nineteenth Century History* 21, no. 2 (April 2020): 1–39; and "Sunday Regulation and the Formation of German American Identity," *Missouri Historical Review* 107, no. 1 (Oct. 2012): 23–40.

Chapter 1: The Valley of Decision

1. See Gordon S. Wood, *The Radicalism of the American Revolution* (New York: Vintage Books, 1991). Epigraph from Lyman Beecher to Catharine Beecher, Boston, July 8, 1830, in Lyman Beecher, *Autobiography, Correspondence, etc.,* ed. Charles Beecher, 2 vols. (New York: Harper & Brothers, 1865), 2:167.

2. See Pauline Maier, *American Scripture: Making the Declaration of Independence* (Vintage Books, 1998).

3. "Religious Affiliation of the Founding Fathers of the United States of America," Adherents.com, http://www.adherents.com/gov/Founding_Fathers_Religion.html.

4. See Steven K. Green, *The Second Disestablishment: Church and State in Nineteenth-Century America* (New York: Oxford University Press, 2010); Amanda Porterfield, *Conceived in Doubt: Religion and Politics in the New American Nation* (Chicago: University of Chicago Press, 2012); and Charles Taylor, *A Secular Age* (Cambridge, MA: Belknap Press of Harvard University Press, 2007).

5. See David Sehat, *The Myth of American Religious Freedom* (New York: Oxford University Press, 2011).

6. Green, *Second Disestablishment.*

7. John Fletcher Darby, *Personal Recollections of Many Prominent People Whom I Have Known, and of Events—Especially of Those Relating to the History of St. Louis—During the First Half of the Present Century* (St. Louis: G. I. Jones, 1880), 8–12. For a study on colonial St. Louis, see Patricia Cleary, *The World, the Flesh, and the Devil: A History of Colonial St. Louis* (Columbia: University of Missouri Press, 2011). For more on the role of Frenchmen in early nineteenth-century Missouri, see Jay Gitlin, *The Bourgeois Frontier: French Towns, French Traders, and American Expansion* (New Haven, CT: Yale University Press, 2010).

8. Russel L. Gerlach, *Immigrants in the Ozarks: A Study in Ethnic Geography* (Columbia: University of Missouri Press, 1976), 27, 41. For more on America as the new Canaan, see Robert Bellah, *The Broken Covenant: American Civil Religion in Time of Trial* (Chicago: University of Chicago Press, 1992); and Bellah, "Civil Religion in America," *Religion in America* 96, no. 1 (Winter 1967): 1–21. For an analysis of "manifest destiny," see John Craig Hammond, *Slavery, Freedom, and Expansion in the Early American West* (Charlottesville: University of Virginia Press, 2007); and Thomas Hietala, *Manifest Design: Anxious Aggrandizement in Late Jacksonian America* (Ithaca, NY: Cornell University Press, 1985).

9. John A. Gurley, "Emigration from Europe," *Star in the West* (Cincinnati), July 18, 1846, 9, 15, Rare Book, CMC.

10. See Bernard Bailyn, *The Peopling of British North America: An Introduction* (New York: Random House, 1986).

11. James P. Shenton and Kevin Kenny, "Ethnicity and Immigration," in *New American History,* ed. Eric Foner (Philadelphia: Temple University Press, 1997), 353–73.

12. See Henry Nash Smith, *Virgin Land: The American West as Symbol and Myth* (Cambridge, MA: Harvard University Press, 1950); and Leo Marx, *The Machine in the Garden: Technology and the Pastoral Ideal* (New York: Oxford University Press, 2000).

13. For studies analyzing patterns of American settlement, particularly in regards to evangelical organization in urban areas after the Second Great Awakening, see Terry D. Bilhartz, *Urban Religion and the Second Great Awakening: Church and Society in Early National Baltimore* (London: Associated University Presses, 1986); Jon Butler, "Protestant Success in the New American City, 1870–1920: The Anxious Secrets of Rev. Walter Laidlaw, Ph.D.," in *New Directions in American Religious History,* ed. Harry S. Stout and D. G. Hart (New York: Oxford University Press, 1997), 296–333; Robert Wuthnow and Tracy L. Scott, "Protestants and Economic Behavior," ibid., 260–98; and Mark A. Lause, *Young America: Land, Labor, and the Republican Community* (Urbana: University of Illinois Press, 2005).

14. Jon Gjerde, *The Minds of the West: Ethnocultural Evolution in the Rural Middle West, 1830–1917* (Chapel Hill: University of North Carolina Press, 1997), 25.

15. Rev. Charles B. Boynton, Vine St. Congregational Church, Cincinnati, to Natick Congregation Church, Natick, MA, Aug. 11, 1854, Early American Broadside 9075, SLU. For more on the development of Chicago, see William Cronon, *Nature's Metropolis: Chicago and the Great West* (New York: W. W. Norton, 1991).

16. Shenton and Kenny, "Ethnicity and Immigration"; Campbell Gibson and Kay Jung, "Historical Census Statistics on the Foreign-Born Population of the United States: 1850 to 2000," U.S. Census Bureau, Population Division, Working Paper 81 (Washington, DC: Feb. 2006): 1–119. One contemporary source accurately estimated the number of German and Irish immigrants to the United States between 1820 and 1855. See William J. Bromwell, *History of immigration to the United States, exhibiting the number, sex, age, occupation, and country of birth, of passengers arriving . . . by sea from foreign countries, from September 30, 1819 to December 31, 1855; compiled entirely from official data: with an introductory review of the progress and extent of immigration to the United States prior to 1819, and an appendix, containing the naturalization and passenger laws of the United States* (New York: Redfield, 1856), General Collection, CMC.

17. Gottfried Düden, *Report on a Journey to the Western States of North America, and a Stay of Several Years Along the Missouri (During the Years 1824, '25, '26, and 1827),* ed. and trans. James W. Goodrich, George H. Kellner, Elsa Nagel, Adolf E. Schroeder, and W. M. Senner (Columbia: University of Missouri Press, 1980).

18. Carl E. Schneider, *The German Church on the American Frontier: A Study in the Rise of Religion among the Germans of the West Based on the History of the Evangelischer Kirchenverein des Westens (Evangelical Church Society of the West), 1840–1866* (St. Louis: Eden Publishing House, 1939); Charles Van Ravenswaay, *The Arts and Architecture of German Settlements in Missouri: A Survey of Vanishing Culture* (Columbia: University of Missouri Press, 2006), 21–57.

19. Gjerde, *Minds of the West*, 41–42.

20. Darrell W. Overdyke, *The Know-Nothing Party in the South* (Baton Rouge: Louisiana State University Press, 1950), 11.

21. Charles O. Gerrish, St. Louis, to Stephanus, July 30, 1858, St. Louis History Papers, MHS.

22. Seventh Census of St. Louis, 1850, in Audrey Olson, *St. Louis Germans, 1850–1920: The Nature of an Immigrant Community and Its Relation to the Assimilation Process* (New York: Arno, 1980), 14.

23. Calvin Stowe, "On the Education of Emigrants," *Transactions of the Fifth Annual Meeting of the Western Literary Institute and College of Professional Teachers, October, 1835* (Cincinnati: 1836), 68–69, in James W. Fraser, *Pedagogue for God's Kingdom: Lyman Beecher and the Second Great Awakening* (Lanham, MD: University Press of America, 1985), 184–85; "Transactions of the Western Literary Institute, 1836," in *American Writings on Popular Education,* ed. Rush Welter (Indianapolis: Bobbs-Merrill, 1971), 57–61.

24. "A Native American," *Republic: A Magazine for the Defence of Civil and Religious*

Liberty, Aug. 1845, Circular 1. (Philadelphia: S. C. Atkinson, 1845), 4, Special Collections, NL.

25. Daniel Walker Howe, *What Hath God Wrought: The Transformation of America, 1815–1848* (New York: Oxford University Press, 2007), 194, 320; Shenton and Kenny, "Ethnicity and Immigration," 353–73.

26. See Michael Pasquier, *Fathers on the Frontier: French Missionaries and the Roman Catholic Priesthood in the United States, 1789–1870* (New York: Oxford University Press, 2010); Jay Dolan, *In Search of an American Catholicism: A History of Religion and Culture in Tension* (New York: Oxford University Press, 2002); Dolan, *The Irish Americans: A History* (New York: Bloomsbury, 2008); Dolan, *Catholic Revivalism: The American Experience, 1830–1900* (Notre Dame, IN: University of Notre Dame Press, 1979); John R. Dichtl, *Frontiers of Faith: Bringing Catholicism to the West in the Early Republic* (Lexington: University Press of Kentucky, 2008); and John T. McGreevy, *Catholicism and American Freedom: A History* (New York: W. W. Norton, 2003).

27. Archdiocese of St. Louis, *Archdiocese of St. Louis: Three Centuries of Catholicism, 1700–2000* (Strasbourg, France: Editions du Signe, 2001).

28. Gregory M. Franzwa, *The Old Cathedral* (St. Louis: Archdiocese of St. Louis, 1965).

29. Bishop Chabrat, Bardstown, to Right Reverend Joseph Rosati, June 22, 1838, Diocese of Bardstown, KY, Records, folder 2, FHS.

30. Bishop Chabrat, Bardstown, to Right Reverend Joseph Rosati, May 12, 1839, Diocese of Bardstown, KY, Records, folder 2, FHS.

31. Bishop Benedict Joseph Fenwick, Boston, to Bishop Rosati, St. Louis, Nov. 6, 1837, St. Louis Archdiocesan Archives, in William Barnaby Faherty, *The St. Louis German Catholics* (St. Louis: Reedy, 2004), 6. See also *An Account of the Progress of the Catholic Religion in the Western States of North America: With Extracts from Several Letters Addressed to the Right Rev. Dr. Edward Fenwick* (London: Kenting and Brown, 1824), Pamphlets in American History, CA 1299, SLU.

32. Bishop Peter Kenrick, St. Louis, to Milde, Dec. 10, 1844, St. Louis Archdiocesan Archives, in Faherty, *St. Louis German Catholics*, 11.

33. The Metropolitan Catholic Almanac, "Summary of the Catholic Church in the United States," in *Catholic Telegraph*, Dec. 28, 1844, 13, no. 52 (Archdiocese of Cincinnati and Louisville), 415, Microfilm, PLC.

34. Shenton and Kenny, "Ethnicity and Immigration," 353–73.

35. See Sydney E. Alhlstrom's seminal work, *A Religious History of the American People* (New Haven, CT: Yale University Press, 1972).

36. For more on anti-Catholicism during the colonial era, see Francis D. Cogliano, *No King, No Popery: Anti-Catholicism in Revolutionary New England* (Westport, CT: Greenwood, 1995); and Colin Haydon, *Anti-Catholicism in Eighteenth-Century England, c.1714–80: A Political and Social Study* (Manchester, UK: Manchester University Press, 1993).

37. See Daniel Walker Howe, "Protestantism, Voluntarism, and Personal Identity in

Antebellum America," in Stout and Hart, *New Directions in American Religious History*, 206–38; Dale T. Knobel, *"America for the Americans": The Nativist Movement in the United States* (New York: Twayne, 1996); and McGreevy, *Catholicism and American Freedom*.

38. "A Native American," *Republic*, 7, Special Collections, NL.

39. Rev. Edward Norris Kirk, *The Church Essential to the Republic: A Sermon in Behalf of the American Home Missionary Society* (New York: Leavitt Trow, 1848), 6.

40. Archbishop Francis Patrick Kenrick of Philadelphia endorsed Browson's *Review* from 1849 through the 1850s, as did Archbishop of St. Louis Peter Richard Kenrick, Coadjutor of Louisville Martin John, Bishop of Nashville Richard Pius, Bishop of Cincinnati John Baptist, Bishop of New York John Hughes, Bishop of Chicago James Oliver, Bishop of Milwaukee John M. Henni, Bishop of Cleveland Amadeus, Coadjutor Administrator of Detroit Peter Paul, and others. Pope Pius IX endorsed the *Review* on April 29, 1854: "As a token of our so great benignity, and *as a pledge of our gratitude to you for the service you have done for us*, we add our apostolic benediction, which we lovingly impart, with the poured-forth affection of our fraternal heart, to you yourself, beloved son, and to your whole family." Rev. James L. Chapman [minister of the Methodist Episcopal Church, South], *Americanism versus Romanism; or, The Cis-Atlantic Battle between Sam and the Pope* (Nashville: Published for the author, 1856), 69.

41. Orestes Brownson, *Brownson's Quarterly Review* (Boston), Jan. 1854, in Chapman, *Americanism Versus Romanism*, 71, 79. See also Orestes Brownson, *An Oration on Liberal Studies, Delivered Before the Philomathian Society of Mount Saint Mary's College, Maryland, June 29th, 1853* (Baltimore: Hedian & O'Brien, 1853); Brownson, *The Convert; or, Leaves from Experience* (New York: E. Dunigan & Brother, 1857); and Brownson, *The American Republic: Its Constitution, Tendencies and Destiny*, ed. Peter Augustine Lawler (Wilmington, DE: ISI Books, 2003).

42. See Brownson, *American Republic*.

43. These questions arose before Pope Pius IX defined the dogma of papal infallibility in the First Vatican Council of 1870. In 1876 Archbishop of Cincinnati John Baptist Purcell later approved the *Little Catechism on the Infallibility of the Sovereign Pontiff*, which announced that the pope reserved the power to speak *ex cathedra*, without error, when it concerned matters of faith and morals. The catechism rejected the question of the dispensing of allegiance as "a vain fear," however, because "infallibility, that is, authority *in teaching*, is one thing, and supreme authority *in governing* is another, and a quite different thing." The catechism criticized nativists' accusations against papal infallibility, particularly that the pope might any day "absolve his subject from their allegiance and plunge us again into the middle ages," as being intentionally designed "to confuse the question and render Infallibility odious to modern society." Purcell, *Little Catechism on the Infallibility of the Sovereign Pontiff* (Cincinnati: Benziger Brothers, 1876), 6, 10, 16, Pamphlet, CMC. For more on the infallibility debates among Catholics, see Kenneth Parker and Michael J. Pahls, *Authority, Dogma, and History: The Role of the Oxford Movement Converts and the Infallibility Debates of the Nineteenth Century, 1835–1875* (Bethesda, MD: Academica, 2008).

44. Rev. Nicholas Murray, D.D., *American Principles on National Prosperity: A Thanksgiving Sermon Preached in the First Presbyterian Church, Elizabethtown, November 23, 1854* (New York: Harper & Brothers, 1854), 24, Pamphlets, General Collections, NL. Reverend Murray was also the author of *Romanism at Home: Letters to the Hon. Roger B. Taney, Chief Justice of the United States* (New York: Harper & Brothers, 1852), ibid. See also Archbishop John Hughes's response to Murray in *Kirwan Unmasked: A Review of Kirwan in Six Letters, Addressed to the Reverend Nicholas Murray, D.D. of Elizabethtown, N.J.*, 4th ed. (New York: Edward Dunigan & Brother, 1851), Early American Imprints, Pamphlets CA 132, SLU.

45. For more on evangelicalism, millennialism, and the West, see Howe, *What Hath God Wrought*, 285–327, 701–43; Robert H. Azbug, *Cosmos Crumbling: American Reform and the Religious Imagination* (New York: Oxford University Press, 1994); Jon Butler, *Awash in a Sea of Faith: Christianizing the American People* (Cambridge, MA: Harvard University Press, 1990); William M. Shea, *The Lion and the Lamb: Evangelicals and Catholics in America* (New York: Oxford University Press, 2004), 14–23, 55–82; Fraser, *Pedagogue for God's Kingdom*; and William J. Phalen, "But They Did Not Build This House: The Attitude of Evangelical Protestantism towards Immigration to the United States, 1800–1924" (PhD diss., Rutgers State University of New Jersey, New Brunswick, 2010).

46. Charles Peabody, American West Travel Diary, vol. 1, Oct. 29, 1846, Mar. 23, 1847, MHS.

47. D. McNaughtan, Louisville, to John Brunton [merchant tailor], Edinburgh, North Britain, Mar. 24, 1840, FHS.

48. One tract, for example, described a dystopic future reminiscent of Martin Robespierre's godless Reign of Terror during the French Revolution, featuring a "prostitute" as a biblical allusion to the "whore of Babylon" in Revelation 17. American Reform Tract and Book Society, *Have We Any Need of the Bible*, no. 25 (Cincinnati: 1857), 24, Pamphlet, CMC.

49. For example, see American Protestant Society, *A Book of Tracts, Containing the Origin and Progress, Cruelties, Frauds, Superstitions, Miracles, Ceremonies, Idolatrous Customs, &c. of the Church of Rome: With a Succinct Account of the Rise and Progress of the Jesuits* (New York: American and Foreign Christian Union, 1856).

50. John F. Schermerhorn and Samuel J. Mills, "A correct view of that part of the United States which lies west of the Allegany Mountains, with regard to religion and morals" (Hartford, CT: 1814), in Fraser, *Pedagogue for God's Kingdom*, 37.

51. Luther Dana Barker, Louisville, to Maj. John Mills, Marietta, Washington County, OH, Oct. 13, 1820, FHS.

52. Peabody, American West Travel Diary, vol. 1, Apr. 29, 1847, MHS.

53. In its 1849 report the American Home Missionary Society defined the West as an area comprising the states of Kentucky, Ohio, Tennessee, Indiana, Illinois, Missouri, Arkansas, Texas, Iowa, Michigan, and Wisconsin. It did not include the new territories in the Southwest and Pacific coast acquired from Mexico in 1849. American Home Missionary Society, *Our Country* (New York: 1849), Early American Imprints, Broadside 7257, SLU.

54. Rev. Abel Stevens, *An Alarm to American Patriots: A Sermon on the Political Tendencies of Popery, Considered in Respect to the Institutions of the United States, Delivered in the Church Street Church, Boston, November 27, 1834; Being the Day of Annual Thanksgiving*, 2nd ed. (Boston: David H. Ela, 1835), 13, General Collections, NL.

55. Joshua Belden, St. Louis, to Dorothy Belden, Newington, CT, July 13, 1830, St. Louis Early Days, MHS.

56. Lyman Beecher, *A Plea for the West*, 2nd ed. (Cincinnati: Truman & Smith, 1835).

57. Lyman Beecher to Catharine Beecher, Boston, July 8, 1830, in Beecher, *Autobiography*, 2:167. For more on Beecher and his family, see Stephen H. Snyder, *Lyman Beecher and His Children: The Transformation of a Religious Tradition* (New York: Carlson, 1991); Altina Waller, *Reverend Beecher and Mrs. Tilton: Sex and Class in Victorian America* (Amherst: University of Massachusetts Press, 1982); Milton Rugoff, *The Beechers: An American Family in the Nineteenth Century* (New York: Harper & Row, 1981); and Marie Caskey, *Chariot of Fire: Religion and the Beecher Family* (New Haven, CT: Yale University Press, 1978).

58. D. A. Parker, Springfield, IL, to Lemon Parker [brother], Galena, IL, July 7, 1832, box 1, Parker-Russell Papers, FHS.

59. American Tract Society, *Fifth Annual Report* (New York: 1830), 41, in Fraser, *Pedagogue for God's Kingdom*, 38.

60. R. Cauffman, Vine Cottage, IL, to Susan H. Cauffman, Sussex County, DE, July 4, 1843, Cauffman Papers, CHS.

61. American Home Missionary Society, *Our Country*, Early American Imprints, Broadside 7257, SLU.

62. See Ray Allen Billington, "Anti-Catholic Propaganda and the Home Missionary Movement, 1800–1860," *Mississippi Valley Historical Review* 22, no. 3 (Dec. 1935): 361–84; and Gjerde, *Minds of the West*, 1–17, 25–49. For contemporary literature on the dangers of Catholic power in the West, see *Rome's Policy Towards the Bible; or, Papal Efforts to Suppress the Scriptures in the Last Five Centuries, Exposed; by an American Citizen* (Philadelphia: James M. Campbell, 1844), Pamphlets in American History, SLU; Rev. Rufus Wheelright, *Popery and the United States, Embracing an Account of Papal Operations in Our Country, With a View of the Dangers Which Threaten our Institutions* (Boston: J. V. Bean, 1847); Robert Fleming, *Apocalyptical Key: An Extraordinary Discourse on the Rise and Fall of Papacy; or, The Pouring out of the Vials, in the Revelation of St. John* (Philadelphia: James M. Campbell, 1843), SLU; Rev. Herman Norton, *Startling Facts for American Protestants! Progress of Romanism since the Revolutionary War; Its Present Position and Future Prospects* (New York: American Protestant Society, 1844); Noah Porter, *The Educational Systems of the Puritans and Jesuits Compared: A Premium Essay, Written for the Society for the Promotion of Collegiate and Theological Education at the West* (New York: M. W. Wood, 1851), SLU; Christopher Wordsworth, *The Church of Rome; or, The Babylon of the Apocalypse* (Philadelphia: Herman Hooker, 1853); Rev. Robert Gault, *Popery, the Man of Sin, and the Son of Perdition: Being the Second Prize*

Essay of the Evangelical Alliance (New York: American and Foreign Christian Union, 1854), Regenstein Library, University of Cincinnati; Frederick Saunders and Thomas Bangs Thorpe, *A Voice to America; or, The model republic, its glory, or its fall: with a review of the causes of the decline and failure of the republics of South America, Mexico, and of the Old World; applied to the present crisis in the United States* (E. Walker, 1855); and American Protestant Society, *Book of Tracts*.

63. For more on Postmillennialism, see Howe, *What Hath God Wrought*, 285–327; and Douglas M. Strong, *Perfectionist Politics: Abolitionism and the Religious Tensions of American Democracy* (Syracuse, NY: Syracuse University Press, 1999). For studies on Dispensationalism, see Russell R. Reno, *In the Ruins of the Church: Sustaining Faith in an Age of Diminished Christianity* (Grand Rapids, MI: Brazos, 2002); Azbug, *Cosmos Crumbling;* Randall Herbert Balmer, *Mine Eyes Have Seen the Glory: A Journey into the Evangelical Subculture* (New York: Oxford University Press, 1993); and Larry V. Crutchfield, *The Origins of Dispensationalism: The Darby Factor* (Lanham, MD: University Press of America, 1992).

64. *The Humble Advice of the Assembly of Divines, Now by Authority of Parliament fitting at Westminster, Concerning a Confession of Faith: With the Quotations and Texts of Scripture annexed* (London: Evan Tyler, 1647). Also see "Adopting Act of 1729," in John Baird, *Digest of the Acts and Deliverances of Assembly,* chap. 2. (Philadelphia: Presbyterian Board of Publication, 1856).

65. Daniel's vision was recorded in the book of Daniel, chapter 7. Historians dispute the actual boundaries, defining characteristics, and legitimacy of political entities after the collapse of the Roman Empire. It is likely Reverend Schmucker consulted Edward Gibbon, *The History of the Decline and Fall of the Roman Empire,* 5 vols. (New York: A. L. Burt, 1845).

66. Rev. Samuel Simon Schmucker, *The Papal Hierarchy, Viewed in the Light of Prophecy and History; Being a Discourse Delivered in the English Lutheran Church, Gettysburg, February 2, 1845* (Gettysburg, PA: H. C. Neinstedt, 1845), 12–13, 31–32, Sermons & Papers against the Roman Catholic Church, 1833–1852, General Collections, NL.

67. Boynton, *Oration on Liberal Studies,* 11–19.

68. Andre Lacocque, *The Book of Daniel* (Atlanta: John Knox, 1979); John Collins, *Daniel: A Commentary* (Minneapolis: Fortress, 1993).

69. See Bernard McGinn et al., *The Continuum of Apocalypticism* (New York: Continuum, 2003); and Jonathan Kirsch, *A History of the End of the World* (San Francisco: Harper, 2006).

70. Here is the passage from the King James Version of Daniel 7:13–14: "I saw in the night visions, and, behold, one like the Son of man came with the clouds of heaven, and came to the Ancient of days, and they brought him near before him. And there was given him dominion, and glory, and a kingdom, that all people, nations, and languages, should serve him: his dominion is an everlasting dominion, which shall not pass away, and his kingdom that which shall not be destroyed." *Thirteenth Annual Report of the Foreign*

Mission Society of the Valley of the Mississippi: Auxiliary to the American Board of Commissioners for Foreign Missions; Presented at Circleville, Ohio, Sept. 28, 1845 (Cincinnati: C. Clark, 1845), 8, Pamphlet, CMC.

71. Dr. Skinner to Lyman Beecher, Philadelphia, Feb. 16, 1832, in Beecher, *Autobiography*, 2:189.

72. See King James Version of Joel, chap. 3V. According to Numbers 25:1–3, the Israelites camped in the valley of Shittim before they entered Canaan, where they disobeyed God by comingling with the daughters of Moab and worshipping Baalpeor.

73. Dr. Skinner to Lyman Beecher, Philadelphia, Feb. 16, 1832, in Beecher, *Autobiography*, 2:189.

74. Samuel Finley Breese Morse [Brutus], *Foreign Conspiracy against the Liberties of the United States: The Numbers of Brutus* (New York: Arno, 1977). Billington made this point in *The Protestant Crusade, 1800–1860: A Study of the Origins of American Nativism* (Chicago: Quadrangle Books, 1938), 123.

75. Rev. William Wiener, D.D. [pseud., "Native American"], *Fatal Mistake: A Pamphlet in Four Numbers Showing the Nature, Political Bearing, Object and Tendency of Popery in this Country* (1835), 15, Special Collections, NL.

76. Samuel B. Smith [Late a Popish Priest], *The Flight of Popery from Rome to the West* (New York: 1836). Smith also authored *Renunciation of Popery,* 6th ed. (Philadelphia: Stereotyped by L. Johnson, for the author, 1833), Sermons & Papers against the Roman Catholic Church, 1833–1852, General Collection, NL.

77. Wiener, *Fatal Mistake,* 14, Special Collections, NL.

78. Smith, *Flight of Popery from Rome to the West.* Smith also authored *Renunciation of Popery; A Synopsis of the Moral Theology of the Church of Rome, Taken from the Works of St. Ligori, and Translated from the Latin into English* (New York: Office of the Downfall of Babylon [Pittsburgh: Patterson, Ingram], 1836); and *The Escape of Sainte Frances Patrick, Another Nun from the Hotel Dieu Nunnery of Montreal; to which is appended, a decisive confirmation of the Awful Disclosures of Maria Monk: Embellished with Six Engravings* (New York: Office of the Downfall of Babylon, 1836).

Chapter 2: Culture War

1. Epigraphs come from Lewis D. Campbell, *Americanism: Speech of Hon. Lewis D. Campbell of Ohio; delivered at the American mass meeting, held in Washington City, February 29th, 1856, as reported and published in the "American Organ"* (Washington, DC: Buell & Blanchard, 1856), 3, Political Pamphlets, vol. 2, no. 18, CHS; and Rev. Charles Brandon Boynton, *Address before the Citizens of Cincinnati: Delivered on the Fourth Day of July, 1855* (Cincinnati: Cincinnati Gazette Company Print, 1855), 26–27, Pamphlets, ibid.

2. See Carl Bankston and Stephen Caldas, *Public Education, America's Civil Religion: A Social History* (New York: Teachers College Press, 2009); Carl F. Kaestle, *Pillars of the*

Republic: Common Schools and American Society, 1780–1860 (New York: Hill and Wang, 1983); and Lawrence Arthur Cremin, *American Education: The National Experience, 1783–1876* (New York: Harper & Row, 1980), viii.

3. Thomas Jefferson, "Bill for the More General Diffusion of Knowledge, 1779," in Roy Honeywell, *The Education Work of Thomas Jefferson* (Cambridge, MA: Harvard University Press, 1931), 199.

4. Thomas Jefferson to Joseph Cabell, 1816, in *American Writings on Popular Education,* ed. Rush Welter (Indianapolis: Bobbs-Merrill, 1971), 9–10.

5. Cremin, *American Education,* 104, 369. For more on Jefferson's views on education, see Mark Wenger, "Thomas Jefferson, the College of William and Mary, and the University of Virginia," *Virginia Magazine of History and Biography* 103 (July 1995): 339–74; David W. Robson, *Educating Republicans: The College in the Era of the American Revolution, 1750–1800* (Westport, CT: Greenwood, 1985); and James Gilreath, ed., *Thomas Jefferson and the Education of a Citizen* (Washington, DC: Library of Congress, 1999).

6. Joshua Belden, St. Louis, to Dorothy Belden, Newington, CT, July 13, 1830, St. Louis Early Days, MHS.

7. Calvin Stowe, *The Religious Element in Education* (Boston: 1844), 26, in James W. Fraser, *Pedagogue for God's Kingdom: Lyman Beecher and the Second Great Awakening* (Lanham, MD: University Press of America, 1985), 183.

8. "Transactions of the Western Literary Institute, 1836," in Welter, *American Writings on Popular Education,* ed57–61.

9. See Cremin, *American Education,* 107–47. For more on the American tradition of religious civility, see Chris Beneke, "America's Whiggish Religious Revolution: An Instance in the Progress of History," *Historically Speaking* 10, no. 3 (June 2009): 31–35.

10. Howe, *What Hath God Wrought,* 191–92.

11. For more on the early career of George Sibley, see Jeffrey E. Smith, *Seeking a New World, 1808–1811: The Fort Osage Journals and Letters of George Sibley* (St. Charles, MO: Lindenwood University Press, 2003).

12. George C. Sibley Lindenwood, to William Russell, May 23, 1836, Letter book of George Sibley, Sibley Papers, MHS.

13. Mary Sibley, Diary, Mar. 24, Apr. 19, May 4, 1833, Feb. 24, 26, 1834, Mar. 3, 1834, Dec. 28, 1835, LU.

14. George Sibley explained that he had a conversion experience sometime in 1834, after which he joined the Presbyterian church his wife, Mary, already attended. George C. Sibley, Lindenwood, to William Russell, Oct. 24, 1834, Letter book of George Sibley, Sibley Papers, MHS.

15. William Russell, Crystal Springs, to Mrs. Mary E. Sibley, St. Charles, May 22, 1836, Lindenwood Collection, MHS.

16. Russell to Sibley, May 22, 1836, Lindenwood Collection, MHS.

17. Sibley, Diary, July 1, 1832, Mar. 28, Apr. 24, 1834, Dec. 28, 1835; George C. Sibley, Lindenwood, to William Russell, Oct. 24, 1834, Letter book of George Sibley, Sibley

Papers, MHS. For more on the relationship between educational outreach and charity, see Kaestle, *Pillars of the Republic*, 30–61.

18. Mary Sibley, Diary, Apr. 22, 1832, LU.

19. Sibley, Diary, Mar. 3, 31, 1834. She also wrote a piece regarding the "sin" of "worshipping" the Virgin Mary.

20. Sibley, Diary, Feb. 10, Aug. 4, 1834.

21. Sibley, Diary, July 15, 1832, Apr. 7, 19, Nov. 8, 1833, Mar. 28, Apr. 24, 1834.

22. Sibley, Diary, July 5, 1832, Sept. 5, 1833, LU.

23. Elijah P. Lovejoy [Waldo], *St. Louis Observer,* in Paul Simon, *Freedom's Champion: Elijah Lovejoy* (Carbondale: Southern Illinois University Press, 1994), 18, 25; Elijah P. Lovejoy, St. Louis, to Elizabeth Lovejoy [Mother], Maine, ibid.,10.

24. Founded in 1827, Lovejoy's *St. Louis Observer* relocated to Alton, Illinois, in 1837. A proslavery mob attacked a warehouse holding one of the paper's printing presses on November 7, 1837, and shot Lovejoy to death, for which he became known as the first martyr of abolition.

25. Elijah P. Lovejoy, *St. Louis Observer,* Aug. 27, 1835, in *Memoir of the Reverend Elijah P. Lovejoy: Who Was Murdered in Defence of the Liberty of the Press, at Alton, Illinois, Nov. 7, 1837,* ed. Joseph Cammet and Owen Lovejoy (New York: Arno, 1969), 113–14.

26. Elijah P. Lovejoy [Waldo], "Popish Zeal for Education," *St. Louis Observer,* Nov. 27, 1834.

27. Rev. David Todd Stuart, Diary, Jan. 2, Feb. 7, Mar. 2, 16, 22–23, Aug. 24, Dec. 18, 1854, FHS.

28. Catharine E. Beecher, *Essay on the Education of Female Teachers; Written at the Request of the American Lyceum and Communicated at Their Annual Meeting, New York, May 8, 1835* (New York: Van Nostrand & Dwight, 1835), 12–13, 18.

29. Sarah Josepha Hale, "Convents Are Increasing," *Ladies Repository* (1834), 561, 564. See also Carol Mattingly, "Uncovering Forgotten Habits: Anti-Catholic Rhetoric and Nineteenth-Century American Women's Literacy," *College Composition and Communication* 58, no. 2 (Dec. 2006): 160–81. For an analysis of the connections between female-led evangelism and reform and anti-Catholicism in Philadelphia, see Bruce Dorsey, *Reforming Men and Women: Gender in the Antebellum City* (Ithaca, NY: Cornell University Press, 2002), 195–244.

30. See Anne M. Boylan, *Sunday School: The Formation of an American Institution, 1790–1880* (New Haven, CT: Yale University Press, 1988); Daniel Walker Howe, "Church, State, and Education in the Young American Republic," *Journal of the Early Republic* 22, no. 1 (Spring 2002): 1–24; Howe, *What Hath God Wrought: The Transformation of America, 1815–1848* (New York: Oxford University Press, 2007), 449–50; and Kaestle, *Pillars of the Republic,* 45.

31. R. Laurence Moore, "Bible Reading and Nonsectarian Schooling," *Journal of American History* 86 (March 2000): 1591, 1595. See Stephen Green, *The Bible, the School, and the Constitution: The Clash that Shaped Modern Church-State Doctrine* (New York: Oxford University Press, 2012); Stephen Green, *The Second Disestablishment: Church*

and State in Nineteenth-Century America (Oxford University Press, 2010); and Philip Hamburger, *Separation of Church and State: A Theologically Liberal, Anti-Catholic, and American Principle* (Chicago: University of Chicago Law School, 2002).

32. See John T. McGreevy, *Catholicism and American Freedom: A History* (New York: W. W. Norton, 2003), 38–42; and Ira M. Leonard and Robert D. Parmet, *American Nativism, 1830–1860* (New York: Van Nostrand Reinhold, 1971), 65–84.

33. See Mark Noll, *America's God: From Jonathan Edwards to Abraham Lincoln* (New York: Oxford University Press, 2002); and William M. Shea, "Biblical Christianity as a Category in Nineteenth-Century American Apologetics," *American Catholic Studies* 115, no. 3 (2004): 1–21.

34. Mark Noll, *The Scandal of the Evangelical Mind* (Grand Rapids, MI: William B. Eerdmans, 1994), 96; Noll, *America's God*, 367–85.

35. A "Know-Nothing," *Know-Nothing Platform: Containing an Account of the Encroachments of the Roman Catholic Hierarchy, on the Civil and Religious Liberties of the People in Europe, Asia, Africa, and America, Showing the Necessity of the Order of Know-Nothings; With a Valuable and Interesting Appendix* (Philadelphia: Published for the author, 1854), 52, General Collections, NL.

36. George C. Sibley, Lindenwood, to William Russell, Oct. 24, 1834, Letter book of George Sibley, Sibley Papers, MHS; George C. Sibley, Lindenwood, to William Russell, June 1, 1836, ibid.

37. Rev. Nicholas Murray, *American Principles on National Prosperity: A Thanksgiving Sermon Preached in the First Presbyterian Church, Elizabethtown, November 23, 1854* (New York: Harper & Brothers, 1854), 8–11, 25, Pamphlets, General Collections, NL.

38. William C. Woodbridge, *Modern School Geography* (1844), 151, in Sister Marie Leonore Fell, "The Foundations of Nativism in American Textbooks, 1783–1860" (PhD diss., Catholic University of America, 1941), 183, 205.

39. Archbishop Hughes to the New York City Board of Alderman, "Petition of the Catholics of the City of New York," Sept. 21, 1840, in Welter, *American Writings on Popular Education,* 103–5.

40. Fell, " Foundations of Nativism in American Textbooks," 176.

41. Archbishop Hughes to the New York City Board of Alderman, "Petition of the Catholics," 103–5.

42. Horace Bushnell, *Common Schools: A Discourse on the Modifications Demanded by the Roman Catholics, Delivered in the North Church, Hartford, March 25, 1853* (Hartford, CT, 1853), in Welter, *American Writings on Popular Education,* 188–89.

43. For example, see Henry Jefferson, *Louisville High School Monthly Report,* Feb. 28, 1851, FHS.

44. Horace Mann, *Common School Journal* 3 (1841), 15, in Cremin, *American Education,* 137.

45. *American Writings on Popular Education,* ed. Rush Welter, The American Heritage Series, eds. Leonard W. Levy and Alfred F. Young (Indianapolis: The Bobbs-Merrill Company, Inc., 1971), xvi.

46. Kaestle, *Pillars of the Republic,* 98. See also Daniel Walker Howe, "Classical Education and Political Culture in Nineteenth-Century America," *Intellectual History Newsletter* 5 (Spring 1983): 9–14, 21–22; Howe, "Church, State, and Education in the Young American Republic," 14; R. Laurence Moore, "Bible Reading and Nonsectarian Schooling," *Journal of American History* 86 (Mar. 2000): 1581–99; Cremin, *American Education,* 133–43, 154–57; and Burke Aaron Hinsdale, *Horace Mann and the Common School Revival in the United States* (New York: Charles Scribner's Sons, 1900), 210–32.

47. Charles Keemle, *The St. Louis Directory for the Years 1840–1* (St. Louis: Charles Keemle, 1840), 72, MHS; James Green, *Green's Saint Louis Directory for 1845* (St. Louis: James Green, 1844), xxvii, ibid.

48. *Schaffer's Advertising Directory for 1839–40* (Cincinnati: 1840), PLC.

49. John Moses and Joseph Kirkland, *History of Chicago, Illinois,* vol. 2 (Chicago: Munsell, 1895), 330. See also Ray Allen Billington, *The Protestant Crusade, 1800–1860: A Study of the Origins of American Nativism* (Chicago: Quadrangle Books, 1938), 142–57.

50. Rev. Nicholas Murray [pseudonym, Kirwan], *Letters to the Right Reverend John Hughes, Roman Catholic Bishop of New-York* (New York: Leavitt, Trow, 1847), 29, 79. Reverend Murray also authored *Romanism at Home: Letters to the Hon. Roger B. Taney, Chief Justice of the United States* (New York: Harper & Brothers, 1852), General Collection, NL. See also Archbishop John Hughes, *Kirwan Unmasked: A Review of Kirwan in Six Letters, Addressed to the Reverend Nicholas Murray, D.D. of Elizabethtown, N.J.,* 4th ed. (New York: Edward Dunigan & Brother, 1851), Early American Imprints, Pamphlet 132, SLU.

51. Rev. G. W. Quinby, "The Bible and the Printing Press," *Star in the West* (Cincinnati), May 28, 1853, 16, no. 9, Unbound Newspapers, CMC.

52. Records of the Rehoboth Society of Walnut Hills, Sept. 1819, CMC.

53. "Second Annual Report of the Louisville and Vicinity Bible Society, Auxiliary to the American Bible Society: Presented April 8, 1839" (Louisville: N. H. White, 1839), Louisville and Vicinity Bible Society Records, vol. 1, FHS.

54. Records of the Young Men's Bible Society of Cincinnati, vol. 2, Dec. 12, 1844 to Dec. 5, 1848, CMC.

55. "Second Annual Report of the Louisville and Vicinity Bible Society," 7.

56. Rev. Edward P. Humphrey, *A Discourse of the Spiritual Power of the Roman Catholic Clergy, Delivered Before the Synod of Kentucky, Oct. 13, 1849* (Louisville: Hull & Brother, 1850), 5–6, Sermons & Papers against the Roman Catholic Church, 1833–1852, General Collections, NL. See also Noah Porter, *The Educational Systems of the Puritans and Jesuits Compared: A Premium Essay, Written for the Society for the Promotion of Collegiate and Theological Education at the West* (New York: M. W. Wood, 1851), SLU; and Richard Baxter's classic, *Jesuit Juggling: Forty Popish Frauds Detected and Disclosed,* 1st American ed. (Cincinnati: Corey & Webster, 1835).

57. Lyman Beecher, *A Plea for the West* (Cincinnati: Truman & Smith, 1835), 48–56, 72, 87, 127–29, 145.

58. Lyman Beecher, *An Address Delivered at the Tenth Anniversary Celebration of the Union Literary Society of Miami University, September 29, 1835* (Cincinnati: *Cincinnati Journal* Office, 1835), 6, 18–19, 35, Pamphlet, CMC.

59. Edward Purcell, "Burning of Bibles," *Catholic Telegraph,* Jan. 21, 1843, 12, no. 3 (Archdiocese of Cincinnati and Louisville), 20, PLC, microfilm.

60. The Jehovah's Witnesses and Seventh Day Adventists emerged from Millerism soon thereafter. See Reinder Brinsma, *Seventh-Day Adventist: Attitudes toward Roman Catholicism, 1844–1965* (Berrien Springs, MI: Andrews University Press, 1994).

61. Edward Purcell, "Some Protestant Misconceptions Corrected," *Catholic Telegraph,* Jan. 28, 1843, 12, no. 4 (Archdiocese of Cincinnati and Louisville), 29, PLC, microfilm.

62. Phebe Daugherty, Lancaster, OH, to Rev. Edward Purcell, Cincinnati, July 19, 1859, Phebe Wood Coburn Papers, folder 5, FHS.

63. Pope Pius VI to Archbishop of Florence, Letter, 1778, in Sen. James L. D. Morrison, *Senate of Illinois: Senator Morrison on the Know-Nothings* (1852), 8, 10–12, Pamphlets, CHS.

64. Edward Purcell, "Western Protestant Association," *Catholic Telegraph,* Feb. 25, 1843, 12, no. 8 (Archdiocese of Cincinnati and Louisville), 62, PLC, microfilm; Purcell, "Western Protestant Association," ibid., Feb. 18, 1843, 51.

65. Rev. J. Perry [Catholic pastor of Aston-le-Walls, South Northamptonshire, Eng.], *The Protesting Christian, Standing Before the Judgment-Seat of Christ, to Answer for His Protest Against that Parent Church which Christ Built upon a Rock, with the Promise: "The gates of Hell SHALL NOT prevail against it,"* (Cincinnati: Catholic Society for the Diffusion of Useful Knowledge, 1840), 4–10, Pamphlet, CMC. In 1850s Cincinnati, Germans constituted a third of the city's population (not counting the second generation). A coalition of German Catholics, Evangelicals, Lutherans, and Freethinkers— strange bedfellows, indeed—forced the education board to change its curriculum. In 1839 the Board of Cincinnati declared that the Holy Scriptures (King James Version) "are all read in the schools, and their moral precepts inculcated as principles of conduct and duty." But in 1855 the Irish bishop of Cincinnati, John Purcell, and German freethinker John Stallo joined together to force the board to concede that "the pupils of the Common Schools may read such versions of the Sacred Scriptures as their parents or guardians may prefer." This concession did little to placate the German demand for public monies to fund their parochial schools, however, which resumed with renewed fervor in the decades after the Civil War. *Report of the Board of Trustees and Visitors of the Common Schools—Tenth Annual Report* (1839), 8–9, University of Cincinnati Library, also quoted in Nancy R. Hamant, "Religion in the Cincinnati Schools, 1830–1900," *Bulletin of the Historical and Philosophical Society of Ohio* 21 (Cincinnati: Oct. 1963): 240; *Report of the Board of Trustees and Visitors of the Common Schools—Twenty-Sixth Annual Report* (1855), 122, University of Cincinnati Library, also quoted in Hamant, "Religion in the Cincinnati Schools," 241. See also Thomas L. Rodgers, "Recollections

of St. Louis, 1857–1860," St. Louis History Papers, MHS; and Carl Wittke, "The Germans of Cincinnati," *Bulletin of the Historical and Philosophical Society of Ohio* 20, no. 1 (Jan. 1962): 3–14.

66. Bishop Chabrat, Bardstown, to Right Rev. Joseph Rosati, May 12, 1839, Diocese of Bardstown, KY, Records, folder 2, FHS; Chabrat, Bardstown, to Rosati, June 22, 1838, ibid.

67. For more on early Catholic development in the West, see Michael Pasquier, *Fathers on the Frontier: French Missionaries and the Roman Catholic Priesthood in the United States, 1789–1870* (New York: Oxford University Press, 2010).

68. Samuel Finley Breese Morse [Brutus], *Foreign Conspiracy Against the Liberties of the United States: The Numbers of Brutus* (1835; repr., New York: Arno, 1977).

69. For more on the Austrian Leopold Foundation in America, see Edward John Hickey, *The Society for the Propagation of the Faith: Its Foundation, Organization, and Success, 1822–1922* (Charleston, SC: BiblioBazaar, 2011); and Billington, *Protestant Crusade*, 118–40. See also William Barnaby Faherty, *The St. Louis German Catholics* (St. Louis: Reedy, 2004).

70. Bishop Edward Fenwick, undated letter, in American Education Society, *Quarterly Register and Journal of the American Education Society*, vol. 2 (Flagg and Gould, 1830), American Libraries, Harvard University, Cambridge, MA.

71. Bishop John Baptist Purcell, Diary, Jan. 24, Feb. 28, 1834, quoted in William A. Baughin, "Nativism in Cincinnati before 1860" (PhD diss., University of Cincinnati, 1963), 23, CMC.

72. See Francis X. Curran, *The Return of the Jesuits: Chapters in the History of the Society of Jesus in Nineteenth Century America* (Chicago: Loyola University Press, 1966). For more on the Jesuit Restoration in Europe, see Geoffrey Cubitt, *The Jesuit Myth: Conspiracy Theory and Politics in Nineteenth-Century France* (Oxford: Clarendon, 1993); and John W. Padberg, *Colleges in Controversy: The Jesuit Schools in France from Revival to Suppression, 1815–1880* (Cambridge, MA: Harvard University Press, 1969).

73. The largest Jesuit-run university in the United States was Georgetown University in Washington, DC.

74. William Barnaby Faherty, "Nativism and Midwestern Education: The Experience of Saint Louis University, 1832–1856," *History of Education Quarterly* 8, no. 4 (winter 1968): 447–458.

75. Green, *Green's Saint Louis Directory for,* xxxi, MHS.

76. Victor Carr Lane, St. Louis College, to Mrs. William Carr Lane [mother], June 11, 1844, William Carr Lane Collection, MHS. See also Mattingly, "Uncovering Forgotten Habits," 160–81; and Kathleen A. Mahoney, *Catholic Higher Education in Protestant America: The Jesuits and Harvard in the Age of the University* (Baltimore: Johns Hopkins University Press, 2003).

77. See Jose Casanova, "Roman and Catholic and American: The Transformation of Catholicism in the U.S.," *International Journal of Politics, Culture, and Society* 6,

1 (Fall 1992): 75–111; Steven Conn, "'Political Romanism': Reevaluating American Anti-Catholicism in the Age of Italian Revolution," *Journal of the Early Republic* 36, 3 (Fall 2016): 521–548; Patrick Carey, "Recent American Catholic Historiography: New Directions in Religious History," in *New Directions in American Religious History*, eds. Harry S. Stout and D.G. Hart (New York: Oxford University Press, 1997), 445–61; and McGreevy, *Catholicism and American Freedom*.

78. See Steven Green, *The Second Disestablishment: Church and State in Nineteenth-Century America* (New York: Oxford University Press, 2010).

79. See Werner Sollors, ed., *The Invention of Ethnicity* (New York: Oxford University Press, 1989); and Kathleen Neils Conzen et al., "The Invention of Ethnicity in the United States," in *Major Problems in American Immigration and Ethnic History*, ed. Jon Gjerde (Boston: Houghton Mifflin, 1998), 23–24.

80. For the theory of the "other," see Alfred Schuetz, "The Stranger: An Essay in Social Psychology," *American Journal of Sociology* 49 no. 6 (May 1944): 499–507; Tzvetan Todorov, *The Conquest of America: The Question of the Other*, trans. Richard Howard (New York: Harper & Row, 1984); and Peter Burke, *Cultural Hybridity* (Cambridge: Polity, 2009).

81. Conzen et al., "Invention of Ethnicity," 23–24. For more on "ethnicity," immigration, and nativism in nineteenth-century America, see Dale T. Knobel, "The Relationship between the Portrayal of Irish Americans and Citizenship at Midcentury," in Gjerde, *Major Problems in American Immigration and Ethnic History*, 160–69; Knobel, *Paddy and the Republic: Ethnicity and Nationality in Antebellum America* (Middletown, CT: Wesleyan University Press, 1986); John Higham, "Ethnicity and American Protestants: Collective Identity in the Mainstream," in *New Directions in American Religious History*, ed. Harry S. Stout and D. G. Hart (New York: Oxford University Press, 1997), 239–59; Leonard Dinnerstein, *Natives and Strangers: Ethnic Groups and the Building of America* (New York: Oxford University Press, 1979); Werner Sollors, *Beyond Ethnicity: Consent and Descent in American Culture* (New York: Oxford University Press, 1986); David A. Gerber, *The Making of An American Pluralism: Buffalo, New York, 1825–1860* (Urbana: University of Illinois Press, 1989); Lawrence H. Fuchs, *The American Kaleidoscope: Race, Ethnicity, and the Civil Culture* (Hanover, NH: Wesleyan University Press, 1990); David A. Hollinger, *Postethnic America: Beyond Multiculturalism* (New York: Basic Books, 1995); and David Thelen, *Paths of Resistance: Tradition and Democracy in Industrializing Missouri* (Columbia: University of Missouri Press, 1991).

82. Heinrich Börnstein, *Memoirs of a Nobody: The Missouri Years of an Austrian Radical, 1849–1866*, trans. and ed. Steven Rowan (St. Louis: Missouri Historical Society Press, 1997), 148. The *Anzeiger des Westens* avowed socialism and "free-thinking," an intellectual movement that rejected all religious authority, creeds, and tradition and instead judged religion on the basis of reason alone. Some German freethinkers held spiritual beliefs, while others like Börnstein avowed agnosticism or atheism.

83. Börnstein, *Memoirs of a Nobody*, 148–50. Börnstein and reporters for the

Whiggish and nativist *St. Louis Republican* disagreed on the exact numbers of Germans involved in the parade and festival. Börnstein estimated eight thousand Germans in the procession, while one writer in the *Republican* reported only three hundred. See "The Sunday Procession," *St. Louis Republican*, July 5, 1852. Both authors had clear motives to misreport the numbers: Börnstein's estimation was probably exaggerated, while the *Republican*'s report probably downplayed the size of the event.

84. "Sunday Parade," *St. Louis Republican*, July 2, 1852.

85. "Of Offenses Affecting Public Peace and Quiet," in *The Revised Ordinances of the City of St. Louis: Revised and Digested by the City Council, In the Year 1850, with the constitutions of the United States and of the state of Missouri; the various charters of, and laws applicable to the town and city of St. Louis*, rev. John M. Krum (St. Louis: Chambers & Knapp, 1850) 1–8, 290–91; "Sunday Parade," *St. Louis Republican*, July 1, 1852.

86. "The Sunday Procession," *St. Louis Republican*, July 5, 1852.

87. See "Doings in honor of the Fourth of July," *St. Louis Republican*, July 6, 1852; and Kathleen Neils Conzen, *Immigrant Milwaukee, 1836–1860: Accommodation and Community in a Frontier City* (Cambridge, MA: Harvard University Press, 1976), 212.

88. "The Foreign Movement on the Sunday Question," *Harper's Weekly Journal of Civilization*, Sept. 24, 1859, 3, 143 610.

89. See James Neal Primm and Steven Rowan, introduction to *Germans for a Free Missouri: Translations from the St. Louis Radical Press, 1857–1862*, trans. Steven Rowan (Columbia: University of Missouri Press, 1983), 26.

90. Stanley Nadel, *Little Germany: Ethnicity, Religion, and Class in New York City, 1845–1880* (Urbana: University of Illinois Press, 1990), 132. See also John Bodnar, *The Transplanted: A History of Immigrants in Urban America* (Bloomington: Indiana University Press, 1985), 197–98.

91. Börnstein, *Memoirs of a Nobody*, 198.

92. See Kyle G. Volk, "Majority Rule, Minority Rights: The Christian Sabbath, Liquor, Racial Amalgamation, and Democracy in Antebellum America" (PhD diss., University of Chicago, 2008).

93. Although "Puritan Sabbatarianism" arose as a pejorative description of religious dissidents in England, it still serves as a useful label because the emergence of English Puritanism and Sabbatarianism became interconnected movements. See John Primus, *Holy Time: Moderate Puritanism and the Sabbath* (Macon, GA: Mercer University Press, 1989), 12–13.

94. The origin of the term "blue law" dates back to the seventeenth century. It either refers to the blue paper on which the original Sunday laws were written, or the color blue denoted constancy, fidelity, and stubbornness. See David N. Laband and Deborah H. Heinbuch, *Blue Laws: The History, Economics, and Politics of Sunday-Closing Laws* (Lexington, MA: Lexington Books, 1987), 8.

95. "Crimes and Punishments," *The Revised Statutes of the State of Missouri, revised and digested by the eighth general assembly, during the years one thousand eight hundred and thirty-four, and one thousand eight hundred and thirty-five. Together with the*

constitutions of Missouri and the United States, 3rd ed. (St. Louis: Chambers & Knapp, 1841), 209. These statutes were reiterated in the 1845, 1856, and 1866 editions with only minor revisions. The Ohio statutes prohibited on Sunday "sporting, rioting, quarreling, hunting, fishing, shooting, or common labor" as well as the sale of any "spirituous liquors" and any disturbance of religious meetings gathered "for the purpose of worship." See "An Act for the prevention of certain immoral practices, June 1, 1831," *The Revised Statutes of the State of Ohio, of a General Nature*, ed. Joseph S. Swan (Cincinnati: Robert Clarke, 1870), 447–48. The New York statutes also outlawed the disturbance of religious meetings, drinking, and frolicking on Sundays. See *The Revised Statues of the State of New York*, ed. Amasa J. Parker, George Wolford, and Edward Wade (Albany: Banks & Brothers, 1859), 934–35.

96. Richard R. John, "Taking Sabbatarianism Seriously: The Postal System, the Sabbath, and the Transformation of American Political Culture," *Journal of the Early Republic* 10 (1990): 530–31.

97. See Richard R. John, *Spreading the News: The American Postal System from Franklin to Morse* (Cambridge, MA: Harvard University Press, 1995).

98. Michael Frank, "Satan's Servant or Authorities' Agent? Publicans in Eighteenth-Century Germany," *The World of the Tavern: Public Houses in Early Modern Europe*, ed. Beat Kuemin and B. Ann Tlusty (Burlington, VT: Ashgate, 2002), 31.

99. For more on teetotalers in England and the United States in the nineteenth century, see Brian Harrison, *Drink and the Victorians: The Temperance Question in England, 1815–1872* (Pittsburgh: University of Pittsburgh Press, 1971), 107–246.

100. B. Ann Tlusty, *Bacchus and Civic Order: The Culture of Drink in Early Modern Germany* (Charlottesville: University Press of Virginia, 2001), 6, 18, 150.

101. For more on the temperance reform movement and immigrant resistance, see Robert H. Abzug, *Cosmos Crumbling: American Reform and the Religious Imagination* (New York: Oxford University Press, 1994); and Joseph R. Gusfield, *Symbolic Crusade: Status Politics and the American Temperance Movement* (Urbana: University of Illinois Press, 1963).

102. Bodnar, *The Transplanted*, 198.

103. See Eviatar Zerubavel, *The Seven Day Circle* (Chicago: University of Chicago Press, 1985); Alexis McCrossen, *Holy Day, Holiday: The American Sunday* (Ithaca, NY: Cornell University Press, 2000); and Craig Harline, *Sunday: A History of the First Day from Babylonia to the Super Bowl* (New York: Doubleday, 2007).

104. George Helmuth Kellner, "The German Element on the Urban Frontier: St. Louis, 1830–1860" (PhD diss., University of Missouri–Columbia, 1973), 279.

105. Ernst D. Kargau, *The German Element in St. Louis: A Translation from German of Ernst D. Kargau's* St. Louis in Former Years: A Commemorative History of the German Element, ed. Don Heinrich Tolzmann, trans. William G. Bek (Baltimore: Clearfield, 2000), 9, 124–25.

106. Audrey Olson, *St. Louis Germans, 1850–1920: The Nature of an Immigrant Community and Its Relation to the Assimilation Process* (New York: Arno, 1980), 20.

107. Kargau, *German Element in St. Louis*, 125, 149.

108. The German wine industry in Missouri experienced rapid growth in the 1850s. German vineyards could be found within sixty miles of St. Louis. See Elliott, "Vine and Fruit Growing in Missouri," *St. Louis Genesee Farmer*, December, 1858. For more on suburban escape in general, see Leo Marx, *The Machine in the Garden: Technology and the Pastoral Ideal in America* (New York: Oxford University Press, 1964).

109. Kargau, *German Element in St. Louis*, 150.

110. "Result of Sabbath Desecration," *Farmer's Cabinet*, July 19, 1849, 47, 49 (Amherst, NH).

111. "Willis's Letter from New York," *Berkshire County Whig*, Sept. 12, 1844, 4, 28 (Pitttsfield, MA).

112. "The Foreign Movement on the Sunday Question," *Harper's Weekly Journal of Civilization*, Sept. 24, 1859, 3, 143 (New York): 610.

113. "German Gardens," *Pittsfield (MA) Sun*, Nov. 3, 1859, 60, 3085.

114. Seventh Census of St. Louis, 1850, cited in Olson, *St. Louis Germans*, 14.

115. Quoted in Ada M. Klett, "Belleville Germans Look at America (1833–1845)," *Journal of the Illinois State Historical Society* 40, no. 1 (Mar. 1947): 28–29.

116. Kellner, "German Element on the Urban Frontier," 143–50. For more on St. Louis additions from 1840 to 1860, see James Neal Primm, *Lion of the Valley: St. Louis, Missouri* (Boulder, CO: Pruett, 1981), 148–53.

117. Emil to Edward, Oct. 15, 1840 (Letter 10), Apr. 29 (Letter 11), Oct. 31 (Letter 12), 1841, Jan. 25, 1844 (Letter 16), Aug. 30, 1846 (Letter 20), Jan. 21, 1847 (Letter 21), MHS.

118. Börnstein, *Memoirs of a Nobody*, 119–23, 217, 226–27.

119. Börnstein's novel underwent six German-language editions, sold two thousand copies, and entertained a community of more than three thousand German readers during its initial serial publication in the *Anzeiger des Westens* from February to June 1851. Popular conspiratorial literature on Jesuitical infiltrations into the U.S. government, evil nun convents that systematically aborted unwanted babies, and Austrian plots to destroy America's free institutions proliferated when Börnstein wrote *The Mysteries of St. Louis*. The protagonist in his novel, Mr. Boettcher, faces a hyperbolic Jesuit plot to steal the "treasure" of the "Prairie des Noyers." The treasure is a metaphor for the dream of land and freedom in the West, which greedy businessmen and sectarians constantly sought to control. "Prairie des Noyers" is the old French name for the common grounds just west of St. Louis. Boettcher, who secures his own homestead in the Prairie des Noyers, is constantly plagued by an Anglo-American conspirator named Jeremiah Smartborn. See Heinrich Börnstein, *The Mysteries of St. Louis: A Novel*, trans. Friedrich Münch (1852; modern ed. by Steven Rowan and Elizabeth Sims, Chicago: Charles H. Kerr, 1990), 123.

120. Friedrich Münch, "Emigration from Germany to America," Mar. 16, 1859, *Mississippi Blätter*, Mar. 27, 1859, in *Germans for a Free Missouri*, 74–77.

121. Conzen, *Immigrant Milwaukee*, 212. For more on the conservative and religious character of German immigrants in St. Louis, see Kellner, "German Element on the

Urban Frontier"; Brent O. Peterson, *Popular Narratives and Ethnic Identity: Literature and Community in* Die Abendschule (Ithaca, NY: Cornell University Press, 1991); Nadel, *Little Germany;* and Faherty, *St. Louis German Catholics.*

122. Kargau, *German Element in St. Louis,* 24.

123. William L. Montague, *St. Louis Business Directory, 1853–1854* (St. Louis: E. A. Lewis, 1853), 126–31; Kargau, *German Element in St. Louis,* 217; Augustus J. Prahl, "The Turner," in *The Forty-Eighters: Political Refugees of the German Revolution of 1848,* ed. A. E. Zucker (New York: Columbia University Press, 1950): 79–110; Joseph Wandel, *The German Dimension of American History* (Chicago: Nelson-Hall, 1979), 81–94.

124. See Bruce Levine, *The Spirit of 1848: German Immigrants, Labor Conflict, and the Coming of the Civil War* (Urbana: University of Illinois Press, 1992). Anglo-American "anti-Sabbatarian" groups also challenged Sunday legislation. See *Proceedings of the Anti-Sabbath Convention, Held in the Melodeon, March 23 and 24,* as reported by Henry M. Parkhurst (Boston: Andrews & Prentiss, 1848). For a brief analysis of the proceedings of the Anti-Sabbath Convention, see McCrossen, *Holy Day, Holiday,* 21–37.

125. Boynton, *Address before the Citizens of Cincinnati,* 26–27, Pamphlets, CHS.

126. Alfred B. Ely, *American Liberty, Its Sources – Its Dangers, and the Means of Its Preservation: An Oration, Delivered at the Broadway Tabernacle, in New-York, Before the Order of United Americans, on the 22d of February, AD 1850, Being the 118th Anniversary of the Birthday of Washington* (New York: Seaman & Dunham, Printers, 1850).

127. Charles O. Gerrish, St. Louis, to Stephanus, July 30, 1858, St. Louis History Papers, MHS.

128. Rodgers, "Recollections of St. Louis," St. Louis History Papers, MHS.

129. Luther M. Kennett, "Mayor's Message," Oct. 14, 1850, *Message of the Mayor of the City of Saint Louis, and Reports of City Officers, Delivered to the City Council,* 2nd Stated Sess. (St. Louis: Missouri Republican Office, 1850), 5, St. Louis Public Library.

130. Criminal cases of selling liquor on Sundays tallied from the St. Louis Criminal Court Records, vol. 6, Jan. 7, 1850, to Dec. 15, 1851, and vol. 7, Dec. 16, 1851, to Dec. 24, 1853, MSA; Seventh Census of St. Louis, 1850, cited in Olson, *St. Louis Germans,* 14–15. See also John C. Schneider, "Riot and Reaction in St. Louis 1854–1856," *Missouri Historical Review* 68 (Jan. 1974): 171–85.

131. See St. Louis Criminal Court Records, Sunday Case Files, 1850–1860, MSA; Criminal Court Records, Sept. 9, 1853, 7:507–8, MSA; Börnstein, *Memoirs of a Nobody,* 198–202, 249–52. Börnstein's case is documented in the Criminal Court Records, Sept. 8, 1853, 7:507–8, MSA.

132. Tyler Anbinder, *Nativism and Slavery: The Northern Know-Nothings and the Politics of the 1850s* (New York: Oxford University Press, 1992). See also Dale T. Knobel, *"America for the Americans": The Nativist Movement in the United States* (New York: Twayne, 1996); Gusfield, *Symbolic Crusade;* Harrison, *Drink and the Victorians;* and Abzug, *Cosmos Crumbling.*

133. Richard Edwards and Merna Hopewell, *Edwards' Great West and Her Commercial Metropolis Embracing a General View of the West, and a Complete History of St. Louis*

(St. Louis: Trubner, 1860), 432. See also Frank Towers, *The Urban South and the Coming of the Civil War* (Charlottesville: University of Virginia Press, 2004), 103–8, 125–27.

134. Börnstein, *Memoirs of a Nobody*, 208–9.

135. Kargau, *German Element in St. Louis*, 149.

136. For more on the nuances of German American politics during the Civil War era, see Alison Clark Efford, *German Immigrants, Race, and Citizenship in the Civil War Era* (Washington, DC: German Historical Institute; Cambridge: Cambridge University Press, 2013); Kristen L. Anderson, *Abolitionizing Missouri: Germans Immigrants and Racial Ideology in Nineteenth-Century America* (Baton Rouge: Louisiana State University Press, 2016); and Susanne Martha Schick, "'For God, Mac, and Country': The Political Worlds of Midwestern Germans during the Civil War Era" (PhD diss., University of Illinois, 1994).

137. See Prahl, "The Turner," 79–110; Walter D. Kamphoefner, *The Westfalians: From Germany to Missouri* (Princeton, NJ: Princeton University Press, 1987); Olson, *St. Louis Germans;* Kellner, "German Element on the Urban Frontier"; Hartmut Keil, ed., *German Workers' Culture in the United States, 1850 to 1920* (Washington, DC: Smithsonian Institution Press, 1988); Linda Schelbitzki Pickle, *Contented among Strangers: Rural German-Speaking Women and Their Families in the Nineteenth-Century Midwest* (Urbana: University of Illinois Press, 1996); Daniel L. Padberg, "German Ethnic Theatre in Missouri: Cultural Assimilation" (PhD diss., Southern Illinois University, 1980); and Charles van Ravenswaay, *The Arts and Architecture of German Settlements in Missouri* (Columbia: University of Missouri Press, 2006).

138. Kargau, *German Element in St. Louis*, 125; Emil to Edward, Jan. 21, 1847 (Letter 21), MHS.

139. Willis L. Williams was a land attorney, and many of his cases involved land disputes between Missouri locals and the Pacific Railroad. Willis L. Williams, "Great Speech of a Know-Nothing Delivered at Hillsboro, Missouri, During the Late Term of the Circuit Court," 1856, John F. Darby Papers, MHS.

140. *Die Nativisten und General Taylor* (Nativism and General Taylor), ca. 1849, OHS.

141. "Know-Nothing Party Platform," ca. 1854, *The Know-Nothing and American Crusader* (Boston: Edward W. Hinks, 1854), Early American Imprints, SLU.

Chapter 3: The Power of Nativist Rhetoric

1. Epigraph from Know-Nothing Party, "The Natives Are Up, D'Ye See" (campaign song "Dedicated to the Native American Party, by R—," ca. 1855), Broadsides, CHS.

2. Alexis de Tocqueville, *Democracy in America,* trans. Harvey C. Mansfield and Delba Winthrop (Chicago: University of Chicago Press, 2000), 280–81.

3. For more on the Christian American "myth," see Allison O'Mahen Malcolm, "Anti-Catholicism and the Rise of Protestant Nationhood in North America,

1830–1871" (PhD diss., University of Illinois–Chicago, 2011); Elizabeth Fenton, *Religious Liberties: Anti-Catholicism and Liberal Democracy in Nineteenth-Century U.S. Literature and Culture* (New York: Oxford University Press, 2011); William M. Shea, *The Lion and the Lamb: Evangelicals and Catholics in America* (New York: Oxford University Press, 2004); John T. McGreevy, *Catholicism and American Freedom: A History* (New York: W. W. Norton, 2003); Francis D. Cogliano, *No King, No Popery: Anti-Catholicism in Revolutionary New England* (Westport, CT: Greenwood, 1995); Jenny Franchot, *Roads to Rome: The Antebellum Protestant Encounter with Catholicism* (Berkeley: University of California Press, 1994); Robert N. Bellah, *The Broken Covenant: American Civil Religion in Time of Trial* (Chicago: University of Chicago Press, 1992); and Ray Allen Billington, *The Protestant Crusade, 1800–1860: A Study of the Origins of American Nativism* (Chicago: Quadrangle Books, 1938).

4. Dale T. Knobel, *"America for the Americans": The Nativist Movement in the United States* (New York: Twayne, 1996), 2.

5. Samuel Finley Breese Morse, "an American," *Imminent Dangers to the Free Institutions of the United States through Foreign Immigration, and the Present State of the Naturalization Laws* (New York: E.B. Clayton, 1835), 8, 24. Also see Samuel Morse, *Our Liberties Defended: The Question Discussed, Is the Protestant or Papal System Most Favorable to Civil and Religious Liberty? By a Protestant, under the signature of Obsta Principiis, and a Roman Catholic, under the signature of Catholicus* (New York: John S. Taylor, 1841). For more on Morse's political career, see Ira M. Leonard and Robert D. Parmet, *American Nativism, 1830–1860* (New York: Van Nostrand Reinhold, 1971), 54–63; and Billington, *Protestant Crusade*, 122–25. Many Protestant leaders elaborated on Morse's conspiracy in the mid-1830s. For example, see Rev. W. C. Brownlee, *Popery: An Enemy to Civil Religious Liberty; and Dangerous to Our Republic* (New York: New York Protestant Press, 1836); and Samuel B. Smith's exposé on Catholic power in the Trans-Mississippi West, *The Flight of Popery from Rome to the West* (New York: 1836), accessed via Hathi Trust Digital Library, Harvard University. Smith also authored *Renunciation of Popery*, 6th ed. (Philadelphia: Stereotyped by L. Johnson, for the author), 1833, Sermons & Papers against the Roman Catholic Church, 1833–1852, General Collection, NL.

6. See Tyler Anbinder, *Nativism and Slavery: The Northern Know-Nothings and the Politics of the 1850s* (New York: Oxford University Press, 1992); Knobel, *"America for the Americans";* and Billington, *Protestant Crusade*.

7. Maria Monk's *Awful Disclosures of the Hotel Dieu Nunnery* (1836) sold more than 300,000 copies prior to the Civil War, which earned it the nickname the "Uncle Tom's Cabin of Know-Nothingism." See Billington, *Protestant Crusade*, 90–108. See also Maria Monk, *Awful Disclosures of the Hotel Dieu Nunnery* (Hamden, CT: Archon Books, 1962). Other popular nineteenth-century nun tales include Samuel B. Smith, *The Escape of Sainte Frances Patrick, Another Nun from the Hotel Dieu Nunnery of Montreal; to which is appended, a decisive confirmation of the Awful Disclosures of Maria Monk: Embellished with Six Engravings* (New York: Office of the Downfall of Babylon, 1836), WU;

and Josephine M. Bunckley, *The Testimony of an Escaped Novice from the Sisterhood of St. Joseph, Emmettsburg, Maryland: The Mother-House of the Sisters of Charity in the United States* (New York: Harper & Brothers, 1855), SLU.

8. Archbishop John Hughes, *A Letter on the Moral Causes that Have Produced the Evil Spirit of the Times; Addressed to the Honorable James Harper, Mayor of New-York; Including a Vindication of the Author from the Infamous Charges Made Against Him by James Gordon Bennett, William L. Stone, and Others* (New York: J. Winchester, New World Press, 1844), 15, Pamphlets, General Collections, NL.

9. Hughes, *Letter on the Moral Causes*, 15–18, 22.

10. Phelim Fearnought O'Flash, *The Only Genuine and Authenticated Report of Mogue More O'Molahan's Dream on the School Question, As dreamed by him on the night of the 3rd, or morning of the 4th of November, A.D. 1841; with a biographical sketch of Mr. O'Molohan Himself, and some of the Pharaoh-like manner in which "The thing had gone from him," while in the act of changing 'his weary side'; together with its miraculous restoration to his memory by the use of "The Apollo Pill, or Mental Regenerator"* (New York: Casserly & Sons, 1841), 11–12, Religious Education, General Collections, NL.

11. *Address of the General Executive Committee of the American Republican Party of the City of New-York; To the People of the United States* (New York: Printed by J. F. Trow, 1845), 9–10, Sabin Americana 54053, WU.

12. Anbinder, *Nativism and Slavery*, 106.

13. Henry Winter Davis, *The Origins, Principles, and Purposes of the American Party* (1855), 7–8, 20, 22, 25. See also *Address of the General Executive Committee*, 9–10.

14. James B. Wallace, Christian County, KY, to Thomas Henry Wallace, Crittenden County, KY, July 13, 1855, Wallace Family Papers, folder 24, FHS.

15. Billington, *Protestant Crusade*, 220–33; Leonard and Parmet, *American Nativism*, 66–68.

16. For contemporary accounts of the Philadelphia Riots of 1844, see *The Full Particulars of the Late Riots, With a View of the Burning of the Catholic Churches, St. Michaels & St. Augustines* (Philadelphia, 1844), Early American Imprints, Pamphlet 1153, SLU; *The Truth Unveiled; or, A Calm and Impartial Exposition of the Origin and Immediate Cause of the Terrible Riots in Philadelphia, on May 6th, 7th, and 8th, A.D. 1844; By a Protestant and Native Philadelphian* (Philadelphia: M. Fithian, 1844), Pamphlet 80, ibid.; Edwin Hubbell Chapin, *A Discourse Preached in the Universalist Church, Charlestown, on Sunday, May 12, 1844, in Reference to the Recent Riots in Philadelphia* (Boston: A. Tompkins, 1844), Pamphlet 852, ibid.; and John Hancock Lee, *The Origin and Progress of the American Party in Politics; Embracing a Complete History of the Philadelphia Riots in 1844 and a Refutation of the Arguments Founded on the Charges of Religious Proscription and Secret Combinations* (Philadelphia: Elliott & Gihon, 1855).

17. "Thursday, November 21, 1844: Proscription," *Cincinnati Weekly Herald and Philanthropist*, Nov. 27, 1844, American Periodicals, WU. For more on the Charlestown convent burning and the Philadelphia Bible Riots, see Katie Oxx, *The Nativist*

Movement in America: Religious Conflict in the Nineteenth Century (New York: Routledge Taylor & Francis, 2013).

18. M.J.S., "Retrospect of the Past Year," *U.S. Catholic Magazine and Monthly Review* 4, no. 1 (Jan. 1845), American Periodicals, WU. Archbishop John Hughes of New York also criticized the nativists for making the Bible a party ensign. See Hughes, *Letter on the Moral Causes,* 15–18, Pamphlets, General Collections, NL.

19. "An Address to the Native Americans of the Fayette Congressional District" (Georgetown, KY: 1847), Broadsides of the Know-Nothing Party, FHS.

20. American Republican Party, "American Republican Manifesto" (ca. 1847), Broadsides of the Know-Nothing Party, FHS.

21. S. Medary, "Prospectus of the Ohio Statesman, Session Paper for 1844–5," Nov. 5, 1844 (Columbus, OH), Unbound Newspaper, CMC.

22. Unknown, Louisville, to William Bodley, Aug. 7, 1844, Bodley Family Papers, folder 31, FHS.

23. "To the Freemen of the Eighth Congressional District," *Kentucky Yeoman,* July 28, 1849 (Frankfort, KY: Kentucky Yeoman Office, 1849), Broadside, FHS.

24. Charles Morehead later won the governorship on the American ticket in 1855, and Know-Nothing Humphrey Marshall won a congressional seat that same year. For more on Trabue's candidacy, see P. H. Cooney, "To S. F.J. Trabue, Esq., Candidate for Congress," *Kentucky Commonwealth,* July 17, 1849, Broadside, FHS.

25. Hamilton Rowan Gamble was a lawyer, secretary of the state of Missouri (1824), judge, Know-Nothing representative, and the provisional governor of Missouri during the Civil War (1861–64). He was a member of the Whig Party. Gamble was elected to the Missouri Supreme Court in 1851 but resigned in 1855 due to "ill health." He temporarily moved to Philadelphia, returning to Missouri in 1861.

26. Charles Keemle, *The St. Louis Directory for the Years 1840–1* (St. Louis: Charles Keemle, Book and Job Printer, 1840), 75, MHS; Mary E. Sibley, St. Charles, to Judge Hamilton R. Gamble, St. Louis, May 24, 1854, Gamble Papers, box 8, folder 9, MHS; Stacey G. Potts, NJ, to Hamilton R. Gamble, St. Louis, June 2, 1849, ibid., folder 5; National American Party, Minute Book of the Grand Council of the State of Missouri, Oct. 20, 1855, Solomon Smith Collection, MHS.

27. "American Republican Ticket," 1846, Case Family Papers, MHS.

28. Newspaper clipping, 1874, Case Family Papers, MHS.

29. Charles Peabody, American West Travel Diary, vol. 1, Mar. 13, 1849, MHS; *Thirteenth Annual Report of the Foreign Mission Society of the Valley of the Mississippi: Auxiliary to the American Board of Commissioners for Foreign Missions; Presented at Circleville, Ohio, Sept. 28, 1845* (Cincinnati: Printed for the Society by C. Clark, 1845), Pamphlets, CMC.

30. Beriah Cleland, *A Historical Account of All the Mayors, Since the Formation of the City Government of St. Louis to the Present Date-1846* (St. Louis: 1846), John Darby Papers, MHS.

31. National American Party, Minute Book of the Grand Council of the State of Missouri, 1854–57, Solomon Smith Collection, MHS; James Green, *Green's Saint Louis Directory for 1845* (St. Louis: James Green, 1844), xxxii.

32. Indenture, Records of the First Presbyterian Society of Cincinnati, Dec. 21, 1843, CMC.

33. James D. Taylor, "Mission Statement," *Cincinnati Dollar Weekly Times* (Cincinnati: C. W. Starbuck, 1856), Early American Imprints, Broadsides 9192, SLU.

34. Taylor, ed., *The Cincinnati Dollar Weekly Times,* 1855. Also see Anbinder, *Nativism and Slavery,* 24.

35. Charles Peabody, Diary, Mar. 18, 1847, MHS.

36. Rev. Charles Brandon Boynton, *Oration, Delivered on the Fifth of July, 1847, Before the Native Americans of Cincinnati* (Cincinnati: Tagart & Gardner, printers, 1847), 19–20, 23, Broadsides, CMC.

37. For a historical and theological perspective on the Catholic American and Protestant American myths, see Shea, *Lion and the Lamb,* 14–23, 55–82. This theme will be more fully explored in chapter 6. For a discussion of the nineteenth-century relationship between Protestantism and the growth of modern capitalism, see Max Weber, *The Protestant Ethic and the Spirit of Capitalism,* trans. Talcott Parsons (New York: Charles Scribner's Sons, 1958).

38. *Startling Facts for Native Americans Called "Know-Nothings," or a Vivid Presentation of the Dangers of American Liberty, to Be Apprehended from Foreign Influence* (New York: Published at 128 Nassau Street, 1855), 11.

39. Boynton, *Oration,* 11–19, Broadsides, CMC. For studies on Dispensationalism, see Russell R. Reno, *In the Ruins of the Church: Sustaining Faith in an Age of Diminished Christianity* (Grand Rapids, MI: Brazos, 2002); Randall Herbert Balmer, *Mine Eyes Have Seen the Glory: A Journey into the Evangelical Subculture* (New York: Oxford University Press, 1993); and Larry V. Crutchfield, *The Origins of Dispensationalism: The Darby Factor* (Lanham, MD: University Press of America, 1992).

40. Boynton, *Oration,* 6–10, Broadsides, CMC.

41. The OUA eventually merged with the Order of the Star-Spangled Banner (also known as the Order of Know-Nothings).

42. Brother Alfred Brewster Ely, *American Liberty, Its Sources—Its Dangers, and the Means of Its Preservation: An Oration, Delivered at the Broadway Tabernacle, in New-York, Before the Order of United Americans, on the 22d of February, AD 1850, Being the 118th Anniversary of the Birthday of Washington* (New York: Seaman & Dunham, Printers, 1850), 30. See Anbinder, *Nativism and Slavery,* 13–14, 20–24. For more on the rituals of the Order of United Americans and the Order of the Star-Spangled Banner in New York, see Carleton Beals, *Brass-Knuckle Crusade: The Great Know-Nothing Conspiracy, 1820–1860* (New York: Hastings House, 1960), 129–45.

43. Ely, *American Liberty,* 5–16.

44. Ely, *American Liberty,* 5–16.

45. For example, Missouri nativist leader Henry W. Williams, who was elected the president of the Know-Nothing Bunker Hill Council, no. 5, in 1854 and a national delegate by Missouri's Grand Council for the first district of St. Louis in 1855, kept a list of books in his library, which included Maria Monk, *Awful Disclosures by Maria Monk, of the Hotel Dieu Nunnery of Montreal* (New York: By the author, 1836); Anna Ella Carroll, *The Great American Battle; or, The Contest between Christianity and Political Romanism* (New York: Miller, Orton, & Mulligan, 1856); George Lynn-Lachlan Davis, *Day-Star of American Freedom: The Birth and Early Growth of Toleration in the Province of Maryland* (New York: C. Scribner, 1855); Justin Dewey Fulton, *The Outlook of Freedom; or, The Roman Catholic Element in American History* (Cincinnati: Printed for the Author by Moore, Wilstach, Keys, & Overend, 1856); Thomas Richard Whitney, *A Defence of the American Policy, as Opposed to the Encroachments of Foreign Influence: and Especially to the Interference of the Papacy in the Political Interests and Affairs of the United States* (N.p.: De Witt & Davenport, 1856); Lee, *Origin and Progress of the American Party in Politics;* William Henry Ryder, ed., *Our Country; or, The American Parlor Keepsake* (Boston: J. M. Usher, 1854); Rev. James L. Chapman, *Americanism Versus Romanism; or, The Cis-Atlantic Battle between Sam and the Pope* (Nashville, TN: By the author, 1856); Thomas D'Arcy McGee, *Catholic History of North America: Five Discourses; To Which Are Added Two Discourses on the Relations of Ireland and America* (Boston: Patrick Donahoe, 1855); Augusta Theodosia Drane, ed., *Catholic Legends: A New Collection Selected, Translated, and Arranged from the Best Sources* (London: Burns and Lambert, 1855); and the sermons of Rev. Lyman Beecher and papers of the famous nativist statesman Henry Winter Davis. Henry W. Williams, Williams's Library, n.d., box 1, folder 49, Papers of Henry Williams, MHS.

46. Carroll, *Great American Battle,* viii.

47. "Miller, Orton & Mulligan will publish on February 22d, The Great American Battle, by Anna Ella Carroll of Maryland, with fine steel portraits" (New York: Miller, Orton, & Mulligan, 1856), Early American Broadside, Pius Library, SLU. Anna Carroll even served as Abraham Lincoln's advisor in 1861. Her pro-Union work, *Reply to Breckenridge,* inspired President Lincoln to demand government funding for the distribution of 50,000 copies of her book throughout the states. Sydney Greenbie and Marjorie Barstow Greenbie, *Anna Ella Carroll and Abraham Lincoln* (Tampa: University of Tampa Press, 1952). For more on Carroll's political career, see Janet L. Coryell, *Neither Heroine nor Fool: Anna Ella Carroll of Maryland* (Kent, OH: Kent State University Press, 1990).

48. For more on the Carroll family, see Maura Farrelly, *Papist Patriots: The Making of an American Catholic Identity* (New York: Oxford University Press, 2012); Ronald Hoffman, *Princes of Ireland, Planters of Maryland: A Carroll Saga, 1500–1782* (Chapel Hill: University of North Carolina Press, 2000); Steven M. Avella and Elizabeth McKeown, eds., *Public Voices: Catholics in the American Context* (Maryknoll, NY: Orbis Books, 1999); Anne M. Butler, Michael E. Engh, and Thomas W. Spalding, eds., *The Frontiers and Catholic Identities* (Maryknoll, New York: Orbis Books, 1999); Scott McDermott,

Charles Carroll of Carrollton: Faithful Revolutionary (New York: Scepter, 2002); and Joseph Agonito, *The Building of an American Catholic Church: The Episcopacy of John Carroll* (New York: Garland, 1988).

49. Carroll, *Great American Battle,* viii, x.

50. Carroll, *Great American Battle,* v.

51. Anna Ella Carroll, *The Romish Church Opposed to the Liberties of the American People; With a Biographical Sketch of the Hon. Erastus Brooks; His Celebrated Controversy With Archbishop Hughes, &c.* (Boston: James French, 1856), Sabin Americana, Olin Library, WU.

52. Anna Ella Carroll, *The Union of the States* (Boston: James French, 1856), Olin Library, WU.

53. Carroll conflated the Pilgrims, who arrived in 1620, with the Puritan exodus a decade later.

54. Carroll, *Union of the States.*

55. For an analysis of "manifest destiny," see John Craig Hammond, *Slavery, Freedom, and Expansion in the Early American West* (Charlottesville: University of Virginia Press, 2007); and Thomas Hietala, *Manifest Design: Anxious Aggrandizement in Late Jacksonian America* (Ithaca, NY: Cornell University Press, 1985).

56. See Richard Hakluyt, "Inducements to the lykinge of the voyadge intended to that parte of America which lyeth between 34. and 36. degree," in *New American World,* ed. David B. Quinn, vol. 3 (New York: Arno, 1979): 62–64. For more on the founding of Jamestown, see David Harris Sacks, "Discourses of Western Planting: Richard Hakluyt and the Making of the Atlantic World," in *The Atlantic World and Virginia, 1550–1624,* ed. Peter C. Mancall (Chapel Hill: University of North Carolina Press, 2007), 410–53; Peter C. Mancall, *Hakluyt's Promise: An Elizabethan's Obsession for an English America* (New Haven, CT: Yale University Press, 2007); and Edmund S. Morgan, *American Slavery, American Freedom: The Ordeal of Colonial Virginia* (New York: Norton, 1975).

57. Carroll, *Union of the States,* 7–8.

58. See Alan Taylor, "Squaring the Circles: The Reach of Colonial America," in *American History Now,* ed. Eric Foner and Lisa McGirr (Philadelphia: Temple University Press, 2011); Jack P. Greene, *Pursuits of Happiness: The Social Development of Early Modern British Colonies and the Formation of American Culture* (Chapel Hill: University of North Carolina Press, 1988); and Morgan, *American Slavery, American Freedom.*

59. Fulton, *Outlook of Freedom,* iii–iv.

60. Edward G. Lengel, *Inventing George Washington: America's Founder, in Myth and Memory* (New York: Harper Collins, 2011), 13, 22–25, 78; Gerald E. Kahler, *The Long Farewell: Americans Mourn the Death of George Washington* (Charlottesville: University of Virginia Press, 2008). For more on civil religion, see Sanford Kessler, *Tocqueville's Civil Religion: American Christianity and the Prospects for Freedom* (Albany: State University of New York Press, 1994); Martin E. Marty, ed., *Civil Religion, Church and State* (New York: K. G. Saur, 1992); and Richard V. Pierard and Robert D. Linder, *Civil Religion and the Presidency* (Grand Rapids, MI: Academie Books, 1988).

61. For example, see "One of 'Em,'" ed., *The Wide-Awake Gift: A Know-Nothing Token for 1855; "Put None but Americans on Guard to-night"* (Cincinnati: H. W. Derby, 1855), MHS; and Lengel, *Inventing George Washington*, 86–91.

62. Ely, *American Liberty*, 25, 30–31.

63. For more on Washington's "prayer" at Valley Forge as Mason Locke Weem's fabrication, see Lengel, *Inventing George Washington*, 77–91.

64. "Order of United Americans Certificate of Membership for William W. Dilks by Continental Chapter no. 12 of New York, Jan. 17, 1850" (New York: Printed by Nagel & Weingaertner, 1850), Broadside, CHS.

65. "Prospectus," *Weekly American Ensign* (New York: 1844), Broadsides, Early American Imprints 6383, Pius Library, SLU.

66. Boynton, *Oration*, 9–11, Broadsides, CMC. See Mark A. Noll, *America's God: From Jonathan Edwards to Abraham Lincoln* (New York: Oxford University Press, 2002), 53–160; and Malcolm, "Anti-Catholicism and the Rise of Protestant Nationhood."

67. Carroll, *Romish Church*, 6, Sabin Americana, Olin Library, WU. For more on Washington's "supplication" as Weem's fabrication, see Lengel, *Inventing George Washington*, 86–91.

68. Ely, *American Liberty*, 25, 29.

69. For example, see American Party, "Andrew Johnson's Position Condemned by Jefferson's Teachings," in *Facts for the People! Read Before You Vote!! Americans Should Govern America!!* (Published by the Executive Committee of the American Party of Tennessee, 1856), Pamphlet, OHS.

70. James B. Wallace, Christian County, KY, to Thomas Henry Wallace, Crittenden County, KY, July 13, 1855, Wallace Family Papers, folder 24, FHS.

71. Rev. William Wiener [Native American], *Fatal Mistake: A Pamphlet in Four Numbers Showing the Nature, Political Bearing, Object and Tendency of Popery in this Country* (New York, 1835), 4–5, Special Collections, NL.

72. Boynton, *Oration*, 19, Broadsides, CMC. See also Daniel Walker Howe, *What Hath God Wrought: The Transformation of America, 1815–1848* (New York: Oxford University Press, 2007), 285–327; Grant Wacker, "Religion in Nineteenth-Century America," *Religion in American Life: A Short History*, ed. Jon Butler, Grant Wacker, and Randall Balmer (New York: Oxford University Press, 2003), 165–330; Robert H. Azbug, *Cosmos Crumbling: American Reform and the Religious Imagination* (New York: Oxford University Press, 1994); Charles Sellers, *The Market Revolution: Jacksonian America, 1815–1846* (New York: Oxford University Press, 1991), 301–31; and Ruth H. Bloch, *Visionary Republic: Millennial Themes in American Thought, 1756–1800* (Cambridge: Cambridge University Press, 1985).

73. For more on Sabbatarianism and the Bible in public schools, see Steven K. Green, *The Bible, the School, and the Constitution: The Clash That Shaped Modern Church-State Doctrine* (New York: Oxford University Press, 2014). Richard R. John demonstrates the significance of early Sabbatarianism in the American opposition to postal operations on Sundays in *Spreading the News: The American Postal System from Franklin to Morse*

(Cambridge, MA: Harvard University Press, 1995). Kyle G. Volk examined the issue of the Sunday laws, drinking, and minority rights in "Majority Rule, Minority Rights: The Christian Sabbath, Liquor, Racial Amalgamation, and Democracy in Antebellum America" (PhD diss., University of Chicago, Illinois, 2008). For more on the place of religion in early American government, see David Sehat, *The Myth of American Religious Freedom* (New York: Oxford University Press, 2011); Steven K. Green, *The Second Disestablishment: Church and State in Nineteenth-Century America* (New York: Oxford University Press, 2010); and Tracy Fessenden, *Culture and Redemption: Religion, the Secular, and American Literature* (Princeton, NJ: Princeton University Press, 2007).

74. Rev. Abel Stevens, *An Alarm to American Patriots: A Sermon on the Political Tendencies of Popery, Considered in Respect to the Institutions of the United States, Delivered in the Church Street Church, Boston, November 27, 1834; Being the Day of Annual Thanksgiving*, 2nd ed. (Boston: Printed by David H. Ela, 1835), 3–4, 8, General Collections, NL.

75. Daniel Raymond, "Prospectus of the Western Statesman," *Cincinnati Western Statesman*, Nov. 12, 1842, 1, Unbound Newspapers, CHS.

76. Boynton, *Oration*, 17, Broadsides, CMC.

77. Distinguished Virginian, *Twelve Letters, Over the Signature of 'Madison,' on the American Question*, ca. 1855, American Party no. 9, p. 22, General Collections, NL.

78. Wiener, *Fatal Mistake*, 4–5.

79. Rev. Nicholas Murray, D.D. [Kirwan], *The Decline of Popery and Its Causes: An Address Delivered in the Broadway Tabernacle, on Wednesday Evening, January 15, 1851* (New York: Harper & Brothers, 1851), Sermons & Papers against the Roman Catholic Church, 1833–52, 6, General Collections, NL. For more on the use of "popery" as a literary device, see Franchot, *Roads to Rome;* and Susan Griffin, *Anti-Catholicism and Nineteenth-Century Fiction* (Cambridge: Cambridge University Press, 2004).

80. Murray, *Decline of Popery*.

81. Rev. J. Balmes, *Protestantism and Catholicity Compared in Their Effects on the Civilization of Europe* (Baltimore: 1842), 27, qtd. in McGreevy, *Catholicism and American Freedom*, 35.

82. Bishop Martin J. Spalding, *Miscellanea: Comprising Reviews, Lectures and Essays, on Historical, Theological and Miscellaneous Subjects* (Louisville: 1855), xli, 390, qtd. in McGreevy, *Catholicism and American Freedom*, 35, 37.

83. American Citizen, *Reverend Cha's B. Boynton on Nativism*, 9, 17. See also Farrelly, *Papist Patriots;* and J. Moss Ives, *The Ark and the Dove: The Beginning of Civil and Religious Liberties in America* (New York: Cooper Square, 1969).

84. The Glorious Revolution in England (1688–90) spilled over into the American colonies, including Maryland. See Farrelly, *Papist Patriots;* and David S. Lovejoy, *The Glorious Revolution* (New York: Harper and Row, 1972).

85. George Lynn-Lachlan Davis, *The Day-Star of American Freedom; or, The Birth and Early Growth of Toleration in the Province of Maryland; With a Glimpse of the Numbers and General Stats of Society, of the Religion and Legislation, of the Life and Manners*

of the Men Who Worshiped in the Wilderness at the First Rude Altar of Liberty (New York: C. Scribner, 1855), 36–37.

86. George Washington and Bishop Charles Carroll, "Address of the Roman Catholics of America to George Washington, and His Reply," in McGee, *Catholic History of North America,* 194–98. See also McGreevy, *Catholicism and American Freedom.*

87. American Citizen, *Reverend Cha's B. Boynton on Nativism,* 4–9, 15, 18.

88. American Citizen, *Reverend Cha's B. Boynton on Nativism,* 4–9, 15–18. For more on the creation of an American Catholic identity in colonial Maryland, see Farrelly, *Papist Patriots.* See also McDermott, *Charles Carroll of Carrollton.*

89. Father Edward Purcell, "Washington's Birth Day," Feb. 18, 1843, *Catholic Telegraph* 12, no. 7 (Archdiocese of Cincinnati and Louisville): 51, Microfilm, PLC.

90. Father Edward Purcell, "Fourth of July," July 8, 1843, *Catholic Telegraph* 12, no. 27 (Archdiocese of Cincinnati and Louisville): 214, Microfilm, PLC. See also Adam Criblez, *Parading Patriotism: Independence Day Celebrations in the Urban Midwest, 1826–1876* (Dekalb: Northern Illinois University Press, 2013); and Father Edward Purcell, "The Presbyterian of the West," *Catholic Telegraph,* Jan. 23, 1845, 14, no. 3 (Archdiocese of Cincinnati and Louisville): 23, Microfilm, PLC.

91. See Doran Hurley, "Was Washington a Catholic?" *I.C.B.U. Journal* 71 (1957): 2–6; and Lengel, *Inventing George Washington,* 86–91.

92. Father Edward Purcell, "American Principles and Religious Proscription," *Catholic Telegraph,* Aug. 26, 1854, 23, no. 34 (Archdiocese of Cincinnati and Louisville): 4, Microfilm Reel 7, PLC.

93. Hughes, *Letter on the Moral Causes,* 15–18, 22, Pamphlets, General Collections, NL.

94. James Lowery Donaldson Morrison (1816–88) had an interesting political career. He served as a Whig in the Illinois house of representatives in 1844. He was elected to the state senate in 1848. He unsuccessfully ran as a Whig candidate for lieutenant governor of Illinois in 1852. When the Whig Party collapsed, he defected to the Democrat Party and was elected to the state house of representatives again in 1856. He unsuccessfully ran as a Democratic candidate for governor in 1860. Sen. James L. D. Morrison, *Senate of Illinois: Senator Morrison on the Know-Nothings* (1852), 2–3, 6–8, Pamphlets, CHS.

95. Nativists discussed this controversial statement in a special meeting outside Chicago in September 1854. See Maj. Jack Downings Letters, no. 5, Prairyville, IL, to Pres. Franklin Pierce, Washington D.C., Sept. 26, 1854, draft prepared for the *St. Louis Intelligencer,* Henry Williams Papers, MHS.

Chapter 4: The Order of Know-Nothings and Secret Democracy

1. Epigraph from William Russell Smith, *The American Party and Its Mission: Speech of Mr. Smith of Alabama, Delivered in the U.S. House of Representatives, Jan. 15, 1855,* 7, Pamphlet, CMC.

2. See David Bennett, *The Party of Fear: From Nativist Movements to the New Right in American History* (Chapel Hill: University of North Carolina Press, 1988); and Peter Schrag, *Not Fit for Our Society: Immigration and Nativism in America* (University of California Press, 2010).

3. See Bennett, *Party of Fear;* Schrag, *Not Fit for Our Society;* and Jenny Franchot, *Roads to Rome: The Antebellum Protestant Encounter with Catholicism* (Berkeley: University of California Press, 1994).

4. Senator from Virginia, Speech, Untitled Newspaper Excerpt, ca. 1855, in James Stone Chrisman, Scrapbook, FHS. See Franchot, *Roads to Rome.*

5. See Michael F. Holt, "The Politics of Impatience: The Origins of Know-Nothingism," *Journal of American History* 60, no. 2 (Sept. 1973): 309–31.

6. "Know-Nothing Passwords," ca. 1854, OHS.

7. Tyler Anbinder, *Nativism and Slavery: The Northern Know-Nothings and the Politics of the 1850s* (New York: Oxford University Press, 1992), 21. For more on Horace Greeley's opinions on party realignment and the Know-Nothings, see Gregory A. Borchard, *Abraham Lincoln and Horace Greeley* (Carbondale: Southern Illinois University Press, 2011); and the New York Tribune, *Horace Greeley and the Republican Party, 1853–1861* (New York: Octagon Books, 1965).

8. Dale Knobel, *"America for the Americans": The Nativist Movement in the United States* (New York: Twayne, 1996).

9. One early biographer noted the national reputation Ned Buntline gained for his own nativist newspaper and the "unfaltering Americanism" of the secret organization he led in New York. Westerners read about Buntline's Order rioting outside a theater on Astor Place, because it employed "foreign" actors, in May 1849. Fred E. Pond (pseud., Will Wildwood), *Life and Adventures of "Ned Buntline" with Ned Buntline's Anecdote of "Frank Forester" and a Chapter of Angling Sketches* (New York, 1919), 2–3. For accounts of the Astor Place Riot of 1849, see Jay Monaghan, *The Great Rascal: The Life and Adventures of Ned Buntline* (Boston: Little, Brown, 1952), 172–81; "Convicted," *New Hampshire Patriot* (Concord), Oct. 4, 1849, 2; and "Good," *Semi-weekly Eagle* (Brattleboro, VT), Oct. 4, 1849, 2.

10. The beginnings of the Order of the Star-Spangled Banner in New York City might have traced to as early as 1847. See Anbinder, *Nativism and Slavery,* 21; and Carleton Beals, *Brass-Knuckle Crusade: The Great Know-Nothing Conspiracy, 1820–1860* (New York: Hastings House, 1960), 130–45.

11. By mid-1855, most Know-Nothing councils had lowered the age requirement from twenty-one to eighteen years old.

12. "The Know-Nothings," *St. Louis Liberty Tribune,* Oct. 6, 1854.

13. A Know Something, Late of the Grand Council, *An Expose of the Secret Order of Know-Nothings: The Most Ludicrous and Startling Yankee 'Notion' Ever Conceived* (New York: Stearns, 1854), 7–8, 31.

14. Lemuel C. Porter, Diary, July 1855, 37, Minutes of the Bowling Green Lyceum, FHS.

15. David Todd Stuart, Diary, Aug. 7–10, 1854, FHS.

16. Albert Seaton Berry, Miami University, OH, to Cousin Thomas Berry Buckner, KY, Sept. 18, 1854, Buckner Family Papers, folder 19, FHS. Albert Seaton Berry, born February 13, 1836 (died 1908), the son of James T. Berry and Elizabeth V. Berry, graduated from Miami University two years later, served in the Confederate army during the Civil War, and went on to political fame as the mayor (1874–80, 1888) of Newport, Kentucky; state senator (1880–88), and U.S. representative (1893–1901). His cousin Thomas Berry Buckner was also a Know-Nothing.

17. *Proceedings of the Grand Council of Ohio: From the Organization, April 23d. to August 1st, 1854* (Cincinnati: Printed by Tidball, Turner, & Gray, Odd Fellows' Literary Casket Office, 1854), Pamphlet, CMC.

18. National American Party, Minute Book of the Grand Council of the State of Missouri, 1854–57, Solomon Smith Collection, MHS (hereafter cited as Missouri Grand Council Minute Book).

19. Thomas Spooner, *Address to Executive Council at Cleveland,* June 2, 1855, Pamphlet, CMC; William E. Gienapp, "Salmon P. Chase, Nativism, and the Formation of the Republican Party in Ohio," *Ohio History* 93, no. 6 (Winter 1984): 5–39. For more on the rise of the Know-Nothing Party in the Old Northwest, see Sister M. Evangeline Thomas, "Nativism in the Old Northwest, 1850–1860" (PhD diss., Catholic University of America, 1936).

20. Garrett Davis, *An Address on "Securing the Blessings of Liberty to Ourselves and to Our Posterity"; or, The Oneness of the American People, Against Alien and Papal Aggressions* (Louisville, KY: 1855), 35, Rare Pamphlet, FHS. Another leading Know-Nothing politician used precisely the same language as Garrett Davis in a speech before Congress earlier that year: "When you fight the devil, you have a right to fight him with fire." Smith, *American Party and Its Mission,* 7, Pamphlet, CMC.

21. Popular nineteenth-century nun tales include Maria Monk, *Awful Disclosures of the Hotel Dieu Nunnery,* ed. Ray Allen Billington (Hamden, CT: Archon Books, 1962); Charles W. Frothingham, *Six Hours in a Convent; or, The Stolen Nuns!: A Tale of Charlestown in 1834,* 8th ed. (Boston: Graves & Weston, 1855), SLU; George Bourne, *Lorette: History of Louise, Daughter of a Canadian Nun, Exhibiting the Interior of Female Convents,* 6th ed. (New York: Charles Small, 1834); Scipio de Ricci, *Female Convents: Secrets of Nunneries Disclosed,* ed. Thomas Roscoe (New York: D. Appleton, 1834); Samuel B. Smith, *The Escape of Sainte Frances Patrick, Another Nun from the Hotel Dieu Nunnery of Montreal; to which is appended, a decisive confirmation of the Awful Disclosures of Maria Monk: Embellished with Six Engravings* (New York: Office of the Downfall of Babylon, 1836), WU; Rachel McCrindell, *The School-Girl in France; or, The Snares of Popery: A Warning to Protestants Against Education in Catholic Seminaries,* 2nd ed. (New York: J. K. Wellman, 1845); McCrindell, *The Convent: A Narrative, Founded on Fact* (London: Aylott and Jones, 1848); Theodore Dwight, *Open Convents; or, Nunneries and Popish Seminaries Dangerous to the Morals, and Degrading to the Character of a Republic Community* (New York: Van Nostrand and Dwight, 1852); Hannah Corcoran, *Hannah Corcoran, The Missing Girl of Charlestown: The Mysterious Disappearance*

Unraveled; the Convent and the Confessor attempt at Abduction Foiled!; A Full and Complete Report of the Riot in Charlestown, ed. Thomas F. Caldicott (Boston: Palfrey, 1853), SLU; *A Narrative of the Conversion and Sufferings of Sarah Doherty, Illustrative of Popery in Ireland and of the Power of Evangelical Truth* (New York: American and Foreign Christian Union, 1854); Andrew Boyd Cross and Thomas Parkin Scott, *Priests' Prisons for Women, or a Consideration of the Question, whether unmarried foreign priests ought to be permitted to erect prisons, into which, under pretence of religion, to seduce or entrap, or by force compel young women to enter, and after they have secured their property, keep them in confinement, and compel them, as their slaves, to submit themselves to their will, under the penalty of flogging or the dungeon? In Twelve Letters to T. Parkin Scott, Esq., Member of the Baltimore Bar, and Vice Consul of the Pope* (Baltimore: Printed by Sherwood, 1854); *Sister Agnes; or, The Captive Nun: A Picture of Convent Life, by a Clergyman's Widow* (New York: Riker, Thorne, 1854), SLU; and Josephine M. Bunckley, *The Testimony of an Escaped Novice from the Sisterhood of St. Joseph, Emmettsburg, Maryland: The Mother-House of the Sisters of Charity in the United States* (New York: Harper & Brothers, 1855), SLU. See also Rebecca Theresa Reed, *Veil of Fear: Nineteenth-Century Convent Tales of Rebecca Reed and Maria Monk* (West Lafayette, IN: Notabell Books, 1999). Interestingly, Maria Monk's story was investigated and proved to be false. See Robert William Wilson, *A Complete Refutation of Maria Monk's Atrocious Plot: Concerning the Hotel Dieu Convent, in Montreal, Lower Canada, by Col. Stone, a Protestant Gentleman of New York; to which is added, documentary evidence chiefly upon oath, of the vile impositions and profligate conduct of the said Maria Monk for the last four years; with a short introductory address to the friends of truth* (Nottingham: Printed and sold by J. Shaw, 1837). For a comprehensive analysis of the nineteenth-century nun tales, see Cassandra L. Yacovazzi, *Escaped Nuns: True Womanhood and the Campaign against Convents in Antebellum America* (New York: Oxford University Press, 2019).

22. Samuel Finley Breese Morse [Brutus], *Foreign Conspiracy against the Liberties of the United States: The Numbers of Brutus* (1835; repr., New York: Arno, 1977); Samuel B. Smith [Late a Popish Priest], *The Flight of Popery from Rome to the West* (New York: 1836), Hathi Trust Digital Library, Harvard University. https://babel.hathitrust.org/cgi/pt?id=hvd.hnnazn&view=1up&seq=11.

23. See Antonia Fraser, *Faith and Treason: The Story of the Gunpowder Plot* (New York: Nan A. Talese/Doubleday, 1996); Fraser, *The Gunpowder Plot: Terror and Faith in 1605* (London: Weiddenfeld and Nicolson, 1996); Alan Haynes, *The Gunpowder Plot: Faith in Rebellion* (Stroud, Eng.: A. Sutton, 1994); and Philip Caraman, *Henry Garnet, 1555–1606, and the Gunpowder Plot* (New York: Farrar, Straus, 1964).

24. Rev. Abel Stevens, *An Alarm to American Patriots: A Sermon on the Political Tendencies of Popery, Considered in Respect to the Institutions of the United States, Delivered in the Church Street Church, Boston, November 27, 1834; Being the Day of Annual Thanksgiving,* 2nd ed. (Boston: Printed by David H. Ela, 1835), 15, General Collections, NL.

25. Rev. Samuel Simon Schmucker, *The Papal Heirarchy, Viewed in the Light of Prophecy and History; Being a Discourse Delivered in the English Lutheran Church, Gettysburg,*

February 2, 1845 (Gettysburg: Printed by H. C. Neinstedt, 1845), 14, Sermons & Papers against the Roman Catholic Church, 1833–52, General Collections, NL.

26. The Second Battle of Arklow occurred on June 9, 1798, during the Irish colonial rebellion against the British. A force of about 10,000 United Catholic Irishmen from Wexford attacked the British-held town of Arklow in an attempt to spread the rebellion in the county and capture the capital of Dublin.

27. A Former French Roman Catholic, but Now a Protestant and Colporteur [G. A. Seigneur], *A Startling Disclosure of the Secret Workings of the Jesuits; Together with the Secret Seal of the Confessional, the Obligations of the Confessor and the Confessed; the Creed and Oaths of Popery; the Secret Instructions of the Jesuits, and Much Other Useful Information* (Published by the author, 1854), 28, 70–71, Sabin Americana, WU.

28. Former French Roman Catholic, *Startling Disclosure,* 28, 70–71.

29. *Startling Facts for Native Americans Called "Know-Nothings," or a Vivid Presentation of the Dangers of American Liberty, to Be Apprehended from Foreign Influence* (New York: Published at 128 Nassau Street, 1855), 58. See also Thomas W. Whitley, *The Jesuit: A National Melo-drama, in three acts, Founded on Incidents Growing Out of the War Between the United States and Mexico* (New York: Democratic Review, 1850), Pamphlets in American History 1033, SLU; Giacinto Achilli, *Dealings with the Inquisition; or, Papal Rome, Her Priests, and Her Jesuits: with important disclosures* (New York: Harper, 1851), SLU; *Helen Mulgrave; or, Jesuit Executorship: Being Passages in the Life of a Seceder from Romanism, an Autobiography* (New York: DeWitt & Davenport, 1852), SLU; Hamilton, *Carlington Castle: A Tale of the Jesuits* (New York: Bunce & Brother, 1854); John Claudius Pitrat, *Americans Warned of Jesuitism; or, The Jesuits Unveiled,* 3rd ed. (Boston: Edward W. Hinks, 1855); American Protestant Society, *A Book of Tracts, Containing the Origin and Progress, Cruelties, Frauds, Superstitions, Miracles, Ceremonies, Idolatrous Customs, &c. of the Church of Rome: With a Succinct Account of the Rise and Progress of the Jesuits; with other instructive and interesting matter* (New York: American and Foreign Christian Union, 1856); and Luigi de Sanctis, *Rome, Christian and Papal: Sketches of its Religious Monuments and Ecclesiastical Hierarchy, with Notices of the Jesuits and the Inquisition* (New York: Harper & Brothers, 1856).

30. Rev. Charles Brandon Boynton, *Address before the Citizens of Cincinnati: Delivered on the Fourth Day of July, 1855* (Cincinnati: Cincinnati Gazette Company Print, 1855), 12, 14, 18, Pamphlet, CHS.

31. Approximately 150,000 immigrants arrived in the United States per year in the 1850s—many of them Catholic. In 1855 one anonymous Know-Nothing estimated that there were "2,500,000 Papists under the government of the pope of Rome." By 1860, the Catholic population in the United States reached 3 million. The same man also estimated that the Catholic Archdiocese of Baltimore ministered to 90,000 people, and the Archdiocese of New York to more than 200,000 Catholics. Alarming increases occurred in western cities too. This anonymous Know-Nothing author estimated that about one-third of America's population occupied the Old Northwest and that "it is chiefly to the western states that this mighty stream of emigration tends." In the West "the battle must

be fought, which is to decide whether this land is to be occupied for Christ, or whether it is to become the stronghold of Popery." That year, 1855, the Diocese of Cincinnati held about 65,000 Catholics; Chicago 50,000; Louisville 30,000; and St. Louis an impressive 100,000. *Startling Facts for Native Americans Called "Know-Nothings,"* 61–65.

32. Sidney D. Maxwell, Diary, Sept. 24, 1854, Maxwell Papers, box 5, folder 19, CMC.

33. Maxwell, Diary, Jan. 10, 1855, Maxwell Papers, box 5, folder 19, 191, CMC.

34. James S. Armstrong [or Richard Miller], Cincinnati, to unknown, Aug. 25, 1854, James Armstrong Papers, box 1, folder 2, CMC.

35. Lemuel C. Porter, Diary, July 1855.

36. Davis, *Address on "Securing the Blessings of Liberty to Ourselves and to Our Posterity,"* 4, Rare Pamphlet, FHS. See also Garrett Davis, *Speeches of Hon. Garrett Davis, Upon His Proposition to Impose Further Restrictions Upon Foreign Immigrants: Delivered in the Convention to Revise the Constitution of Kentucky, December 15th and 17th, 1849* (Frankfort, KY: A. G. Hodges, 1855), Rare Pamphlet, FHS.

37. Davis, *Address on "Securing the Blessings of Liberty to Ourselves and to Our Posterity,"* 6–9, 11, 35.

38. See Anbinder, *Nativism and Slavery*.

39. See William Gannaway Brownlow, *Americanism Contrasted with Foreignism, Romanism, and Bogus Democracy, in the Light of Reason, History, and Scripture; in which Certain Demagogues of Tennessee, and Elsewhere, Are Shown Up in Their True Colors* (Nashville: Published for the author, 1856); and Thomas Richard Whitney, *A Defence of the American Policy, as Opposed to the Encroachments of Foreign Influence: and Especially to the Interference of the Papacy in the Political Interests and Affairs of the United States* (DeWitt & Davenport, 1856). See also Schrag, *Not Fit for Our Society*.

40. Ely, *American Liberty*, 20–22.

41. Henry Winter Davis, *The Origins, Principles, and Purposes of the American Party* (1855), 13, 19, 36.

42. James L. Chapman, *Americanism Versus Romanism; or, The Cis-Atlantic Battle between Sam and the Pope* (Nashville: By the author, 1856), 36, 322–23.

43. Chapman, *Americanism Versus Romanism*, 36, 322–23. For more on German American politics, see Alison Clark Efford, *German Immigrants, Race, and Citizenship in the Civil War Era* (Cambridge: Cambridge University Press, 2013); Kristen L. Anderson, *Abolitionizing Missouri: Germans Immigrants and Racial Ideology in Nineteenth-Century America* (Baton Rouge: Louisiana State University Press, 2016); and Susanne Martha Schick, "'For God, Mac, and Country': The Political Worlds of Midwestern Germans during the Civil War Era" (PhD diss., University of Illinois, Urbana-Champaign, 1994).

44. Davis, *The Origins, Principles, and Purposes of the American Party*, 13, 19, 36.

45. Chapman, *Americanism Versus Romanism*, 36, 322–23; Davis, *Origins, Principles, and Purposes of the American Party*, 31.

46. Chapman, *Americanism Versus Romanism*, 36, 322–23.

47. American Party, *Platform Adopted by the National Council of the American Party:*

Ratification of the National Platform by the State Council of Missouri with Declaration of Principles, Constitution and By-laws of the State Council of Missouri, Ritual of the Order (St. Louis: Ustick, Studley, 1855), 36–37, Pamphlet, MHS (hereafter cited as *Ratification of the National Platform by the State Council of Missouri*).

48. *Report of the Committee on Constitution and By-Laws to the State Council of Ohio* (1854), 15, Pamphlet, CMC.

49. *Proceedings of the Grand Council of Ohio,* Pamphlet, CMC.

50. *Ratification of the National Platform by the State Council of Missouri,* 29–37, Pamphlet, MHS.

51. *Ratification of the National Platform by the State Council of Missouri,* 37–44, Pamphlet, MHS.

52. John F. Weishampel, *The Pope's Stratagem, "Rome to America!": An Address to the Protestants of the United States Against Placing the Pope's Block of Marble in the Washington Monument, Containing also Important Suggestions to Both the Roman Catholic and Protestant Churches in our Country Relative to the Monument, by an American Citizen,* 2nd ed. (Philadelphia: 1852), Pamphlets in American history, CA 714, SLU.

53. Katie Oxx, *The Nativist Movement in America: Religious Conflict in the Nineteenth Century* (New York: Routledge, Taylor, & Francis Group, 2013), 83–110.

54. *Proceedings of the Grand Council of Ohio,* May 17, 1854, Pamphlet, CMC.

55. Missouri Grand Council Minute Book, Apr. 20, 1855.

56. *Proceedings of the Grand Council of Ohio,* May 17, 1854, Pamphlet, CMC.

57. John R. Mulkern, *The Know-Nothing Party in Massachusetts: The Rise and Fall of a People's Movement* (Boston: Northeastern University Press, 1990), 183. See also Dale Knobel, *"America for the Americans,"* 30–33.

58. Smith, *American Party and Its Mission,* 6–7, Pamphlet, CMC.

59. *Proceedings of the Grand Council of Ohio,* July 31–Aug. 1, 1854, 17, Pamphlet, CMC; Thomas Spooner, E. M. Gregory, and Charles Grant, *Report of Committee on Constitution and By-Laws,* 1–16, Pamphlet, CMC; *Ratification of the National Platform by the State Council of Missouri,* 11–18, Pamphlet, MHS; and Mulkern, *Know-Nothing Party in Massachusetts,* 63–64.

60. William B. Napton, Diary, Feb. 23, 1855, MHS.

61. This stricture on voting changed in most states by late 1855, when Know-Nothing orders released their members to vote for whomever they wished.

62. *Proceedings of the Grand Council of Ohio,* Pamphlet, CMC; Spooner, Gregory, and Grant, *Report of Committee on Constitution and By-Laws,* 1–16, ibid.; and *Ratification of the National Platform by the State Council of Missouri,* 11–18, Pamphlet, MHS.

63. *Proceedings of the Grand Council of Ohio,* July 31, 1854, 17, Pamphlet, CMC; and *Ratification of the National Platform by the State Council of Missouri,* 25, Pamphlet, MHS.

64. Spooner, Gregory, and Grant, "Rules of the Order," in *Report of Committee on Constitution and By-Laws,* 12–16, Pamphlet, CMC.

65. Missouri Grand Council Minute Book, Sept. 29–30, Oct. 19–20, 1854.

66. Missouri Grand Council Minute Book, Apr. 16, 1856.

67. William Finney of St. Louis wrote, "Parsons is preaching among us with great acceptability." William Finney, St. Louis, to son Thomas, Jan. 21, 1856, Alphabetical File, MHS; Missouri Grand Council Minute Book, Aug. 26, 1854.

68. Solomon Smith temporarily held the grand presidency of the Missouri State Council in 1856 before stepping down. He was a respected theater manager in Cincinnati, New Orleans, and St. Louis. Parsons had met Solomon Smith previously while operating his own theater business in Natchez, Mississippi, and Cincinnati in the 1830s. Parsons later dropped the theater business and became a Methodist minister. Over the years, he bantered with Smith in private correspondence, critiquing actors and plays, railing against heavy drinkers—"you know how I hate drunkards"—and taking the occasional jab at Catholicism—"City Directories are no more to be relied upon for their 'infallibility' than the Pope." Charles B. Parsons, Natchez, MS, to Solomon Smith, St. Louis, Dec. 28, 1836, Solomon Smith Papers, box 5, MHS; Charles B. Parsons, Natchez, to Sol Smith, St. Louis, Feb. 26, 1837, ibid.; Charles B. Parsons, St. Louis, to Sol Smith, St. Louis, Nov. 15, 1855, ibid.

69. Allen Wright, Lexington, MO, to Gen. George R. Smith, Feb. 28, 1856, Gen. George R. Smith Papers, MHS. Born in Virginia and educated as a lawyer in Kentucky, George Smith came to Missouri in 1833 with his wife and two little girls. He settled in Georgetown in Pettis County, where he promoted the Pacific Railroad and founded Sedalia in 1856. Smith was in the Santa Fe freighting business from 1848 to 1852. He was a candidate for Congress for the Whig Party in 1846 and later the American Party in both 1856 and 1858. He belonged to the Know-Nothing order in Missouri and served as alternate U.S. representative of St. Louis's Fifth District for the Grand Council. Under Provisional Governor Hamilton R. Gamble, Smith served as adjutant general for three months in 1861. Although a slaveholder, he was strongly unionist and a nominal abolitionist. Smith died July 11, 1879. Many forms of nativist propaganda included the mantra "America for the Americans." One St. Louis broadside from 1854 declared, *"None but Americans shall govern America!"* "Sam's Principles" (ca. 1854), Broadside, MHS.

70. See Mark A. Tabbert, *American Freemasons: Three Centuries of Building Communities* (New York: New York University Press, 2005); and Jasper Godwin Ridley, *The Freemasons: A History of the World's Most Powerful Secret Society* (New York: Arcade, Distributed by Time Warner, 2001).

71. Mark C. Carnes, *Secret Ritual and Manhood in Victorian America* (New Haven, CT: Yale University Press, 1989), 72.

72. See Carnes, *Secret Ritual and Manhood in Victorian America*.

73. Edward Purcell, "Secret Societies," *Catholic Telegraph*, Jan. 7, 1854, 23, no. 1 (Archdiocese of Cincinnati and Louisville): 2, PLC.

74. Purcell, "Secret Societies."

75. Edward Purcell, "Odd Fellows," *Catholic Telegraph*, Feb. 15, 1849, 18, no. 7 (Archdiocese of Cincinnati and Louisville): 50, PLC.

76. For example, see M. W. William B. Dodds, grand master, *Proceedings of the Grand*

Lodge of Free and Accepted Masons of the State of Ohio: Held at Chillicothe, October 17th–20th, 1854 (Columbus: Printed by the Ohio State Journal, 1854).

77. The Odd Fellows referenced Matthew 18:20, "For where two or three are gathered together in my name, there am I in the midst of them." *Constitution of the R.W. Grand Lodge of Ohio, of the Independent Order of Odd Fellows; Adopted January 10, 1846* (Cincinnati: Printed by Order of the Grand Lodge, 1846), 12, 21.

78. P. G. Edson B. Olds of Circleville, Ohio, *An Address Delivered Before Hamilton Lodge, No. 17, I.O.O.F., at their Celebration at Hamilton, May 23d, 1846* (Columbus, OH: Published by a Committee of the Lodge, 1846), 16, CMC.

79. "Odd Fellows' Hall," *St. Louis Weekly Reveille*, Nov. 19, 1848, St. Louis History Papers, MHS.

80. Olds, *Address Delivered Before Hamilton Lodge*, 17–18.

81. Olds, *Address Delivered Before Hamilton Lodge*, 12–16. Rachel Devereux, *An Essay on Masonry: Particularly Addressed to the Fair Sex* (Albany: 1858), Pamphlets in American History 10099, SLU. See also Mary P. Ryan, *Cradle of the Middle Class: The Family in Oneida County, New York, 1790–1865* (Cambridge: Cambridge University Press, 1981); and Carnes, *Secret Ritual and Manhood in Victorian America*.

82. The Ancient Order of Druids was a secret fraternal society similar to the Masons founded in England in 1781. Druids were mythological priest-like figures in Iron Age Celtic paganism. The order was not pagan, however, as it forbade any discussion of religion in lodge rooms. Like the Order of Free Masons and Odd Fellows, the Ancient Order of Druids also became more democratic and socially conscientious in the 1840s. See Ronald Hutton, *Blood and Mistletoe: The History of the Druids in Britain* (New Haven, CT: Yale University Press, 2009).

83. *The Chicago City Directory and Business Advertiser* (Chicago: Robert Fergus, Book & Job Printers, 1855), 199–201.

84. John B. Jegil, *John B. Jegil's Louisville, New-Albany, Jeffersonville, Shippingport and Portland Directory, For 1845–1846* (Louisville: Office of the Louisville Journal, 1845), 35.

85. John A. Paxton, *The St. Louis Directory and Register* (St. Louis: Printed for the publisher, 1821), MHS; Charles Keemle, *The St. Louis Directory for the Years 1838-9* (St. Louis: Charles Keemle, 1838), 63–64, MHS; Keemle, *The St. Louis Directory for the Years 1840-1* (St. Louis: Charles Keemle, 1840), 79–80, MHS; William L. Montague, *The Saint Louis Business Directory for 1853-4* (St. Louis: E. A. Lewis, Printer, 1853), 127–28, MHS; *The St. Louis Directory for the Years 1854-5* (St. Louis: Printed by Chambers & Knapp, 1854), 256, MHS; Missouri Grand Council Minute Book, Apr. 18, 1855.

86. While many Know-Nothing councils were named after their location, many others honored American heroes and events during the Revolution and the founding era as well as certain American symbols. Council names in Ohio included Lexington no. 4, Yorktown no. 5, Plymouth Rock no. 8, E Pluribus Unum no. 18, Fate no. 28, Madison no. 54, Mount Vernon no. 55, Eagle no. 85, Tea Party no. 110, Trenton no. 113, Uncle Sam no. 122, and Fidelity no. 126. Kentucky councils included names such as Henry Clay no. 2,

Concord no. 6, and Jackson no. 7. Council names in Missouri included Tea Party no. 1, Saratoga no. 6, Hancock no. 12, Star no. 27, and Liberty no. 28. *Proceedings of the Grand Council of Ohio,* Pamphlet, CMC; Missouri Grand Council Minute Book.

87. *Proceedings of the Grand Council of Ohio,* Pamphlet, CMC.

88. Davis, *Address on "Securing the Blessings of Liberty to Ourselves and to Our Posterity,"* 21.

89. American Party, *Principles and Objects of the American Party* (New York: 1855), 7–20, General Collections, NL.

90. Maj. Jack Downing, Prairyville, Illinois, to President Franklin Pierce, Washington D.C., Sept. 26, 1854, unpublished letter prepared for the *St. Louis Intelligencer,* Henry Williams Papers, Downing Letters no. 5, MHS.

91. Foe to Despotism [S. D. T. Willard], *The Red Cross of Catholicism in America: Startling Expose of an Infernal Catholic Plot; Know-Nothings Set at Defiance, Uses of Firearms in Cathedrals, Confessions and Secret Correspondence* (Boston: Published by Federhen, 1854), American Party, 22, General Collections, NL.

92. *The Know-Nothing?* (Cleveland: Jewett, Proctor, & Worthington, 1855), 71, 85, 116, 136, 145, 214.

93. *The Know-Nothing?*, 147–48, 213, 215–16.

94. Maj. Jack Downing to President Franklin Pierce, Sept. 26, 1854.

95. *The Know-Nothing?*, 229–30, 345–47.

96. Edward Purcell, "Religious Secret Societies," *Catholic Telegraph,* Dec. 10, 1853, 22, no. 51 (Archdiocese of Cincinnati and Louisville): 51, PLC. Also see Purcell, "The Catholics and Natives," ibid., Dec. 21, 1844, 13, no. 51 p. 413; and Purcell, "American Principles and Religious Proscription," ibid., Aug. 26, 1854, 23, no. 24 p. 4.f

97. Rev. G. Reed, Hiram, OH, to brother, Dec. 25, 1855, OHS.

98. William B. Napton, Diary, Jan. 7, 1855, Jan. 7, 1856, MHS.

99. Most archbishops endorsed *Brownson's Quarterly Review,* including Bishop of St. Louis Peter Richard Kenrick, Coadjutor of Louisville Martin John Spalding, Bishop of Nashville Richard Pius Miles, Bishop of Cincinnati John Baptist Purcell, Bishop of Chicago James Oliver, Bishop of Milwaukee John M. Henni, Bishop of Cleveland Amadeus, Coadjutor Administrator of Detroit Peter Paul, and others. Pope Pius IX endorsed the *Review* on April 29, 1854: "as a token of our so great benignity, and *as a pledge of our gratitude to you for the service you have done for us,* we add our apostolic benediction, which we lovingly impart, with the poured-forth affection of our fraternal heart, to you yourself, beloved son, and to your whole family." See Chapman, *Americanism Versus Romanism,* 69. Also see Orestes Brownson, "Know-Nothingism; or Satan Warring Against Christ," *Brownson's Quarterly Review,* 2, no. 4 (Oct. 1, 1854): 453.

100. Orestes A. Brownson's essays appear, for example, on a list of the private library of St. Louis Know-Nothing Henry W. Williams. See Henry W. Williams, Library, n.d., St. Louis, Henry W. Williams Papers, box 1, folder 49, MHS. For more on Brownson's notoriety across America, see Peter Augustine Lawler's introduction to Orestes A. Brownson, *The American Republic: Its Constitution, Tendencies and Destiny,* vol. 1, in

Works in Political Philosophy, ed. Gregory S. Butler (Wilmington, DE: ISI Books, 2003), 1–10; Franchot, *Roads to Rome,* 337–49; and Mark A. Noll, *America's God: From Jonathan Edwards to Abraham Lincoln* (New York: Oxford University Press, 2002), 406–9.

101. Orestes Brownson, "A Few Words on Native Americanism; New Orleans, 1854," *Brownson's Quarterly Review* 2, no. 3 (July 1854): 348.

102. Napton, Diary, Feb. 23, 1855.

103 A Foreigner, *Emigration, Emigrants, and Know-Nothings* (Philadelphia: Published for the author, 1854), 37–44, Sabin Americana 22493, WU.

104. Henry A. Wise, *Religious Liberty: Equality of Civil Rights Among Native and Naturalized Citizens, The Virginia Campaign of 1855, Governor Wise's Letter on Know-Nothingism, and His Speech at Alexandria* (1855), 5–7, MHS.

105. *Extracts from the Speeches of Several Members of the New-York Legislature, Renouncing and Exposing the Anti-Republican Order of Know-Nothings or American Jesuits* (Printed at the "Banner of Liberty" Office, 1855), 4, Pamphlets, CHS. For the full publication, see *U.S. Senatorial Question: Speeches Delivered in the Assembly of the State of New-York, By the Honorables Messrs. C. C. Leigh, C. P. Johnson, J. W. Stebbins, D. C. Littlejohn, A. W. Hull, S. B. Cole, W. Gleason, M. L. Rickerson, L. S. May, H. Baker, R. M. Blatchford, S. Smith, E. Fitch, and Others, in Exposition of the Oaths, Obligations and Rituals of the Know-Nothings, During the Debate on the U.S. Senatorial Question, February 1, 2, 3, 5 and 6, 1855* (Albany: Weed, Parsons, Printers, 1855), American Party, General Collections, NL.

106. "National Democratic Platform of 1856; Adopted at Cincinnati, June 6, 1856," John B. Bruner Collection, folder 8, FHS.

107. "Pope's Ticket," *Columbian,* Oct. 11, 1854, qtd. in William A. Baughin, "Nativism in Cincinnati before 1860" (PhD diss., University of Cincinnati, 1963), 183, CMC.

Chapter 5: Crime, Poverty, and the Economic Origins of Political Nativism

1. Epigraph from "An Address to the Native Americans of the Fayette Congressional District" (Georgetown, KY: 1847), Broadsides of the Know-Nothing Party, oversize, FHS.

2. See Hidetaka Hirota, *Expelling the Poor: Atlantic Seaboard States and the 19th-Century Origins of American Immigration Policy* (New York: Oxford University Press, 2017).

3. For nativism as xenophobia, see Ray Allen Billington, *The Protestant Crusade, 1800–1860* (1938; repr., Chicago: Quadrangle Books, 1964); Richard Hofstadter, *The Paranoid Style in American Politics and Other Essays* (New York: Alfred A. Knopf, 1952); Hofstadter *Anti-Intellectualism in American Life* (New York: Alfred A. Knopf, 1962); Seymour Martin Lipset and Earl Raab, *The Politics of Unreason: Right Wing Extremism in America* (New York: Harper and Row, 1970); and Carleton Beals, *Brass-Knuckle Crusade: The Great Know-Nothing Conspiracy, 1820–1860* (New York: Hastings House,

1960). For nativism as nationalism, see John Higham, *Strangers in the Land: Patterns of American Nativism, 1860–1925* (1955; repr., New Brunswick, NJ: Rutgers University Press, 2008); Dale T. Knobel, *Paddy and the Republic: Ethnicity and Nationality in Antebellum America* (Middletown, CT: Wesleyan University Press, 1986); Knobel, *"America for the Americans": The Nativist Movement in the United States* (New York: Twayne, 1996); Matthew Frye Jacobson, *Whiteness of a Different Color: European Immigrants and the Alchemy of Race* (Cambridge, MA: Harvard University Press, 1998); Noel Ignatiev, *How the Irish Became White* (New York: Routledge, 1995); and Peter Kolchin, "Whiteness Studies: The New History of Race in America," *Journal of American History* 89, no. 1 (June 2002): 154–73. For more on the relationship between nativism and immigration policy, see Mae M. Ngai, *Impossible Subjects: Illegal Aliens and the Making of Modern America* (Princeton, NJ: Princeton University Press, 2004); and Peter Schrag, *Not Fit for Our Society: Immigration and Nativism in America* (Berkeley: University of California Press, 2010). For nativism as political expediency, see Tyler Anbinder, *Nativism and Slavery: The Northern Know-Nothings and the Politics of the 1850s* (New York: Oxford University Press, 1992); Ira Leonard and Robert Parmet, *American Nativism, 1830–1860* (New York: Van Nostrand Reinhold, 1971); Michael F. Holt, "The Politics of Impatience: The Origins of Know-Nothingism," *Journal of American History* 60, no. 2 (Sept. 1973): 309–31; Holt, *Forging a Majority: The Formation of the Republican Party in Pittsburgh, 1848–1860* (New Haven, CT: Yale University Press, 1969); David Morris Potter, *The Impending Crisis, 1848–1861* (New York: Harper & Row, 1976); Stephen E. Maizlish, *The Triumph of Sectionalism: The Transformation of Ohio Politics, 1844–1856* (Kent, OH: Kent State University Press, 1983); Stephen E. Maizlish and John J. Kushma, eds., *Essays on American Antebellum Politics* (College Station: Texas A&M University Press, 1982); Paul Kleppner, *The Cross of Culture: A Social Analysis of Midwestern Politics, 1850–1900* (New York: Free Press, 1970); Kleppner, *The Third Electoral System, 1853–1892: Parties, Voters, and Political Cultures* (Chapel Hill: University of North Carolina Press, 1979); Frederick C. Luebke, *Ethnic Voters and the Election of Lincoln* (Lincoln: University of Nebraska Press, 1971); William E. Gienapp, *The Origins of the Republican Party, 1852–1856* (New York: Oxford University Press, 1987); and Darrell W. Overdyke, *The Know-Nothing Party in the South* (Baton Rouge: Louisiana State University Press, 1950).

4. See Hidetaka Hirota's excellent study of immigration, crime, and nativism in antebellum Massachusetts and New York, *Expelling the Poor,* and Joel Fetzer, *Public Attitudes toward Immigration in the United States, France, and Germany* (New York: Cambridge University Press, 2000), 90.

5. "Know-Nothing" riots also erupted in Baltimore in 1856; Washington, D.C., in 1857; and New Orleans in 1858. For two broad studies on recurring patterns of riots in American history, see Paul A. Gilje, *Rioting in America* (Indianapolis: Indiana University Press, 1996); and Gilje, *The Road to Mobocracy: Popular Disorder in New York City, 1763–1834* (Chapel Hill: University of North Carolina Press, 1987).

6. For scholarship on political nativism in the Northeast, see John R. Mulkern, *The Know-Nothing Party in Massachusetts: The Rise and Fall of a People's Movement* (Boston:

Northeastern University Press, 1990); Knobel, *Paddy and the Republic;* Holt, " Politics of Impatience," 309–31; and Oscar Handlin, *Boston's Immigrants, 1790–1880* (Cambridge, MA: Harvard University Press, 1959). For studies that cover nativism in the West, at least partially, see Jay Dolan, *The Irish Americans: A History* (New York: Bloomsbury, 2008); Dolan, *The American Catholic Experience* (New York: Crown, 1987); David H. Bennett, *The Party of Fear: From Nativist Movements to the New Right in American History* (Chapel Hill: University of North Carolina Press, 1988); Leonard and Parmet, *American Nativism;* and Billington, *Protestant Crusade.* Dissertations on antebellum nativism in the West include Thomas, "Nativism in the Old Northwest," and McGann, "Nativism in Kentucky to 1860."

7. Missouri State Penitentiary Records, 1836–1931, MSA.

8. Luther M. Kennett, "Mayor's Message," May 13, 1850, in *Message of the Mayor of the City of Saint Louis, and Reports of City Officers, Delivered to the City Council* (St. Louis: Intelligencer Office, 1850), SLPL.

9. See Allen Eugene Wagner, *Good Order and Safety: A History of the St. Louis Metropolitan Police Department, 1861–1906* (Missouri History Museum Press, 2008); and Board of Police Commissioners, comp., *History of the Metropolitan Police Department of St. Louis, 1810–1910* (St. Louis: Skinner & Kennedy, 1910), SLPL.

10. Henry Hitchcock, St. Louis, to Miss Ellen Erwin, Nashville, TN, Aug. 15, 1854, Hitchcock Collection, MHS.

11. "Police Department," *St. Louis City Directory* (1854), 244.

12. Heinrich Börnstein, *Memoirs of a Nobody: The Missouri Years of an Austrian Radical, 1849–1866,* trans. and ed. Steven Rowan (St. Louis: Missouri Historical Society Press, 1997), 203.

13. *Mayor's Message, with Accompanying Documents, Submitted to the Common Council of the City of Saint Louis,* First Stated Session, May 1872 (St. Louis: Missouri Democrat Office, 1872), 30, SLPL.

14. John G. Schneider, "Riot and Reaction in St. Louis, 1854–1856," *Missouri Historical Review* 68 (Jan. 1974), 184.

15. Luther M. Kennett, "Mayor's Message," Oct. 14, 1850, in *Message of the Mayor of the City of Saint Louis* (1850), 3, SLPL.

16. Luther M. Kennett, "Mayor's Message," May 10, 1852, in *Mayor's Message, with Accompanying Documents, Submitted to the City Council of the City of Saint Louis,* First Stated Session, May 10, 1852 (St. Louis: Missouri Republican Office, 1852), 3, SLPL; John How, "Mayor's Message," *Mayor's Message, with Accompanying Documents, Submitted to the City Council of the City of Saint Louis,* Second Stated Session, Oct. 10, 1853 (Republican Book and Job Office, 1853), 4, SLPL.

17. *The Revised Ordinances of the City of St. Louis* (St. Louis: George Knapp, 1853).

18. *Revised Ordinances of the City of St. Louis,* 669–70.

19. J. A. Dacus and Dames W. Buel, *A Tour of St. Louis; or, The Inside Life of a Great City* (St. Louis: Western, Jones & Griffin, 1878), 406–18.

20. Dacus and Buel, *Tour of St. Louis,* 393–94, 418.

21. Ernst D. Kargau, *The German Element in St. Louis: A Translation from German of Ernst D. Kargau's* St. Louis in Former Years: A Commemorative History of the German Element, in ed. Don Heinrich Tolzmann, trans. William G. Bek (Baltimore: Clearfield, 2000), 43.

22. Dacus and Buel, *Tour of St. Louis,* 406–18.

23. Dacus and Buel, *Tour of St. Louis,* 445, 474. See also St. Louis Criminal Court Indexes, "Bawdy Houses," MSA, St. Louis, Missouri. For an account of the Almond Street Riot of 1860, see Steven Rowan, *Germans for a Free Missouri* (Columbia: University of Missouri Press, 1983).

24. *Message of the Mayor of the City of Saint Louis, and Reports of City Officers, Delivered to the City Council* (St. Louis: Saint Louis Daily Union Office, 1849), 17.

25. *Mayor's Message,* First Stated Session, May 12, 1851 (1851).

26. *Mayor's Message,* First Stated Session, May 10, 1852, 3.

27. *Mayor's Message,* First Stated Session, May 9, 1853, 20.

28. John How, "Mayor's Message," May 9, 1853, *Mayor's Message,* First Stated Session, May 9, 1853; How, "Mayor's Message," Oct. 10, 1853, *Mayor's Message,* Second Stated Session (1853), 5.

29. Luther M. Kennett, "Mayor's Message," Oct. 13, 1851, *Message of the Mayor of the City of Saint Louis* (1851), 5, SLPL.

30. "Arrested Persons," St. Louis Police Department Reports, in *Mayor's Message* (1865–72), SLPL.

31. "Rules for the Guidance of Sergeants and Patrolmen," in Board of Police Commissioners, *History of the Metropolitan Police Department of St. Louis,* 170–71.

32. J. E. D. Couzins, "Report of the Chief of Police," June 16, 1864, in *Mayor's Message,* First Stated Session, May 1864 (St. Louis: M'Kee, Fishback, 1864), 66, SLPL.

33. See Hirota, *Expelling the Poor.*

34. Hirota, *Expelling the Poor,* 6–7, 14.

35. Joseph Kett, *Merit: The History of a Founding Ideal from the American Revolution to the Twenty-First Century* (Ithaca, NY: Cornell University Press), 101.

36. *Message of the Mayor of the City of Saint Louis, and Reports of City Officers, Delivered to the City Council* (St. Louis: Saint Louis Daily Union Office, 1849), SLPL; Auditor's Report, *Mayor's Message,* First Stated Session, May 12, 1851 (1851), 12; Auditor's Report, *Mayor's Message,* First Stated Session, May 10, 1852 (1852), 9; Auditor's Report, *Mayor's Message, with Accompanying Documents, Submitted to the City Council of the City of Saint Louis,* First Stated Session, May 14, 1855 (St. Louis: Missouri Democrat Office, 1855), 13; and Auditor's Report, *Mayor's Message, with Accompanying Documents, Submitted to the City Council of the City of Saint Louis,* First Stated Session, May 11, 1858 (St. Louis: Missouri Democrat Book and Job Office, 1858), 20.

37. See Gilje, *Rioting in America,* and Gilje, *Road to Mobocracy.* For theoretical discussions on the social significance of popular-crowd action, see Lynn Hunt, ed., *The New Cultural History: Essays by Aletta Biersack* (Berkeley: University of California Press,

1989); and William Pencak, Matthew Dennis, and Simon P. Newman, eds., *Riot and Revelry in Early America* (University Park: Pennsylvania State University Press, 2002).

38. See George Helmuth Kellner, "The German Element on the Urban Frontier: St. Louis, 1830–1860" (PhD diss., University of Missouri, Columbia, 1973), 149.

39. Testimony of Henry Clunk, St. Louis Criminal Court, reprinted in "Ned Buntline Arrested Upon an Indictment Found Twenty Years Ago," *St. Louis Times*, Dec. 27, 1872.

40. See Jay Monaghan, *The Great Rascal: The Life and Adventures of Ned Buntline* (Bonanza Books, 1951), 198–203.

41. "Dutch" was a derogatory term used to refer to the Germans.

42. Testimony of Luther M. Kennett, St. Louis Criminal Court, reprinted in "Arrest of Ned Buntline," *Missouri Democrat* (St. Louis), Dec. 27, 1872.

43. "Ned Buntline Arrested Upon an Indictment Found Twenty Years Ago," *St. Louis Times*, Dec. 27, 1872.

44. Börnstein, *Memoirs of a Nobody*, 179.

45. Testimony of David Robinson, St. Louis Criminal Court, reprinted in "Arrest of Ned Buntline," *Missouri Democrat* (St. Louis), Dec. 27, 1872; Monaghan, *Great Rascal*, 199.

46. "Arrest of Ned Buntline," *Missouri Democrat* (St. Louis), Dec. 27, 1872.

47. Testimony of David Robinson and James Ames, St. Louis Criminal Court, reprinted in "Ned Buntline Arrested Upon an Indictment Found Twenty Years Ago," *St. Louis Times*, Dec. 27, 1872.

48. Testimony of Robinson and Ames, St. Louis Criminal Court, reprinted in "Ned Buntline Arrested Upon an Indictment Found Twenty Years Ago," *St. Louis Times*, Dec. 27, 1872.

49. Henry Niemeier later testified that the gunshot came from a house adjoining his coffeehouse and that the bullet that killed Joseph Stevens came from an unaffiliated German bunkered in his tavern for protection from the nativist rioters. One newspaper reported, "There were no guns or pistols fired from his premises." "The Disturbances in the First Ward," *Missouri Republican* (St. Louis), Apr. 8, 1852.

50. Monaghan, *Great Rascal*, 198–99.

51. "Election at St. Louis—Disgraceful Riot," *New York Times*, Apr. 7, 1852.

52. "Terrible Riot in St. Louis," *Barre (MA) Patriot*, Apr. 9, 1852.

53. Börnstein, *Memoirs of a Nobody*, 181–82. Börnstein wrote, "There were the most dreadful threats in the American papers against me, against the *Anzeiger*, against [Alexander] Kayser and against all Germans whomsoever." Ibid., 178.

54. "'Facts' from the *Anzeiger*," *Missouri Republican* (St. Louis), Apr. 9, 1852. For accounts of the St. Louis Election Riot of 1852, see "Ned Buntline Arrested Upon an Indictment Found Twenty Years Ago," *St. Louis Times*, Dec. 27, 1872; "The Disturbances in the First Ward," *Missouri Republican* (St. Louis), Apr. 8, 1852; Börnstein, *Memoirs of a Nobody*, 178–82; and Pardon Dexter, St. Louis, to Hannah Kerr Tiffany, Apr. 6, 1852, Tiffany Family Papers, box 1, folder 16, MHS.

55. Monaghan, *Great Rascal*, 150.

56. British author George Reynolds wrote the first "penny part" mysteries serial in London. Eugene Sue made the genre popular in France when he published *Les mysteres de Paris* [The mysteries of Paris] in 1842. In Germany alone in 1844 there were thirty-six different urban mysteries. A year after Börnstein became editor of the *Anzeiger* in March 1850, he wrote the *Mysteries of St. Louis: The Jesuits on the Prairie des Noyers, A Western Tale*. When Buntline arrived in St. Louis in 1851 and launched *Ned Buntline's Novelist*, he may have been disappointed to discover that Börnstein had beat him to writing a mystery novel of the city. The first-part reprints of *Mysteries of St. Louis* sold for twenty-five cents in March 1851. The second part concluded on the eve of the municipal election of April 8, 1851, which produced a Whig victory. Börnstein wrote in the *Anzeiger* that the election had been such a disaster that he had to take a break from writing. He finished the series in June. Though Anglo-Americans considered the novel too scandalous due to its graphic sex scenes, it went through six German-language editions and sold more than two thousand copies in St. Louis alone. A German Forty-Eighter in New Orleans, Baron Ludwig von Reizenstein, wrote *Mysteries of New Orleans* in 1854 and 1855, which included a lesbian sex scene. His novel pushed the limits of the genre to extremes that even Börnstein was unwilling to cross. Börnstein himself thought the novel contributed to his initial success in St. Louis. Later, in 1869, a concert troupe at the Apollo Theater in St. Louis performed a stage version of Börnstein's *Mysteries,* and in 1871 German papers reprinted *Mysteries* in a new series. See Steven Rowan, introduction to Heinrich Börnstein, *Mysteries of St. Louis: A Novel,* trans. Friedrich Muench (1852; modern ed.by Steven Rowan and Elizabeth Sims, Chicago: Charles H. Kerr, 1990 [1851–52]), ix–x; and Börnstein, *Memoirs of a Nobody,* 127.

57. Monaghan, *Great Rascal,* 193.

58. Börnstein, *Memoirs of a Nobody,* 177.

59. Rowan, introduction to Börnstein, *Memoirs of a Nobody,* 14.

60. Rowan, introduction to Börnstein, *Memoirs of a Nobody,* 14.

61. William B. Faherty, S.J., *Better the Dream, St. Louis: University and Community, 1818–1968* (St. Louis: St. Louis University, 1968), 101. See also Rowan, introduction to Börnstein, *Memoirs of a Nobody,* 20–22; and James M. Bergquist, "German Communities in American Cities: An Interpretation of the Nineteenth-Century Experience," *Journal of American Ethnic History* 4, 1 (Fall 1984): 14.

62. Börnstein, *Mysteries of St. Louis,* 160.

63. Kargau, *German Element in St. Louis,* 24.

64. Mark Alan Neels, "We shall be literally 'sold to the Dutch': Nativist Suppression of German Radicals in Antebellum St. Louis, 1852–1861," *Confluence* 1 (Fall 2009), 22; Börnstein, *Memoirs of a Nobody,* 178–79; "'Facts' from the Anzeiger," *Missouri Republican* (St. Louis), Apr. 9, 1852.

65. A report sent to the *New York Times* on Tuesday, April 6, from St. Louis announced that Mayor Kennett had been reelected "by six or seven hundred majority." See "Election at St. Louis—Disgraceful Riot," *New York Times,* Apr. 7, 1852.

66. Börnstein, *Memoirs of a Nobody*, 181.

67. Börnstein, *Memoirs of a Nobody*, 178.

68. Börnstein, *Memoirs of a Nobody*, 180–81.

69. Pardon Dexter, St. Louis, to Hannah Kerr Tiffany, Apr. 6, 1852, Tiffany Family Papers, box 1, folder 16, MHS.

70. "The Election Riots of Monday," *Missouri Republican* (St. Louis), Apr. 10, 1852.

71. Quoted in Monaghan, *Great Rascal*, 202.

72. Kellner, " German Element on the Urban Frontier," 95–96. For a social history of German immigrants in St. Louis, see Audrey Olson, *St. Louis Germans, 1850–1920: The Nature of an Immigrant Community and Its Relation to the Assimilation Process* (New York: Arno, 1980). Tyler Anbinder notes: "Historians once attributed the increase [of German immigrants] to the revolutions of 1848. However, German emigration did not grow significantly from pre-revolutionary levels until 1852, long after authorities had quelled the uprising. Furthermore, the sources of greatest emigration do not correspond to the areas of revolutionary unrest." *Nativism and Slavery*, 7.

73. "The Spirit of the German Press," *Missouri Republican* (St. Louis), Apr. 9, 1852. For more on the election riot, see "Order and Quiet," ibid., Apr. 8, 1852. Judge Treat served on the Court of Common Pleas in the early 1850s. See Börnstein, *Memoirs of a Nobody*, 181; "'Facts' from the Anzeiger," *Missouri Republican* (St. Louis), Apr. 9, 1852; "The Election Riots of Monday," ibid., Apr. 10, 1852; and "The Military," ibid., Apr. 6, 1852. The Whig *Republican* added its own accusations. The newspaper's journalists followed up on the witnesses Börnstein listed in his accounts, and apparently no one saw Roever mistreated as Börnstein had described. According to the *Republican*'s account, the two Americans said to have provoked the disturbances at the Soulard election polls offered alibis to confirm their innocence. As for the Americans smashing the ballots on Monday afternoon, several witnesses testified that the accused did not mishandle any ballots once they overtook the polls. The Whig newspaper claimed that Germans maltreated "every man who came to vote the Whig ticket or who was supposed to favor it; and from sneers, jeering and hustling, they finally commenced pelting their political opponents with mud, and then with stones, until no man could deposit his vote except at the risk of his life." "The Election Riots of Monday," ibid., Apr. 10, 1852; and "Manufacturing Votes," ibid., Apr. 8, 1852. The *Republican* printed a relatively accurate chart proving that immigrants were naturalizing in the weeks before the April election. Its journalists prepared the chart from Court of Common Pleas records. It was, however, probably a dubious claim that immigrants were illegally voting in large numbers.

74. Pardon Dexter, St. Louis, to Hannah Kerr Tiffany, Apr. 6, 1852, Tiffany Family Papers, MHS.

75. "State of Missouri v. Edward Judson (alias Ned Buntline), Bob Mc'OBlennis, Joseph McBride, etc.," June 1, 1852, St. Louis Criminal Court Records, vol. 7, 1851–53, Case 68, MSA. For more on Ned Buntline's dime novels about "Buffalo Bill" and his "Wild West" shows, see Louis S. Warren, *Buffalo Bill's America: William Cody and the Wild West Show* (New York: Alfred A. Knopf, 2005).

234234234234 *Notes*

76. Henry Hitchcock, St. Louis, to Ellen Erwin, Nashville, TN, Aug. 14–15, 1854, MHS. Irishmen pronounced "blackguard" *blaggard,* and over time the slang word came to mean a generic persona of bad repute.

77. Some of the following material originally appeared in Luke Ritter, "The St. Louis 'Know-Nothing' Riot of 1854: Political Violence and the Rise of the Irish," *Gateway Magazine* 32 (2012): 26–35.

78. Mayor John How, "Proclamation to the Citizens of St. Louis," *Missouri Republican* (St. Louis), in "The Riot at St. Louis—More Bloodshed," *New York Times,* Aug. 14, 1854; "Particular of the Mob," *St. Louis Globe Democrat,* Aug. 9, 1854. Captain Eaton served as president over the Patrick Henry Council in the St. Louis chapter of the National American Party. See National American Party, Grand Council of the State of Missouri, No. 13, Sept. 5, 1854, MHS. That Captains Eaton and Lyttleton Cooke commanded the special police surprised Henry Hitchcock because the men were Know-Nothings. He wrote: "How could I omit to mention that Lyttleton Cooke, Esq. was a captain, or else Lieutenant, of one of the companies of the special police! As I mentioned, he was on the 'Know-Nothing' Ticket,—and is supposed to be one of the Know-Nothings himself." Hitchcock to Erwin, Aug. 14–15, 1854, MHS.

79. Case File, Edward Murphy, St. Louis Criminal Court, 1848, C43019, MSA, St. Louis, MO.

80. Case File, Henry B. Belt and John M. Wimer, St. Louis Circuit Court, 1852, 11, 93.

81. Case File, Thomas Tremble, St. Louis Criminal Court, 1853, Criminal Index vols. 7–8, 202–203.

82. See Richard Franklin Bensel, *The American Ballot Box in the Mid-Nineteenth Century* (New York: Cambridge University Press, 2004); and W. J. Rorabaugh, *The Alcoholic Republic: An American Tradition* (New York: Oxford University Press, 1979).

83. "Bloody Riot in St. Louis," *St. Louis Intelligencer,* Aug. 8, 1854, in *New York Times,* Aug. 12, 1854.

84. Search "Riot," Criminal Court Records Index, Vol. 7, MHS.

85. "The Elections," *La Revue de l'Ouest,* Aug. 2, 1854, trans. Debra Ritter, Microfilm Department, SLCL.

86. "Great Mob—Intense Excitement—Several of our Citizens Killed, and a Number Wounded!," *St. Louis Globe Democrat,* Aug. 8, 1854; "The Riots," ibid., Aug. 10, 1854.

87. George Engelmann, St. Louis, to Soulard, Nov. 24, 1854, Soulard Papers, MHS.

88. Newspapers reported at least ten people killed, thirty to one hundred others wounded, and ninety businesses and houses destroyed. But journalists deliberately stopped calculating the damages after the initial reports. There were at least ten casualties published in local newspapers. In addition, there were about ten people severely wounded and thought unable to recover. One St. Louis newspaper reported twenty killed on Tuesday night alone. See "The Riot at St. Louis—More Bloodshed," *New York Times,* Aug. 14, 1854, 5. Also, another commented on how it was "utterly impossible to estimate the number of persons wounded in the whole affair, or even to say how many have been killed," because people dragged bodies from the scene in a hurry. See "Great

Mob—Intense Excitement—Several of Our Citizens Killed, and a Number Wounded!,"
St. Louis Globe Democrat, Aug. 8, 1854.

89. *St. Louis City Directory, July, 1854–Jan., 1856* (St. Louis: Printed by Chambers and Knapp, 1854).

90. Hitchcock to Erwin, Aug. 14–15, 1854, MHS.

91. "A Disgraceful Riot—Account of the Know-Nothing Riots," *St. Louis Pilot,* in *Liberty Tribune* (Clay County, MO), Aug. 18, 1854, Early American Newspapers, Pius Library, SLU.

92. Kargau, *German Element in St. Louis,* 27.

93. Case Files 85, 321, 322, 325, 334, 383, 384, 385, 386, Criminal Court Records, Aug.–Nov. 1854, MSA; Naturalization Records, MSA.

94. "Great Mob—Intense Excitement—Several of our Citizens Killed, and a Number Wounded!," *St. Louis Globe Democrat,* Aug. 7, 1854; "The Riots," ibid., Aug. 10, 1854.

95. Hitchcock to Erwin, Aug. 14–15, 1854, MHS; Hitchcock to H. J. Spanhorst, Nov. 27, 1891, MHS. See also Ellen Meara Dolan, *The St. Louis Irish* (St. Louis: Old St. Patrick's, 1967), City Hall, St. Louis, Microfilm Department, MSA.

96. "Great Mob—Intense Excitement—Several of our Citizens Killed, and a Number Wounded!," *St. Louis Globe Democrat,* Aug. 7, 1854; "The Riots," ibid., Aug. 10, 1854.

97. Mayor John How, "Proclamation to the Citizens of St. Louis," *St. Louis Republican,* in "The Riot at St. Louis—More Bloodshed," *New York Times,* Aug. 14, 1854, 5.

98. "Discharged," *St. Louis Globe Democrat,* Aug. 14, 1854. See also *John Cox v. City of St. Louis,* Court of Common Pleas, Sept. term, 1854, Case 321, MSA; John Bourke, ibid. Case 325; "Auditor's Report," *City Ordinances, 1850–1855,* Apr. 9–Oct. 1, 1855, reels 2391–3320, p. 17, City Hall, St. Louis, Microfilm Department, MSA; and "Ordinance no. 3303," Mar. 22, 1855, sec. 2, ibid.

99. John How, "Mayor's Message," *Board of Alderman Minutes,* Oct. 9, 1854, Board of Alderman Minute Books and Records, 1839–56, 118–20, City Hall, St. Louis, Microfilm Department, MSA.

100. LaMotte, Ringgold Barracks, to Wife Ellen, Sept. 16, 1854, Lamotte-Coppinger Papers, MHS.

101. Schneider, "Riot and Reaction in St. Louis," 181.

102. Richard Edwards and Merna Hopewell, *Edwards' Great West and Her Commercial Metropolis Embracing a General View of the West, and a Complete History of St. Louis* (St. Louis: Trubner, 1860), 432. Also see Frank Towers, *The Urban South and the Coming of the Civil War* (Charlottesville: University of Virginia Press, 2004), 103–8, 125–27.

103. "Committee of Claims," *Journal of the Board of Delegates, Charter Convention, 1854–1864,* Oct. 9, 1854, p. 47, City Hall, St. Louis, Microfilm Department, MSA.

104. German Americans were strongest in the Ninth, Tenth, Eleventh, Twelfth, and Thirteenth Wards of Cincinnati in the north and west, while Irish dominated the Third Ward along the Ohio River front. See William A. Baughin, "Nativism in Cincinnati before 1860" (PhD diss., University of Cincinnati, 1963), 139.

105. William A. Baughin, "Bullets and Ballots: The Election Day Riots of 1855," *Bulletin of the Historical and Philosophical Society of Ohio* 21 (Oct. 1963): 272.

106. Anbinder, *Nativism and Slavery,* 24.

107. *Cincinnati Gazette,* Mar. 30, 1855, in Baughin, "Bullets and Ballots," 268.

108. For more on the Maine Law, temperance, and the nativist movement, see Joseph R. Gusfield, *Symbolic Crusade: Status Politics and the American Temperance Movement* (University of Illinois Press, 1986); Brian H. Harrison, *Drink and the Victorians: The Temperance Question in England, 1815–1872* (Pittsburgh: University of Pittsburgh Press, 1971); and Anbinder, *Nativism and Slavery.*

109. Thomas M. Keefe, "Chicago's Flirtation with Political Nativism, 1854–1856," *Records of the American Catholic Historical Society of Philadelphia* 82, no. 3 (Sept. 1971): 131–58.

110. Levi Boone, Speech, Mar. 13, 1855, in Keefe, "Chicago's Flirtation with Political Nativism," 141.

111. Richard Wilson Renner, "In a Perfect Ferment: Chicago, the Know-Nothings, and the Riot for Lager Beer," *Chicago History* 5, no. 3 (Fall 1976): 163–64.

112. In Richard English, "When Drunkards Revolt: The Chicago Lager Riot of 1855," *Modern Drunkard Magazine* 52, http://drunkard.com/52-no-beer/, accessed Nov. 22, 2013.

113. See Jed Dannenbaum, *Temperance Reform in Cincinnati from the Washingtonian Revival to the WCTU* (Urbana: University of Illinois Press, 1984); and Renner, "In a Perfect Ferment," 161–70.

114. James Speed, Louisville, to William K. Thompson, Shepherdsville, KY, Sept. 8, 1855, Speed Family Papers, folder 4, FHS.

115. Speed to Thompson, Sept. 8, 1855, Speed Family Papers.

116. Lewis A. Walter, "Bloody Monday," 1936, Lewis Allahwyn Walter Papers, folder 9, FHS.

117. Sister Agnes Geraldine McGann, "The Know-Nothing Movement in Kentucky," *Records of the American Catholic Historical Society* 49, no. 4 (Dec. 1938): 320.

118. See Leslie Ann Harper, "Lethal Language: The Rhetoric of George Prentice and Louisville's Bloody Monday," *Ohio Valley History* 11, no. 3 (Fall 2011): 24–43.

119. Edward Ayars, "Time and Memorandum Book," Aug. 6–12, 1855, Jefferson County, KY, FHS.

120. J. H. Ashbaugh, Napa County, CA, to Jacob H. Weller, Louisville, Sept. 26, 1855, Weller Family Papers, folder 7, FHS.

121. J. H. Ashbaugh, Napa County, CA, to Jacob H. Weller, Louisville, Oct. 15, 1855, Weller Family Papers, folder 7, FHS.

122. H. Cox, Carollton, KY, to Norvin Green et al. [all Kentucky Democrats], Oct. 22, 1855, Norvin Green Papers, folder 12, FHS.

123. See Benedict Joseph Webb, *The Catholic Question in Politics: Comprising a Series of Letters Addressed to George D. Prentice, Esq. (of the Louisville Journal); by a Kentucky*

Catholic (Louisville: Webb, Gill, & Levering, 1856), Pamphlets in American History, CA 686, SLU.

124. Board of Alderman Minutes, Louisville, 1855, Information File 4, 345–75, FHS.

125. Board of Alderman Minutes, Louisville, 1855, Information File 4, 363, FHS.

126. For more on the professionalization of the police in America, see Eric H. Monkkonen, *Police in Urban America, 1860–1920* (Cambridge: Cambridge University Press, 1981); Wagner, *Good Order and Safety;* and Schneider, "Riot and Reaction in St. Louis."

127. Katharine T. Corbett, *In Her Place: A Guide to St. Louis Women's History* (St. Louis: Missouri Historical Society Press, 1999), 65–73.

128. For a detailed description of St. Louis's notable charitable organizations in the 1860s and 1870s, see Dacus and Buel, *Tour of St. Louis,* 482–526.

Chapter 6: From Anti-Catholicism to Church-State Separation

1. Epigraph from American Party, *Proceedings of the Grand Council of Kentucky,* Frankfort, 1856, Rare Pamphlet, FHS.

2. For more on the Know-Nothing Party in Massachusetts, see John R. Mulkern, *The Know-Nothing Party in Massachusetts: The Rise and Fall of a People's Movement* (Boston: Northeastern University Press, 1990).

3. See Carroll John Noonan, "Nativism in Connecticut, 1829–1860" (PhD diss., Catholic University of America, 1938); Robert D. Parmet, "The Know-Nothings in Connecticut" (PhD diss., Columbia University, 1966); Thomas R. Bright, "The Anti-Nebraska Coalition and the Emergence of the Republican Party in New Hampshire, 1853–1857," *Historical New Hampshire* 27 (1972); and Larry A. Rand, "Know-Nothing Party in Rhode Island," *Rhode Island History* 23 (1964): 102–16.

4. See Darrell W. Overdyke, *The Know-Nothing Party in the South* (Baton Rouge: Louisiana State University Press, 1950).

5. In the April elections of 1855, residents of Chicago reelected Mayor Levi Boone on the Know-Nothing ticket. In Louisville Know-Nothing mayor Barbee took office, and Know-Nothing mayor Washington King won in St. Louis.

6. Know-Nothing candidates elected as U.S. representatives were, from Illinois, James Knox (1855–57) and Jesse O. Norton (1855–57); from Ohio, Lewis D. Campbell (1855–58) and Timothy Crane Day (1855–57); from Missouri, Samuel Caruthers (1855–57), James Johnson Lindley (1855–57), John Gaines Miller (1855–57), Mordecai Oliver (1855–57), Thomas Peter Akers (1856–57), Thomas Lilbourne Anderson (1857–59), and Samuel H. Woodson (1857–1861); and from Kentucky, Francis Bristow (1855–57), John P. Campbell Jr. (1855–57), Leander Cox (1853–57), Alexander Marshall (1855–57), Humphrey Marshall (1855–59), Samuel F. Swope (1855–57), and Warner Underwood (1855–59). Independent candidates who later became associated with the Know-Nothing Party included William Clayton Anderson (1859–61), Green Adams (1859–61), Robert Mallory (1859–61),

and Laban T. Moore (1859–61). Sen. John B. Thompson from Kentucky was a member of his state's Know-Nothing order (1853–59).

7. See Peyton Hurt, "The Rise and Fall of the 'Know-Nothings' in California," *California Historical Society Quarterly* 9, no. 1 (Mar. 1930): 16–49.

8. The largest third-party turnout in American political history belonged to Teddy Roosevelt's Progressive Party in 1912, which gained approximately 27 percent of the popular vote. After the American Party, Ross Perot's independent ticket led the third-largest third party in American history in 1992, garnering roughly 18 percent of the popular vote.

9. Samuel H. Woodson, Independence, MO, to General Smith, Feb. 23, 1856, George R. Smith Papers, MHS.

10. "American Platform of Principles," in *The True American's Almanac and Politician's Manual for 1857*, ed. Tisdale (New York: 1857).

11. For more on the development of civil religion, the rise of modern church-state doctrine, and the embedding of anti-Catholicism into law and public policy, see Steven Green, *The Bible, the School, and the Constitution: The Clash that Shaped Modern Church-State Doctrine* (New York: Oxford University Press, 2013); Green, *The Second Disestablishment: Church and State in Nineteenth-Century America* (New York: Oxford University Press, 2010); David Sehat, *The Myth of Religious Freedom* (New York: Oxford University Press, 2011); Tracy Fessenden, *Culture and Redemption: Religion, the Secular, and American Literature* (Princeton, NJ: Princeton University Press, 2007); Philip Hamburger, *Separation of Church and State: A Theologically Liberal, Anti-Catholic, and American Principle* (Chicago: University of Chicago Law School, 2002); and Robert N. Bellah, "Civil Religion in America," *Journal of the American Academy of Arts and Sciences* 96, no. 1 (Winter 1967): 1–21. For more on the problems Catholics and Jews posed to American civil religion, see David Hollinger, "Jewish Intellectuals and the De-Christianization of American Public Culture in the Twentieth Century," in *New Directions in American Religious History,* ed. Harry S. Stout and D. G. Hart (New York: Oxford University Press, 1997), 462–86; and Will Herberg, *Protestant, Catholic, Jew: An Essay in American Religious Sociology* (Garden City, NY: Anchor Books, 1960).

12. For a recent essay distinguishing the difference between ideological anti-Catholicism and anti-Catholic bigotry, see Steven Conn, "'Political Romanism': Reevaluating American Anti-Catholicism in the Age of Italian Revolution," *Journal of the Early Republic* 36, no. 3 (Fall 2016): 521–48.

13. For more on the development of civil religion in nineteenth-century America, see Bruce T. Murray, *Religious Liberty in America: The First Amendment in Historical and Contemporary Perspective* (Amherst: University of Massachusetts Press in Association with the Foundation for American Communications, 2008); Sanford Kessler, *Tocqueville's Civil Religion: American Christianity and the Prospects for Freedom* (Albany: State University of New York Press, 1994); Robert N. Bellah [et al.], *The Good Society* (New York: Alfred Knopf, 1991); Herberg, *Protestant, Catholic, Jew*; Robert N. Bellah, *American Civil Religion in Time of Trial* (Chicago: University of Chicago Press, 1975);

Bellah, "Civil Religion in America," 1–21; Carl Bankston and Stephen Caldas, *Public Education, America's Civil Religion: A Social History* (New York: Teachers College Press, 2009); William Cavanaugh, *The Myth of Religious Violence: Secular Ideology and the Roots of Modern Conflict* (New York: Oxford University Press, 2009); Tisa Wenger, *We Have a Religion: The 1920s Pueblo Indian Dance Controversy and American Religious Freedom* (Chapel Hill: University of North Carolina Press, 2009); Peter Gardella, *American Civil Religion: What Americans Hold Sacred* (New York: Oxford University Press, 2014); and Philip Gorski, *Fall and Rise of Civil Religion in America* (Princeton, NJ: Princeton University Press, 2015). See also these primary-source readers *Civil Religion in Political Thought: Its Perennial Questions and Enduring Relevance in North America* (Washington, DC: Catholic University of America Press, 2010); and Mark A. Noll and Luke E. Harlow, eds., *Religion and American Politics: From the Colonial Period to the Present* (New York: Oxford University Press, 2007).

14. For more on the tensions surrounding the Kansas-Nebraska Act and the rearrangement of the two-party system from 1854 to 1856, see David Morris Potter, *The Impending Crisis, 1848–1861* (New York: Harper & Row, 1976), 199–266.

15. William Seward, *Speech of William H. Seward, On the Admission of California: Delivered in the Senate of the United States, March 11, 1850* (Washington, DC: Printed by Buell & Blanchard, 1850), Nineteenth Century Collection, Law Library, SLU.

16. Anbinder, *Nativism and Slavery*. Many Know-Nothings in the Northwest believed that "popular sovereignty" in Kansas and Nebraska was an affront to precedents dating back to the Northwest Ordinance of 1787 and the Missouri Compromise of 1820, which prohibited slavery above the $36°$ $30'$ parallel. Previous Whig congressmen had attempted to legally extend this precedent to the West, including David Wilmot, who in 1846 proposed the "Wilmot Proviso" to prohibit the extension of slavery into all of the new territories acquired by the United States. But with strong proslavery factions on the Democratic side and internal disagreement within their own party, Whig leaders struggled in the early 1850s to establish a clear policy on the matter. For more on antislavery sentiment and the collapse of the Whig Party in the 1850s, see Thomas G. Mitchell, *Antislavery Politics in Antebellum and Civil War America* (Westport, CT: Praeger, 2007); and Michael F. Holt, *The Rise and Fall of the American Whig Party: Jacksonian Politics and the Onset of the Civil War* (New York: Oxford University Press, 1999).

17. For example, see William E. Gienapp, *The Origins of the Republican Party, 1852–1856* (New York: Oxford University Press, 1987); Michael Holt, *The Political Crisis of the 1850s* (New York: Norton, 1983); Stephen E. Maizlish, *The Triumph of Sectionalism: The Transformation of Ohio Politics, 1844–1856* (Kent, OH: Kent State University Press, 1983); Potter, *Impending Crisis*; Eric Foner, *Free Soil, Free Labor, Free Men: The Ideology of the Republican Party before the Civil War* (New York: Oxford University, 1970); Michael F. Holt, "The Politics of Impatience: The Origins of Know-Nothingism," *Journal of American History* 60, no. 2 (Sept. 1973): 309–31; Stephen E. Maizlish, "The Meaning of Nativism and the Crisis of the Union: The Know-Nothing Movement in the Antebellum North," in *Essays on American Antebellum Politics, 1840–1860,* ed. Stephen E.

Maizlish and John J. Kushma (College Station: Texas A & M University Press, 1982): 166–98; and Pearl T. Ponce, *To Govern the Devil in Hell: The Political Crisis in Territorial Kansas* (DeKalb: Northern Illinois University Press, 2014).

18. James Rollins, Columbia, MO, to Gen. George R. Smith, St. Louis, May 24, 1855, George R. Smith Papers, MHS.

19. Luther M. Kennett, Washington, DC, to Henry W. Williams, St. Louis, June 29, 1856, Henry W. Williams Papers, box 1, folder 4, MHS.

20. William Carr Lane, "Citizens of St. Louis," *St. Louis Intelligencer,* Apr. 6, 1857, Newspaper Clipping, William Carr Lane Collection, MHS.

21. Anna Ella Carroll, *The Union of the States* (Boston: James French, 1856), 7–17, Olin Library, WU.

22. For more on the Cincinnati Know-Nothing Convention of 1854, see John Bennett Weaver, "Nativism and the Birth of the Republican Party in Ohio, 1854–1860" (PhD diss., Ohio State University, 1982).

23. For more on fusionism in Ohio antebellum politics, see Maizlish, *Triumph of Sectionalism,* 187–224.

24. William E. Gienapp, "Salmon P. Chase, Nativism, and the Formation of the Republican Party in Ohio," *Ohio History* 93 (Winter-Spring 1984): 5–39.

25. See Anbinder, *Nativism and Slavery,* 53–68, 87–102. See also Mulkern, *Know-Nothing Party in Massachusetts.* For more on Massachusetts's immigration policy during the height of Know-Nothing power in the state, see Hidetaka Hirota, *Expelling the Poor: Atlantic Seaboard States and the 19th-Century Origins of American Immigration Policy* (New York: Oxford University Press, 2017).

26. For more on the role of Chase, German Protestants, and Know-Nothings in Opposition Party of Ohio, see Maizlish, *Triumph of Sectionalism,* 187–224.

27. Henry Roedter, Memoirs, CMC.

28. Joseph Medill, Cleveland, OH, to Oran Follett, May 29, 1854, Oran Follett Papers, box 2, CMC.

29. By selectively emphasizing the perspective of Freethinkers and Republican Party leaders, past studies on German American politics in the mid-1850s have ignored the existence of a Democrat constituency and thus exaggerated the extent to which antislavery sentiment compelled German Americans to overcome their discomfort with nativism. Many German Democrats in the West, Susanne Schick has pointed out, remained faithful to the party during the election of 1860 and all the way through the Civil War period. For more on the German Democrats in Ohio, see Susanne Martha Schick, "'For God, Mac, and Country': The Political Worlds of Midwestern Germans during the Civil War Era" (PhD diss., University of Illinois, Urbana-Champaign, 1994). For more on German American racial attitudes and political solidarity, see Kristen Layne Anderson, "German Americans, African Americans, and the Construction of Racial Identity in Nineteenth-Century St. Louis" (PhD diss., University of Iowa, 2009), via Proquest; Russell A. Kazal, *Becoming Old Stock: The Paradox of German-American Identity* (Princeton, NJ: Princeton University Press, 2004); Matthew Frye Jacobson, *Whiteness of a*

Different Color: European Immigrants and the Alchemy of Race (Cambridge, MA: Harvard University Press, 1998); Reinhold Grimm and Jost Hermand, eds., *Blacks and German Culture* (Madison: University of Wisconsin Press, 1986); and Sander L. Gilman, *On Blackness without Blacks: Essays on the Image of the Black in Germany* (Boston: G. K. Hall, 1982).

30. "Resolves of the Cincinnati German Democratic Anti-Nebraska Meeting," *Cincinnati Gazette,* July 13, 1854.

31. See Anderson, "German Americans, African Americans, and the Construction of Racial Identity," 24.

32. "Platform of the Free Germans," Louisville, KY, ca. 1856, in *Americanism Versus Romanism; or, The Cis-Atlantic Battle between Sam and the Pope,* by James L. Chapman (Nashville: By the author, 1856), 304–7.

33. Heinrich Börnstein, *Mysteries of St. Louis: A Novel,* trans. Friedrich Muench, (1852; modern ed. by Steven Rowan and Elizabeth Sims, Chicago: Charles H. Kerr, 1990), 160.

34. "The Pope's Nuncio: Bedini's Character," 1853, Early American Imprints, Broadside 8649, SLU.

35. For accounts of the Cincinnati Riot of 1853, see Father Edward Purcell, "An Attempt at a Riot," *Catholic Telegraph* (Archdiocese of Cincinnati and Louisville), Dec. 31, 1853, 4; "Monsignor Bedini," ibid., Jan. 7, 1854, 5; and "The Law of Brute Force," ibid., Jan. 14, 1854, 5. For more on the significance of Bedini's tour of America that year, see David J. Endres, "Know-Nothings, Nationhood, and the Nuncio: Reassessing the Visit of Archbishop Bedini," *U.S. Catholic Historian* 21, no. 4 (Fall 2003): 1–16.

36. James F. Connelly, *The Visit of Archbishop Gaetano Bedini to the U.S.A., June 1853–February 1854* (Roma: Universita Gregoriana, 1960).

37. Samuel Portland Chase, Cincinnati, to unknown, June 23, 1855, CMC; Chase, quoted in Gienapp, " Chase, Nativism, and the Formation of the Republican Party in Ohio," 26.

38. His brother, Edwin Ruthven Campbell, was also a prominent nativist, having served as a delegate for the national convention of the old Native American Party in 1845. Edwin Campbell challenged Catholic power in his stridently anti-Catholic, anti-foreign Cincinnati newspaper. See his private criticism of Germans in the West in Edwin Ruthven Campbell, Washington, DC, to Will, Jan. 10, 1852, CMC. Unlike his brother, Lewis, Edwin was apparently a pious evangelical Christian. See Edwin Ruthven Campbell, "Let There Be Light!" (poem), CMC. See also William E. Van Horne, "Lewis D. Campbell and the Know-Nothing Party in Ohio," *Ohio Valley History* 76 (1967): 205.

39. Lewis D. Campbell, Hamilton County, OH, to Samuel Galloway, Columbus, OH, May 14, 1855, CMC.

40. Lewis D. Campbell, Hamilton County, OH, to Samuel Galloway, Columbus, OH, June 21, 1855, CMC.

41. See Gienapp, " Chase, Nativism, and the Formation of the Republican Party in Ohio," 27–28.

42. Joseph Medill, Cleveland, to Oran Follett, Jan. 27, 1855, Oran Follett Papers, box 2, p. 169, CMC.

43. Medill to Follett, Apr. 18, 1855, Oran Follett Papers, box 2, CMC.

44. Anbinder, *Nativism and Slavery,* 75–87.

45. *Principles and Objects of the American Party* (New York: 1855), American Party, 7, 15, 20, General Collections, NL. The New York Know-Nothing Order suggested that secrecy was inherent to American Party politics and not really the same kind of threat as Catholicism. The New York Know-Nothings argued that, unlike the Roman Catholic Church, their organization harbored independent patriots, not devotees subservient to plotting priests: "we have no doubt of the fact that [the Roman Catholic Church] exhibits in its brotherhood a more submissive obedience to its guides, a greater dependence upon authority for its direction and conduct, and a closer inter-relation of personal sympathy and identity of end and object, than any other fraternity in our land." And besides, they could also accuse the major-party organizations of being "altogether secret" in their conventions.

46. Historian Eugene H. Rosebom has pointed out that Know-Nothings in the East generally formed independent parties, while in Ohio—and areas in Illinois, Kentucky, and Missouri as well—they often worked hand in hand with other fusion parties, such as the Republicans in Ohio and various opposition parties in the other western border-states. See Rosebom, "Salmon P. Chase and the Know-Nothings," *Mississippi Valley Historical Review* 25, no. 3 (Dec. 1938): 335–50. While Rosebom interpreted the People's Party nomination of Republican Salmon P. Chase for governor in July 1855 as a sign of waning Know-Nothing control of Ohio's fusion party, William E. Gienapp has pointed out that nativism remained a strong political force through the mid-1850s and that the "Republican Party in Ohio rested on a substantial Know-Nothing foundation." See Gienapp, " Chase, Nativism, and the Formation of the Republican Party in Ohio," 5–39.

47. Thomas Spooner, *Address to Executive Council at Cleveland,* June 2, 1855, Pamphlet, CMC.

48. Spooner, *Address to Executive Council at Cleveland,* Pamphlet, CMC.

49. Cushing's resolution was tabled in 1854, but a similar one was passed in 1855. See American Party, *Platform Adopted by the National Council of the American Party: Ratification of the National Platform by the State Council of Missouri* (St. Louis: Ustick, Studley, 1855), 25, Pamphlet, MHS; and *Proceedings of the Grand Council of Ohio: From the Organization, April 23d. to August 1st, 1854* (Cincinnati: Printed by Tidball, Turner, & Gray, Odd Fellows' Literary Casket Office, 1854), 17, Pamphlet, CMC.

50. Thomas Spooner, *To the Members of the American Order in Ohio,* (Cincinnati: July 23, 1855), Pamphlet, CMC.

51. *Cincinnati Times,* Aug. 3, 1854, quoted in Rosebom, "Salmon P. Chase and the Know-Nothings," 336.

52. *Proceedings of the Grand Council of Ohio,* Pamphlets, CMC.

53. Joseph Medill, Cleveland, to Oran Follett, Apr. 18, 1855, Oran Follett Papers, box 2, CMC.

54. Spooner, *Address to Executive Council at Cleveland,* Pamphlet, CMC.

55. Thomas Spooner et al., *Resolutions of the Executive Council of Ohio,* (Cleveland: June 4, 1855), Pamphlet, CMC.

56. National American Party, Minute Book of the Grand Council of the State of Missouri, Apr. 18–21, 1855, St. Louis, Solomon Smith Collection, MHS.

57. Overdyke, *Know-Nothing Party in the South,* 229–32.

58. W. M. Corry, Cincinnati, to Mr. Sanders, June 19, 1855, Sanders Family Papers, folder 11, FHS.

59. Rev. Thomas Horace Cleland, Memorandum Book, Nov. 4, 1856, Cleland-Howard Family Papers, folder 2, FHS.

60. "Platform and Principles of the American Party; Adopted by the National Council at Philadelphia, June 15, 1855" (Louisville: C. Settle, 1855), Broadsides of the Know-Nothing Party, FHS.

61. National American Party, "Philadelphia Platform," June 5, 1855, in American Party, *Facts for the People!* (Nashville: Printed at the Daily Gazette Book and Job Office, 1856) American Party, General Collections, NL.

62. Alcee Fortier, *A History of Louisiana,* vol. 3 (New Orleans, 1903), 254–55; *New Orleans Daily True Delta,* Sept. 8, 1855; Leon Cyprian Soulé, *The Know-Nothing Party in New Orleans: A Reappraisal* (Baton Rouge: Louisiana Historical Association, 1961), 66.

63. Charles Gayarré, *Address on the Religious Test to the Convention of the American Party Assembled in Philadelphia on the 5th of June, 1855* (New Orleans, 1855); Gayarré, "Religious Toleration," *De Bow's Review* 19 (1855): 32–36.

64. For more on Catholic voting patterns, see Kenneth J. Zanca, comp. and ed., *American Catholics and Slavery, 1789–1866: An Anthology of Primary Documents* (Lanham, MD: University Press of America, 1994); Andrew H. M. Stern, *Southern Crucifix, Southern Cross: Catholic-Protestant Relations in the Old South* (Tuscaloosa: University of Alabama Press, 2012); and Noel Ignatiev, *How the Irish Became White* (New York: Routledge, 1995).

65. Charles B. Boynton, *Address Before the Citizens of Cincinnati: Delivered on the Fourth Day of July, 1855* (Cincinnati: Cincinnati Gazette Company Print, 1855), 19, 21, 24, Pamphlets, CHS.

66. Thomas Spooner to the State Council of Ohio, Jan. 3, 1856, PLC, in Anbinder, *Nativism and Slavery,* 47.

67. Chapman, *Americanism Versus Romanism,* 33–36.

68. Lane, "Citizens of St. Louis," *St. Louis Intelligencer,* Apr. 6, 1857, Newspaper Clipping, William Carr Lane Collection, MHS.

69. Anbinder, *Nativism and Slavery,* 167–69.

70. Van Horne, "Lewis D. Campbell and the Know-Nothing Party in Ohio," 209.

71. Anbinder, *Nativism and Slavery,* 167–68.

72. Michael F. Holt, *Political Parties and American Political Development from the Age of Jackson to the Age of Lincoln* (Baton Rouge: Louisiana State University Press, 1992), 131–37. This resolution was signed by representatives from Maine, New Hampshire, Vermont, Massachusetts, Rhode Island, Connecticut, Ohio, Indiana, Illinois, Michigan, Iowa, and Wisconsin. See Lewis D. Campbell, Hamilton County, OH, to Samuel Galloway, Columbus, OH, June 21, 1855, CMC.

73. Samuel H. Woodson, Independence, MO, to Gen. Georg. R. Smith, St. Louis, July 1, 1856, George R. Smith Papers, box 1, MHS.

74 Luther M. Kennett, Washington, DC, to Henry W. Williams, St. Louis, June 29, 1856, Papers of Henry W. Williams, box 1, folder 4, MHS.

75. Francis P. Blair Jr., St. Louis, to James M. Stone, 1855, Francis Preston Blair Papers, MHS.

76. For more on Sen. Thomas Hart Benton's leadership role in the West, see Ken S. Mueller, "Benton and the People: White Nationalism on the Jacksonian Frontier, 1782–1848" (PhD diss., Saint Louis University, 2007); and Justin Wolff, *Thomas Hart Benton: A Life* (New York: Farrar, Straus, and Giroux, 2012).

77. Chapman, *Americanism Versus Romanism*, 44, 149.

78. Madison [A Distinguished Virginian], *Twelve Letters, Over the Signature of 'Madison,' on the American Question*, ca. 1855, American Party, no. 9, 20–21, General Collections, NL. See also William Russell Smith, *The American Party and Its Mission: Speech of Mr. Smith of Alabama, Delivered in the U.S. House of Representatives, January 15, 1855* (1855), Pamphlet, CMC.

79. Madison, *Twelve Letters*, 20–21, General Collections, NL.

80. Lemuel C. Porter, Diary, July 1855, Minute Book of the Bowling Green Lyceum, FHS.

81. William W. Danenhower was the president of the Illinois State Know-Nothing Council from 1854 to 1856 and the editor of the anti-Catholic *Chicago Literary Budget* in 1854. William Danenhower, *Chicago Literary Budget*, Feb. 17, 1855, in Thomas M. Keefe, "Chicago's Flirtation with Political Nativism, 1854–1856," *Records of the American Catholic Historical Society of Philadelphia* 82, no. 3 (Sept. 1971): 137.

82. James D. Taylor, ed., *The Cincinnati Dollar Weekly Times*, 1855 (Cincinnati: Published by C. W. Starbuck, 1855), Early American Imprints, Broadside 9192, SLU.

83. Madison, *Twelve Letters*, 20–21, General Collections, NL.

84. Charles Gayarré, *Address to the General Assembly of the Know-Nothing Party Held in Philadelphia, May, 1854*, 1–4, in Overdyke, *Know-Nothing Party in the South*, 219.

85. Overdyke, *Know-Nothing Party in the South*, 220.

86. American Party, *Proceedings of the Grand Council of Kentucky* (Frankfort: 1856), Rare Pamphlet, FHS.

87. American Party, *Proceedings of the Grand Council of Kentucky* (Frankfort: 1856), Rare Pamphlet, FHS.

88. "Sam's Principles," ca. 1855, St. Louis, Broadsides, MHS.

89. "Sam's Principles," ca. 1855, St. Louis, Broadsides, MHS.

90. American Party, "Report of the Committee of the State Council of Missouri, on National Platform," in *Platform Adopted by the National Council of the American Party*, 8, Pamphlet, MHS; National American Party, Minute Book of the Grand Council of the State of Missouri, Apr. 18–21, 1855, St. Louis, Solomon Smith Collection, MHS.

91. For example, see William B. Napton, Diary, Jan. 10, 1855, MHS.

92. *Constitution of the National American Association of Hamilton County* (Cincinnati: Ben Franklin Steam Printing, 1857), Pamphlets, CHS.

93. American Party, *Proceedings of the Grand Council of Kentucky*, (Frankfort: 1856), Rare Pamphlet, FHS.

94. Henry Winter Davis, *The Origins, Principles, and Purposes of the American Party* (1855), 26.

95. James Brooks, "Defence of President Fillmore: Before a Meeting of the American Party, Held at Cincinnati, Friday Evening, May 30, 1856" (Cincinnati: Reported by T. Shinkwinm, 1856), Broadsides 119, CMC.

96. Lewis D. Campbell, *Americanism: Speech of Hon. Lewis D. Campbell of Ohio; delivered at the American mass meeting, held in Washington City, February 29th, 1856, as reported and published in the "American organ"* (Washington, DC: Buell & Blanchard, Printers, 1856), in Political Pamphlets, vol. 2, no. 18, Pamphlets, CHS.

97. Chapman, *Americanism Versus Romanism*, vii.

98. Davis, *Origins, Principles, and Purposes of the American Party*, 27–29.

99. For more on the development of the modern church-state doctrine and embedding of anti-Catholicism into law and public policy, see Green, *Bible, the School, and the Constitution;* Sehat, *Myth of Religious Freedom;* Green, *Second Disestablishment;* Fessenden, *Culture and Redemption;* and Hamburger, *Separation of Church and State.* See also Pauline Maier, *American Scripture: Making the Declaration of Independence* (New York: Knopf, 1997).

100. Cleland, Memorandum Book, July 17, 1855, Cleland-Howard Family Papers, folder 2, FHS.

101. Holt, *Political Parties*, 138–48.

102. Thomas C. Ware, James C. Hall, and Osgood Mussey [Committee of the Plymouth Council No. 8, Cincinnati], "To the American Party of Ohio: Address and Resolutions of the Plymouth Rock Council, Adopted Wednesday evening, December 12, 1855," (Cincinnati: Dec. 12, 1855), Broadsides, General Politics, CMC.

103. The National Council nominated Millard Fillmore four days later, on February 22, 1856—Washington's Birthday. During the election of 1856, Fillmore ran on the Know-Nothing ticket, and John C. Frémont ran as the Republican Party's candidate. Know-Nothing propaganda accused Frémont of being a crypto-Catholic, though he was actually Anglican. See American Party, *Fremont's Romanism Established: Acknowledged by Archbishop Hughes* (1856), Rare Campaign Pamphlet, UMSL. For campaign paraphernalia on Fillmore, see Edwin Barbour Morgan, *Mr. Fillmore's Political History and Position: Speech of Hon. E. B. Morgan, of New York, in U.S. House of Representatives, August 4, 1856* (Washington, DC: Republican Association, 1856), Rare Book, FHS; and

Thomas Ware, C. H. Sargent, and W. B. McKenzie, *To Make Known the Principles and Promote the Success of the National American Party; and Chiefly to Advance and Secure the Election of our Distinguished Fellow Citizens, Millard Fillmore and Andrew Jackson Donelson, to the Presidency and Vice-Presidency of the United States, we recommend the immediate formation and establishment of Fillmore and Donelson Clubs....* (Cincinnati: 1856), Broadside, Cincinnati Politics, CMC. For nativist propaganda supporting Fillmore, see Millard Fillmore Campaign Ephemera, 1856, FHS; Morgan, *Fillmore's Political History and Position;* Ware, Sargent, and McKenzie, *To Make Known the Principles and Promote the Success of the National American Party;* and American Party, *Facts for the People!.*

104. James S. Rollins, Columbia, MO, to Gen. George R. Smith, Jan. 30, 1856, Gen. George R. Smith Papers, box 1, MHS; Abel Rathbone Corbin, Washington, DC, to Thomas C. Reynolds, St. Louis, July 27, 1856, Thomas Caute Reynolds Papers, folder 1, MHS; and Walter D. Kamphoefner, "St. Louis Germans and the Republican Party, 1848–1860," *Mid-America* 57, no. 2 (Apr. 1975): 72–73.

105. *Chicago Free West,* Mar. 15, 1855, in Thomas M. Keefe, "Chicago's Flirtation with Political Nativism, 1854–1856," *Records of the American Catholic Historical Society of Philadelphia* 82, no. 3 (Sept. 1971): 131–58.

106. See Weaver, "Nativism and the Birth of the Republican Party in Ohio."

Epilogue: The Specter of Anti-Catholicism, New Nativism, and the Ascendancy of Religious Freedom

1. Epigraphs from Rt. Rev. Msgr. Fulton J. Sheen, D.D., Preface to *Radio Replies in Defence of Religion: Given from the Catholic Broadcasting Station 2SM, Sydney Australia,* Rev. Dr. Rumble and Rev. Charles Mortimer Carty (1938); and "Understanding Shariah," Islamic Circle of North America, 2012. https://www.icna.org/defending-religious-freedom-understanding-shariah/.

2. Dwight D. Eisenhower, *New York Times,* Dec. 23, 1952, in Will Herberg, *Protestant, Catholic, Jew: An Essay in American Religious Sociology* (Garden City, NY: Anchor Books, 1960), 84. See Stephen Green, *The Second Disestablishment: Church and State in Nineteenth-Century America* (New York: Oxford University Press, 2010).

3. See, for example, William J. Murray, *The Pledge: One Nation under God* (Chattanooga: Living Ink Books, 2007); and Tricia Raymond, *Saving One Nation under God: The Role of the Pledge of Allegiance in America's Fight against Socialism* (Madison, MS: Sametilon, 2011).

4. Theodore Sorensen, *Kennedy* (New York: Harper and Row, 1965), 9–17.

5. Theodore H. White, *The Making of the President 1960* (New York: Atheneum, 1988), 258–61. Also see Albert J. Menendez, *The Religious Factor in the 1960 Presidential Election: An Analysis of the Kennedy Victory over Anti-Catholic Prejudice* (Jefferson, NC: McFarland, 2011).

6. For a contemporary anti-Catholic work, see Paul Blanshard, *American Freedom and Catholic Power* (Boston: Beacon Press, 1949). See also Rev. George Harold Dunne, *Religion and American Democracy: A Reply to Paul Blanshard's* American Freedom and Catholic Power (New York: America Press, 1949). For more on the rise of fundamentalism in twentieth-century America, see Adam Laats, *Fundamentalism and Education in the Scopes Era: God, Darwin, and the Roots of America's Culture Wars* (New York: Palgrave Macmillan, 2010); Anne C. Loveland, "Later Stages of the Recovery of American Religious History," in *New Directions in American Religious History,* ed. Harry S. Stout and D. G. Hart (New York: Oxford University Press, 1997), 487–502; Karl Keating, *Catholicism and Fundamentalism: The Attack on "Romanism" by "Bible Christians"* (San Francisco: Ignatius, 1988); and George Marsden, *Fundamentalism and American Culture: The Shaping of the Twentieth Century Evangelicalism, 1870–1925* (New York: Oxford University Press, 1980).

7. For an analysis of civil religion in Kennedy's campaign, see Robert N. Bellah, "Civil Religion in America," *Journal of the American Academy of Arts and Sciences* 96, no. 1 (Winter 1967): 1–21.

8. John F. Kennedy, Inaugural Address, Jan. 20, 1961, in Bellah, "Civil Religion in America," 1–2.

9. Katie Oxx, *The Nativist Movement in America: Religious Conflict in the Nineteenth Century* (New York: Routledge, 2013), 104.

10. See Philip Jenkins, *The New Anti-Catholicism: The Last Acceptable Prejudice* (New York: Oxford University Press, 2003), 10; and Mark Massa, *Anti-Catholicism in America: The Last Acceptable Prejudice* (New York: Crossroad, 2003).

11. Andrew M. Greeley, "An Ugly Little Secret Revisited: A Pretest on Anti-Catholicism in America," in *American Catholics, American Culture: Tradition and Resistance* (Sheed and Ward, 2004), 162 (emphasis added); Kenneth L. Woodward, "Anti-Catholicism: The Last Acceptable Prejudice? Yes," ibid., 171. See also Steven Conn, "'Political Romanism': Reevaluating American Anti-Catholicism in the Age of Italian Revolution," *Journal of the Early Republic* 36, no. 3 (Fall 2016): 521–48.

12. Conn, "'Political Romanism,'" 547.

13. For more on Christianity's persecution complex, see Alan Noble, "The Evangelical Persecution Complex: The Theological and Cultural Roots of a Damaging Attitude in the Christian Community," *The Atlantic,* Aug. 4, 2014, https://www.theatlantic.com/national/archive/2014/08/the-evangelical-persecution-complex/375506/, accessed July 30, 2017.

14. Stephen Kobasa, Jonah House, 2005, http://www.jonahhouse.org/archive/Kobasa_conscience.htm, accessed Aug. 25, 2015.

15. William T. Cavanaugh, speech, "Religious Freedom and the Security State," February 26, 2014, University of St. Thomas. <https://www.youtube.com/watch?v=q70_0V6130w>. Also see Cavanaugh, *The Myth of Religious Violence: Secular Ideology and the Roots of Modern Conflict* (New York: Oxford University Press, 2009).

16. Archdiocese of Baltimore, http://www.usccb.org/issues-and-action/religious-lib-

erty/fortnight-for-freedom/fortnight-freedom-prayer-resources.cfm, accessed Aug. 25, 2015 (page removed); and United States Conference of Catholic Bishops, Religious Liberty-Prayer Resources, http://www.usccb.org/issues-and-action/religious-liberty/prayer -resources.cfm, accessed May 5, 2020. For an example of the "Patriotic Rosary," see Sacred Heart Catholic Church, Milledgeville, GA, http://www.sacredheartmilledgeville .org/Freedom%20Rosary%20and%20Litany.pdf, accessed Aug. 25, 2015.

17. Cavanaugh, "Religious Freedom and the Security State," University of St. Thomas. Also see Cavanaugh, *Myth of Religious Violence.*

18. For example, see Jose Casanova, Nativism and the Politics of Gender in Catholicism and Islam," in Herzog H., Braude A., eds. Gendering Religion and Politics (New York: Palgrave Macmillan, 2009), 21-50; and Katie Oxx, *The Nativist Movement in America: Religious Conflict in the Nineteenth Century.*

19. Besheer Mohamed, "A New Estimate of the U.S. Muslim Population," Pew Research Center, Fact Tank: News in the Numbers, Jan. 6, 2016, http://www.pewresearch .org/fact-tank/2016/01/06/a-new-estimate-of-the-u-s-muslim-population/, accessed July 30, 2017; and "Demographic Portrait of Muslim Americans," Pew Research Center, Religion and Public Life, July 26, 2017, https://www.pewforum.org/2017/07/26/demo graphic-portrait-of-muslim-americans/, accessed September 1, 2017.

20. Phillip Connor, "United States Admits Record Number of Muslim Refugees in 2016," Pew Research Center, Fact Tank: News in the Numbers, Oct. 5, 2016, http:// www.pewresearch.org/fact-tank/2016/10/05/u-s-admits-record-number-of-muslim -refugees-in-2016/, accessed July 30, 2017.

21. Andrew Buncombe, "Donald Trump Claims He Is a 'Big Fan of Hindu'—before Saying He Means India," *Independent,* Oct. 16, 2016, http://www.independent.co.uk /news/world/americas/us-elections/donald-trump-claims-he-is-a-big-fan-of-hindu -republican-hindu-coalition-a7364526.html, accessed July 30, 2017.

22. See"5th Republican Debate Transcript, Annotated: Who Said What and What It Meant," *Washington Post,* Dec. 15, 2016, https://www.washingtonpost.com/news /the-fix/wp/2015/12/15/who-said-what-and-what-it-meant-the-fifth-gop-debate-anno tated/?utm_term=.7ed43d1b542a, accessed July 30, 2017.

23. Each year between 1840 and 1860, the foreign-born population of the U.S. averaged about 14–15%. The foreign-born population of the U.S. dropped to 4.7% in 1970, but since it has been steadily rising, due to a law passed in 1965 that replaced immigration policy based on a national quota system. In 1990, the foreign-born population rose above 8%. In 2017, the Pew Research Center reported 35.2 million legal, permanent immigrants, out of a total population of 325.7 million, or 10.8%. The number of illegal immigrants significantly raises the estimate of the foreign-born population in the United States. Jynnah Radford and Luis Noe-Bustamante, "Facts on U.S. Immigrants, 2017: Statistical Portrait of the Foreign-born Population in the United States," Pew Research Center, Hispanic Trends, June 3, 2019, https://www.pewresearch.org /hispanic/2019/06/03/facts-on-u-s-immigrants/, accessed May 6, 2020; and Jynnah Radford, "Key Findings about U.S. Immigrants," Pew Research Center, Fact Tank: News

in the Numbers, June 17, 2019, https://www.pewresearch.org/fact-tank/2019/06/17/key-findings-about-u-s-immigrants/, accessed May 6, 2020.

24. Mohamed, " New Estimate of the U.S. Muslim Population," Pew Research Center, accessed July 30, 2017.

25. Joseph C. G. Kennedy, ed., *Population of the United States in 1860; Compiled from the Original Returns of the Eighth Census* (Washington, DC: Government Printing Office, 1864).

26. See CAIR—Council of American-Islam Relations, www.cair.com.

27. Editors, "9/11 Families Reject Towering Mosque Planned for Ground Zero Site," 9/11 Families for a Safe and Strong America, May 24, 2010, https://911familiesforamerica.org/911-families-reject-towering-mosque-planned-for-ground-zero-site/, accessed July 30, 2017. Katie Oxx uses this example in *Nativist Movement in America,* 83.

28. Liz Farmer, "Alabama Joins Wave of States Banning Foreign Laws," Governing: The Future of States and Localities, Nov. 4, 2014, http://www.governing.com/topics/elections/gov-alabama-foreign-law-courts-amendment.html, accessed July 30, 2017.

29. Andrea Elliott, "The Man behind the Anti-Shariah Movement," *New York Times,* July 30, 2011, https://www.nytimes.com/2011/07/31/us/31shariah.html, accessed August 1, 2017.

30. James C. McKinley, "Judge Blocks Oklahoma's Ban on Using Shariah Law in Court," *New York Times,* Nov. 29, 2010, http://www.nytimes.com/2010/11/30/us/30oklahoma.html, accessed July 30, 2017.

31. Erik Eckholm, "Oklahoma: Court Upholds Blocking of Amendment against Shariah Law," *New York Times,* Jan. 10, 2012, http://www.nytimes.com/2012/01/11/us/oklahoma-court-upholds-blocking-of-amendment-against-shariah-law.html, accessed July 30, 2017.

32. "Understanding Shariah," Why Islam?, Dec. 15, 2014, www.whyislam.org/brochures/understanding-shariah/, accessed August 20, 2017.

33. Radhika Sanghani, "Burka Bans: The Countries Where Muslim Women Can't Wear Veils," *The Telegraph,* Aug. 17, 2017, http://www.telegraph.co.uk/women/life/burka-bans-the-countries-where-muslim-women-cant-wear-veils/, accessed Aug. 26, 2017.

INDEX

American Party, 134, 147, 148–52,
237–38; admission requirements of,
152, 157–62; platforms of, 59, 149,
160–64, 167–72
American Republican Party, 63–65, 67
Anbinder, Tyler, *Nativism and Slavery*,
by, 3, 57, 233
antebellum West, 3–4, 11–19
anti-Catholicism, 11, 21–24, 26–29,
76, 149–50; American identity, the
formation of, 66–72; among Germans,
154–55; as perverse imitation, 82,
93–94, 100; popular literature, 28–29,
61, 67, 69–70, 86–87, 131, 213, 219–20,
232; recent, 176–79
anti-Islamicism, 179–84

Barbee, John, Mayor, 144, 146
Beecher, Lyman, Reverend, 9, 25, 27,
42–43, 65; *Plea for the West*, 25, 42, 70
Benton, Thomas Hart, Governor, 131,
154, 165
Bible, King James: American identity,
38–43; Douay-Rheims Bible, 39, 43,
62; school curriculum, 38, 40–41,
62, 64, 201
Billington, Ray Allen, *The Protestant
Crusade*, by, 2, 64
blue laws. *See* Sunday closing laws
Boernstein, Henry, 47–48, 54–56, 114,
130–33, 141, 154–55, 203–4, 206, 233
Boone, Levi, Mayor, 142–43
Boynton, Charles B., 13, 31, 66, 68,
73–76, 88, 162

Brownson, Orestes, 23, 102
Buntline, Ned, 84, 129–33, 218

Camden, Peter G., Mayor, 65
Campbell, Lewis, 31, 156, 170
Carroll, Anna Ella, 67, 69–73, 152, 213
Catholicism, American, 6–7, 16, 23,
221; apologetics, 43–44, 77–80, 98,
102–3, 161–62; education, 44–46,
62–64; recent, 174–79; in the West, 17,
19–21, 44–46
Chabrat, Guy Ignatius, Bishop, 20, 44
Chapman, James, *Americanism versus
Romanism; or, the Cis-Atlantic Battle
between Sam and the Pope*, by, 90–91,
163, 165, 167
church-state separation, 6, 9–10, 75–76,
79, 149–50, 161–62, 166–70, 173,
175–76, 181–84
crime. *See* prisons

Davis, Henry Winter, 63, 90–91, 169
deportation, 105, 115–16
Douglas, Stephen A., 151, 153, 173

Ely, Alfred Brewster, 67–69, 72–73, 77,
90
evangelicalism: education, 33–37,
41–42; missions, 24–26, 97;
post-millennialism, 26–28, 69; valley
campaign, 24–28

Fillmore, Millard, 70, 149, 172, 245
Finney, Charles Grandison, 97

First Amendment, U.S. Constitution, 10,
166, 174–75, 178, 182–84
First West. *See* antebellum West
French, missions, 12, 17, 71; in New
Orleans, 45, 160–62, 167; in St. Louis,
12, 19, 46, 114, 138, 159

Gamble, Hamilton Rowan, 65, 211
Germans: beer, 51, 54–56, 142–43; crime,
56–57, 110, 118, 120–21; language,
57–58; politics, 90–91, 130–31, 141,
146, 153–59, 163, 172, 240; recreation,
47–56, 131, 143; riots, 64, 128–30, 132–
33, 140–46, 155; schools, 35, 38, 201; in
the West, 14–15, 19, 53–54, 57–58, 112,
114, 117–18, 136–38, 146–47

Hibernians, 138
house of refuge. *See* prisons
How, John, 115, 119, 134, 141
Hughes, John, Archbishop, 62–63, 80

immigration, 12–18, 106–9, 179, 221, 248
Irish: crime, 110, 120–21, 134–35; politics,
90–91, 141, 146, 163; poverty, 105,
116–18, 121–22, 124; riots, 64, 128,
133–34, 138–41, 143–46; schools, 38,
64; in the West, 15, 112, 114, 116–18,
136–38, 146–47

Jesuit: conspiracy, 28–29, 86–88, 131, 155,
232; Saint Louis University, 35, 45–46,
140

Kennedy, John F., 175–76
Kennett, Luther M., Mayor, 56, 110, 115,
118–19, 129–30, 132, 141, 151
Kenrick, Peter, Bishop, 20, 81, 141, 192
Kenrick, Francis P., Bishop, 64, 192
King, Washington, Mayor, 57, 114, 141
Know-Nothing Order, 5, 83–85;
elections, 90–91, 95–96, 133–34,

142–46; literature, 100–101; rituals,
92–97, 99, 225; similarity to Masonry,
97–101; in the West, 85, 88–89, 94, 99,
133–34, 142–47, 152–60
Know-Nothing Party. *See* American Party

Lovejoy, Elijah Parish, Reverend, 34,
36–37

Marshall, Humphrey, 65, 144, 211, 237
Mississippi River Valley, Upper. *See*
antebellum West
Morse, Samuel Finley Breese, 28, 45;
*Foreign Conspiracy against the
Liberties of the United States*, 28, 61, 86

Native American Party. *See* American
Republican Party
nativism, 1–3, 61–62, 82–83, 106, 227–28
naturalization, 10, 89–90, 134–40,
147, 156

Order of Free Masons, 97–99
Order of Odd Fellows, 98–99
Order of the Star-Spangled Banner,
83–84, 89, 218
Order of United American Mechanics,
130
Order of United Americans, 67–69,
72–73, 84, 92, 212

pauperism. *See* poverty
police, St. Louis, 110–13, 116, 141;
demographic of arrests, 115, 118–23,
125–26; reforms of, 141, 146–47
Pope's Stone, 93–94, 176
poverty: demographic of, 114–20, 122–27;
laws, 114–16
prisons: demographic of, 107, 110–13;
St. Louis, 108, 110, 114–15, 118–22,
125–26, 147
Purcell, Edward, 43–44, 79, 98, 102

ABOUT THE AUTHOR

LUKE RITTER is an assistant professor at New Mexico Highlands University. He received his Ph.D. in American history from Saint Louis University. He specializes in the history of immigration, nativism, and religion in the mid-nineteenth-century United States. Ritter received the William E. Foley Research Fellowship in 2019, the Environment in Missouri History Fellowship in 2016, and the Filson Fellowship in 2013. He is the author of numerous articles published in the *Journal of American Ethnic History, American Nineteenth Century History,* the *Journal of Early American History,* and the *Missouri Historical Review.*

Luke Ritter, *Inventing America's First Immigration Crisis:*
Political Nativism in the Antebellum West

Gerald J. Beyer, *Just Universities: Catholic Social Teaching Confronts*
Corporatized Higher Education

CPSIA information can be obtained
at www.ICGtesting.com
Printed in the USA
JSHW021401171120
9648JS00001B/16